P9-DMF-959

A True Republican

A TRUE REPUBLICAN

THE LIFE OF PAUL REVERE

Jayne E. Triber

UNIVERSITY OF MASSACHUSETTS

Amherst

This book is published with the support and
cooperation of the University of Massachusetts, Boston

Copyright © 1998 by
The University of Massachusetts Press
All rights reserved
Printed in the United States of America
LC 97-32621
ISBN 1-55849-139-2
Designed by Milenda Nan Ok Lee
Set in Adobe Caslon
Printed and bound by Braun-Brumfield, Inc.
Library of Congress Cataloging-in-Publication Data

Triber, Jayne E., 1955–
A true Republican : the life of Paul Revere / Jayne E. Triber.
p.   cm.
Includes bibliographical references (p.   ) and index.
ISBN 1-55849-139-2 (alk. paper)
1. Revere, Paul, 1735–1818.   2. Statesmen—Massachusetts—
Biography.   3. Massachusetts—Biography.   4. United States—
History—Revolution, 1775–1783—Biography.   I. Title.
F69.R43T75   1998
974.4'03'092—dc21
[b]   97-32621
                                                                  CIP

British Library Cataloguing in Publication data are
available.

CONTENTS

List of Illustrations   vii
Acknowledgements   ix
Introduction   1

CHAPTER ONE
Clark's Wharf   7

CHAPTER TWO
An Artisan and a Freemason   21

CHAPTER THREE
The Political Awakening of Paul Revere   37

CHAPTER FOUR
A Son of Liberty   55

CHAPTER FIVE
"My Worthy Friend Revere"   73

CHAPTER SIX
"Mr. Revere Will Give You the News"   89

CHAPTER SEVEN
"Am Obliged to Be Contented in This State's Service"   107

CHAPTER EIGHT
No Laurels on His Brow   123

CHAPTER NINE
Paul Revere, Esq.   141

CHAPTER TEN
A True Republican   159

CHAPTER ELEVEN
"In My Last Stage, How Blest Am I, to Find Content and Plenty By"   177

Notes   197
Bibliography   279
Index   295

ILLUSTRATIONS

1. Sugar bowl and cream pot, 1761, Paul Revere   28

2. "A View of the Year 1765," engraving by Paul Revere   49

3. Copley portrait of Paul Revere, 1768   52

4. Liberty bowl, 1768, Paul Revere   65

5. Paul Revere House, Boston   70

6. "The Bloody Massacre," 1770, engraving by Paul Revere   79

7. Two salt spoons from set of eight, 1796, Paul Revere   144

8. Edmund Hartt tea service, 1799, Paul Revere   164

9. Trade card of Paul Revere and Son, c. 1796–1803   165

10. Saint-Memin mezzotint of Paul Revere, c. 1800   180

11. Pen-and-ink sketch of Paul Revere's mill property and dwelling
    house in Canton   183

12. Stuart portrait of Rachel Revere, 1813   195

13. Stuart portrait of Paul Revere, 1813   195

ACKNOWLEDGMENTS

Growing up in Revere, Massachusetts, I have been aware of Paul Revere almost from the beginning, but it was not until I worked at the Paul Revere House in the summer of 1976 that I was introduced to his life and the possibility of history as a career. When I returned to work at the Paul Revere House after college, I became more immersed in Revere's life, and in 1981 I wrote a monograph and helped design an exhibit on the history and folklore of Paul Revere's "Midnight Ride." I put Paul Revere aside for many years until 1989, when I proposed writing a dual biography of Revere and a Loyalist for my dissertation at Brown University. It was Gordon Wood who suggested a full-length biography of Paul Revere instead.

Financial support from the History Department and Graduate School at Brown University and a Society of the Cincinnati Fellowship from the Massachusetts Historical Society greatly assisted my research. The contributions of Gordon Wood, John Thomas, and Naomi Lamoreaux, who read this work in its dissertation stage at Brown, exemplified the phrase "constructive criticism." I thank them for that and for their unfailing encouragement. Irving Bartlett, whose contributions as mentor helped me receive an M.A. in American civilization from the University of Massachusetts, Boston, in 1985, offered his scholarly expertise on this manuscript as he has on countless other occasions.

Several individuals at libraries, repositories, and historic sites went way beyond the call of duty in helping me. From beginning to end of this project, Nina Zannieri, Patrick M. Leehey, and Edith J. Steblecki of the Paul Revere Memorial Association assisted me through their excellent published work on Revere, their abundant willingness to share their considerable expertise on all aspects of Revere's life, and their invitation to present my ideas at part of the Lowell Lecture

Series at the Old South Meeting House in Boston in September 1991. The entire staff of the Massachusetts Historical Society justifiably deserve the thanks they invariably receive in acknowledgments. In particular, I thank Peter Drummey, Edward Hanson, Richard Ryerson, Virginia Smith, Chris Steele, and Conrad Wright for their invaluable assistance during my residence as a research fellow and throughout the research and writing of this work. Cynthia Alcorn, librarian and curator of the Samuel Crocker Lawrence Library at the Grand Lodge of Massachusetts A.F. & A.M., and Ward Williamson, formerly associated with the library, unlocked a wealth of materials on Revere's Masonic career and provided a delightful place to do research.

Questions and comments from students, professors, and classmates at workshops and seminars at Brown University and Boston University added useful information and refined my ideas. Colleagues at the wonderfully informative and convivial meetings of the Boston Area Seminar in Early American History at the Massachusetts Historical Society offered both scholarly advice and social communion. My students at Brown University, the University of Massachusetts in Boston, and Suffolk University were a receptive audience for my latest theories, research findings, and status reports on Paul Revere. There was only occasional eye-rolling as I worked Paul Revere into another lecture.

In addition to the value of observations from friends, students, and colleagues in the academic community, I gained many insights from members of the general public who attended my lectures at Boston's Old South Meeting House and the Lynn (Massachusetts) Historical Society. During much of the research stage, I worked part-time for the National Park Service as a park ranger at the Longfellow National Historic Site in Cambridge, Massachusetts. I benefited tremendously by discussing my work on Revere with my fellow rangers and the many visitors from around the world whom I led on tours.

For their sound advice, unflagging support, sense of humor, and patience, thank you to Paul Wright, my editor at the University of Massachusetts Press; my friends Leslie Lindenauer, Chris Mathias, Ken Turino, and Pat Zingariello; and my family. My mother, "Marksy" Triber, my sister and brother-in-law, Karen and Kenny Meola, and especially my nieces, Kristin, Karly, and Marisa Meola, are probably nearly as happy as I am to see the completion of this work!

A True Republican

INTRODUCTION

PAUL REVERE'S ascent into the realm of folklore surely began when Henry Wadsworth Longfellow climbed the tower of Boston's Old North Church on April 5, 1860. In his journal, this preeminent American poet wrote: "From this tower were hung the lanterns as a signal that the British troops had left Boston for Concord." The next day, Longfellow began writing "Paul Revere's Ride." On April 19 he noted: "I wrote a few lines in 'Paul Revere's Ride'; this being the day of that achievement."[1] With the publication of the poem in the January 1861 issue of *Atlantic Monthly* and also in *Tales of a Wayside Inn* in 1863, Longfellow inspired his countrymen with a romantic vision of America's Revolutionary struggle against British tyranny. In the process, he also created an enduring symbol of America's Revolutionary ideals in the person of Paul Revere, a daring horseman who, "with a cry of defiance and not of fear," rallied his countrymen in defense of liberty.[2] The poet did not explain what attracted Paul Revere to the Revolutionary cause, how Revere interpreted the republican principles of the Revolution, or how those principles shaped his life after April 19, 1775. Those were the questions that I set out to answer.[3]

As a historian and biographer, I have always been fascinated by what abstract terms like "liberty," "equality," "republicanism," and "democracy" meant to real people from different segments of society at various points in American history. I have also been drawn to the study of individuals who do not neatly fit into the disciplines or categories that we historians create. The intellectual historian will discover that the master goldsmith Paul Revere was intelligent but not intellectual, and that his ideology must be deciphered as much through his actions as through his words. The meaning and attraction of republicanism for Paul Revere will be found in a handful of letters and speeches but even more so in his political cartoons, as well as his choice of professions, political affiliations, and charitable associations. The social historian must employ a more sophisticated analysis of the role of artisans and laborers in the American Revolution in order to find a place for Paul Revere, a master artisan in the highly skilled goldsmith's trade.

The man that emerges from his own words and deeds, contemporary descriptions, and socioeconomic analysis was a proud, ambitious master artisan whose desire for prosperity, independence, and social distinction drew him to the republican ideals of liberty and equality of opportunity based on individual merit. At the same time, his correspondence, charitable associations, and professional pursuits reveal his equally fervent belief in the necessity of virtue—the sacrifice of private interest to the public good—in order to sustain republicanism. Understanding the tension between ambition and virtue seemed to be one key to defining Paul Revere's conception of the promise, responsibilities, and danger of republicanism as well as a key element in understanding his own life.[4]

When I raised the issue of ambition as a central theme in Revere's life during a lecture at Boston's Old South Meeting House in September 1991, members of the audience immediately condemned ambition as a negative trait and seized upon Revere's relevance to the twentieth century: He was just a money-grubbing social climber. It was a reaction I neither expected nor wanted. While acknowledging some unattractive examples of Revere's ambition, I tried to point out that ambition was not necessarily negative. Ambition could indeed be an "eager and sometimes inordinate desire for . . . preferment, honor, superiority, power, fame, wealth, etc.," and Revere struggled mightily and not always successfully to contain this aspect of his ambition. But ambition could also be a more general and positive "desire to distinguish oneself in some way." For Revere, his ambition also pushed him to earn laurels in his own time and for posterity for his public service during and after the American Revolution.[5]

Paul Revere and his fellow artisans who joined the patriot cause in the 1760s and 1770s were men who had already attained modest levels of property and independence through their hard work and talent. When they became Sons of Liberty, it was to protect their rights and liberties but even more so to advance their hopes for the future. What republicanism offered these master artisans, mariners, and shopkeepers was the prospect that their merit, virtue, and devotion to liberty would be rewarded not only with wealth but with social mobility and recognition as respected members of society.

Perhaps it is easier to understand Revere as an ambitious parvenu who raised himself up the social ladder from master goldsmith to merchant and manufacturer of bells, cannon, and copper and who, according to his letters and recollections, reveled in the elevated status that came with his patriotic activities and business achievements. Yet, to divorce Revere's ambition from its more positive elements—

the desire for honor, fame, and reputation in his own time and for posterity balanced by the restraining influence of virtue—is to misunderstand both the man and his culture. To do so is to ignore the man who delighted in the economic success he earned while serving the public good as a manufacturer of useful products and the man who, as a republican and a member of the Ancient and Honorable Society of Freemasons, practiced many acts of benevolence as an individual and through his charitable and fraternal affiliations.[6]

The search for Paul Revere's interpretation of republicanism also allowed me to leap into the historical debate over the definitions and the role of republican ideology in early American history. In the early 1990s Daniel T. Rodgers carefully reviewed and dissected the history, strengths, and weaknesses of the marvelously elastic term "republicanism." During the era of the American Revolution and the Early Republic, individuals of opposing political parties both claimed to be republicans and charged the other with subverting republican principles, and historians of every era and discipline in American history have turned to republicanism as an explanatory concept. Does such a concept have any validity at all when its very definitions have been so "slippery and contested," as Rodgers notes?[7]

The mantle of "true republicanism" does indeed seem "slippery and contested," if not downright absurd, when it can be claimed by members of antagonistic political parties. In 1796 a friend described the Federalist Paul Revere as "a *true Republican*," while in 1801 the Republican Elbridge Gerry rejoiced at the prospect of the presidential election of Thomas Jefferson, a man whose politics Revere deplored. Gerry welcomed the election of his fellow Republican because Jefferson "has always appeared to me a man of abilities and integrity, a firm friend to his country and a true republican." Yet it is precisely because Paul Revere and Thomas Jefferson and other Federalists and Republicans fought over the title of "true republicans" that we must try to decipher their republican principles.[8]

For Paul Revere, republicanism ensured a society based on social order and harmony, virtue and benevolence, and the opportunity for advancement based on achievement. It was an idealistic view, but not a hopelessly naive one, for Revere's belief in the promise of republicanism was always tempered by his awareness of the frailty of the human condition. After all, "man is," as he wrote his friend Thomas Ramsden in 1804, "an uneasy Animal." Such a glorious future rested, of course, on the guidance of the Federalists, with their realistic view of human nature, and was threatened by dangerous Jeffersonian notions of social equality and individualism that undermined true republicanism.[9]

The search for the sources that shaped Revere's definition of republicanism involved his family, socioeconomic status, occupation, and fraternal associations. In several pages of engaging reading, Revere biographer Esther Forbes suggests that Revere's zeal for liberty and independence was an inheritance from his French Huguenot father, who emigrated to Boston to escape religious persecution, or from a host of his mother's Hichborn ancestors, who defended their rights and liberties with energy, defiance, and cantankerousness. A genetic predisposition toward liberty is difficult to prove, but perhaps knowledge of family tradition did play a part in shaping Revere's political beliefs.[10]

The artisanal culture of Boston's North End was a more important factor in influencing Revere's beliefs. Certainly "artisanal culture," "artisanal republicanism," or the "artisan community" are categories too monolithic to contain all the individuals encompassed in those terms. Differences in wealth, rank, and ideology separated the master artisan from the journeyman and apprentice, and there was a hierarchy of trades that elevated Paul Revere, master goldsmith, over George Robert Twelves Hewes, shoemaker. Revere's "artisan republicanism" emerged and evolved from his socioeconomic status as a master artisan in the prestigious goldsmith's trade. What he shared with other master artisans was a pride in "a life defined by productive labor"; a fierce protectiveness of his liberty, independence, and aspirations for upward mobility; and a strong communal bond that offset the centrifugal tendencies of his ambition.[11]

His identity as a master artisan in an elite trade contributed to Revere's definition of republicanism, but so too did his identity as a Freemason. Freemasonry gratified Revere's desire for status by opening its ranks to all men of merit and character, regardless of their social standing, and by offering him opportunities to exercise leadership as a Masonic officer, leadership that was not readily available to a master artisan in his society. Yet, Freemasonry was also a very hierarchical organization in its structure and principles. The emphasis on both equality and hierarchy and the dedication to the ideal of a universe based on order, reason, and brotherly love that Revere learned as a Freemason were reinforced by Revolutionary rhetoric and affected his post-Revolutionary conception of republicanism.[12]

Although Paul Revere is best known to the general public for his "Midnight Ride," I am far more interested in his life after April 19, 1775. What did republicanism mean, not in theory, but in practice, and did those ideals change Revere's life for the better? The simple answer is that republican notions of "liberty," "equality," and "opportunity" did indeed improve Revere's life, which consisted of several successful attempts at upward mobility. He rose from the artisans' ranks to become a prosperous merchant, manufacturer, and public-spirited citizen whose leadership abilities were recognized in church committees, town meetings, and Masonic circles. But his failure to receive either a Continental Army officer's commission or patronage positions in the Washington and Adams administrations—sources of great disappointment in his life—also remind us of the limits of a young republic that still retained a sense of deference toward those of superior breeding and education.[13]

On May 21, 1846, Henry Wadsworth Longfellow wrote in his journal: "The most interesting books to me are the histories of individuals and individual minds." I share the poet's enthusiasm for biography, believing that it can be the intersection between history and personality. Paul Revere's story is the chronicle of a master artisan whose ambition for economic success and social distinction drew him to the republican ideals of liberty and equality; who found a sense of purpose, enhanced social status, and exhilaration in his role as a Son of Liberty and messenger of the American Revolution; and who discovered both the opportunities and the limitations of post-Revolutionary republicanism. Revere's story is also a larger chronicle of the historical events and cultural developments that transformed him from colonial subject to citizen of the new republic.[14]

CHAPTER ONE

CLARK'S WHARF

CROWDED AND NOISY, Boston's North End was dominated by wharves and shipyards and peopled with mariners, ropemakers, housewrights, and silversmiths, along with wealthy merchants like the Hutchinsons. Here Paul Revere, the second child and first son of Paul and Deborah Hichborn Revere, was born on December 21, 1734. His family was probably living on North Street (now Hanover) opposite Clark Street near the corner of Love Lane (now Tileston Street), where his father practiced the goldsmith's trade. In 1743 the Reveres moved to Clark's Wharf, where they rented a house or part of a house from Dr. John Clark. Young Paul grew up surrounded by the hustle and bustle of Boston's waterfront and by the numerous Hichborn clan. His world was bounded by family, the New Brick Church, the North Writing School, and a sense of his place in a stratified world.[1]

Paul's father, a French Huguenot, was born Apollos Rivoire in Riocaud, France, near Bordeaux, on November 30, 1702. On November 21, 1715, Apollos left his birthplace in the center of French Protestantism to join his Uncle Simon, who had emigrated to the English Channel Island of Guernsey ten years earlier. Simon Rivoire then paid for his nephew's passage to Boston and for his apprenticeship to goldsmith John Coney. In late 1715 or early 1716, thirteen-year-old Apollos Rivoire arrived in his new home. The warehouses and wharves, the densely packed streets, and the mingled voices of ship's captains, fishermen, merchants, and tradesmen speaking a foreign language must have bewildered a young French boy from the vineyard region of Bordeaux. Still, by the early 1700s, Boston was not an entirely alien city for French Huguenots.[2]

In the summer of 1686, less than a year after Louis XIV revoked the Edict of

Nantes, which had provided religious toleration for French Protestants since 1598, the first group of Huguenots arrived in Boston. Soon after their arrival, they organized a church, although they did not erect a building until approximately the time that Apollos Rivoire landed in Boston. The Bowdoins, Johonnots, and Sigourneys became successful merchants and respected citizens. Peter Faneuil, a merchant, inherited the sizable estate of his Uncle Andrew and, in 1742, built a new market near the town dock. Donated to the town of Boston, Faneuil Hall is the most visible reminder of the Huguenot presence in Boston. By the time Peter Faneuil built his market, the Huguenots, small in number to begin with, had become thoroughly integrated into the Anglo-American society of Boston. Apollos Rivoire followed this pattern of anglicizing his name, joining an English church, and marrying into an English family.[3]

Settled into Mr. Coney's house on Anne Street near Dock Square, Apollos learned his craft from one of Boston's finest goldsmiths. When Coney died in August 1722, Apollos Rivoire had become anglicized enough to call himself Paul Rivoire and successful enough to be able to buy out the remainder of his apprenticeship from Coney's widow. Paul Rivoire spent the next few years establishing himself in his trade and establishing himself in Anglo-American society.[4]

When it came time to join a church, the French émigré did not join the Huguenot church of the Faneuils, Boutineaus, and Johonnots. Paul Rivoire became a member of the New Brick Church, also known as the Cockerel because of the shape of its 172-pound weathervane fashioned by Deacon Shem Drowne. In 1720 the New North Church, which had been established by seventeen "substantial mechanics" in 1714, installed the Reverend Peter Thacher of Weymouth as assistant pastor. Dissenting members of New North disapproved of Thacher's leaving his congregation for a better position in Boston, claiming, "Ministers shall not be vagrants, nor intrude themselves of their own authority into any place which best pleaseth them." Ten dissenters formed the New Brick Church, which was gathered on May 22, 1722. Largely composed of artisans, New Brick also numbered the Hutchinsons among their congregation. Indeed, Thomas Hutchinson's sister married William Welsteed, pastor of New Brick Church from 1728 to 1753.[5]

Paul Rivoire integrated himself into his Anglo-American community in another way in 1729, when he subscribed to *The Life of the Very Reverend and Learned Cotton Mather*, by Samuel Mather. In a list of subscribers top-heavy with ministers, scholars, and gentlemen, the name of Paul Rivoire stands out as one of two goldsmiths and two apothecaries who had the financial means and intellectual curiosity to purchase a life of Cotton Mather, the paragon of Calvinist rectitude. His subscription may testify to a young artisan's interest in improving himself with books, a habit inherited by his son. He may also have looked to Cotton Mather as a model of Christian piety, charity, and ethics. As Mather taught his children to act by "Principles of Reason and Honour" and "to fear God, to serve Christ and shun Sin," so too may Paul Rivoire have instructed his children. By the time his first son was born, Paul Revere, as he now called himself, was a thoroughly respectable member of the community. The first Paul Revere gave his son a good name, a church, and a trade that would establish his place in the community. But it was his mother's family that supplied Paul's Anglo-American heritage and dominated his childhood.[6]

Paul Revere's father must have known the Hichborns long before he married Deborah on June 19, 1729. Deborah's father, Thomas, owned Hichborn Wharf on Ann Street, along with several other buildings. A joiner by trade, he was also licensed to sell liquor from his house on Hichborn Wharf. The Hichborns descended from a long line of mariners, artisans, and entrepreneurs. Paul's great-great-grandfather Thomas Dexter possessed both an entrepreneurial spirit in business and a defiant attitude in politics. He was a substantial farmer and promoter of the Saugus Iron Works, whose purchase of Nahant from an Indian for a suit of clothes involved Massachusetts in lawsuits for forty years. Shortly after his arrival from England, he was fined for his "insolent carriage and speeches" to Governor Simon Bradstreet and later "sett in the bilbows, disfranchized and fined for speaking reproachfull and seditious words against the government . . . saying this captious government will bring all to naught, adding that the best of them was but an attorney." Dexter's lack of deference so outraged John Endecott that Endecott slapped him. Endecott conceded that it was unlawful to strike Dexter, but as he explained to John Winthrop, "if you had seen the manner of his carriage, with such daring of me, with his arms akimbo, it would have provoked a very patient man."[7]

As the oldest son in an artisan's family of nine children, Paul would most likely assume his father's trade and eventually become a master goldsmith.[8] If he were a younger son who showed exceptional intelligence or a particular talent, like his cousin Benjamin Hichborn, his family might educate him for the ministry, medicine, or law. Paul Revere's formal education began and ended at the North Writing School, but Benjamin Hichborn, a boatbuilder's son, graduated from Harvard in 1768 and became a lawyer and a gentleman. During the Revolutionary War, Paul Revere rose no higher than lieutenant colonel in the Massachusetts militia. Benjamin Hichborn held the rank of colonel in the elite Independent Cadets, the second-oldest military organization in Massachusetts after the Ancient and Honorable Artillery Company. Clark's Wharf and the New Brick Church may have been good enough for the other Hichborns and Reveres, but by the 1780s Benjamin Hichborn and his family owned a house on Brattle Street, a summer home in Dorchester, and sometimes attended King's Chapel. Paul Revere, whose boyhood was shaped by the North Writing School, the New Brick Church, and apprenticeship with his father, seemed destined for a future as a master goldsmith, an elite among his fellow artisans, but a man of mere middling rank in colonial society.[9]

As a boy growing up in Boston's North End, Paul could not help being aware of the differences that separated the ranks of his society. Artisans like the Reveres rented or owned two-story wooden houses with a central chimney and two rooms on each floor. In 1770, when Paul could finally afford to buy a house, something that his father never achieved, he purchased a seventeenth-century wooden row house in North Square. Built around 1680 for Robert Howard, a wealthy merchant, the house had been at the height of fashion in its day, but that day was long past by the time Revere bought the house. Yet, in the very same neighborhood of modest wooden row houses stood two of the finest mansions in Boston: the Clark-Frankland and the Hutchinson houses.[10]

William Clark, the merchant who gave his name to Clark's Wharf and Clark Square, built his handsome three-story brick dwelling in 1711, before he lost his fortune in the French wars. In 1756 his heirs sold the house to Sir Charles Henry Frankland, collector of Boston under Governor William Shirley. Its twenty-six rooms contained porcelain fireplaces, mantelpieces of Italian marble, floors inlaid with alternating pine and cedar squares, and walls ornamented with fluted columns and gilded pilasters and cornices. The equally magnificent Hutchinson house next door was built at the end of the seventeenth century by John Foster, a Boston merchant and grandfather of Thomas Hutchinson, the future governor of Massachusetts. The painted brick mansion ornamented with four Corinthian pilasters and the Crown of Britain surmounting each window contained an entrance hall with carved and gilded arch ornamented with busts and statues and a library decorated with a tapestry commemorating the coronation of George II, with gardens extending to Hanover and Fleet Streets. The Reveres and people like them would have to be content with their less fashionable houses filled with simple wooden furniture embellished with an occasional piece of plate, glass, or china.[11]

A gentleman and an artisan were immediately distinguished by their difference in dress. A gentleman was resplendent in his powdered wig, cocked hat, and clothing that was either imported from London or based on London designs. He wore a white ruffled silk or linen shirt, a richly embroidered and brilliantly hued broadcloth waistcoat, silk hose, and brocade, velvet, or silk breeches fastened at the knee with silver buckles made by silversmiths like the Reveres. His elegant lady made her appearance in an imported brocade, damask, or velvet gown with whalebone stays and hoop skirts, brightly colored shoes, and elaborate coiffure piled atop a frame erected on her head. In contrast, an artisan and his wife wore clothing more for practicality than appearance. While he helped his father make silver knee buckles for wealthy customers, Paul wore a rough linen shirt, leather apron, and leather knee breeches. His mother and his sisters wore linen or wool dresses, petticoats, and an undergarment called a shift. The homespun clothing of artisans and their families lacked the fine texture and bright color that marked the clothing of the gentleman and gentlewoman.[12]

Once inside their beautifully appointed homes, Boston's elites enjoyed lavish dining and drinking, perhaps from silver plate made by the Reveres. Their other leisure pursuits included tea drinking, needlework, theater, concerts, and dancing. Master craftsmen like the Reveres and their families enjoyed their tea, although they did not own the assemblage of imported utensils and commodities that their wealthier neighbors seemed to require for their tea-drinking rituals. Mrs. Revere's needlework was not simply a form of recreation or symbol of feminine accomplishment but a necessary part of the household economy. The Reveres did not attend the theater, concert hall, or dances with the Hutchinsons, Hancocks, or Apthorps, but they had their own amusements. At their taverns, Boston artisans enjoyed liquor and conversation, backgammon, billiards, cards, and traveling shows with their displays of camels, tame bears, or other unusual animals. As young Paul and his friends wandered about Clark's Wharf, they could see such wonders as a polar bear, a "sapient dog," and even a pirate's head "in a pickle." They could visit Mrs. Hiller's waxworks with its representations of kings and queens or the more exciting waxworks of John Dyer with its "Lively Representation" of the Countess of Heininburg, who had 365 children at one birth. For amusement as well as the chance to earn some money, Paul and six of his friends worked as bell ringers at Christ Church.[13]

Compared with English society, colonial society was less hierarchical, and it was easier for a master craftsman to acquire the property that would make him theoretically independent from the control of his social superiors. Certainly the Reveres lived more comfortably than the families of the laboring poor on Boston's waterfront, with adequate food, housing, and recreation, but they were still dependent on the merchants, whose success or failure affected their own economic situation. A decline in maritime activity, along with illness or death of the head of household, or a household with too many children could spell distress or disaster for an artisan's family. An artisan might well envy the gentleman for his independence, his life of contemplation and amusement, and the deference paid to him as a natural leader of society. A bright, ambitious boy need not resign himself to permanent status as an artisan, however. As Daniel DeFoe pointed out: "Wealth however got in England makes Lords of mechanics, gentlemen of rakes." In the more open social structure of the colonies, there were even more ways to rise in the world without benefit of family wealth or pedigree.[14]

At the same time that Apollos Rivoire was serving his apprenticeship to John Coney, another Boston apprentice was making his way in the world. Thomas Hancock, son of the esteemed Reverend John Hancock of Lexington, did not follow his father or two brothers into the socially respectable but financially precarious position of a country parson. In a society that valued education and books as a means of attaining upward mobility and social status, the trade of bookseller could be a bridge to the world of gentlemen. Apprenticed to Colonel Daniel Henchman, a prosperous Boston bookbinder and bookseller, Thomas Hancock took the first step upward by marrying Henchman's daughter, Lydia. He soon expanded his horizons in the 1730s by investing in trading vessels. When war broke out in 1740 between England and its perennial enemy, France, Hancock was well positioned to make his fortune by profiting from the bounty of his privateers on the high seas and the inflated prices of wartime contracts. His ability to curry favor with Massachusetts governor William Shirley resulted in Hancock's success in obtaining supply contracts for the British assault on Louisburg, Nova Scotia, in 1745. By war's end, Thomas Hancock's profits exceeded £12,000 sterling. His immense fortune, estimated at £100,000 and bequeathed to his nephew John Hancock, enabled the latter to grow up a gentleman instead of the impoverished orphan of a country minister.[15]

Thomas Hancock proved that a socially advantageous marriage, choice of the right trade, patronage, and the acquisition of enormous wealth could help a man of modest origins become a man of influence. Granted, his wealth was also the result of ruthless and questionable business practices and his proficiency at profiting from a war that brought an astonishing loss of life for Massachusetts recruits and severe economic anguish for those at the bottom of the social structure. Paul Revere Sr., an industrious, religious man and an admirer of Cotton Mather, might well disapprove of Thomas Hancock's life of acquisitiveness and luxury and hope that his son would find another model of success.[16]

While Paul Revere's father was establishing himself as a master goldsmith, another Boston apprentice was aspiring to a loftier status than that of a Boston printer. Born in 1706, Benjamin Franklin, a tallow-chandler's son, showed early promise as a scholar. His father sent him to grammar school in preparation for a potential career as a minister. But the expense of a college education persuaded Josiah Franklin to transfer his youngest son to a writing school in anticipation of a more probable future as an artisan. After several false starts in choosing a craft, Josiah Franklin decided that his son's "Bookish Inclination" would make the trade of printer an appropriate one. Benjamin soon chafed under the autocratic rule of his master, his older brother James. Abandoning his apprenticeship and Boston, Franklin found more pleasing opportunities in Philadelphia. Aided by his own hard work, the generous assistance of numerous patrons, and the more open, entrepreneurial society of Philadelphia, Franklin acquired sufficient wealth to retire from business at age forty-two. It was not wealth, however, that Franklin craved, but the kind of life that wealth supplied.[17]

As he surveyed the world around him, Franklin saw laborers dependent on employers, tenant farmers on landlords, and artisans on customers. His own father was an "ingenious" man with a "sound Understanding and solid Judgment in prudential Matters, both in private and public affairs." Unfortunately, his large family and the "straitness of his circumstances" meant that Josiah Franklin lacked the independence to hold public office. In a largely dependent world, only gentlemen had the independence to pursue the kind of life denied to those of the middling and lower ranks. Living off the profits of land ownership or investments, a gentleman devoted himself to a liberal education, scientific and agricultural experiments, and public service. Franklin expected to assume all the responsibilities of a gentleman's life and to enjoy all its advantages, especially access to political power and preferment.[18]

Royal officials, members of Parliament, and even the members of the Royal Society who scoffed at his paper on electricity never acknowledged Benjamin Franklin as a gentleman. He was the product of a society that had very different ideas about social structure and social mobility. In the colonies, individuals expected personal independence and upward mobility. A printer or a goldsmith could become a merchant and a gentleman through hard work and self-improvement. In this process of upward mobility, education played a crucial role.[19]

In Europe and England, education prepared a man for his station in life. While an individual of middling or lower status received a utilitarian education that taught him all he needed to know for his particular role in society, a gentleman received a "liberal" education, one that freed his mind from the narrow limits imposed by time, geographic boundaries, or dependence on one's social superiors. Colonel Thomas Hutchinson, father of Thomas Hutchinson, who later became governor of Massachusetts, helped found two schools in Boston following the traditional pattern of educating children to assume their proper station in life. He donated the building for a Latin school, where his son and his son's future political opponent, Samuel Adams, studied Latin, Greek, grammar, rhetoric, mathematics, and geography, in preparation for Harvard and the assumption of their roles as natural leaders of their society. Colonel Hutchinson and his brother also built the North Writing School, where Paul Revere learned to read, write, and "cipher," in preparation for his proper place in society as an artisan.[20]

Revere and his contemporaries, throughout the Revolutionary period and the Early Republic, believed that the leaders of their society should be men whose liberal education provided them with the ability to think broadly, clearly, and independently about the problems of their society. In 1776 John Adams proposed James Bowdoin, Harvard Class of 1745, amateur astronomer and scientist, and a future founder of the American Academy of Arts and Sciences, as an excellent choice for governor because the office "will require the clearest and coolest Head and the firmest and Steadyest Heart, the most immoveable Temper and the Profoundest Judgment." That Bowdoin was the scion of a prominent mercantile family also pleased Adams, who stated his belief that the governor "ought to have

a Fortune too, and extensive connections." Deferential though he was to an educated gentleman, Adams did not, however, believe that education was the exclusive province of the rich and wellborn. In American society, a gentleman could be
made as well as born, and education could assist an individual in his aspirations.[21]

In Paul Revere's world, then, status and profession were not necessarily permanent. Benjamin Franklin, a tallow-chandler's son, rose from printer to scientist,
statesman, and gentleman. Henry Knox, the orphaned son of a Boston shipmaster, rose from bookseller to Continental Army general to secretary of war. David
Rittenhouse, the son of a Pennsylvania farmer, became an instrument maker,
astronomer, mathematician, and, in 1793, the first director of the United States
Mint, a position that Paul Revere sought unsuccessfully. All three men achieved
prominence because of their intelligence and talent and because they were products of a society that encouraged education, both formal and informal, as an
instrument of improvement and social mobility.[22]

Franklin supplemented his modest formal education by voracious reading and
the formation of the Junto, a club of mutual instruction. He and fellow members
Thomas Godfrey, a glazier and "self-taught mathematician" who published an
almanac and invented a quadrant, and William Parsons, a shoemaker turned
surveyor who loved reading and "acquired a considerable Share of Mathematics,"
wrote essays and discussed topics of moral, political, and natural philosophy.
Knox's formal education ended at age twelve, when his father died, but through
books and conversations with patrons at his bookstore, he became a student of
military science. In his autobiography, John Adams recalled that Knox "had been
a youth who had attracted my notice by his pleasing manners and inquisitive turn
of mind." Adams was so "impressed with an opinion of your Knowledge and
Abilities in the military Way for several years" that he assisted Knox in obtaining a
commission as colonel in the artillery regiment of the Continental Army, a commission that Revere hoped he would receive. Rittenhouse had limited schooling
but showed exceptional mathematical and mechanical ability, which was apparently stimulated by the inheritance of a chest of books and tools from an uncle.
Through a combination of reading and his own powers of observation, Rittenhouse acquired proficiency in theoretical and practical astronomy. Admired for his
celebrated orrery designed in 1767, his telescope, and his contributions to mathematics and astronomy, Rittenhouse became an educational and political leader in
Pennsylvania.[23]

Revere's rudimentary education at the North Writing School, which probably
ended at age thirteen, also helped his transformation from artisan to manufacturer.
Like Franklin, Knox, and Rittenhouse, Paul Revere used the knowledge contained
in books as ideas to be tested against the reality of observation and experimentation. His eventual success as a bell and cannon founder and copper manufacturer
was a combination of trial-and-error experimentation and the application of les-

sons learned from reading such works as Watson's *Chemical Essays*. In the 1790s, as he developed his expertise in metallurgy, he enjoyed corresponding with educated experts on the subject, even writing to Reverend Richard Watson to correct an error in his chemistry text. In memoranda books, he jotted down "recipes" for silver copper and formulas for casting bells and cannons. When coppersmiths told him that copper could not be melted and hammered hot, Revere "determined if possible to gain the secret." He succeeded, not by finding the formula in a book, but "after a great many tryals and very considerable expense."[24]

For Revere, books and education were not just tools to make his way in the world. He maintained a lively interest in books, newspapers, and ideas throughout his life. His education did not end at the North Writing School but continued through his own reading and discussions at his shop, taverns, political clubs, and town meetings. Explaining to his cousin John Rivoire of Guernsey why the colonies had to fight a war with England, Revere offered a lengthy review of the Imperial Crisis, which seems to have been the result of an extensive reading of newspapers and pamphlets, along with attendance at political meetings. To support his interpretation of the American Revolution, he even cited Voltaire's assessment of the English as "the *Savages* of Europe." After the Revolution, he continued his course of self-education and monitored the progress of Freemasonry and republicanism, two causes to which he devoted a considerable part of his life, through subscriptions to numerous newspapers and magazines, membership in the Boston Library Society, and careful readings of Masonic discourses.[25]

Intelligent and well informed, Paul Revere was still largely a self-educated man who, like many self-educated people, had great respect for formal education. His own lack of education and social refinement meant that Revere would never quite become a gentleman, but he saw to it that his children were educated to fulfill his social ambitions. His sons Joshua, Joseph Warren, and John all graduated from the Boston Public Latin School. John continued his education at Harvard and the University of Edinburgh, where he received his medical degree, in preparation for a career as a physician, scientist, medical editor, and educator. Revere sent his younger daughters, Maria and Harriet, to William Turner's dancing school, perhaps hoping to instill in them one of the more important attributes of gentility. Maria also attended the Young Ladies' Academy in Woburn, where she studied reading, writing, grammar, history, geography, mathematics, needlework, painting, and drawing.[26]

With his formal schooling finished at age thirteen, Paul Revere entered the next stage of his education with his apprenticeship to his father. First by observation and then by practice, he learned to make flatware, tankards, buckles, buttons, thimbles, tea sets, children's whistles, and surgeon's instruments. He also learned to clean and burnish silver and mend everything from buttons to earrings to the lock on a pocketbook. His craft required a laborer's brawn for the incessant hammering necessary to turn silver sheets into tankards and coffeepots and an artist's discerning eye and delicate hand to design an object and cover it with surface ornamentation. Both a mechanic who made buckles and mended buttons for fellow artisans and their families and an artist who designed rococo-style "scalop'd salvers" for the merchant elite, the goldsmith moved back and forth between the worlds of artisans and gentlemen. The nature of his work made Paul Revere a useful bridge between the upper and lower echelons of his society, a point that would not escape the attention of leaders of the American Revolution.[27]

Paul Revere's customers ranged from merchants and ship's captains to his Hichborn relations and Clark's Wharf neighbors. His dual role as artist and mechanic enabled him to adapt to fluctuations in the economy. At a time when cash was chronically in short supply and the value of currency was unstable, the goldsmith was something of a banker who transformed specie into objects of lasting value that could be used or melted down to make new objects. In prosperous times, Revere made a silver sugar dish and a pair of silver canns for the merchant Benjamin Greene and a silver coffeepot and a silver child's porringer for Captain John Collings. In leaner years, he survived by making an almost continuous supply of buckles and buttons, repairing spectacles and picture frames, and cleaning silver for his family, friends, and neighbors. The richly ornamented rococo-style silver that Revere made for Boston's merchants and ship's captains brought him greater financial reward and eventually ended up in museum collections. But it was the steady stream of buckles, buttons, and other commonplace objects that he made for Uncle Thomas Hichborn, a boatbuilder, Joshua Brackett, a coppersmith who later became the owner of the Cromwell Head Tavern on School Street, and many other artisans and mariners that sustained him through good years and bad.[28]

As a master goldsmith who worked in gold and silver, Revere had better than average prospects of success. Although most artisans never rose above the middling rank, master goldsmiths, distillers, tanners, ropemakers, and sugar refiners were often very well-to-do, with personal property averaging about two-and-a-half times the amount generally left by artisans and twice the amount for most colonists. A skilled metal craftsman possessed talents that were in demand in several auxiliary areas. In addition to making teapots and coffeepots, Revere could also engrave copperplates to produce bookplates, songbooks, and political cartoons; make false teeth fastened with gold or silver wire; and provide metal objects for clockmakers, saddlers, silversmiths, and other artisans.[29]

His specialized talents and the prosperity that often accompanied him made the master goldsmith an aristocrat among artisans. But in the overall social hierarchy, he stood in the middle ranks. Property and wealth could help an artisan move upward, but the absence of the other attributes of gentility would block his entrance into the highest ranks of society. Paul Revere might grow up to be a wealthy artisan, but he still lacked the liberal education, good breeding, refined manner, and independence from labor that marked the gentleman. Although his craft allowed Revere a certain degree of creativity and independence in the design and ornamentation of his silver, he was nonetheless confined to interpreting and adapting the English and European styles favored by Boston's merchant elite. He might be able to vary the design of finials and handle tips on his tankards, but in the end, he was dependent on the demands and whims of customers like Andrew Oliver, who wanted him to make a sugar dish out of an ostrich egg. Paul Revere, master goldsmith, could never forget—nor would many a true gentleman let him forget—that for all the artistry involved in the design and production of his silver, he still wore a leather apron and worked with his hands as he hammered, soldered, cleaned, and filed each piece of silver.[30]

As he grew up in the 1740s, the young apprentice learned of events beyond his family or his neighborhood. From customers' conversations, from newspapers lying about his father's shop or on a tavern table, and from gossip in the streets, he heard about the latest London fashions, the state of trade, and politics. At first, the awareness that he was part of a wider world—that of the British Empire—came in small ways. On November 5 he and his friends and neighbors observed Pope's Day, in commemoration of the failed gunpowder plot to blow up James I and Parliament in 1605 to avenge the persecution of Roman Catholics. Rival gangs from the North and South Ends erected platforms and carriages with figures of the pope, monks, and the Devil, which were burned in effigy at the conclusion of the celebration. With their rambunctious ceremony, the rowdy young men and boys showed their contempt for popery and their allegiance to the Crown and Protestantism. Colonial citizens also marked the king's birthday, the anniversary of his coronation, and the anniversary of the execution of Charles I on January 30, 1649, the last event commemorated as a day of atonement for the murder of the king. As Englishmen, they took pride and delight in their victory over the French at Louisburg in 1745. Of course their connection to the Crown meant more than merely observing royal anniversaries or raising a toast to the king. It also meant that the Reveres and their neighbors were affected by royal policies concerning war, politics, and the economy.[31]

Their involvement in King George's War (1744–48), England's war against Spain and France, had far-reaching effects on the lives and livelihoods of the colonists. The war brought an influx of paper money, a financial windfall for privateers and those who supplied provisions for royal military expeditions, but suffering and privation for those who served in and paid for colonial campaigns. On August 14, 1744, the inhabitants of Boston petitioned for relief from heavy taxation, complaining that even the richest inhabitants were "groaning under the weight of them." The situation of the "middling sort" was even worse, with "many of them Sinking into extream Poverty. . . . many honest Tradesmen are without

Employ, the Trade of Building Houses being in a manner stagnated, as well as that of Building Ships." Thomas Hancock and other wealthy merchants, anticipating the great fortunes to be made, rallied around Governor William Shirley's plans to fortify the Maine frontier, supply Britain's Caribbean expeditions, and capture the French fortress at Louisburg. As they left Boston on April 4, 1745, the primarily lower-class recruits who made up the largest expeditionary force ever assembled in the colonies were fired up with patriotism, Protestant zeal, and visions of the plunder that awaited them at Louisburg. The successful six-week campaign against papist France was a time for Englishmen on both sides of the Atlantic to rejoice, but joy in Massachusetts was short lived, as the colony soon faced the aftermath of war.[32]

The heavy loss of life, estimated at about 2 percent of the colony's population, plagued the inhabitants of Massachusetts for years to come. The number of taxable polls decreased from 3,395 in 1738 to 2,972 in 1741 to about 2,660 in 1745. The artisans and shopkeepers of the North End would have to make up the losses with an increased tax burden. On May 14, 1746, the Boston town meeting appointed a committee to draw up a petition to the General Court "that the Town may be Relieved as to their Proportion of the publick Taxes." The middling ranks feared the tax burden of war, but it was the mariners and laborers who were pressed into service to fight the Crown's wars who had the most to lose by prolonged periods of war. Against this background, it is not surprising that mariners and laborers rioted against the Crown's efforts at impressment, or that people of the middling ranks supported them.[33]

In November 1747 Commodore Charles Knowles, commander of the royal squadron that fought at Louisburg, put into port at Boston for the purpose of impressing colonial seamen to replace royal deserters. Knowles should have expected trouble, for the inhabitants of Boston's waterfront had rioted against impressment several times since 1741. A mob surrounded Governor Shirley's mansion on suspicion that royal officers had taken refuge there, and the militia ignored the governor's order to suppress the mob, forcing Shirley to seek safer quarters at Castle William in Boston Harbor. The danger of insurrection passed only when the General Court approved resolutions supporting the governor, the militia assured the governor of its protection, and Commodore Knowles, forced to acknowledge the governor's authority over military affairs in the province, released the impressed seamen. The Knowles riot could be dismissed as an example of lower-class antiauthoritarianism no different from the street politics of England. But it also revealed particular views about colonial society and government that were troubling to royal officials.[34]

Where Commodore Knowles saw the necessity of colonial submission to royal authority, the inhabitants of Massachusetts saw the invasion of their individual rights and colonial sovereignty. They invoked an interpretation of the proper authority over royal military forces in the province that was at odds with the Crown's view. After the Glorious Revolution of 1688, moderate Whigs in England accepted the necessity of a professional army to defend England, as long as it was under parliamentary control. The inhabitants of Massachusetts also accepted the presence of royal military forces, but in their interpretation of moderate Whig thought, they substituted the provincial legislatures for Parliament. They directed their anger at Knowles for ignoring colonial laws against impressment. Governor Shirley came in for his share of abuse from the mob and the militia because he had not stopped Knowles from landing his press gang in Boston. The Knowles riot showed that the reciprocal bond of protection and allegiance between the Crown and its colonial subjects was a fragile one that often hinged on colonial interpretations of that bond. The riot also showed how "men of all orders"—from "Persons of Mean and vile Condition" to artisans of the middling ranks to "Persons of Influence in the Town"—could unite in defense of their interpretation of the rights of Englishmen. That lesson would not be lost on Samuel Adams and Dr. Joseph Warren when they mobilized "men of all orders"— among them, Paul Revere—in the patriot cause of the 1760s and 1770s.[35]

Within a short time of the Knowles riot, another controversy broke out in Massachusetts over the actions of one of the Reveres' North End neighbors. In 1748, with the end of King George's War, Parliament granted Massachusetts £183,649 sterling as its share of war compensation. When Thomas Hutchinson drafted a bill for the immediate retirement of all paper currency, the mass of ordinary Bostonians saw that their interests would be sacrificed to the interests of wealthy merchants hoping to profit by their purchase of depreciated paper currency. Perhaps they also remembered that in 1740–41, when shopkeepers, artisans, and the working poor supported a land bank that would issue bills of credit backed by land, Thomas Hutchinson had opposed their interests by supporting a silver bank, whose bills of credit would be backed by silver. In the May 1749 elections, the Boston electorate withdrew its allegiance by voting Hutchinson and other supporters of immediate redemption out of office.[36]

Young Paul Revere might not have understood the issues of paper money, land banks, taxes, royal sovereignty, and colonial liberties that he heard discussed at the family dinner table, in his father's shop, or on the streets. But perhaps he wondered why a crowd of Bostonians shouted insults at Governor Shirley, why the militia ignored orders from a royal governor, and why people were so adamant that Commodore Knowles release colonial subjects from service to the Crown. He might also have wondered why his neighbors were so angry at Thomas Hutchinson for proposing immediate redemption that they threatened to let his house burn in 1748 and later forced him to withdraw to the safety of his country house in Milton. It is difficult to know when Paul Revere's political awakening began, but family tradition says that his attendance at the sermons of Dr. Jonathan Mayhew may have been a turning point.[37]

According to family tradition, Paul's father beat his fifteen-year-old son for attending Dr. Mayhew's West Church instead of the family's New Brick Church. Paul Sr. might have objected to his son's attendance at Mayhew's church on theological grounds, for Dr. Mayhew's enlightened views on religion and his belief in human goodness, reason, and ability to work with God toward salvation conflicted with the elder Revere's orthodox Calvinism, emphasizing human beings' depravity and inability to achieve their own salvation. But there were additional objections when Mayhew's pronouncements crossed the line from theology to politics, and he introduced dangerous ideas about resistance to authority.[38]

On January 30, 1749, the citizens of Massachusetts observed the anniversary of the execution of Charles I. For those in attendance at Dr. Mayhew's West Church, it was not an occasion for atonement or humiliation but an opportunity to consider the grounds of "Unlimited Submission and Non-Resistance to the Higher Powers." Dr. Mayhew based his discourse on Romans 13: "For there is no power but of God: the powers that be are ordained of God. Whosoever therefore resisteth the power, resisteth the ordinance of God." Mayhew preached that submission was due "only to those who *actually* perform the duty of rulers, by exercising a reasonable and just authority, for the good of human society." When magistrates "act contrary to their office" and "rob and ruin the public . . . they cease to be the *ordinance* and *ministers of God.*" To resist Charles I, whose reign was marked by "wicked councellors and ministers," taxes without parliamentary consent, arbitrary courts, and unjust imprisonment, was not rebellion "but a most righteous and glorious stand, made in defence of the natural and legal rights of the people." Dr. Mayhew proposed that his audience observe January 30 not as a day to atone for their ancestors' treason against the king but rather as "a standing *memento,* that *Britons* will not be *slaves,* and a warning to all corrupt *councellors* and *ministers,* not to go too far in advising to arbitrary, despotic measures."[39]

Paul Revere Sr. may have thought that Dr. Mayhew's notions about submission to rightful authority were dangerous ideas for a fifteen-year-old boy. They would be no less dangerous when Paul Revere Jr. grew up and thought even more deeply about the rights of colonial Englishmen.

CHAPTER TWO

AN ARTISAN
AND A FREEMASON

AT NINETEEN, Paul Revere was nearing the end of his apprenticeship and entering manhood when his father died on July 22, 1754. The former Apollos Rivoire, dead at fifty-two, "left no estate, but he left a good name, and seven children." His father's death left Paul in an awkward situation. He was now the head of the household, with responsibility for his mother and younger brothers and sisters, including the apprenticeship of his younger brother Thomas. Although burdened with adult responsibilities, Paul was not legally an adult and could not open his own silversmith shop. Possibly he ran a shop under his mother's name, or he might have worked for the silversmith Nathaniel Hurd. Whatever the circumstances, Paul's entrance into adulthood was not easy, and difficult economic times lay ahead.[1]

King George's War, which ended in 1748, had brought substantial profits to merchants, supply contractors, and privateers, but the postwar depression brought hardship to families in the middling ranks. The Reveres were among those affected, as the newly widowed Deborah Revere paid her rent to Dr. John Clark with a combination of a silver thimble, rum, and cash. For the next quarter's rent, her oldest son paid the debt with cash and by making ten rings for his landlord. Over the next two years, Paul Revere, like so many other young artisans and farmers' sons, would be caught between dependence and independence. Not yet old enough to run a business or inherit the family farm, these young men would work for their families and await the day when they would be on their own. That day may have looked very distant, for it seemed that only war brought temporary prosperity and independence in the form of supply contracts, credit, and ready cash at the end of military service. It is no wonder that provincial military service was an enticement for many young men.[2]

Unlike earlier wars, where the colonies were dragged into England's European disputes, the French and Indian War began in the colonies, as French and English colonists raced to settle the trans-Allegheny West. What began in 1754 as a colonial response by Virginia and Massachusetts to French activity in the northern Ohio valley broadened to worldwide war, known as the Seven Years' War, when England declared war against France and her allies in May 1756. When Massachusetts governor William Shirley authorized the enlistment of volunteers to seize the French fortification at Crown Point on Lake Champlain, Paul Revere answered the call. On February 18, 1756, the young silversmith became Second Lieutenant Paul Revere in Richard Gridley's artillery train.[3]

Two years before his death, Paul Revere recalled his youthful military service in a brief account. It is not an old man's wistful recollection of glorious military exploits but a matter-of-fact description of his military service in which he simply noted that he was twenty-one years old when he enlisted in the army commanded by General Winslow and that he was stationed at Fort William Henry on Lake George from May to November 1756. From the many journal entries in which provincial volunteers described the people and places they saw in their journey from Boston through western Massachusetts to Albany, it seems that boredom and a longing for adventure might have been a motive for some young men to enlist. Other volunteers heeded the call of New England's ministers that they should, like the Israelites, take the field against God's and England's enemies. If boredom, patriotism, and religious enthusiasm were not sufficient reasons to enlist, there were always the lure of money.[4]

On February 11, 1756, a committee of the Boston town meeting drafted a petition to the General Court asking for a reevaluation of estates, complaining that although in the past there were "near four thousand Polls who paid Taxes, now there are but few more than two thousand." The shipbuilding trade had declined drastically in a short time from "thirty or forty mostly large vessels on the stocks" to "but six vessels," and Boston was losing its monopoly on distilling molasses and refining sugar to competition from several other towns and colonies. The loss of trade affected coopers, bakers, hatters, tanners, chandlers, truckmen, and porters, "all of which having full employ chearfully paid their part of the Taxes." As a consequence, poor relief had soared from £1000–1500 per year to £10,000–12,000 per year.[5]

Under these circumstances, many a young farmer, cooper, or silversmith saw military service as the best way to support his family. The provincial private in 1756 earned the equivalent of a laborer's daily wage, but unlike the laborer, the soldier had a guaranteed daily wage plus an enlistment bounty for his six- to eight-month's service, for an average compensation of more than fifteen pounds lawful money. As an artillery lieutenant, Paul Revere would be more richly compensated, receiving five pounds six and eight per month (£5.6.8), or thirty-two pounds for his six months of service, at a time when the rent on his family's house was sixteen pounds per year. Revere, who later zealously but unsuccessfully sought a Continental officer's commission and used his Revolutionary War rank as lieutenant colonel in the Massachusetts Militia to the end of his life, may have been motivated to enlist by visions of glory or the status of a junior officer's rank, in addition to wishing to help his family. Whatever their motives, Lieutenant Paul Revere and his fellow volunteers would find that duty as a provincial soldier in His Majesty's service was not always what they expected.[6]

Provincial Englishmen, especially in Massachusetts, had many examples from seventeenth-century English and colonial history to support their belief in the danger of standing armies. Charles I, Cromwell, and Charles II had all maintained their rule with the help of a standing army. In December 1686 Sir Edmund Andros, appointed governor-general of the Dominion of New England by the Catholic monarch James II, arrived in Boston with a company of soldiers and authority over all legislative, judicial, and military affairs. To the colonists, regular soldiers were a dangerous body of drunkards, convicts, and vagrants who had no property or stake in the community. They were to be feared and despised as the unwitting tools of despotic monarchs, kept under control only by the brutal discipline of their aristocratic officers. In contrast, the colonists venerated the citizen-soldiers who volunteered for royal expeditions and served in the militia as the best defense against foreign or Indian attack and their community's rightful upholders of liberty and order. Provincial soldiers were a safe and stabilizing force because they were citizens who knew why they were fighting, they took orders from officers of their own choice, and unlike the standing army, they were subject to the control of representative colonial legislatures.[7]

While provincials complained about the arrogance and contempt of British officers and the brutishness of their men, British regulars condemned provincial solders as dirty, cowardly, insubordinate, and inferior in every way to regular soldiers. In 1755 the Newcastle ministry dispatched Major General Edward Braddock and two regular regiments to Virginia to assume command of what had been a colonial effort against the French. Benjamin Franklin, who helped Braddock procure horses and wagons for his campaign, thought the general was "a brave Man" but had "too much self-confidence, too high an Opinion of the Validity of Regular Troops, and too mean a One of both Americans and Indians." After Braddock outlined his ambitious plans to defeat the French, Franklin diplomatically tried to warn the general of the danger of Indian ambush on the exposed flanks of the British lines. In his autobiography, Franklin recalled that Braddock "smiled at my Ignorance, and replied, 'These Savages may indeed be a formidable Enemy to your raw American militia; but upon the King's regular and disciplined Troops, Sir, it is impossible they could make any Impression.'"[8]

Braddock's confidence proved to be misplaced, as he was killed in the Pennsylvania wilderness during a French and Indian attack at the Monongahela River. His eventual successor, Lord Loudoun, was a veteran professional officer with a similar attitude toward provincial armies. He would use regular regiments to wage war, relegating provincial troops to guard duty, building roads, clearing brush, hauling supplies, and the other "dirty work" of war. Paul Revere and the Massachusetts volunteers would find little glory during their military service. They would also discover that Loudoun had very different ideas about military command and subordination.[9]

With General Braddock's death on July 9, 1755, supreme command in North America had fallen to Governor William Shirley of Massachusetts, who, with characteristic vigor, planned a provincial campaign against the French at Crown Point. When Paul Revere and his fellow soldiers left Boston in May 1756, it was as an army organized by Governor Shirley and the Massachusetts General Court and contracted to serve under the command of General John Winslow. In July 1756 the Crown replaced Shirley as supreme commander in North America with John Campbell, the fourth earl of Loudoun, and Shirley's plans for Crown Point dissolved amid a protracted dispute between Lord Loudoun and the provincial officers over command of the expedition.[10]

When Lord Loudoun took command in July 1756, he assumed that the provincial troops would abide by the Rules and Articles of War, chiefly the provision that provincial officers were subordinate to regular officers of the same rank. Thus, General Winslow, the esteemed veteran of several colonial campaigns against the French, would be subordinate to the most junior regular major general. While Winslow assured Governor Shirley, Major General James Abercromby, the interim commander, and Lord Loudoun of his willingness to follow orders, he tried to explain why the provincial officers and enlisted men were not so inclined. The officers, as he explained to Shirley, considered that the army enlisted for Crown Point was "a proper organized body" and that they, as officers appointed by the several provincial governments, were "executors in trust, which it was not in their power to resign." Furthermore, the privates in the provincial army "universally hold it as one part of the terms on which they enlisted that they were to be commanded by their own officers." Because he needed the provincial troops to defend the New York frontier, Loudoun was forced to accept provincial terms of enlistment. The commander in chief of the provincial army was to be a Massachusetts general, terms of payment would be set by the provincial assemblies, and provincial troops were to be limited to a term of service not longer than twelve months and neither south of Albany nor west or Schenectady.[11]

While Lord Loudoun and the provincial officers waged their endless disputes over rank and subordination to authority, the French took Fort Oswego from the British, the Crown Point expedition never got underway, and the French built Fort Carillon (Ticonderoga) on Lake Champlain, an act that would impede the British advance into Canada for three years. Paul Revere had no chance to test his courage and patriotism or to display his skill in the elite military science of artillery. He returned to Boston in November 1756 with neither laurels on his brow nor war stories that would entertain future grandchildren; nonetheless, service in the Crown Point expedition had its own lessons to teach.[12]

When Revere and the other Massachusetts volunteers joined British regulars in service to the Crown, they discovered that they held notions about rights, obligations, and deference to authority that were profoundly different from those of Lord Loudoun, regular military officers, and other royal officials. Loudoun, an aristocratic, professional officer who deferred to his superiors, expected a similar unquestioned obedience from provincial officers and enlisted men. He was astonished that the provincials "assumed to themselves what they call rights and privileges, totally unknown in the mother country." Loudoun and the British hierarchy were appalled by the fraternization between provincial officers and their men and the provincials' concept of a contract between themselves and their governments. The citizen-soldiers of Massachusetts, who had long fought colonial wars with little assistance from the Crown, and whose more open social structure was at variance with Lord Loudoun's highly stratified world, were unaccustomed to and often dumbfounded by the strict lines of vertical authority and blind submission to one's superiors that was expected of both regular and provincial soldiers. British officers would long remember the insubordination of the provincials, while Paul Revere and the other citizen-soldiers of Massachusetts would not forget the contempt of their fellow Englishmen.[13]

It did not take Revere long to resume civilian life after he returned home in November 1756. On August 4, 1757, he married Sara Orne of Boston, and they moved into his mother's house on Clark's Wharf. Only twenty-two years old, Revere assumed responsibility for his mother and younger sisters, a new wife, and the apprenticeship of his younger brother Thomas. On April 3, 1758, Sara gave birth to their first child, Deborah. Seven more children would be born in the next fourteen years. The prospect of supporting a rapidly growing family in a town still reeling from the financial burden of war was a daunting one. But Paul Revere had certain advantages that laid the foundation for a successful business.[14]

Rising taxes and food prices, currency depreciation, and economic decline because of Boston's loss of supply contracts to New York all threatened the survival of Boston's master craftsmen, shopkeepers, mariners, and laborers. The considerable capital required to stock a goldsmith's shop with bellows, hammer, anvil, tongs, molds, and the multitude of tools necessary for the design and production of silver and gold objects might have prevented many a journeyman goldsmith from opening his own shop in the late 1750s and early 1760s. Revere's father may have "left no estate," but he bequeathed a valuable inheritance to his oldest son by training him and leaving him a fully stocked shop, including molds that his son used throughout his career. Revere also inherited some of his father's customers, including the Boston merchant Benjamin Greene. Greene, who had supplied Paul Revere Sr. with household goods in exchange for silver objects, was one of Paul Jr.'s first customers, and he and his son remained customers until 1796.[15]

Much of Revere's success in the early stages of his career can be attributed to the rich network of family, friends, and neighbors, which provided him with both emotional and economic support. His Hichborn relations—including Uncle Thomas and cousins Thomas Jr. and Nathaniel, all boatbuilders, William, a hatter, and Robert, a sailmaker who became a trader and retailer after the Revolution—were among his earliest and steadiest customers. He engraved copperplates to print "hatt prints" for William Hichborn and made buckles, buttons, spoons, porringers, and teaspoons for the other Hichborns. His friend Joshua Brackett and Clark's Wharf neighbors Captain Samuel Cochran and Isaac Greenwood, an instrument maker and ivory turner, were among the many artisans, mariners, and neighbors who patronized Revere in the early 1760s.[16]

As a resident of Clark's Wharf, Revere knew that much of his livelihood depended on the seagoing trade. Many of his neighbors were mariners, most of them destined to die with little or no property. But among this class of men were many like Paul Revere, ambitious and shrewd men who might save their commissions from selling a merchant's goods, take a risk selling goods on their own, or acquire a small ownership of a sailing vessel. Eventually, they might retire ashore as merchants or landowners. In 1762 Revere's most profitable customers included ship's captains William Tory, who ordered a pair of silver porringers for £17.14.9 on May 10; John Collings, who ordered a silver coffeepot and a child's porringer and spoon for £20.1.0 on June 3; and Barnabas Benney, who ordered a large silver salver worth £19.6.0 on July 3. Ship's captains would continue to be a lucrative source of income for Revere throughout the Revolutionary period and beyond.[17]

Always resourceful, eager to explore new avenues of business, and pressed by the demands of a large family, Revere found another profitable source of opportunity by making items for other silversmiths, who re-marked and sold those items. Silversmiths with less diversified shops or who lacked Revere's particular skill in the art of repoussé, a type of surface ornamentation formed in relief by hammering up from the reverse side, turned to Revere to supply a wide range of objects. In 1762 he made "scalop'd" salvers, a chafing dish, a picture frame and Indian pipe for Nathaniel Hurd, silver canns for John Avery, and two silver waiters for Samuel Minott. Another silversmith, John Coburn, came to Revere throughout the 1760s and 1770s for snuff boxes, teapots, teaspoons, and tea tongs, and for engraving arms and crests on teapots and coffeepots, kettles, tankards, and plates. Revere's alliances with fellow silversmiths, established in the early 1760s and an integral part of his business throughout his career, improved both his business and his artistic reputation.[18]

Only a few years after his return from military service in the French and Indian War, Paul Revere had established a thriving business based on a diversified clientele. He might have considered himself a man of some independence, the head of a small business, responsible for the apprenticeship of his younger brother and two other young men, and a master craftsman producing stock goods for family, friends, and neighbors drawn from the middling ranks of society. But the young master goldsmith could not hope to become a man of means solely by mending stone buttons for Joshua Brackett or making knee buckles for cousin Robert. His long residence on Clark's Wharf had taught Paul Revere that Boston was a mercantile town, and his success or failure also rested on the fortunes of Boston's merchants.[19]

While Boston's citizens complained endlessly about declining tax rolls and increasing poor relief rolls, economic depression did not really hit until the mid-1760s. In the early 1760s trade improved somewhat from the slump of the 1750s, and merchants were not yet feeling the full impact of declining royal military spending and tightened credit. With the fall of Canada in 1761, Boston merchants had reason to be hopeful about the future. Proud of their status as colonial elites and anxious to display their wealth and sophistication, merchants patronized artisans who could design houses, fine furniture, dinnerware, and luxury items copied or adapted from English styles. Paul Revere's skill at surface ornamentation and his overall mastery of the detail and delicacy of the French-influenced rococo style so fashionable in England and its colonies earned him the patronage of some of Boston's most prominent merchant families. The creation of a sugar dish for Lucretia Chandler and the many other fine objects that he made for merchants like Thomas Greene, Zacariah Johonnot, and Foster Hutchinson in the early 1760s were undoubtedly more artistically and financially satisfying to Revere than the buckles and buttons that he made for Boston's artisans and mariners. Yet, it was ultimately Revere's connections to his fellow artisans and men of middling rank that played the larger role in his business, social, and political life.[20]

As Paul Revere established his place in society as a respected master artisan, his world still revolved around the people and institutions of the North End: his wife and children, his mother and Hichborn relations, the New Brick Church, and Clark's Wharf friends, neighbors, and taverns. On September 9, 1760, he became an Entered Apprentice in St. Andrew's Lodge of Freemasons, forming an association that would shape his life for the next forty years. His membership in the

1. Silver sugar bowl and cream pot made by Revere in 1761, apparently as a wedding gift for Lucretia Chandler from her brother-in-law, Benjamin Green. In March 1762 Revere charged Greene for the "sugar dish." Courtesy, Museum of Fine Arts, Boston. Pauline Revere Thayer Collection.

artisan-dominated St. Andrew's Lodge cemented existing ties to family, friends, and neighbors and created new bonds of brotherhood that were reinforced in his business and political life. His standing as a Freemason also moved him beyond the provincial confines of the wharves, shops, and taverns of the North End into a larger realm where he was part of a potentially worldwide movement based on brotherly love and universal benevolence. The tangible rewards of membership in St. Andrew's Lodge included evenings of fellowship with friends, cousins, neighbors, and brother artisans as well as business relationships that sustained him throughout his career. Beyond those benefits, no organization was more important than St. Andrew's Lodge of Freemasons for enhancing Revere's status in the community, allowing him a setting to exhibit his leadership skills, and expanding his cultural and intellectual horizons.[21]

Originating in the medieval stoneworkers' guilds, Freemasonry had become a fraternal order of noncraftsmen by the seventeenth century. Both gentlemen and men of middling status were attracted to Freemasonry's devotion to charity, virtue, and the Enlightenment ideals of order, reason, and the natural ties of affection between men. Masonic lodges multiplied in the colonies during the 1730s, when rapid economic and demographic growth led to uncertainty over one's social status and the need to forge patronage ties in order to rise in the world. Gentlemen, threatened by the influx of new men into their ranks, found confirmation of their status in Freemasonry's conveyance of authority, gentility, and honor through its ideals, rituals, and processions. Artisans, too, were drawn to Freemasonry as a means of acquiring gentility. With membership based solely on character and virtue and advancement in Masonic office based only on merit, Freemasonry conferred status on its brethren. When Revere became a Master Mason on January 27, 1761, it was acknowledgment by his Masonic brethren that he was a man of virtue and character who deserved respect both from his brother Masons and from his fellow citizens.[22]

As a Freemason, Paul Revere, master goldsmith, was linked by bonds of brotherly love to the classically educated attorney James Otis, the merchant John Rowe, and several Gridleys, Quincys, and other members of Boston's elite, although they were not his lodge brothers.[23] With the exception of Dr. Joseph Warren and John Hancock, who only attended meetings for a brief period of time, the brethren of St. Andrew's Lodge were overwhelmingly men of the middling ranks of society. Of fifty-three members of the lodge whose occupations were listed in January 1762, seven were merchants, one was a physician (Dr. Warren), eighteen were "seafaring members," and the remaining twenty-seven were artisans and retailers. Between 1752 and 1775, artisans, retailers, and men in the seagoing trades made up nearly 70 percent of the membership of St. Andrew's Lodge. Revere's lodge brothers included his cousin Nathaniel Hichborn, a boatbuilder; Josiah Flagg, a jeweler and childhood friend who had helped Revere ring bells at Christ Church; Samuel Barrett, a sailmaker; Thomas Crafts Jr., a painter and japanner; and Ezra Collins, a hatmaker and neighbor. Membership in St. Andrew's Lodge of Freemasons surely strengthened Revere's preexisting ties of blood or friendship to his fellow artisans, but it also allowed him to forge a bond of friendship with Dr. Joseph Warren, a man of superior rank and education, that shaped both of their futures in the political struggles of the 1760s and 1770s.[24]

St. Andrew's Lodge, chartered by the Grand Lodge of Scotland on November 30, 1756, was born out of a schism in English Freemasonry dating to 1738, when a group of seceding lodges accused the Grand Lodge of England of corrupting the ancient ritual of Freemasonry. The seceding lodges called themselves Ancient Masons and denounced their opponents as "a Grand Lodge of Modern Masons." When a group of nine men who had been meeting as Masons in Boston decided to form a regular lodge in 1754, they did not petition St. John's Grand Lodge of Massachusetts, a modern grand lodge chartered by the Grand Lodge of England. Instead, they petitioned the Grand Lodge of Scotland, which tried to maintain a neutral position, favoring neither the extreme position of the Ancients nor approving of the changes of the Grand Lodge of England.[25]

The schism between Ancients and Moderns, which originated in opposing interpretations of Masonic ritual, had social overtones as well. By adopting the label of Ancient Masons, the members of St. Andrew's Lodge, including Paul Revere, goldsmith, George Bray, baker, and William Burbeck, a carver and former member of a modern lodge of Freemasons, portrayed themselves as true Freemasons who upheld traditional Masonic ritual and principles while implying that the social elites who made up St. John's Grand Lodge of Modern Masons departed from the ancient ways.[26] St. John's Grand Lodge continued to condemn the nine charter members of St. Andrew's Lodge as "Irregular Masons" until April 10, 1766, when they reversed their decision. They conceded that the members of St. Andrew's Lodge "have acted consistent with their character as Masons" and that the Grand Lodge's previous refusal to admit the brethren of St. Andrew's to visit modern lodges "was directly Subversive of the Principles of Masonry." It appeared that the goldsmiths, bakers, and carvers of St. Andrew's Lodge had a more accurate understanding of Masonic principles than the Grand Master of North America, the Right Worshipful Jeremiah Gridley, Esq., a Harvard-educated lawyer who trained a generation of lawyers, including James Otis.[27]

Revere's admission to St. Andrew's Lodge rested on his reputation as a man of integrity and high moral character, qualities that encouraged his Masonic brothers to patronize his shop. Indeed, Freemasonry brought almost immediate financial benefits to Revere.[28] On January 3, 1761, a little over three months after joining St. Andrew's Lodge, he made a Freemason's medal for James Graham. In 1762 he made Masonic medals for Richard Pulling, James Jackson, and George Stacy. Samuel Barrett, Master of St. Andrew's from 1769 to 1770, was one of Revere's most faithful customers between 1762 and 1765, purchasing items ranging from buttons and shoe buckles to silver teapots and teaspoons. Between 1763 and 1767 Revere mended gold buttons and spectacles, made silver shoe buckles, and engraved a notification of a Masonic meeting in Surinam for Captain Caleb Hopkins, a North End mariner. Throughout his career, Revere relied on the patronage of his lodge brothers and other Masons, who ordered everything from Masonic jewels, seals, and ladles to non-Masonic buttons, buckles, and fine silver dinnerware. He also made a variety of Masonic items for the Massachusetts Grand Lodge and several other lodges.[29] Revere in turn patronized Dr. Samuel Danforth, a member of St. Andrew's since 1765 and a regular customer in the 1770s. In the 1780s he rented out his home to George DeFrance, a member of Friendship Lodge who joined St. Andrew's in 1782, and Joseph Dunkerly, a member of St. Andrew's since 1776.[30]

For a young master goldsmith trying to establish his place in the community, Freemasonry offered Revere a chance to exercise leadership within Masonic circles and elevate his status in the community at large. His lack of education and gentility may have prevented Revere from holding high political office, but it was no obstacle to attaining Masonic offices. Character, merit, and mastery of Masonic principles and traditions gained him the respect of his Masonic brothers, who elected him to progressively higher offices on both the lodge and Grand Lodge level. As he rose through the hierarchy of Masonic offices, preparing Masonic candidates, keeping lodge records, running orderly meetings, and maintaining "the honor and dignity of the Lodge," Revere was learning skills and displaying leadership abilities that would later bring him to the attention of Boston's Revolutionary leaders and gratify his ambition for social distinction.[31]

When Paul Revere and his fellow artisans met at St. Andrew's Lodge, they were not just enjoying convivial evenings or making business contacts. They were also exposing themselves to ideas that would later resonate in the words and actions of the Sons of Liberty, North End Caucus, and other political organizations to which many of them belonged. Much as Benjamin Franklin and the members of the Junto met to discuss moral, political, and philosophical ideals that would elevate their minds and improve their lives, the brethren of St. Andrew's were introduced to Enlightenment ideals of a universe based on order, reason, and bonds of friendship among men of honor and virtue. Instead of a world where men were accorded status because of their money, education, and social refinement, the spread of Freemasonry promised recognition for men whose only criterion for status was their character and talent.[32]

By 1772 twelve members of the North End Caucus were members of St. Andrew's Lodge, including Dr. Joseph Warren and Paul Revere. Certainly, being a Freemason did not automatically propel one into the ranks of the patriot cause. Merchant John Rowe, who became Grand Master of Masons for North America in 1768, practiced a "cautious neutrality"; Benjamin Hallowell Jr., customs commissioner, his brother Robert, and twenty members of the Second Lodge of Modern Masons were among the Loyalists who left Boston for Canada; and Tory lodges prospered in British-held cities throughout the Revolutionary War. But for Paul Revere and many of his fellow artisans and mariners, both the tenets of Freemasonry and the rhetoric of republicanism proposed a future where a vertical, dependent society based on ascribed status would be replaced by a horizontal society based on love, benevolence, and achieved status.[33]

While Paul Revere, master goldsmith and Master Mason, was building a reputation as an enterprising artisan and highly regarded member of the community, military and political events were unfolding that would affect the lives and fortunes of Revere and the artisans of Clark's Wharf and St. Andrew's Lodge. The tide of battle in the Seven Years' War had begun to turn with William Pitt's ministry and his assumption of military affairs in 1758. On October 16, 1759, Bostonians celebrated British brigadier James Wolfe's victory over French forces under Montcalm in the Plains of Abraham engagement. Boston printer John Boyle recorded in his journal that "the Regiment of Militia were mustered, and the Town beautifully illuminated in the Evening." One year after the fall of Quebec, Boston rejoiced over the reduction of Montreal. The inhabitants of the town were justifiably proud of the British capture of New France, since thousands of Massachusetts soldiers had participated in the successful military campaigns of 1760. Once again, the loyal Englishmen of Massachusetts had responded energetically to their government's requests for assistance against England's enemies. Hopes for peace and prosperity were high in 1760, but the effects of war as well as political developments inside and outside of Massachusetts soon altered expectations.[34]

On August 2, 1760, one month before British victory at Montreal, Francis Bernard arrived in Boston to assume his new duties as governor of Massachusetts. Bernard was pleased with his prospects, calling Boston "perhaps the most polished and scientific Town in America." He was also sanguine about political conditions in Massachusetts, informing the Board of Trade: "This people are better disposed to observe their contract with the Crown than any other on the continent I have known." Bernard hoped to rise above the political factions in Massachusetts, but his alliance with the Hutchinson faction soon involved him in political controversy and excited the anger of the loyal subjects of whom he had previously written so fondly.[35]

Governor Bernard hoped to avoid choosing between the Otis and Hutchinson factions in Massachusetts, but when Chief Justice Stephen Sewall died in September 1760, Bernard made his political sympathies known by appointing Thomas Hutchinson to the position instead of James Otis Sr., the merchant, Barnstable Country magistrate, and member of the Governor's Council who had been promised the post by the previous administration. Bernard knew he needed a strong prerogative man on the bench to implement changes in royal government under the new monarch, George III, and rule in favor of the legality of writs of assistance, the general search warrants used by customs officials in their efforts to tighten up imperial trade regulations. With his selection in November 1760 of Thomas Hutchinson—merchant, gentleman, and holder of several royal offices—as chief justice, Governor Bernard incited political debate about power, multiple office-holding, and the fundamental rights of Englishmen.[36]

Paul Revere and the other artisans and laborers of the North End readily deferred to merchants, lawyers, and professional men, whose wealth made them independent thinkers, free from the control of social superiors, and whose education further freed them from provincial and unenlightened views. If, however, gentlemen in power chose their own interests over the public interest, they were no longer considered rightful rulers and no longer deserving of the people's allegiance. Since the 1740s, as a hard-money advocate and loyal prerogative man,

Hutchinson had favored the interests of his class over the people. In May 1760, anticipating the arrival of the new governor, Hutchinson led an unsuccessful movement to abolish Boston's town meeting. He and his "Junto" of wealthy merchants and lawyers anticipated a future where gentlemen of liberal education and sound reason would exercise their rightful rule without the interference of "working Artificers, Seafaring Men, and low sort of people" who, in the words of Governor William Shirley, created a "Mobbish Spirit" in the town meeting. John Adams, writing as Novanglus, indicted Hutchinson, who by 1760 simultaneously held the positions of lieutenant governor, chief justice, member of the Governor's Council, probate judge, and captain of Castle William in Boston Harbor, and his fellow multiple officeholders as "conspirators against the public liberty." In 1749 Dr. Jonathan Mayhew had warned magistrates not to "act contrary to their office" and "not to go too far in advising to arbitrary, despotic measures." Chief Justice Hutchinson, sitting in judgment of the legality of writs of assistance, ignored the warnings.[37]

During the Seven Years' War, royal officials and military officers had been frustrated and angered by colonial violations of the Acts of Trade, on the part of both citizens and their provincial assemblies. Now, in February 1761, under pressure to tighten up enforcement of trade regulations, Boston customs officials turned to the Superior Court to renew the writs of assistance. Chief Justice Hutchinson eventually ruled in favor of the legality of the writs in November 1761, after consultation with London, but the argument of James Otis Jr. against the legality of the writs the preceding February was a turning point in Crown-provincial politics. John Adams, a young lawyer from Braintree only recently arrived in Boston, was so spellbound by Otis that he forgot to take notes as he had planned, but years later he claimed: "The child independence was then and there born [for] every man of an immense crowded audience appeared to me to go away as I did, ready to take up arms against writs of assistance."[38]

Otis had resigned his post as deputy advocate general of the vice-admiralty court, in which smugglers were tried, to join Oxenbridge Thacher in representing Boston merchants opposed to the writs. Rather than argue the legal technicalities of whether the Superior Court could issue the writs, empowering any customs officer accompanied by a peace officer to enter stores, warehouses, or homes on the mere suspicion of smuggled goods, Otis eloquently spoke about the rights of Englishmen, fundamental law, and the danger of royal enslavement. The writs were "against the fundamental principles of law," and any acts of Parliament authorizing them were violations of the constitution and natural law and thus to be considered void. Otis called on the Superior Court to "demolish this monster of oppression, and . . . tear into rags this remnant of star-chamber tyranny." Although he lost the case, Otis emerged as the hero of the people, who elected him to the General Court three months later. Hutchinson remained as the enemy of the people, vilified in the pages of the *Boston Gazette* and in the taverns of the North End.[39]

Although the demands of family and work filled Revere's days, there was still plenty of time for the taverns and clubs of the North End. After a hard day's work, Revere might head over to the Salutation Tavern on Salutation Alley. At this gathering place for North End shipwrights, caulkers, mastmakers, and other artisans, he would enjoy his rum or ale, a pipe, a newspaper, and conversation. Revere, his Hichborn cousins, and their friends, neighbors, and Masonic brothers might discuss the Hutchinson faction's attempt to destroy the town meeting, James Otis's electrifying defense of the rights of Englishmen in the writs of assistance case, or the persistent problem of high taxes and declining trade. But taverns like the Salutation were not just informal spots for artisans and laborers to complain about high taxes or corrupt politicians. They were also the setting for the more formal discussion of ideas and actions carried out by Boston's political caucuses. By 1772, when Bostonians were in the midst of organized resistance to imperial policy, Paul Revere was a member of the North End Caucus, which met first in the Salutation Tavern and later in the Green Dragon Tavern.[40]

The origins of Boston's political caucuses are obscure and open to historical debate. Alan and Katherine Day note that the first date in the records of the North End Caucus is March 23, 1772, but a memorandum in the records states "Began 1767—records lost." In a diary entry in February 1763 John Adams described a meeting of a caucus club at the home of Thomas Dawes of the South End. Other references to caucuses appeared in letters and newspapers in the early 1760s, especially during the Hutchinson faction's attempt to abolish the town meeting in May 1760. Although conclusive evidence of the existence of the caucuses is elusive, both G. B. Warden and Gary Nash point to the existence of the Boston Caucus by the 1720s. Shortly after his election to the General Court in 1718, Elisha Cooke Jr., a Harvard-educated physician and substantial landholder, had begun to organize Boston voters through a secret political club. The Boston Caucus, as it was later known, selected candidates for Boston selectmen and representatives to the General Court and generally mobilized public support on political issues of the day. Yet what is perhaps more important than the original date of Boston's caucuses is how they were organized and operated, and how they united various interests in the community.[41]

Elisha Cooke Jr. and other large landlords in Boston's South End had controlled political organization in the 1720s, but the candidates and issues they supported were also endorsed by artisans, shopkeepers, and laborers. Both the gentlemen who managed the caucus and the men of middling rank who made up the membership supported paper money, the curbing of the royal governor's prerogative and patronage, and the promotion of local manufacturing and public works projects. Through pamphlets, newspaper articles, and tavern meetings, the leaders mobilized public opinion. Though gentlemen still ruled in town and provincial politics, an increasingly well-informed electorate deferred only to leaders who served the public will.[42]

The men who succeeded Elisha Cooke Jr. in the 1760s and 1770s—Samuel and John Adams, James Otis, and Dr. Joseph Warren—had the education and leadership qualities to write political tracts and develop strategies to respond to royal policies during the Imperial Crisis. Their success, however, depended on their ability to articulate the grievances and express the ideas of the diverse segments of Boston society: merchants, professional men, artisans, tradesmen, ship's captains, mariners, and laborers. When the Adamses, Otis, and Warren set out to organize Boston's middling and lower sort against the Crown's trade regulations in the 1760s, they discovered that "the people" often had an agenda of their own. Boston's Revolutionary leaders needed men whose socioeconomic status and cultural outlook allowed them to move among the various ranks of society. As a master artisan with customers ranging from influential merchants to the mariners and artisans of the North End, and a man whose contacts reached deep into the social and political networks that would supply recruits for the cause of liberty, Paul Revere would be a useful bridge between the "bully boys" of Boston's waterfront and the Harvard-educated gentlemen who led the American Revolution.[43]

Revere and his family, friends, and neighbors who became involved in Revolutionary activity were master artisans and mariners. They shared many of the grievances of Boston's waterfront laborers—high taxes and high costs of living, if not low wages. Yet, they also stood somewhat apart from the world of journeymen artisans, laborers, and apprentices. Although Revere's income fluctuated dramatically between 1761 and 1775, from a high of slightly over £294 in 1762 to a low of nearly £11 in 1770, his average yearly income during this period was approximately £85, at a time when a successful journeyman artisan might earn £40–£45, and an urban laborer might earn as much as £30, if he was lucky enough to find steady work. But work was seldom steady, and the cost of urban living was high.[44] The artistic aspects of his work as a master goldsmith also broadened his cultural outlook beyond the immediate confines of Clark's Wharf. Through his knowledge of European and English artistic styles, Revere temporarily left the world of the Salutation Tavern and boisterous Pope's Day celebrations, although he certainly would not be invited into the homes of his wealthy customers to sip tea poured from his elegant teapots.[45]

When Paul Revere joined the cause of liberty, the gentlemen who led the Revolution gained a man whose associations extended from the Salutation Tavern and other gathering places of North End artisans and mariners to "The Ancient and Honorable Society of Freemasonry," dedicated to the gentlemanly ideals of honor, benevolence, and virtue. He was a worthy member of the community, a hard-working artisan, and a man who inspired loyalty from friends and neighbors, both in business and in his private life. Despite his attempts to acquire status and gentility, he also retained a less than genteel readiness to defend his honor or stand up for his rights by the use of harsh rhetoric or his fists.

On May 11, 1761, Thomas Fosdick, a hatter who was married to Revere's cousin Frances Hichborn, swore out a complaint against Revere "for assaulting and beating ye complainant." The circumstances surrounding the brawl are unknown, but after a hearing, Judge Richard Dana found Revere guilty. Dana fined Revere six shillings, eight pence and court costs, ordered him "to keep ye peace and be of good behavior" until the next court session, and asked two reputable citizens to post bond as surety for Revere's good behavior. The men who stood up for Revere were Joshua Brackett, his friend, customer, and, in a few years, fellow Son of Liberty, and Nathaniel Fosdick, brother of Thomas Fosdick, the man whom Revere was accused of assaulting.[46]

Revere's willingness to resort to fisticuffs surely marked him as no gentleman, but it did suggest qualities that would be useful to the patriot cause. His ability to stand up for himself would earn the respect of Boston's artisans, mariners, and laborers, elements of the community that had to be mobilized by the leaders of the Revolution. In the coming years, Dr. Joseph Warren, brother Mason and brother Son of Liberty, would also recognize Revere's value as a man whose actions were tempered by his exposure to Masonic ideals of honor, virtue, order, and brotherly love. His contemporaries eulogized Revere as "cool in thought, ardent in action . . . well adapted to form plans and to carry them into successful execution— both for the benefit of himself and the service of others." "Bold Revere," as he was dubbed by the author of the "Rallying Song of the Tea Party at the Green Dragon," would be a welcome addition to the cause of liberty.[47]

CHAPTER THREE

THE POLITICAL AWAKENING
OF PAUL REVERE

THE FUTURE looked promising for Paul Revere in 1763. The previous year he had made an astounding £294 worth of silver objects for North End artisans, ship's captains, and wealthy merchants and distillers. The business relationships he established in the early 1760s with Samuel Barrett, Captain Caleb Hopkins, Deacon Thomas Hill, a distiller, and Zacariah Johonnot, the merchant/distiller, contributed to Revere's ability to survive the economic hardships of the 1760s and 1770s. He formed another long-term business relationship with the artist John Singleton Copley, an ideal customer who paid promptly in cash for gold and silver picture frames, gold picture cases, and gold bracelets. Starting with a view of the North Battery (c. 1762), he expanded his business to include copperplate engraving. Although Revere's skill as an engraver never approached the artistic heights of his silver work, it provided an additional means to support his family and later brought him to the attention of Boston's Revolutionary leaders, who relied on his political cartoons as an important means of enlightening the community. He was also gaining respect and increasing status among his Masonic brethren, who elected him Junior Deacon of St. Andrew's Lodge in December 1761 and Junior Warden in November 1763. The young master goldsmith, engraver, husband, and father of three children must have felt secure about the future, with a strong sense of his place in the community.[1]

In May 1763 Bostonians received the news that the Seven Years' War was finally over. All Englishmen could take pride in their victory. By the terms of the Peace of Paris, signed on February 10, 1763, Great Britain was now the greatest maritime and colonial power in the world. France lost Minorca in the western Mediterranean and any influence in India, along with all its colonies in mainland North

America. Britain also gained Florida from France's ally Spain. Yet, as in earlier wars, colonial rejoicing over peace was short lived, for once again peace and plenty did not necessarily go hand in hand.[2]

Even before they began to feel the impact of a postwar depression, the colonists were affected by other long-term economic developments. From 1745 to 1760, colonial merchants and consumers had benefited by the rapid growth of the British economy and extraordinarily generous credit terms offered by British merchants. After 1760, however, economic growth began to slow down, and British merchants tightened the flow of colonial credit. The decline of the British economy caused a slump in the West Indian economy, which particularly affected New England farmers and fishermen, whose livestock, lumber, and fish went primarily to West Indian markets. By the summer of 1765 the West Indian trade has dropped by as much as 80 percent, affecting not only merchants but mariners and artisans employed in maritime trades.[3]

The fall of Canada, which brought great pride and joy to the colonists, also added to their financial woes. With the end of the war, colonial citizens and their governments suffered the loss of contracts for weapons and uniforms, along with the withdrawal of British troops and the hard currency they brought with them. Just as their supply of specie was dwindling, their British creditors were demanding payment for goods. In a diary entry on March 8, 1764, John Boyle wrote that "many people" were moving out of Boston "in order to do Business in the Country." Merchants John Scollay and Joseph Scott declared bankruptcy in 1764, and in January 1765 the failure of Boston importer Nathaniel Wheelwright set off more shock waves. An anonymous poet in the *Boston Gazette*, commenting on the domino effect of Wheelwright's collapse on Boston's economy, wrote that his "fiery Tail . . . swept lesser Stars Down from their sev'ral Orbits."[4]

In 1763 Revere earned slightly over £95, a sharp drop from the year before but a respectable sum nonetheless. He made items for John Singleton Copley, canns and porringers for Thomas Green, Esq., and six teaspoons and a pair of butter cups for Deacon Thomas Hill, but most of his orders in 1763 were for cheaper and more mundane objects. He made buckles for his friend Joshua Brackett, mended gold buttons for Captain Caleb Hopkins, a fellow Mason, and produced a steady supply of buckles, spoons, and "hatt prints" for his cousins Thomas and William Hichborn. If Revere could at least maintain the income level of 1763, he could remain safely above the ranks of journeymen artisans or laborers, but political and economic events in the coming year made even that prospect questionable.[5]

The year 1764 began well enough on January 2, with Joseph Barnard's order for a silver tankard and church cup, worth £19.5.0. Then, in February, the Reveres were one of seven families who "have lately been visited with Small-Pox," as John Boyle noted in his journal. Refusing to send his children to the pesthouse, Revere quarantined the family at home, and for the next month he conducted no business. Business picked up after March 4, and he ended the year on a favorable note when Captain Joseph Goodwin ordered a teapot, sugar dish, and several other items for £15.2.18 on December 15, 1764. He recorded a respectable income of £102, and as always, he could rely on the patronage of family, friends, neighbors, and Masonic brothers. Throughout the 1760s and 1770s, Revere could count upon regular customers like Dr. Philip Godfrid Kast, for whom he mended buttons, engraved prints for Kast's fire club, and made spoons, cream pots, thimbles, and a set of surgeon's instruments. But in this year of uncertainty, the Reveres and their neighbors learned that they were to be the source of much-needed revenue for their home government.[6]

Great Britain had emerged victorious from the Seven Years' War, but the cost of victory was a national debt of almost £140,000,000. Faced with an annual debt charge of four to five million pounds and the expense of maintaining military forces to defend the vast Indian lands acquired in the war, the Grenville ministry turned to the colonies as a source of revenue. The Sugar Act of April 5, 1764, proposed duties on foreign molasses and other products, not to regulate trade as in the past, but to raise revenue. The Currency Act (April 19, 1764), passed at the request of British merchants who were tired of receiving payment in depreciated paper currency, forbid the issuance of colonial paper currency. The colonists viewed the Sugar and Currency Acts as dangerous measures that would destroy the rum trade, drain already scarce specie from the colonies, create a bureaucracy that would upset the delicate balance-of-trade interests of the empire, and, above all, threaten their much-cherished rights and privileges as freeborn subjects of Great Britain.[7]

In the summer of 1764 James Otis Jr., one of Boston's representatives to the General Court, responded to the Sugar Act with *The Rights of the British Colonies Asserted and Proved*.[8] Following the precedent of his argument in the writs of assistance case, Otis focused his considerable rhetorical skill on the rights of Englishmen originating in the constitution and natural law. Otis paid homage to "the grandeur of the British constitution . . . by far the best, now existing on earth" and promised colonial obedience to Parliament and the king. The colonists would "submit and patiently bear" such laws till Parliament "will be pleased to relieve us." Yet, in spite of his deference to Crown and Parliament, Otis emphatically upheld the "natural, essential, inherent and inseparable rights" of Englishmen, granted to them by "the law of god and nature, by the common law, and by act of parliament."

Otis asserted that "an original supreme Sovereign, absolute, and uncontroulable *earthly* power . . . is *originally* and *ultimately* in the people." The people had delegated their power to the king, lords, and Commons, but they expected that their rulers would govern "by stated laws," that the laws "should have no other end ultimately, but the good of the people," and, most of all, that "Taxes are not to be laid on the people, but by their consent in person, or by deputation." Otis recommended that the colonies "should not only be continued in the enjoyment of subordinate legislation" but also be represented in Parliament. Unfortunately, neither his solution to the crisis nor his passionate defense of the rights and liberties of Englishmen had any impact in London.

On February 8, 1765, Arthur Savage Jr., writing from London, informed his brother, the merchant Samuel Phillips Savage, that a stamp duty had passed the House of Commons "by a great majority." Savage claimed that James Otis's argument on the rights of the colonies "has not been of any Service. . . . The present Sentiments of the Ministry are such that they will not be Bullied into Opinions contrary to their own." On March 1 Savage expressed his fears that the ministry might "thro in more Troops" and "oblige" the colonists to "maintain them." He warned that "they might prove a powerful Enemy and in fact I believe are determined to keep a good look out that we rise not too far." The Stamp Act became law on March 22, 1765, to go into effect on November 1, 1765. This time, colonial Britons would do more than grumble about the financial burden of another revenue act. Now they would accuse Parliament of tampering with the British constitution and encroaching upon the sacred rights and liberties of Englishmen.[9]

The Sugar Act had indirect impact on the colonists through its effect on trade, but the Stamp Act proposed to touch items that were part of everyday life. His Majesty's subjects in America would pay stamp duties on legal papers, liquor licenses, indentures, cards, dice, pamphlets, newspapers, advertisements, almanacs, academic degrees, and appointments to office. The Stamp Act would have the strongest impact on lawyers, printers, and those in the mercantile trades, but its repercussions would be felt by artisans and laborers as well. Paul Revere would feel the sting of the Stamp Act when he signed a term of indenture with an apprentice, when he played cards and dice at the Salutation Tavern, and when Boston merchants and their wives decided that they could do without his butter cups, teapots, or silver dinnerware.[10]

The depressed trade conditions that reached a low in 1765 led to stagnation or bankruptcy for colonial merchants, unemployment for mariners and laborers, and a decline in the demand for the services of artisans. Paul Revere could still rely on the patronage of Joseph Webb, his neighbor and Master of St. Andrew's Lodge in 1765, who ordered copperplate engravings advertising his ironware store; his other Masonic brethren Samuel Barrett, Increase Blake, and Edward Proctor; and dependable customers like Zacariah Johonnot, Deacon Hill, Dr. Kast, and Epes Sargent, a Gloucester merchant, but his income fell to just over £60 in the year of the Stamp Act's passage. On January 21, 1765, he and Josiah Flagg, his friend and Masonic brother, advertised "A Collection of the Best Psalm-Tunes set in score by Josiah Flagg and engraved by Paul Revere." Unfortunately, Revere chose as his partner a man who owed him over £200, which further contributed to his financial misfortune. By April 15, 1765, Revere was renting out part of his shop to Thomas Beney for £4 a year. On September 13, 1765, the merchant Thomas Fletcher attached his estate for a debt of £10 that dated back to April 13, 1763, when the master goldsmith gave Fletcher a note for £6.14.5 to be paid on demand. The economic results of the Stamp Act on an already depressed economy could not be ignored, but colonial merchants, artisans, and laborers were also frightened and aroused by the Stamp Act's attempt to deprive them of their liberties.[11]

Colonial Englishmen like Paul Revere regarded the Stamp Act with horror as an internal tax unjustly imposed on English citizens without the consent of their local assemblies. Beginning in January 1765, Harbottle Dorr, a North End shop-keeper soon to become a Son of Liberty, began amassing an annotated collection of Boston newspapers, reflecting the views of a man of middling rank toward the developing struggle for liberty. On June 24, 1765, the *Boston Evening Post* re-printed an article from the *New York Gazette* that Dorr claimed "first gave the Alarm about the Stamp Act." The author denied the validity of virtual representa-tion, so forcefully presented by Thomas Whately in his pamphlet "The Regula-tions Lately Made." Colonial Englishmen were loyal adherents to the English constitution, especially the principle "that we have a right to be taxed only by our own consent." The author warned: "The English government cannot long act towards a part of its dominions diametrically opposed to its own, without losing itself in the slavery it would impose upon the colonies." At the end of May, Patrick Henry, member of the Virginia House of Burgesses, upheld the rights of his fellow colonial Englishmen by proposing "that any person who shall, by Speaking or Writing, assert or maintain That any Person or Persons, other than the General Assembly of this Colony . . . have any Right or Authority to lay or impose any Tax whatever on the Inhabitants thereof, shall be Deemed, an *Enemy to his Majesty's Colony.*"[12]

The publication of Henry's resolves, in the mistaken belief that they were adopted by the Virginia House of Burgesses, galvanized Americans against the Stamp Act. Governor Francis Bernard called the resolutions "an Alarm Bell" to the people of New England. Throughout the summer of 1765, Boston newspapers hammered away at the issue of taxation without representation, the invasion of the sacred rights of Englishmen, and the necessity for public spirit and vigilance in the face of impending slavery. Harbottle Dorr enthusiastically endorsed the *New York Gazette* in its call on men "of name and figure . . . to prize public Spirit and Patriots," writing in the margin of his newspaper: "Yes thus lukewarm were many of the great Romans, even when they saw Caesar's sword already waving dread-fully over them." In October 1765 Daniel Dulany, a Maryland lawyer, denied the validity of virtual representation in the colonies, claiming: "There is not that intimate and inseparable relation between the *electors of* Great-Britain, and the *Inhabitants of the colonies,* which must inevitably involve both in the same taxation." Dulany warned his countrymen that "their security as well as honour" made it necessary for them to resist any oppression. Patrick Henry, Daniel Dulany, and Boston's artisans and mariners looked to the British constitution to protect their sacred liberties, a lengthy and often loosely defined list of "natural rights," revolving around the issues of the protection of personal liberty and property, and viewed the Stamp Act as an entering wedge against their liberty and property.[13]

The master artisans, mariners, and shopkeepers who became Sons of Liberty were men of middling means and high aspirations, for whom property was perhaps more precious than it was for the merchant John Hancock because it was so precarious. Among these men who later joined the North End Caucus were Gibbens Sharp, a shipwright, and Asa Stoddard, a bricklayer, both of whom had modest real estate holdings in the North End. Captain Caleb Hopkins called himself a mariner when he bought part of a brick house and land on the corner of Tileston and Unity Streets on July 29, 1762, but he listed himself as a merchant in 1783 and as a gentleman in the 1790s when he purchased additional real estate. Harbottle Dorr, who sold ironmongery, braziery, cutlery, and pewter in the 1760s, became a Boston selectman from 1777 to 1784 and from 1786 to 1791. Paul Revere became a successful manufacturer of bells, cannons, and copper with substantial real estate holdings, but in 1765 the ambitious master goldsmith's hopes of rising in the world seemed very much in doubt. The flourishing business he had worked so hard to create and his hopes for upward mobility were at the mercy of the flagging economy and the corrupt policies of the king's ministers and Parliament. For Paul Revere and his fellow master artisans, the Stamp Act meant enslavement; hard-working, frugal men would now be taxed to support a set of corrupt, luxury-loving placemen and pensioners. A writer in the *Boston Post-Boy and Advertiser* voiced these fears when he asked the stamp man: "Will the Cries of your despairing, dying Brethren be Music pleasing to your Ears? If so, go on! bend the Knee to your Master Horseleach, and beg a Share in the Pillage of your Country."[14]

In Massachusetts, fears of enslavement, corruption, and conspiracy centered on Lieutenant Governor Thomas Hutchinson. Ironically, Hutchinson disapproved of the Stamp Act and worked for its repeal. In a manuscript he sent to Richard Jackson, member of Parliament and colonial agent for Massachusetts, Hutchinson agreed with his enemies that Parliament had no constitutional right to pass the Stamp Act. But his countrymen, who had long memories, found more compelling evidence of Hutchinson's self-interest and betrayal of the public good. They recalled his opposition to paper money in the 1740s, his attempts to abolish the town meeting in 1760, his support for the writs of assistance in 1761, and the servile petition against the Stamp Act that he imposed in place of the General Court's spirited defense of constitutional right. The most damning evidence against Hutchinson, however, was the appointment of the stamp master for Massachusetts: Andrew Oliver, secretary of the colony, member of the council, and—

worst of all—Hutchinson's brother-in-law. When the time came for direct action against the Stamp Act, the people of Massachusetts had ready-made enemies, men who were seen as the instruments of their oppression and the violators of their constitutional rights.[15]

By early summer 1765 a group of men calling themselves the Loyal Nine had organized to resist the Stamp Act: John Avery Jr., a merchant/distiller; Henry Bass, another merchant; Thomas Chase, a distiller; Thomas Crafts, a painter/japanner; Benjamin Edes, one of the printers of the *Boston Gazette*, the influential forum for resistance to the Stamp Act; John Smith and Stephen Cleverly, braziers; and George Trott, jeweler. The ninth member was either Henry Welles, a mariner, or Joseph Field, master of a vessel. With the exception of Avery, who was a Harvard graduate, the other members were men like Paul Revere—artisans, shopkeepers, and men of middling rank whose desires for upward mobility were threatened by political and economic events in 1765. James Otis and Samuel and John Adams certainly must have been aware of the activities of the Loyal Nine, but they had no official connection to the organization. To put their plans into action, the Loyal Nine called upon the services of Ebenezer McIntosh, a South End cordwainer and leader of the South End Pope's Day company. When the government and laws would not serve the interests of the people, the Loyal Nine turned to the people to redress those wrongs.[16]

On the morning of August 14, 1765, Bostonians witnessed a ritual of protest similar to the mocking, world-turned-upside-down festivities of the Pope's Day processions. The Loyal Nine prepared effigies of Andrew Oliver, the stamp master, and Lord Bute, the king's favorite, who, though out of office since the end of 1763, was considered the instigator of the unpopular revenue measures. McIntosh's men, mostly artisans from the lower ranks of the craft hierarchy, laborers, and mariners, hung the effigies from a large elm tree at Essex and Orange Streets in the South End, a tree soon to become famous as Liberty Tree. A label on the breast of Oliver's effigy praised liberty and denounced "Vengeance on the Subvertors of it," and another label warned: "He that takes this down is an enemy to his Country." At sunset, forty or fifty artisans and tradesmen took down the effigies and carried them in a procession to Andrew Oliver's dock, where the mob leveled a building that they believed would be the stamp office, and then to Fort Hill, where they burned the figures. In his journal, John Boyle stressed that the procession was "followed by a great Concourse of People, some of the highest Reputation, and in the greatest order." At this point, the less genteel members of the mob, led by McIntosh and angered by Thomas Hutchinson's attempts to disperse them, proceeded to wreak havoc on Andrew Oliver's house, pulling down fences, breaking windows, looking glasses, and furniture, stripping his trees of fruit, and drinking his wine.[17]

On August 26, after first attacking the homes of William Story, deputy register of the Vice-Admiralty Court, and Benjamin Hallowell, comptroller of customs, McIntosh led his men to the home of Lieutenant Governor Hutchinson, the unfortunate scapegoat of the Stamp Act crisis. Hutchinson, who was lucky to escape with his life, had no time to remove any valuables from his home. By dawn, the mob had destroyed furniture and torn out windows, partitions, wainscoting, roof tiles, and even part of a cupola at the top of Hutchinson's mansion. They also ruined Hutchinson's formal gardens, helped themselves to the contents of his wine cellar, stole £900 sterling, removed every object of value from his house, and scattered or destroyed thirty years' worth of books and papers that Hutchinson had collected for his history of Massachusetts.[18]

Hutchinson's fellow citizens, including those who had long regarded him as an enemy of the people, were aghast at the ferocity of the attack against him. The *Boston Gazette* reported that "most people seem dispos'd to discriminate between the Assembly of the 14th of the Month, and their Transactions, and the unbridled Licentiousness of *this* Mob." Agreeing that "the cause of Liberty requires an extraordinary Spirit to support it," the *Gazette* nonetheless warned that "the pulling down Houses and robbing Persons of their Substance . . . is utterly inconsistent with the first Principles of Government, and subversive of the glorious Cause." Edward Payne, a merchant writing to a correspondent in England, also expressed the belief that the burning of Oliver's effigy "seemed to be approved of by persons of all Ranks" and that the act "was conducted with some prudence and Done only to shew their dislike to the Stamp Act," but that the attack on Hutchinson's house "had no connection" with the events of August 14. Governor Bernard believed that the mob was punishing Hutchinson for his support of the writs of assistance, while others felt the motive was his part in suppressing smuggling. The Reverend William Gordon, among others, proposed that the real motive was that a group of speculators in Maine lands were after the destruction of papers that were unfavorable to their claims. Whatever the motives, it was apparent that McIntosh's men were not simply protesting against abstract notions of constitutional balance and no taxation without consent. They were also unmistakably displaying the contempt and anger of laboring men toward the wealth and power wielded by men like Thomas Hutchinson.[19]

Whether Paul Revere was one of the artisans and tradesmen who carried the effigies of Oliver and Bute in the procession on August 14 is not known, but his reputable standing in the community as a master goldsmith and Freemason and his many ties to the artisans, mariners, and laborers of the North End would have made him an appropriate choice. By the Stamp Act crisis, Revere had connections to two and possibly three members of the Loyal Nine, and within a few years he would join several members of the Loyal Nine in the North End Caucus. John Avery, a Harvard classmate of Dr. Joseph Warren, had purchased a silver tankard from Revere on October 19, 1764, and Thomas Crafts had been a lodge brother at

St. Andrew's since 1761. Captain Henry Welles, who may have been one of the Loyal Nine, was another member of St. Andrew's Lodge. Thomas Chase, who joined St. Andrew's Lodge in 1769, Henry Bass, and Benjamin Edes were later Revere's fellow members of the North End Caucus, and Revere, Chase, and Bass were identified as participants in the Boston Tea Party. Revere may have known Bass, Edes, Chase, and other members of the Loyal Nine even earlier because of geographic proximity and their similar social status. He also listed no business activity between August 1 and September 14, 1765, suggesting that he may have been otherwise occupied with the Stamp Act protest.[20]

While it is possible that Revere participated in the events of August 14, 1765, it does not seem likely that he was involved in the attack on Thomas Hutchinson's home on August 26. As a master artisan, Revere had more in common with the Loyal Nine than with Ebenezer McIntosh and his men. Revere and the members of the Loyal Nine were primarily practitioners of skilled trades and the owners of small businesses. They were not waterfront ruffians who broke into a man's home and stomped on his books and furniture, but responsible men who trained apprentices and supervised journeymen, paid taxes, and attended church and town meetings. Paul Revere, Thomas Chase, Stephen Cleverly, and Benjamin Edes may have lacked the requisite gentility that earned John Avery, Esq. a position as overseer of the poor on March 12, 1765, but their fellow citizens acknowledged their more modest leadership qualifications by electing them clerks of the market, scavengers, constables, and haywards throughout the 1760s and 1770s. Governor Bernard and Lieutenant Governor Hutchinson may have seen no difference between the artisans who carried effigies of Oliver and Bute on August 14, 1765, and the "meaner sort" who destroyed Hutchinson's mansion on August 26, but Boston's Revolutionary leaders, in spite of their belief in a deferential society, began to recognize the qualities that distinguished master artisans from common laborers and made them an asset to the patriot cause.[21]

While the economic deterioration brought about by the postwar depression and the imperial revenue measures of 1764 and 1765 were distressing to Paul Revere, they were potentially devastating for Ebenezer McIntosh, the cordwainer, and the mariners and laborers who demolished Lieutenant Governor Hutchinson's property. The Stamp Act might thwart Revere's ambitions for higher social and economic status, but to McIntosh and his followers it could mean unemployment or debtor's prison. Revere could adjust by renting out part of his shop, making buckles and thimbles instead of silver canns, mending everything from earrings to spectacles, or engraving bookplates, songbooks, and business cards. His multiple skills as a master goldsmith and engraver freed Revere from the economic dependence of laborers, mariners, and other artisans whose fortunes were more closely connected to the mercantile trade. Moreover, the artistic nature of his work—designing, producing, and engraving coffeepots, sugar dishes, teaspoons, and silver trays for members of Boston's merchant elite—elevated him above the world of men who made shoes and barrels, baked bread, or unloaded ships.[22]

Revere's status as a Freemason also gave him values and experiences that made it more probable that he would be found among a closely controlled procession of artisans and tradesmen carrying political effigies than as one of a mob breaking windows at Andrew Oliver's house or flinging Thomas Hutchinson's books and papers into the street. Masonic teachings emphasized social harmony, order, reason, and deference to authority, and those principles were reinforced by Revere's standing as a Masonic officer. As Junior Warden of St. Andrew's Lodge in 1764, Revere collected fees at each lodge meeting, examined visitors, and introduced candidates for membership; and as Senior Warden in 1765, he was second in authority only to the Master of the lodge. In the conduct of his offices, Revere upheld order, virtue, and respect for authority and suppressed raucous debate or disharmony of any sort. Revere may also have seen some similarity between Masonic processions, which demonstrated the principles of authority, gentility, and honor, and the solemn parade of artisans and tradesmen whose dramatic but methodical destruction of the effigies of Oliver and Bute on August 14, 1765, illustrated the honor, power, and dignity of the people defending their liberty. Although he had spent all of his life within sight of Thomas Hutchinson's grand mansion, Paul Revere had no animosity against men of wealth and power, as long as they served the public good, and as long as men like himself had the same chance for success. When he declared his allegiance to the cause of liberty, it would not be by breaking windows or tearing down houses but by participating in organized political protest, engraving political cartoons, and working within the hierarchical structure of the patriotic cause.[23]

The leaders of the Stamp Act resistance needed crowd action because petitioning and other traditional means of redress were sometimes inadequate, but they were also aware that they could not always control individuals of middling and lower-class rank who had their own economic and social grievances. Before the dreaded Stamp Act went into effect, the leaders needed to reassert their authority over the Boston crowd, mobilize respected master artisans, and return to more traditional means of redressing grievances, among them, a Stamp Act Congress that would "consider of a general and united, dutiful, loyal and humble Representation of their Condition to His Majesty and the Parliament; and to implore Relief."[24]

The delegates from nine colonies who met in New York in October 1765 humbly affirmed their "warmest Sentiments of Affection and Duty to his Majesty's Person and Government" and humbly requested the repeal of the stamp duties, but in the statement of their rights, liberties, and grievances, they drew a line between subordination to parliamentary legislation and subordination to parliamentary taxation; they would submit to the former but not to the latter. It was "inseparably essential to the Freedom of a People, and the undoubted Right of *Englishmen,*" that no taxes be imposed without the people's consent. On October 25, 1765, the Massachusetts Assembly firmly stated its belief that the rights of the British constitution were founded "in the law of God and nature . . . and that no law of society can, consistent with the law of God and nature, divest them of those rights." With their principles clearly affirmed, the people of Massachusetts and the leaders of the Stamp Act resistance awaited "the long-expected and long-dreaded First of November."[25]

On October 7 the *Boston Gazette* printed an address to the inhabitants of Massachusetts, urging them to awake and "by a regular and legal opposition defeat the Designs of those who enslave us and our Posterity." The author reminded them: "For great is the Authority, exalted the Dignity, and powerful the Majesty of the People." When the people assembled on November 1 to protest the Stamp Act, there would be none of the mayhem that resulted in the destruction of Lieutenant Governor Hutchinson's home on August 26. An assembly "of near Three Thousand People" escorted effigies of George Grenville and John Huske, a former citizen of Boston who became a member of Parliament and was erroneously believed to have suggested the Stamp Act to Grenville, to the gallows outside the city gates, where they were "rent . . . into a Thousand Fragments, and dispersed . . . on the four Wings of the Air." It was "remarkable," wrote John Boyle, "that amidst this vast Assembly there was not one Weapon of Defence, not the least Token of Insult or Injury offered to any Person whatever." On November 5 McIntosh and Swift, the leaders of the South End and North End mobs, united their forces for a peaceful celebration of Pope's Day. Their social superiors rewarded them with a "Union Feast" at the Royal Exchange Tavern, where they were reminded of their inferior status by the division of the company into several classes: "while those of the first Class were enjoying themselves in Conversation, those of the Class who had formerly been at Variance were joining together with Heart and Hand in flowing Bowls and bumping Glasses."[26]

After the orderly protest on November 1, Boston's opposition to the Stamp Act became more organized and less violent. The *Boston Gazette* expressed its admiration for the merchants of New York and Philadelphia who promised not to import any goods from Great Britain until the Stamp Act was repealed and proudly reported that "above two hundred of the Principal Merchants" of Boston signed their own nonimportation agreement in early December. By December the Loyal Nine had expanded into the Sons of Liberty, adopting their name from a label applied to the colonists by their champion in Parliament, Colonel Isaac Barre. On December 16 "the True-born Sons of Liberty" requested that Andrew Oliver, whose commission as stamp distributor had finally arrived from England, appear under Liberty Tree the following day to "make a public Resignation." They promised that if he complied with their request, "you shall be treated with the greatest Politeness and Humanity. If not ——!" Oliver tried to resign at the town house, but the Sons of Liberty were not going to miss the chance to humiliate him. They dispatched Ebenezer McIntosh to escort Oliver to Liberty Tree, where the ill-fated royal official resigned in a driving rain. As Harbottle Dorr noted on his copy of the *Boston Gazette* of December 23, 1765: "And a Glorious sight it was which I beheld."[27]

Andrew Oliver's public debasement was not exclusively McIntosh's triumph. McIntosh answered to the Loyal Nine, who in turn answered to the merchant and political elite of Boston. Henry Bass of the Loyal Nine wrote fellow merchant Samuel Phillips Savage that the Loyal Nine decided to have Oliver resign under Liberty Tree, and to celebrate their decision they held "a very genteel supper" to which they invited "your very good friends Mr. S. A. [Samuel Adams], E and G [Edes and Gill], and three or four others." Savage was "not a little pleased to hear that McIntosh has the Credit of the whole affair."[28]

The Sons of Liberty throughout the colonies began the year 1766 with vigorous efforts to organize popular resentment against the Stamp Act. The New York Sons of Liberty took the lead in intercolonial resistance by establishing communications with their Boston brethren in January 1766. Sons of Liberty in all the colonies used the press to educate and arouse the public. Between January 1766 and July 1767, Harbottle Dorr abandoned less enthusiastic newspapers in favor of the *Boston Gazette,* which Governor Bernard lamented as "the most factious paper in America." The pages of the *Gazette* contained both straightforward reports of London and colonial news, along with satire and hysterical invective against the Stamp Act and its perpetrators.[29]

In their attempts to keep up the spirit of resistance, the Sons of Liberty used another effective tool—political cartoons. While James Otis used his classical education and rhetorical command to express the ideology of resistance, Paul Revere used his skill as an engraver of political cartoons to proclaim his commitment to the patriot cause. On January 27, 1766, the *Boston Gazette* advertised Revere's engraving "A View of the Year 1765." Adapted from the English caricature "View of the Present Crisis," which expressed opposition to Bute's Excise Bill of 1763, Revere paid tribute to "Boston brave! unstain'd by Placemen's Bribes" who "Attacks the Monster and his venal Tribes." Using a combination of vivid images and graphic language, he dramatically depicted Boston and the united colonies protecting Lady Liberty against the Dragon, wearing the Scottish bonnet of Lord Bute and trampling the prostrate body of John Pym, celebrated for his opposition to the absolute monarchy of Charles I. To the right of the dragon, Revere showed "perfidious H——k [John Husk]" hanging from Liberty Tree.[30]

Throughout the winter and spring of 1766, the Sons of Liberty and their leaders waged their patriotic campaign. On February 20, 1766, the Boston Sons of

2. "A View of the Year 1765," one of Revere's earliest engravings, expressed his commitment to the patriot cause. Courtesy, Massachusetts Historical Society.

Liberty held a trial and found the recently arrived stamped paper "guilty of a Breach of Magna Charta, and a Design to subvert the British Constitution, and alienate the Affections of His Majesty's most loyal and dutiful Subjects." Accordingly, they burned the papers along with effigies of Grenville and Bute. On March 31, 1766, the *Boston Gazette* listed the names of representatives to the Massachusetts General Court, whom they termed "Tools to the Governor." In April the *Gazette* tried to inspire its readers with an account of a meeting in Providence of the "Daughters of Liberty," a group of patriotic ladies who, eschewing imported English finery, spun from "Sunrise until Dark, and displayed a Spirit for saving their sinking Country rarely to be found among Persons of more Age and Experience." In May the publishers of the *Gazette* urged the election of "Friends of Liberty" and recalled that "before the spirit of those without doors was raised and fired," there were many who "yet opposed a manly opposition, and every scheme of our patriots for setting it aside."[31]

The efforts of the patriots were rewarded in the spring elections when they captured the lower house. Voters rejected nineteen of the thirty-two Hutchinsonians listed in the *Gazette,* and in Boston they chose the patriots James Otis Jr.,

Thomas Cushing, Samuel Adams, and John Hancock over Thomas Gray, an incumbent representative, John Ruddock, and John Rowe, all of whom had apparently not shown sufficient zeal for the cause of liberty. A week after the election, Boston received the joyous news that the Stamp Act had been repealed. On May 17, 1766, Paul Revere and his fellow citizens observed the sights and sounds of celebration in Boston: "the Bells in the Town were set a ringing, the Ships in the Harbour display'd their Colours, Guns were discharged in different parts of the Town, and in the Evening were several Bonfires."[32]

Two days later, Bostonians held a more stupendous celebration. The morning began with music, the ringing of church bells, and the discharge of cannon. Flags and streamers decorated ships, houses, and Liberty Tree. In the evening, the town was illuminated and ready for an exhibition of fireworks prepared by William Burbeck, a charter member and Master of St. Andrew's Lodge and an expert in pyrotechnics. The centerpiece of the festivities was an obelisk, a "magnificent Pyramid illuminated by two-hundred-and-eighty lamps," that the Sons of Liberty, possibly including Paul Revere, had erected on Boston Common. Luckily, Revere engraved an illustration of the obelisk for posterity, as this "standing Monument of this Glorious Era" was accidentally destroyed by fire. The oiled papers of the four sides of the obelisk were covered with the now familiar display of heroes and villains and expressions of Whig political sentiment: Pitt and Bute, Liberty Tree and the Devil, and, most of all, "Fair LIBERTY! thou Lovely Goddess." With the total repeal of the Stamp Act and with parliamentary champions like William Pitt, the Sons of Liberty might well savor their victory for the rights and liberties of Englishmen and look forward to the return to private life, but they could not afford to rest on their laurels. Parliament had coupled the repeal of the Stamp Act with a Declaratory Act, affirming their right to have "full power and authority to make laws and statutes . . . to bind the colonies and people of *America*, subjects of the crown of *Great Britain*, in all cases whatsoever."[33]

William Pitt's defense of the colonial position in the debate over the repeal of the Stamp Act was more than any patriot could have desired. Debating Grenville, the hated father of the Stamp Act, Pitt drew the line between legislation and taxation, declaring the distinction "essentially necessary to liberty." He denied the right of Parliament to impose a tax on the colonies while asserting their authority "in every circumstance of government whatsoever." He called the Americans "the sons, not the bastards, of England," dismissed the notion of virtual representation as "the most contemptible idea that ever entered into the head of a man," and urged the total repeal of the Stamp Act "because it was founded on an erroneous principle." The reasons for the Stamp Act's repeal had less to do, however, with Pitt's thrilling defense of the rights of Englishmen than with domestic politics and economics.[34]

When George III succeeded his grandfather to the throne in 1760, the young monarch was determined to rule as a "Patriot King" by banishing corruption and reasserting the royal prerogative, especially in the selection of ministerial appointments. The king's attempts to rise above faction unfortunately led to a period of ministerial instability that greatly affected the colonial situation. The Grenville ministry fell in July 1765, to be replaced by a coalition of "Old Whigs" under the young Marquis of Rockingham. The Rockingham ministry entered office with no clear policy on colonial taxation, but with little following of their own, they were disposed toward conciliation. They would try to stay in power by discrediting Grenville and steering a course between courting the pleasure of George III and that of William Pitt. In an effort to broaden their political base, the Rockingham administration was susceptible to the pressure of English merchants involved in the North American trade, who deluged Parliament with petitions calling for the repeal of the Stamp Act in the hopes of restoring advantageous economic conditions. Rockingham Whigs were more comfortable with basing repeal of the Stamp Act on economic reasons than in bowing to Pitt's support of colonial principles of constitutional liberty.[35]

Although members of both the Rockingham ministry and the opposition had evidence from colonial petitions and pamphlets that the Americans made no distinction between internal and external taxation, they chose instead to rely on skillful political answers supplied by Benjamin Franklin during questioning by the House of Commons. Franklin admitted that "at present" the colonists did not object to Parliament's right of external taxation, but that "in time they may possibly be convinced by these arguments." His questioners focused only on Franklin's statement of colonial objections to internal taxes. In February 1766 Rockingham shrewdly echoed Pitt's call for a declaration of Parliament's legislative authority. By not mentioning taxation powers, Rockingham satisfied all segments of political opinion. Grenville and the majority of Parliament read the Declaratory Act as a confirmation of their belief that there was no distinction between the powers of legislation and those of taxation, while Pitt, his English supporters, and the colonists interpreted the act as an assertion only of Parliament's legislative authority. Parliamentary debates and the ensuing votes revealed how precarious the colonial position was. Parliament passed the Declaratory Act first, but the repeal of the Stamp Act passed only after acrimonious debate and a close vote. Parliament ultimately repealed the Stamp Act, not because they recognized colonial interpretations of the rights and liberties of Englishmen, but because of expediency—that favorite word in the English political dictionary.[36]

James Otis and Samuel Adams, the Loyal Nine, and "True-born Sons of Liberty" like Paul Revere had done their jobs well. Through the use of rhetoric, political organization, carefully controlled crowd action, and political cartoons, they had aroused the people to defend their liberties against tyranny and corruption. It would seem that with the repeal of the Stamp Act they had achieved their

3. In 1768 John Singleton Copley (1738–1815), painted Paul Revere, the master goldsmith and Son of Liberty, at work. Courtesy, Museum of Fine Arts, Boston. Gift of Joseph W. Revere, William B. Revere, and Edward H. R. Revere.

goal and could dissolve their organization. But wiser men knew that the price of liberty was vigilance. Though they had just been "snatch'd from the jaws of . . . political destruction," an essayist in the *Boston Gazette* warned that they could not foresee "what revolutions may in a short time take place in Britain." They must be aware of the danger that "we may inadvertently be drawn in by the designing courtier to give up rights which never could have been wrested from us." The Boston town meeting instructed its representatives to the General Court to use their influence against multiple officeholding and to choose government officers who were "men of integrity and wisdom, lovers of liberty, and of our civil and ecclesiastical constitution." Furthermore, they should "support and encourage seminaries of learning . . . since we apprehend that learning is the surest support of our constitution."[37]

The violence of the Stamp Act riots convinced patriot leaders of the necessity of exploring nonimportation and other alternatives to mob action and of drawing the right kind of men to their cause. Within a year of the Stamp Act riots, Ebenezer McIntosh lost his status as leader of the Boston crowd and ended up in debtor's prison soon after the Boston Massacre. He was replaced by Paul Revere, Gibbens Sharp, Nathaniel Barber, Edward Proctor, and several other respectable citizens from the middling ranks. They were men who were brave and quick to defend their rights, but who also possessed the classical republican virtues of prudence, justice, and temperance. They were men who could move easily between the worlds of gentlemen and of laborers, who expressed political ideas when necessary, but who also knew when to listen and defer to those of superior intellect and education.[38]

Esther Forbes wrote that the leaders of the Revolution in Boston admitted Paul Revere into their society "because they wished the sympathy of the large artisan class with whom he was immensely popular, and he represented an important point of view." His position as a respected master artisan whose ties of business and friendship connected him to Boston's artisans, mariners, merchants, and Freemasons surely made Paul Revere a desirable member of the patriot cause, but at least one of Boston's Revolutionary leaders knew that Revere was more than a token representative of the artisanal class. On November 14, 1765, Dr. Joseph Warren, who had joined St. Andrew's Lodge in September 1761 but only attended occasional meetings through August 1762, was readmitted to membership. From his position as a member and then as Master of St. Andrew's Lodge from 1768 to 1769, Dr. Warren was well positioned to appreciate the qualities that would make Paul Revere a valuable Son of Liberty during the next phase of the defense of the rights and liberties of Englishmen. Revere's Masonic experience had taught him both to know when to defer to those of superior authority and achievement and when and how to exercise leadership. Revere had also learned to appreciate the opportunity of enlightening his mind through reading, discussion, and fellowship with like-minded men. Revere's standing in the community, his personality, and his Masonic experience would all make him a worthy member of the patriot circle.[39]

In 1768 John Singleton Copley painted Paul Revere, the master artisan, Masonic leader, and Son of Liberty. Copley painted a man in the prime of life, dressed in the rough linen shirt and vest of an artisan with his tools spread out before him, firmly holding one of his silver teapots. The hands are those of an artisan—strong, yet delicate, with dirt under the fingernails. He does not look down deferentially but looks the artist right in the eye, proud of his achievements as an artisan and a man. There is intelligence, boldness, and self-assurance in his expression. It was those very qualities that brought Paul Revere to the attention of Boston's Revolutionary leaders, and it would be the Revolutionary cause that increased Revere's confidence in himself and in his worth to the community.[40]

CHAPTER FOUR

A SON OF LIBERTY

WITH THE BIRTH of Frances Revere on February 19, 1766, Paul Revere now had a wife and four young children to support. On May 16, 1766, the same day that Captain Coffin arrived from London with news that the Stamp Act had been repealed, Adam Colson, a North End leather dresser and member of St. Andrew's Lodge, ordered a silver snuffbox from Revere. It was a good sign, for within a month of receiving news of the Stamp Act's repeal, Revere's business began to improve. Wealthier customers like merchant Thomas Brattle, merchant/distiller Zacariah Johonnot, Captain Joseph Goodwin, and Captain Winthrop Sargent ordered gold broaches, punch strainers and ladles, spoons, coffeepots, and canns. Revere's annual income rose to nearly £81. He and his fellow Sons of Liberty temporarily returned to the private world of family, business, and evenings at St. Andrew's Lodge or the Salutation Tavern, but they were reminded in town meeting and in the pages of the *Boston Gazette* of the need to be "vigilant and jealous, of our just rights, liberties, and privileges" and to remember "that before the spirit of those without doors was raised and fired," many of their elected leaders "opposed a manly opposition, and every scheme of our patriots."[1]

Beginning on June 2, 1766, Dr. Joseph Warren, writing as Paskalos in the *Boston Gazette*, launched a relentless campaign against Governor Francis Bernard. Warren rejected dry, dispassionate legal prose in favor of emotional and personal invective, a style aimed at "the spirit of those without doors." The hapless Governor Bernard became the personification of British tyranny and corruption, an unjust ruler who had betrayed the people's trust and a villain whom Warren promised to "pursue . . . through all your Labyrinths, until I have made you as detestable to all good men in Great Britain, as you are to me." The wicked

Bernard stood in marked contrast to the beloved Dr. Jonathan Mayhew, who died on July 9, 1766. Mayhew, "a Friend to Liberty and Learning, a Lover of Mankind, and a uniform Disciple of Jesus Christ," died two months after delivering a sermon on the repeal of the Stamp Act and nearly two decades after warning corrupt rulers "not to go too far in advising to arbitrary, despotic measures." Revere may have hoped that the repeal of the Stamp Act would allow him to exchange the life of a Son of Liberty for that of a master goldsmith who could concentrate on rebuilding his business and planning for his future success. But four months after celebrating the repeal, he and the artisans and mariners of the North End were abruptly reminded of the warnings of "Paskalos" and Dr. Mayhew about the ever-present need to defend their liberties from villains in power.[2]

On the morning of September 24, 1766, Deputy Collector of Customs William Sheafe and Comptroller of His Majesty's Customs Benjamin Hallowell called at the North End home of Captain Daniel Malcolm, a trader and vessel owner. Based on information from an anonymous informant that casks of brandy, wine, and other liquors were concealed in a cellar under Malcolm's house, the customs officers, armed with a writ of assistance, asked to search the premises. Malcolm allowed them to do so, with the exception of a locked room in the cellar that Malcolm was renting to Captain William Mackay. After Mackay claimed he did not have the key to the room, Sheafe and Hallowell ordered Malcolm to open the door. Captain Malcolm, a client of James Otis, who had so ably attacked the tyranny of writs of assistance in 1761, "solemnly swore it should not be" and, in the words of Sheafe and Hallowell, threatened "if any Man attempted it he would blow his Brains out."[3]

The customs officers, along with Sheriff Stephen Greenleaf, a justice of the peace, and two minor customs officers, returned about three o'clock in the afternoon with a search warrant signed by Judge Foster Hutchinson, the younger brother of Lieutenant Governor Thomas Hutchinson and one of Paul Revere's customers back in the prosperous year of 1762. Sheafe and Hallowell testified that they found Malcolm's gate locked and his property surrounded by three or four hundred people. Sheriff Greenleaf stated that the crowd informed him that the customs officers would not be admitted into Malcolm's house unless they would appear before a justice of the peace "and make Oath who their Informer was." The royal officials left about 5:30, after "receiving repeated Intimations from several persons of Credit" that if force were used in breaking into Malcolm's house, "the Officers would be ill used, and it would be attended by fatal consequences." For Sheafe and Hallowell, Governor Bernard, and British treasury officials, the Malcolm incident was a demonstration of the lawlessness of the Boston crowd and the need to strengthen imperial authority in the colonies. Other witnesses in the crowd, Paul Revere among them, presented a very different picture of events outside Captain Malcolm's property.

Sons of Liberty Paul Revere, Nathaniel Barber, and Captain Caleb Hopkins—as might be expected—all described a peaceable, law-abiding gathering of Boston citizens observing what they considered to be Captain Malcolm's lawful defense of his property. Revere, who was in the crowd between three and four o'clock, described Comptroller Hallowell as looking "very angry," while the approximately fifty people outside Malcolm's home "behaved with decency and good order." He testified that he was certain that the people "had not any intent to hinder the officers in the discharge of their duty but would have protected them all that lay in their power." Crown officials did not concur with Revere's depiction of virtuous and loyal citizens quietly assembled in defense of the sacred rights and liberties of Englishmen. Instead, they sought a legal ruling to uphold the writs of assistance and their opinion that the colonists were deliberately flouting the law.[4]

On October 17, 1766, William De Grey, attorney and solicitor general of the Realm, stunned the commissioners of the customs and the treasury by denying the validity of the writs of assistance in the colonies on the grounds that the Acts of Trade did not extend the Court of Exchequer's power of issuing writs to the colonies. The colonists had won another temporary victory, but the Malcolm incident left royal authorities determined to strengthen enforcement of the trade laws. Paul Revere, Daniel Malcolm, William Mackay, Nathaniel Barber, Caleb Hopkins and other patriots were equally determined to resist any future efforts to deprive them of their liberties.[5]

Two days after Daniel Malcolm's successful confrontation with His Majesty's representatives, Paul Revere returned to business, taking an order from Captain Joseph Goodwin for a silver coffeepot and punch ladle. But the economic recovery spurred by the repeal of the Stamp Act was only temporary, and by 1767 the colonial economy was suffering once again from the effects of the postwar slump of the British economy. Revere continued to make buckles for his family, friends, neighbors, and other reliable customers, but he experienced a sharp decline in the demand for luxury items from Boston's merchants and ship's captains compared with the year before. It may have been a source of some consolation in this disappointing year when three new customers who shared either his political or Masonic principles placed orders for luxury items. Gibbens Sharp, a fellow member of the North End Caucus, ordered a silver teapot on January 9; William Palfrey, Revere's Masonic brother at St. Andrew's, merchant and protégé of John Hancock, and future secretary of the Sons of Liberty, commissioned a silver tankard on February 15; and John Symmes, a goldsmith and member of St. Andrew's Lodge and the North End Caucus, ordered a silver salver and beer cups with engraved crests on September 17, 1767. Still, Revere's income dropped to approximately £48 in 1767, and he recorded no orders after September 17. Within the month, the citizens of Boston received the distressing news of Parliament's latest plans for strengthening imperial control over the colonies. Paul Revere would have to continue to juggle his identities as a master goldsmith and a Son of Liberty.[6]

As early as 1754, when he was a junior minister, Charles Townshend had plans for stricter imperial control over the colonies, but it was not until 1767, as chancellor of the exchequer, that he could implement his plans. Colonial resistance to the Stamp Act, the Malcolm incident, and other acts of colonial opposition convinced Parliament of the need to tighten the reins of the British Empire. William Pitt, America's savior for his role in the Stamp Act's repeal, conceded that the colonists had gone too far when, in December 1766, the New York Assembly refused to supply troops as provided under the Mutiny Act on the grounds that it would be acquiescing to another form of internal taxation. "New York has drunk the deepest of the baneful cup of infatuation," wrote the exasperated Pitt, "but none seem to be sober and in full possession of reason." Townshend, then, presented his revenue proposals on May 13, 1767, to a Parliament that was very receptive to any ideas for asserting rightful parliamentary control over the rebellious colonists.[7]

Townshend proposed that, beginning on November 20, 1767, the colonists would pay an external tax on glass, paper, painter's lead, and tea. The estimated annual revenue of £40,000 was a paltry sum, but both supporters and opponents of the Townshend Revenue Acts knew that the amount of revenue was secondary to the goal of increasing imperial control over the colonies. Under the Townshend Acts, Parliament extended the legality of writs of assistance to the colonies, created an American Board of Customs Commissioners based in Boston, suspended the New York Assembly until it agreed to uphold the Quartering Act, and in September 1767 ordered royal governors not to assent to laws passed by colonial assemblies affecting their constitutions. Townshend's most dangerous intent, in colonial eyes, was his bold plan to earmark revenue, creating an emergency fund to selectively pay salaries where royal control was most needed. Finally, Crown officials would be beyond the control of colonial assemblies, and Parliament would have the complete legislative power it claimed in the Declaratory Act. On October 5, 1767, Boston printer John Boyle noted with ironic understatement: "An Opposition to this Act no doubt will take place."[8]

On February 11, 1768, the Massachusetts House of Representatives approved a circular letter to the other colonial assemblies. Drafted by Samuel Adams, the Massachusetts circular letter called for colonial unity against Parliament's continued infringement of the people's right to consent to taxation and asked whether the payment of royal salaries to civil officers "hath not a tendency to subvert the principles of Equity and endanger the Happiness and Security of the Subject." Colonial unity would not be limited to the exchange of circular letters or respectful petitions to the king for the redress of grievances. Boston merchants, joined by their brethren in Massachusetts and their sister colonies, pledged that, beginning in March 1768 and lasting for one year, they would, with a few exceptions, not import European commodities, "encourage the Produce and Manufactures of these colonies," and give preference to "such Persons as shall subscribe to these Resolutions."[9]

Samuel Adams, the publishers of the *Boston Gazette,* and other Revolutionary leaders favored nonimportation because they hoped it would draw the respectable element of Boston's merchant class to the patriot cause and unite the citizens of Massachusetts in "suppressing extravagance, idleness and vice, and in promoting industry, oeconomy and good morals." John Rowe, John Erving Jr., Edward Payne, and the other members of the Committee of Merchants did indeed support nonimportation, but less for constitutional or moral reasons than for economic ones. Months before they learned of the Townshend Act's passage, Boston merchants reminded Parliament of the economic interdependence of the empire: "the Trade of America . . . is really the Trade of great Britain. . . . It is in short a strong Chain of Connection between the Mother Country and the Colonys . . . and consequently every Embarrassment of the American Trade must be a real Injury to Great Britain herself." On April 18, 1768, Thomas Cushing assured Dennys DeBerdt, the colony's agent in England, "it will not be long before the merchants on your side the water will have reason to complain." If Boston merchants could not use their economic leverage to convince Parliament to relax the revenue measures, they could at least temporarily benefit from nonimportation. Colonial merchants found it easier to collect debts from their nonimporting customers and, in turn, to pay their British creditors. Nonimportation was also a means for colonial merchants to further meet the demands of their British creditors by selling the glut of imported goods on their shelves.[10]

The success or failure of nonimportation depended on more than the efforts of colonial merchants. It also rested on the willingness of virtuous citizens like Paul Revere to give up imported luxuries in favor of the less stylish but more patriotic manufactures of their own country. One of these virtuous citizens was William Dawes Jr., who joined Paul Revere in spreading the alarm on April 18–19, 1775. As the publishers of the *Boston Gazette* reported, Dawes admirably displayed his patriotism at his May 1768 wedding to Miss Mehitable May, where he "made a handsome Appearance, dress'd wholly in the Manufactures of this Country, wherein he did Honor to himself, and merits the respect of the Province." A little over a year later and years before their celebrated rides, Revere and Dawes united in a less dramatic but no less patriotic act when they signed their names to a petition promising that they would not patronize merchants who violated nonimportation. Other signers of the nonconsumption pledge of July 31, 1769, included the diligent newspaper annotator Harbottle Dorr, two of Revere's Hichborn cousins, and several of his neighbors, customers, and fellow members of St.

Andrew's Lodge and the North End Caucus, including the respectable artisans and tradesmen Ezra Collins, Thomas Crafts, John Symmes, John Boit, and Abiel Ruddock.[11]

Paul Revere and his family, friends, and fellow artisans who supported nonimportation saw the contrast between the virtuous society of hard-working artisans like William Dawes, proudly dressed in homespun, and the corrupt, luxury-loving world of English placemen and pensioners supported by unconstitutional colonial taxation. On November 6, 1767, John Boyle reported the arrival of "a most unwelcome Cargo" in Boston—Henry Hulton, William Burch, and Charles Paxton, three of the five members of the American Board of Customs Commissioners. Edes and Gill of the *Boston Gazette* reported "it was the universal Opinion" of the representatives in the General Court "that a free People would be in more Danger of being subdued by Pensioners than Soldiers." For enforcing the hated Townshend Acts, the customs commissioners were handsomely rewarded with £500 a year and authorized to employ four clerks whose salaries ranged from £40 to £100 a year.[12]

In 1768 Paul Revere struggled to make the same amount of money as the lowest-paid clerks for the Board of Customs Commissioners earned helping to enforce regulations designed to deprive colonial Englishmen of their property, but Revere at least knew that he earned his money by serving the public good. As demand for his fine silver items declined, Revere turned to dentistry to supplement his income. Informing potential customers that he had learned the skill of making false teeth from John Baker, surgeon-dentist, Revere promised that a set of his teeth "looks as well as the Natural, and answers the End of Speaking to all Intents." Instead of being humiliated by the change of fortune that turned him from a designer and producer of fine rococo-style silver found in some of Boston's most genteel homes to a mechanic who made false teeth, Revere could take pride in providing an inelegant but useful service to his fellow citizens.[13]

While merchants saw nonimportation as a way to reduce their overstock of imported goods and lessen their indebtedness to British creditors, colonial artisans had a stronger and potentially more long-term economic motivation for supporting nonimportation. If they could patiently wait for the merchants to deplete their stock of imported items, colonial artisans would benefit from the increased demand for their products. In the nonimportation agreement of October 28, 1767, the Boston town meeting had included gold and silver buttons, wrought plate, and "Silver Smiths and Jewellers Ware" among its list of prohibited items. On January 5, 1768, Edmund Quincy, merchant, justice of the peace, and uncle of the patriot Josiah Quincy Jr., commissioned Revere to make spoons, sugar tongs, one hundred prints, and to take "the paint out of a punch bowl." On February 5 Quincy ordered spoons, canns, and a cream pot, all engraved with his family crest, and Tristram Dalton, Esq., Newbury merchant and son-in-law of the Tory merchant Robert "King" Hooper, ordered four engraved gravy spoons and two butter ladles. Still, Revere's income was nearly the same as the previous year. In 1769, however, the increase in orders for luxury items from the merchant elite raised Revere's income to almost £79. His dentistry advertisements, which had appeared in the *Boston Gazette* and *Evening-Post* from September to December 1768, disappeared after January 16, 1769, as he returned to the more elegant tasks of making silver coffeepots, teaspoons, and butter cups.[14]

Revere's motives for joining the cause of liberty were always a combination of idealism, altruism, and self-interest, and never was that more so than during the nonimportation movement. Throughout the Revolutionary period and beyond, Revere expressed his fervent and idealistic belief in liberty, virtue, honor, and benevolence, and several of his contemporaries applauded his sincere zeal for the Revolutionary cause. At the same time, Revere's increasing involvement in patriotic activities elevated his status in the community and satisfied his social ambitions. As Freemasonry allowed Revere to ennoble himself by practicing the genteel principles of honor, virtue, and benevolence, so too did his identity as a patriot. When Paul Revere publicly proclaimed his willingness to sacrifice his individual comfort and convenience by giving up English merchandise in order to defend the liberties of all colonial Englishmen, he signaled that a master artisan could be as enlightened and virtuous as any gentleman. Of course, the notion of equality between Paul Revere and the Harvard-educated attorney James Otis would have been equally ridiculous and uncomfortable to both men, but Boston's Revolutionary leaders acknowledged that master artisans would be important contributors in their plans to mobilize all segments of the community against imperial policy.[15]

Long before the Imperial Crisis, Boston's political life revolved around social clubs, taverns, and fire and militia companies. Boston merchant and officeholder Royall Tyler, Harvard classmate of the Revolutionary leaders Dr. Samuel Cooper and James Otis, made the rounds of the mechanics' taverns, mixing in with the conversation and remarking, "Nothing will take them fellows in like it." Tyler also arranged to be invited to fire company suppers, where he was seated at the head table and paid "as much homage as a demi-god." Boasting of his successful electoral methods, he wrote: "You would sometimes laugh your soul out, if you was to see how much I work them poor toads." Paul Revere and the other mechanics who became Sons of Liberty and attended the North End Caucus were certainly not "poor toads" willing to do the bidding of their social superiors for a mug of rum or merely for the glory of being admitted to their august presence. They were capable and talented men who had mastered skilled trades and ran small businesses, and after the American Revolution, they frequently succeeded in rising through the ranks of their society. They had much to gain from joining the cause of liberty, but the cause of liberty also had much to gain from men like Paul Revere, Caleb Champney, and Adam Colson.[16]

From its origins in 1767 and through the 1770s, the North End Caucus chose candidates for office, organized its members in support of street paving and other mundane civic affairs, and formulated and implemented plans for resisting imperial policies. Nearly 40 percent of its members were merchants, lawyers, and physicians. Samuel Adams, Dr. Joseph Warren, and John Adams, a young Braintree lawyer who played an increasingly important role in political activity upon his move to Boston in 1768, used their Harvard educations, exceptional rhetorical and organizational talents, and social and professional respectability to write anonymous articles in the *Boston Gazette* and draft instructions to their representatives in the General Court. However, the leaders of the North End Caucus knew that the patriot cause could not survive without the support of Boston's master artisans, who could mobilize their families, friends, and neighbors to resist British tyranny by electing candidates who will "assert your rights as men and liberties as Englishmen," signing petitions in support of nonimportation, or enforcing resistance to imperial policies through controlled crowd action.[17]

The artisan members of the North End Caucus were members of a hierarchical organization in a society that accepted deference. These master goldsmiths, shipwrights, glaziers, and leather dressers deferred to Samuel and John Adams, James Otis, and Dr. Joseph Warren not only because of their wealth, education, or gentility but also because these men had proved by their words and actions that they were friends of liberty. Thus, Harbottle Dorr praised James Otis not only for his pamphlet *The Rights of the British Colonies* but "for his truly Patriotic conduct in general." Paul Revere and his artisan friends could be mobilized only when the natural leaders of their society articulated the values, hopes, and fears of the artisan ranks of the North End Caucus. Perhaps Paul Revere could not cite natural law, common law, or the British constitution with the ease of James Otis to prove that "no man can take my property from me, without my consent" or that laws "should have no other end ultimately, but the good of the people," but he believed that his property should be protected from the unjust grasp of the Stamp Act, the Townshend Act, and corrupt customs officials, and that a legitimate government would protect his personal and political liberty.[18]

The master artisans and shopkeepers of the North End Caucus were not humble mechanics or the unthinking tools of the "better sort" who led the Revolution. They were men of accomplishment in their private and professional lives and men who had distinct ideas about their future. Gibbens Sharp was a North End shipwright who owned houses and land on Hanover Street. John Boit was a retailer/trader who rose to the rank of merchant after the Revolution. Caleb Champney was a North End plumber/glazier and small property-owner who, by

July 16, 1782, called himself a gentleman when he began building up his real estate holdings on Prince Street. Adam Colson was a leather dresser who became a shopkeeper and innholder after the Revolution. His estate in 1798 was worth $16,864.08, including real estate on Marlboro Street valued at $10,000. Paul Revere, a master goldsmith who supplemented his income as a dentist and engraver during the financial ups and downs of the Revolutionary era, rose to become a hardware retailer, bell-and-cannon founder, and copper manufacturer after the Revolution, leaving an estate worth over $37,000. These were men who joined the patriot cause not only to protect their rights and liberties as Englishmen but also to ensure the hope of a new society based on liberty and equality where men like themselves would rise in the world based only on virtue and merit.[19]

While John Dickinson rallied the colonists to resist imperial policies with his "Letters from a Farmer in Pennsylvania," the patriotic ladies of Newport, Rhode Island, supported nonimportation with their spirited production of homespun linen, patriots throughout North America sang "The Liberty Song" ("Come, join Hand in Hand, brave Americans all, / And rouse your bold Hearts to Fair Liberty's Call . . ."), and Paul Revere engraved political cartoons to awaken Boston's citizens to the danger of British tyranny. He also engraved plates for the hated Tory publisher John Mein and his partner John Fleeming in February 1768, never letting politics interfere with business. Nonetheless, engraving was always much more than a means of supplementing his income to Revere. Engraving allowed Revere, an artisan with limited formal education, to express his political beliefs and to serve an important function in the Revolutionary cause. With his renderings of Lady Liberty, America in distress, and the Devil in the shape of Lord Bute, Revere vividly depicted the Whig ideology that was usually expressed in the more refined language of John Dickinson, James Otis, and other gentlemen of liberal education. All of Revere's assets and talents—his engraving ability, his commitment to the cause of liberty, and his multiple connections in the social and political institutions of the community—would be needed as political events unfolded in 1768.[20]

On Friday evening, June 10, 1768, customs officers seized John Hancock's sloop *Liberty* on a charge of landing undutied goods. John Boyle recorded that a crowd, "exasperated at the Conduct of the Officers of the Customs, particularly Mr. Hallowell," broke a few of Hallowell's windows and burned a pleasure boat belonging to the custom house. Similar to the mob that destroyed Lieutenant Governor Hutchinson's mansion during the Stamp Act crisis, this angry crowd had grievances of their own that went beyond joining Hancock's dispute with the customs officials. According to the *Boston Gazette*, the "mix'd Multitude," including "a Number of Sailors and vagrant Persons," were protesting royal impressment policy, their fears fueled by the news that a press gang had boarded a vessel "just arrived from Glasgow" the previous Sunday. Governor Bernard and Lieutenant

Governor Hutchinson were naturally alarmed by the actions of the mob, but so too were Whig leaders, including the fiery William Molineux, the hardware merchant turned radical Whig leader of the Boston crowd, who apologized to Customs Collector Joseph Harrison for "the Frenzy of the Night." Molineux reminded Harrison, who was beaten by the crowd, that "the Whole is not to be you know condemn'd for the Actions of a few."[21]

One month after the *Liberty* riots, the Boston crowd "waited on" Inspector General John Williams, an especially unpopular customs officer, and demanded that he resign. On July 18, 1768, the *Boston Gazette* printed a notice from the Sons of Liberty in which they emphasized that the crowd "undertook the Business without the Order, Desire or Knowledge of the Sons of Liberty." In town meetings, the pages of the *Boston Gazette,* and in the Boston crowd, Whig leaders tried to regain control over events. They replaced mob action with petitions to the governor, instructions to representatives of the General Court, and letters to Dennys DeBerdt, their agent in England. John Rowe and other moderate Whigs were losing influence to Samuel Adams, Dr. Joseph Warren, and others who were more sensitive to the grievances of Boston's middling and lower ranks, but Adams and Warren would try to more carefully control protests against imperial policy in the future by relying on Paul Revere and other enlightened and disciplined master artisans and Sons of Liberty.[22]

On June 30, 1768, the Massachusetts General Court convened to respond to Secretary of State Hillsborough's order that they rescind their circular letter of February 11, 1768. By a vote of 92 to 17, the members of the General Court voted not to rescind the letter. Both John Rowe and the "trumpeters of sedition" Edes and Gill celebrated the "Massachusetts 92," and in his diary Rowe wrote: "for my own satisfaction I record the seventeen yeas, that were so mean spirited to vote away their Blessings as Englishmen, namely their Rights, Liberty and Properties." Fifteen Sons of Liberty, including Daniel Malcolm, William Mackay, Caleb Hopkins, and Nathaniel Barber, participants in and witnesses to Malcolm's confrontation with Boston customs officers back in September 1766, commissioned their fellow Son of Liberty Paul Revere to fashion a silver punch bowl engraved with words and images in honor of "the glorious NINETY-TWO . . . who, undaunted by the insolent Menaces of Villains in Power, from a strict Regard to Conscience, and the LIBERTIES of their Constituents . . . Voted NOT TO RESCIND."[23]

Revere engraved the Liberty Bowl with a plethora of Whig images and slogans—liberty caps, the Magna Carta, the Bill of Rights, "Wilkes and Liberty," and "No. 45." Massachusetts patriots were now linked with John Wilkes, the British opposition leader whose defense of liberty and the constitution against the encroachments of a corrupt government led to his arrest for libel and the loss of his seat in Parliament. As Wilkes fought against general warrants, James Otis had

4. In 1768 fifteen Sons of Liberty commissioned Paul Revere to make a silver punch bowl—the "Liberty Bowl"—in honor of "the glorious NINETY-TWO" members of the Massachusetts General Court who voted not to rescind their letter of protest against the Townshend Act. Courtesy, Museum of Fine Arts, Boston. Gift by Subscription and Francis Bartlett Fund.

fought against writs of assistance. As Wilkes refused to abandon his defense of liberty in his outlawed *Number 45 North Briton,* the "Glorious Ninety-Two" refused to rescind the circular letter. Revere's Liberty Bowl, placed on display at Nathaniel Barber's insurance office, served as a reminder, as William Palfrey later wrote Wilkes, that "the fate of Wilkes and America must stand or fall together."[24]

In addition to saluting the "Glorious Ninety-Two" with his Liberty Bowl, Revere condemned the seventeen members of the Massachusetts House who voted to rescind the circular letter with his print "A Warm Place—Hell." His portrayal of the Devil prodding the seventeen "Villains" towards the jaws of hell and shouting "push on Tim" to Timothy Ruggles, a Tory member of the House, was an almost exact copy of an English cartoon by the same title that he modified to suit the present political circumstances. Years later, when Ephraim Eliot showed a copy of the print to him, the eighty-year-old Revere recalled that "he was a young man, zealous in the cause of liberty" when he produced the print, and that Dr. Benjamin Church, then thought to be a leading Whig but later proved to be a traitor, wrote the text: "On brave Rescinders! to you yawning Cell, Seventeen such Miscreants, sure will startle Hell."[25]

Shortly after the Massachusetts House issued its circular letter and well before the *Liberty* riots, Customs Commissioner Charles Paxton warned Lord Viscount Townshend that "the Government is as much in the hands of the people as it was in the time of the Stamp Act." His solution to suppressing the disorder in Massachusetts was the dispatch of royal troops to Boston. The arrival of the Fourteenth and Twenty-Ninth Regiments on October 1, 1768, along with the arrival of the Sixty-Fourth and Sixty-Fifth Regiments on November 13, may have temporarily cheered Paxton, Governor Bernard, and Lieutenant Governor Hutchinson, but the presence of the troops also helped the patriot cause by increasing the unity of its members against a common enemy. First, their government attempted to enslave them with unjust revenue acts imposed by corrupt customs officials. Now, the ministerial conspiracy was deepening with the presence of a standing army in peacetime Boston. Samuel Adams, writing as Vindex in the *Boston Gazette*, could consult a copy of Trenchard and Moyle's *Argument, Shewing, that a Standing Army Is Inconsistent with a Free Government* (1697) or Trenchard and Gordon's *Cato's Letters* (1720) to condemn regular soldiers as brutal, debauched mercenaries carrying out the orders of tyrants, but Paul Revere need only remember his service during the Crown Point expedition to understand the dangers of a standing army.[26]

From December 1768 throughout 1769, readers of the *Boston Evening-Post* read about the contrast between the corrupt, dissolute conduct of the king's soldiers and placemen stationed in Boston and the virtuous lives led by the Sons and Daughters of Liberty. In his "Journal of Transactions in Boston," published in the *Evening-Post*, Town Clerk William Cooper recounted the many transgressions committed by the king's troops against the people of Boston. The depraved soldiers stole, drank to excess, assaulted innocent citizens, and behaved "with great rudeness" and "great insolence" toward the ladies. While "the friends of their country" practiced "the strictest oeconomy," Customs Commissioner Paxton and his "company" tried to "establish a weekly and brilliant assembly at Concert Hall." Commissioner Robinson intended to "dazzle" the people by making an appearance in a crimson velvet suit "which will cost him a *sum* that would have been a *full support* to some one of the families, that are almost reduced to poverty themselves, who are yet obliged . . . to feed the hungry and clothe the naked."[27]

In spite of the baneful presence of His Majesty's soldiers, placemen, and pensioners, in many ways 1769 was a good year for Paul Revere. During this period when Boston merchants adopted stricter nonimportation resolutions and Revere vowed not to patronize violators of nonimportation, Revere's business affairs took a turn for the better. Fortunately for Revere, his customers kept business and politics separate, and the patronage of Tory merchants Epes Sargent, Robert Hooper, and the partners Edward Cox and John Berry contributed to Revere's rise in income. He made a silver coffeepot for Sargent on March 4 and coffeepots for

Hooper on May 10 and July 6. New customers Cox and Berry were among the year's best customers, ordering a coffeepot for £5.10.0 on April 26 and silver butter "cupps," four butter ladles, and two silver cups worth £13.18.0 on May 21.[28]

While Revere was working to regain the promising economic situation that he enjoyed in the early 1760s and establishing a reputation as a reliable Son of Liberty, he was also steadily increasing both his knowledge of and stature within Freemasonry. He faithfully attended meetings at St. Andrew's Lodge throughout the 1760s and held a series of successively higher offices, rising to the rank of Secretary of his lodge from 1768 to 1769. Revere's brethren acknowledged his command of Masonic principles and traditions and his leadership skills by appointing him to several committees between 1766 to 1769 charged with developing regulations and procedures on Masonic funerals and charity. Revere's dual desires to broaden his knowledge and achieve higher status also led him to study for the advanced degree of a Royal Arch Mason. St. Andrew's Lodge Royal Arch Chapter received its charter on August 28, 1769, and Paul Revere was made a Royal Arch Mason on December 11, 1769. As a Royal Arch Mason, Revere held an exalted status within Freemasonry. St. Andrew's Lodge Royal Arch Chapter received only five initiates between 1770 to 1773, among them, Dr. Joseph Warren, who received his degree on May 14, 1770.[29]

Revere was also a leading force in the founding of the first Grand Lodge of Ancient Masons in Massachusetts, a role that drew him closer to his Revolutionary associate Dr. Joseph Warren. On November 30, 1768, after St. John's Grand Lodge had repeatedly refused to acknowledge the legitimacy of St. Andrew's Lodge because its charter had been granted by the Grand Lodge of Scotland instead of the Grand Lodge of England, the members of St. Andrew's Lodge voted to consider petitioning the Grand Lodge of Scotland to appoint a Grand Master of Ancient Masons in America. Paul Revere and Dr. Joseph Warren served on an eight-member committee that consulted with the three other Ancient Lodges in Boston that were, ironically enough, military lodges of the detested Fourteenth, Twenty-Ninth, and Sixty-Fourth Regiments. On December 27, 1769, the Grand Lodge of Ancient Masons was organized at the Green Dragon Tavern with Dr. Joseph Warren as the first Grand Master of Ancient Masons "in Boston, New England, and within one hundred miles of the same." Jeremiah French and Ponsonby Molesworth, officers of the Twenty-Ninth Regiment, were chosen Senior and Junior Grand Wardens, respectively, but the majority of Dr. Warren's subordinate officers were also his subordinates in the patriot cause. The Sons of Liberty were well represented by Grand Treasurer Thomas Crafts, Senior Grand Deacon Paul Revere, Grand Stewards Thomas Urann and Caleb Hopkins, and Sword-Bearer Edward Proctor.[30]

Their status as Freemasons and as Sons of Liberty reminded Revere and men of his rank that they lived in a hierarchical society where painters, goldsmiths, ship joiners, mariners, and retail merchants deferred to the gentry leadership of their fraternal and political institutions. Yet, Revere and his artisan brethren who were simultaneously slowly moving up through the ranks of Freemasonry and the patriot cause were becoming aware that theirs was no longer a world sharply divided between patricians and plebeians. In their lodge meetings and in the Grand Lodge, in town meetings and in meetings of the North End Caucus, these Freemasons and Sons of Liberty were achieving ever higher levels of responsibility based on their growing enlightenment in the principles of Freemasonry and the patriot cause and in their proven ability.[31]

Paul Revere was one of 350 Sons of Liberty who dined at Liberty Tree in Dorchester on August 14, 1769. John Adams, one of those in attendance, thought that James Otis and his cousin Samuel Adams were "politick" in holding such an event, "for they tinge the minds of the People, they impregnate them with the sentiments of Liberty. They render the People fond of their Leaders in the Cause, and averse and bitter against all opposers." Sons of Liberty ranging from the Adamses, James Otis, John Hancock, and Dr. Joseph Warren (the "Leaders in the Cause") to Paul Revere and his artisan friends and neighbors ("the People") drank forty-five toasts, including ones to the king and queen, John Wilkes, the Massachusetts Ninety-Two, and *Liberty* without *Licentiousness.*"[32]

At the Liberty Tree dinner, James Otis and Paul Revere, Royall Tyler and Adam Colson, John Adams and Joshua Brackett, gentlemen and artisans, celebrated not only the Stamp Act protest in 1765 and the more recent good news of the departure of Governor Francis Bernard, "the Tool of Lord Hillsborough" and "that Enemy to American Liberty," but their devotion to the principles of liberty. John Adams, who in his younger days had denigrated "Common Persons" with their "vulgar, rustic Imaginations," now believed that the minds of the people could be enlightened by the educational efforts of their leaders. Revere, through his design of exquisite silver articles for Boston's gentry and his devotion to the Masonic ideals of gentility, benevolence, and honor, had been trying mightily to raise himself above the level of common persons in the 1760s. He surely did not see himself as one of Adams's "Common Persons" or Royall Tyler's "poor toads," opening up his ignorant mind to their liberal ideas, but the Liberty Tree dinner was surely affirmation that he had risen above the exclusive company of his artisan neighbors at Clark's Wharf, the New Brick Church, and the Salutation Tavern.[33]

At Liberty Tree, Harvard-educated John Adams and Paul Revere, graduate of the North Writing School, sang "The Liberty Song" and enjoyed a performance of "Mimickry" by the hatter Nathaniel Balch, who "gave us, the Lawyers Head, and the Hunting of a Bitch fox." This "most agreeable Day," as Adams called it, was not only an opportunity for Paul Revere to mix with his social superiors but an occasion to enjoy the company of his fellow artisans, whose existing ties of friendship and Masonic love were now reinforced by the bond of patriotism. Many of those friends, neighbors, customers, and Masonic brothers would join him in future Revolutionary activity. Uncle Thomas and Cousin Thomas Hichborn, the boatbuilders, served with him in the North End Caucus and Committee of Correspondence, Safety, and Inspection. At the Boston Tea Party, Stephen Bruce, husband of his cousin Isanna, and Thomas Chase, Adam Colson, and Edward Proctor, all of St. Andrew's Lodge, helped him dispose of King George's "vile Bohea." Joshua Brackett, coppersmith turned keeper of the Cromwell Head Tavern and also customer and friend, helped Revere organize an intelligence committee to keep track of the movements of the king's troops in 1774.[34]

Just three days after celebrating their patriotism at Liberty Tree, John Hancock and other "Well Disposed Merchants" had to defend their patriotism when John Mein, the despised Tory publisher of the *Boston Chronicle,* began publishing manifests from the customhouse supposedly showing their violations of the nonimportation agreement. The following month, James Otis, another participant at the Liberty Tree dinner, defended his patriotism in the *Boston Gazette* and in the British Coffee House. Otis, whose deepening mental instability was alarming John Adams, became convinced after reading correspondence between former Governor Bernard and Customs Commissioners Henry Hulton and John Robinson that Hulton and Robinson had portrayed him as "inimical to the Crown." On September 5, 1769, one day after Otis attacked the character of the customs officers in the *Boston Gazette,* he met Commissioner Robinson in the British Coffee House on King Street, gathering place for British military and customs officials and Boston Tories. Otis proposed that he and Robinson step outside to "decide this controversy" as gentlemen. Instead, Robinson showed his contempt for Otis by tweaking his nose. Otis, armed with a cane, defended his person and his honor against attack by Robinson and several bystanders, chiefly army, navy, and revenue officers. The *Boston Gazette* concluded that Otis and John Gridley, who came to Otis's aid, "acquitted themselves with a Spirit and Resolution becoming Gentlemen and Men of Honor" as they fought off an onslaught of cutlasses, canes, and other weapons.[35]

On October 4, 1769, Paul Revere recorded his last order for the year: two silver spoons for his brother John. On the same day, the Boston town meeting voted that the names of individuals who refused to sign the nonimportation agreement be entered on the town records "that Posterity may know, who those Persons were that preferred their little private advantage to the common Interest of all the Colonies." One of the individuals who refused to sign the nonimportation agreement was John Mein, who had become "so obnoxious to the People" that he was "oblig'd to go Arm'd." The Tory merchant George Mason was convinced after a conversation with a "no less worthy personage than a Deacon . . . that the Revolution principles were gaining ground daily." On Saturday, October 28, 1769, between four and five in the afternoon, a mob of "many thousands" encouraged by

5. In February 1770 Paul Revere bought this home in North Square. Built around 1680 for the merchant Robert Howard, Revere's home became a tenement by the late nineteenth century. On April 19, 1908, the Paul Revere Memorial Association opened the restored home to the public. The Paul Revere House, 1995. Courtesy, Paul Revere Memorial Association.

"the Principal People in Town," including Selectman Jonathan Mason, and armed with canes, brickbats, and, in one case, a shovel, attacked Mein and his partner, John Fleeming, as they headed toward their print shop on King Street. Mein identified the leaders as William Molineux, the merchant Edward Davis, Captain Ingram, Captain Samuel Dashwood, and Lieutenant Colonel Thomas Marshall of the Boston militia regiment. The mob, stopped only by Mein's possession of a pistol and his retreat into the main guardhouse opposite the town house, later seized a presumed customs informer, tarred and feathered him, and paraded their unfortunate victim from the town house to Liberty Tree, the North

End, West End, and back to the town house. It is not known whether Paul Revere joined Molineux, Davis, Dashwood, and Marshall, his co-celebrants at Liberty Tree in Dorchester on August 14, 1769, in the attack on his customers Mein and Fleeming.[36]

In his ironmongery shop on Union Street, Son of Liberty Harbottle Dorr collected Boston newspapers documenting "the Cruel Treatment of the Colonies, by a despotic Administration" in the years 1770–71. But for another Son of Liberty, Paul Revere, imperial despotism temporarily receded as his personal fortunes rose. In February 1770 Revere, whose goldsmith's tools and his ability to use them were the only property he had ever owned, bought a seventeenth-century house in North Square from Captain John Erving for £213.6.8. Built around 1680 for the merchant Robert Howard, the original two-story house with its leaded casement windows and second-story overhang was at the height of fashion in its day, but that day had long passed by 1770. Still, Revere could take pride in the fact that his entrepreneurial skills had allowed him to overcome the economic impact of the revenue laws in the 1760s and purchase a home for his wife, mother, and five children. That humble house in North Square also provided proof that Revere was no longer one of the "Meaner Sort" of people paying rent in cash or commodities to Doctor Clark, Captain Erving, and John Hancock, or one of Boston's other great property owners. With property came the freedom and happiness that John Dickinson had championed in letter 12 of his "Letters from a Farmer in Pennsylvania," when he wrote *that we cannot be* HAPPY, WITHOUT *being* FREE— that we cannot be free, *without being secure in our property.*"[37]

North Square was just a block inland from Clark's Wharf, where Revere continued to maintain his shop. The Reveres still lived among artisans, mariners, and merchants in a densely settled neighborhood of small row houses, shops, and one of Boston's three town markets. The Old North Meeting House, "the church of the Mathers," stood opposite Revere's house. Within a few years, his cousin Nathaniel Hichborn, a boatbuilder, would buy a three-story brick house two doors away. Comfortably surrounded by Hichborn relations, the New Brick Church, the Masonic brethren of St. Andrew's Lodge, and fellow artisans of the North End Caucus, Revere also found himself living closer to the new scapegoat for "all the calamities of North America" since Governor Bernard had left Boston—Lieutenant Governor Thomas Hutchinson. Given the political events that would intrude on Revere's domestic tranquility within a month of his move to North Square, he could hardly have had warm feelings toward his new neighbor.[38]

CHAPTER FIVE

"MY WORTHY FRIEND REVERE"

W HILE THE REVERES settled into their new home in North Square, the patriot leaders struggled to hold the nonimportation movement together. With the passing of the January 1, 1770, deadline to resume importation, Samuel Adams, William Molineux, and the other leaders used newspapers, town meetings, and coercion to rouse the patriotic spirits of the people and keep pressure on the merchants to continue nonimportation. A letter in the *Boston Gazette* from "The People" urged the Committee of Inspection to "do *your* Duty" against the sons of Lieutenant Governor Hutchinson and other violators of nonimportation. On Wednesday, January 17, 1770, at Faneuil Hall, the inhabitants of Boston condemned several merchants, including Benjamin Greene, one of Revere's customers, and Thomas Fletcher, who had attached Revere's estate back in 1765, for "meanly sacrificing the rights of their country to their own avarice and private interest." William Molineux proposed a mass visit to Lieutenant Governor Hutchinson's home to demand that his sons deliver up their contraband tea, but Josiah Quincy, heretofore "esteem'd a violent partizan" of the Sons of Liberty, called Molineux's plan "an Act of high treason." In the end, Molineux, Samuel Adams, and Dr. Thomas Young prevailed; only the people, Molineux proclaimed, could "save the liberties" of their country. Their actions—against the Hutchinsons and, one month later, against Theophilus Lillie—took place in Paul Revere's new neighborhood.[1]

In early February, as the *Boston Gazette* reported, "upwards of one hundred Ladies at the North Part of this Town" showed their patriotism by signing an agreement not to drink tea "till the Revenue Acts are repealed." In addition to such peaceful and genteel protests, Boston's patriot leaders relied on mobs who practiced more direct methods of coercion against William Jackson, Theophilus Lillie, and other violators of the nonimportation agreement. The rowdy school-boys, joined by countrymen who streamed into Boston on market days, were very different from the men who carried effigies of Oliver and Bute on August 14, 1765, or erected an obelisk on Boston Common on May 16, 1766, to celebrate the Stamp Act's repeal. They were not politically enlightened, as Paul Revere was, by attend-ing town meetings and political caucuses. Nor were they restrained from hooli-ganism by their respectable positions as master artisans and responsible members of the church and community in Boston. They did, however, prove useful tools for enforcing nonimportation through picketing the shops of importers, breaking shop windows, or smearing the houses of their targets with a mixture of urine and excrement known as Hillsborough paint. The pageantry, playfulness, and ritualis-tic violence of their acts reinforced the image of the saucy boys who paraded effigies and mocked authority on Pope's Day. If this made their attacks on their victims seem nothing more than naughty pranks, it also made them convenient political martyrs when their victims retaliated against them.[2]

On February 22, 1770, one day after the entry of Revere's deed to his North Square home in Suffolk County records, "a Number of Boys" descended upon the shop of Theophilus Lillie, located behind Revere's house, near the New Brick Church on Middle Street. They erected a large wooden head carved with the figures of four persons representing merchants who had violated the nonimporta-tion agreement. When Ebenezer Richardson, a neighbor of Lillie's, appeared on the scene about 10 A.M., the mob found a more suitable target of their wrath. Sons of Liberty had long reviled Richardson as a reprobate and customs informer who had supposedly leaked information that led to Captain Daniel Malcolm's con-frontation with customs officers on September 24, 1766. William Palfrey called him "a fellow of a most infamous and abandoned character; who has for many years been employ'd as a Spy and informer," and John Adams repeated rumors that adultery, incest, and perjury were among Richardson's crimes.[3]

After an unsuccessful attempt "to take down the Pageantry," during which the schoolboys showered him with a variety of missiles, Richardson fled to his house, but not before an encounter with three Sons of Liberty: Thomas Knox, John Matchett, and Edward Proctor. All three men had joined Revere at the Liberty Tree dinner on August 14, 1769; Matchett and Proctor were fellow members of the North End Caucus, and Knox and Proctor were both members of St. Andrew's Lodge. Richardson accused Proctor of perjury and blacklisting Lillie as an impor-ter, threatening "to make it too hot for you before night." While the crowd pelted his house with sticks, stones, brickbats, eggs, and fruit peelings, Richardson made good on his threat of violence. He "discharged a loaded Gun into the midst of the people, saying at the same time, 'By God I'll make a Lane through you.'" His actions resulted in "a barbarous murder . . . committed on the Body of a young lad about eleven Years of Age." Christopher Seider (or Snider) was the victim, and the Sons of Liberty gained a martyr to their cause.[4]

On Monday, February 26, at 5 P.M., 400–500 schoolboys led Seider's funeral procession from Liberty Tree. Samuel Adams and the Sons of Liberty had full control of the solemn and symbolic occasion, carefully modeled on the funeral of a similar young victim of the St. George's Field Massacre in London. The procession of over thirteen hundred schoolboys, "sorrowful Relatives," "particular Friends of the Youth," "Principal Gentlemen," and "a great Number of other respectable Inhabitants of this Town" ended at the Old Granary Burying Ground. In case the citizens of Boston missed the significance of Richardson's murder of Seider, the Sons of Liberty "ordered a board affixed to Liberty Tree" bearing the biblical quotations: "Thou shall take no Satisfaction for the Life of a MURDERER; He shall surely be put to Death. Though *Hand join in Hand,* the wicked shall not pass *unpunish'd.* The Memory of the Just is *Blessed.*"[5]

Paul Revere did not note his presence in the crowd outside Ebenezer Richardson's house on February 22 or his participation in Seider's funeral procession, but he certainly had the proximity to the site of Seider's murder and the credentials as a Son of Liberty to be an observer or participant in both events. What is clear is that business was not consuming much of Revere's time in 1770, for he only recorded income of approximately £11 as a goldsmith or engraver in his waste book. He produced three engravings for Edes and Gill and made a pair of stone buttons set in gold for John Joy. He began advertising his dentistry skills again, and newspaper advertisements also note other work as an engraver, but Revere did not record income from these activities. In 1769 nonimportation had led to a dramatic revival of Revere's business, but political events in the critical year of 1770 had the opposite effect. Revere's quest for upward mobility, so recently confirmed by the purchase of his North Square home, was once again in jeopardy.[6]

On March 5, 1770, Edes and Gill of the *Boston Gazette* devoted so much space to reporting on Seider's funeral that they had to omit "Particulars of several Rencountres between the Inhabitants and the soldiery the Week past." The first of these "rencountres" occurred between 10 and 11 A.M. on Friday, March 2, when William Green, "one of the hands" at John Gray's Ropewalks, approached Patrick Walker of the Twenty-Ninth Regiment and asked: "Will you work?" When the soldier said he would, Green replied: "Then go and clean my s——t house." Walker "swore by the Holy Ghost that he would have recompence" and returned with reinforcements from the barracks. After several encounters, in which the ropemakers, wielding stout sticks used in rope twisting, bested their opponents each time, a "single corporal had influence enough to put an end" to the quarrel. The next day, there was "another fray" in MacNeil's Ropewalks between three grenadiers and six or seven ropemakers "in which the ropemakers again had the advantage." At a meeting on Sunday, March 4, John Gray agreed to dismiss his trouble-making employee, William Green, and Lieutenant Colonel William Dalrymple, commander of the king's troops, promised Gray he "should do everything in his power to keep his soldiers in order."[7]

Patriots and Tories alike agreed that the brawls at Gray's Ropewalks led up to what the patriots called the Horrid Massacre on King Street on March 5, 1770. Both patriots and Tories were avid students of Anglo-American history and politics, believing that the events of March 5, 1770, were the result of a conspiracy. Boston patriots recounted the imposition of the Stamp Act and the presence of troops in peacetime among the many violations of their liberties culminating on the evening of March 5, when vengeful soldiers seemed "to have formed a combination to commit some outrage upon the inhabitants of the town indiscriminantly." Tories condemned the Sons of Liberty for their nonimportation movement and its attack on those who opposed it by "a licentious and deluded populace" and for "a degree of cruelty" practiced against the king's troops that peaked on March 5, when the townspeople "seem to have intended to draw the soldiers out of their barracks to a general engagement."[8]

Despite a foot of snow on the ground and chilly temperatures on Monday, March 5, Boston's streets were swarming with citizens and soldiers between 6:30 and 9:00 P.M. At the customhouse, Private Hugh White, the sentry on duty, struck Edward Garrick in the head with his musket after the young apprentice to peruke maker John Piemont falsely accused Captain Lieutenant John Goldfinch of the Fourteenth Regiment of not paying Piemont for his services. While Private White held off the gathering crowd, another confrontation was taking place at Murray's Barracks on Draper's Alley between Cornhill and Brattle Streets. Henry Bass of the Loyal Nine and the North End Caucus described the grenadiers charging from their barracks as "stout men . . . armed with large naked cutlasses" who "made at every body coming in their way cutting and slashing." In contrast, Sergeant Major William Davies of the Twenty-Ninth Regiment described a large mob near the market, "tearing up the butchers stalls for clubs, swearing they would murder the first officer or soldier they met." A third crowd assembled at Dock Square near Royal Exchange Lane. Thomas Marshall, one of the leaders of the mob that attacked John Mein, saw "ten or twelve soldiers, in a tumultuous manner . . . flourishing their arms, and *saying damn them where are they*, and crying 'fire.'" The crowd from Dock Square, fired up by the speech of a mysterious figure in white wig and red cloak, and the Murray's Barracks crowd joined the angry crowd taunting Private White at the customhouse.[9]

The ringing of bells at the Brattle Square and Old Brick Churches shortly after nine brought a stream of apprentices, sailors, and respectable townspeople to King Street. Revere's customer and friend Nathaniel Fosdick was at home with his family when he heard the bells ringing for fire and "ran out to assist the inhabitants." Samuel Maverick, a seventeen-year-old apprentice to Isaac Greenwood,

Revere's customer and Clark's Wharf neighbor, also headed to King Street to see the fire. Robert Patterson, a sailor whose trousers had been torn by a shot from Ebenezer Richardson's musket less than two weeks ago, was at Captain McNeil's in the North End when he heard the bells and soon joined the North End mob that surged toward the customhouse. While some in the crowd carried fire buckets to King Street, others carried more lethal weapons. Crispus Attucks, a 6'2" mulatto, armed himself with a thick cordwood stick before leading twenty or thirty sailors, some similarly armed, up Cornhill.[10]

Nathaniel Fosdick was temporarily relieved when Captain Thomas Preston and a relief party of Corporal William Wemms and six privates came to the aid of Private White at the customhouse, where the beleaguered sentry was the object of an onslaught of snowballs from the crowd. Captain Preston later wrote that he "went to that fatal place . . . to passify the Mob if possible, to support the Sentry . . . and restrain the Soldiers by my presence," but patriot witness Henry Knox thought that Preston "seemed in great haste and much agitated." While Preston was assuring Richard Palmes of the North End Caucus that he did not intend that the soldiers should fire on the crowd, Palmes saw "a piece of snow or ice fall among the soldiers, on which the soldier at the officer's right hand stept back and discharged his gun." Palmes heard the word "Fire," although he admitted that he did not know who said it. Nonetheless, Palmes charged that Preston "had full time to forbid the other soldiers not to fire, but I did not hear him speak to them at all."[11]

With the mob advancing toward the soldiers, and Captain Preston no longer in front of them, the soldiers began firing randomly. Private Matthew Kilroy and Samuel Gray, a ropemaker, had both been involved in the brawls at Gray's Ropewalks on March 2. Now, on March 5, a shot from Private Kilroy instantly killed Samuel Gray. Crispus Attucks and James Caldwell, a sailor who had come to the customhouse after paying a courtship call, were both also killed instantly. As young Samuel Maverick ran toward the town house, he received a mortal chest wound and died the following day. A neighbor had persuaded Patrick Carr, an Irish immigrant familiar with soldiers and mobs, to leave behind a small cutlass before he headed to King Street. As he crossed King Street with Charles Connor, a shipmaster, Carr was mortally wounded. Carr, the final victim of the Boston Massacre, died nine days later, on March 14.[12]

At eleven o'clock, Lieutenant Governor Thomas Hutchinson made his way from his North End home to the town house, where he assured the crowd that he would "do all in his power that Justice should be done and the Law have its Course." By morning, Captain Preston and the eight soldiers under his command were under arrest, and the process of removing the Fourteenth and Twenty-Ninth Regiments from Boston had begun. Boston's patriot leaders then turned their attention to planning funerals for the Massacre victims and organizing propaganda efforts to arouse patriots throughout the colonies and publicize their cause in England. On March 8, as John Boyle noted, the funeral procession for four of the Massacre victims left Faneuil Hall at four o'clock, passing through King Street, "the Theatre of that inhuman Tragedy," to the Granary Burying Ground. John Rowe remarked: "Such a Concourse of People I never saw before—I believe Ten or Twelve thousand." On March 17 another procession bore the body of Patrick Carr to the Granary to join his fellow martyrs.[13]

Despite such masters of propaganda as Samuel Adams and Edes and Gill on their side, the patriots were not as quick as the Tories to publicize their version of the events of March 5. Customs Commissioner John Robinson sailed for London on March 16, carrying the government's report on the confrontation between the citizens and soldiers. But what they lost in time, the patriots made up for by the quantity and quality of their depositions. Of the twenty-seven depositions in the Tory narrative, twenty were from officers, soldiers, or persons in some way affiliated with the Fourteenth and Twenty-Ninth Regiments. In contrast, the patriots printed ninety-six depositions drawn from individuals of all ranks: the merchant Edward Payne, Selectman Jonathan Mason, apprentice Benjamin Broaders, Nathaniel Fosdick, a hatter, several women, and Cato, a "Negro Man servant to Tuthil Hubbart, Esq." Six depositions were from men who were not from Boston and thus presumably were not interested parties to the political disputes in the town. Thomas Marshall, one of John Mein's attackers, and Robert Patterson, one of Ebenezer Richardson's victims, were in the crowd, but men of their ilk were far outnumbered by more reputable and genteel Sons of Liberty like Richard Palmes, Henry Bass, and Henry Knox and a host of apparently respectable and innocent townspeople who were either enjoying an evening stroll or a visit with friends or drawn into the street by the threat of fire when they witnessed the Boston Massacre.[14]

Neither Paul Revere nor any of the patriot witnesses mentioned whether Revere himself was present at King Street with Nathaniel Fosdick, Henry Knox, Richard Palmes, or the many other nameless inhabitants of the town who came to the customhouse armed with fire buckets, clubs, or just plain curiosity. In 1887 Mellen Chamberlain, librarian at the Boston Public Library, identified Revere as the draftsman of a detailed diagram of the Massacre scene, which may have been intended for use at the soldiers' trials. Possibly Revere was in the crowd, for he correctly located the victims' bodies, excluding Patrick Carr, who died more than a week later. However, he could also have gathered the information from any number of witnesses in the crowd, including his friend Nathaniel Fosdick or North End Caucus colleagues Henry Bass and Richard Palmes. Even if Revere was in the crowd at King Street, whatever testimony he might have given to the patriot committee was not nearly as valuable as his pictorial representation of "The BLOODY MASSACRE perpetrated in King Street."[15]

The following text appears within the engraving:

The BLOODY MASSACRE perpetrated in King — Street BOSTON on March 5th 1770, by a party of the 29th REGt

BUTCHER'S HALL

Engrav'd Printed & Sold by PAUL REVERE BOSTON

Unhappy BOSTON! see thy Sons deplore,
Thy hallow'd Walks besmear'd with guiltless Gore:
While faithless P——n and his savage Bands,
With murd'rous Rancour stretch their bloody Hands;
Like fierce Barbarians grinning o'er their Prey,
Approve the Carnage and enjoy the Day.

If scalding drops from Rage from Anguish Wrung
If speechless Sorrows lab'ring for a Tongue,
Or if a weeping World can ought appease
The plaintive Ghosts of Victims such as these;
The Patriot's copious Tears for each are shed,
A glorious Tribute which embalms the Dead.

But know, FATE summons to that awful Goal,
Where JUSTICE strips the Murd'rer of his Soul:
Should venal C——ts the scandal of the Land,
Snatch the relentless Villain from her Hand,
Keen Execrations on this Plate inscrib'd,
Shall reach a JUDGE who never can be brib'd.

The unhappy Sufferers were Mess⁵ SAM¹ GRAY SAM¹ MAVERICK, JAM⁵ CALDWELL, CRISPUS ATTUCKS & PAT⁵ CARR
Killed. Six wounded, two of them (CHRIST⁵ MONK & JOHN CLARK) Mortally

6. "The Bloody Massacre," Revere's engraving of the Boston Massacre on March 5, 1770, is probably his best-known engraving, but it was heavily "borrowed" from "an Original Print . . . taken from the Spot" by painter and engraver Henry Pelham. Courtesy, Massachusetts Historical Society.

On the front page of the March 12, 1770, edition of the *Boston Gazette,* Edes and Gill reported "the recent and melancholy Demonstration of the destructive Consequences of quartering Troops among Citizens in a Time of Peace." To accompany the story, they printed a black border around the text and Revere's illustration of the coffins of four of the Massacre victims. The March 19 edition of the *Gazette* carried Revere's illustration of the coffin of Patrick Carr, the fifth victim of the Boston Massacre. On March 26 Edes and Gills advertised Revere's print of the Boston Massacre. In Revere's engraving, Captain Preston appears to be inciting the soldiers of the Twenty-Ninth Regiment, standing in front of the aptly named Butcher's Hall, to fire at a peaceful gathering of Boston's inhabitants, including a liberty-loving dog. It was a masterful work of propaganda, but what is probably Paul Revere's most famous engraving was not an original work. As he had done in the past, Revere "borrowed" from another artist.[16]

A week after they advertised Revere's print, Edes and Gill offered "the Fruits of Arbitrary Power, an Original Print . . . taken from the Spot." The artist was Henry Pelham—painter, engraver, and half-brother of the artist John Singleton Copley, one of Revere's customers. Pelham had loaned Revere his print, thinking "I had intrusted it in the hands of a person who had more regard to the dictates of Honour and Justice than to take the undue advantage you have done of the confidence and Trust I reposed in you." In copying Pelham's print without attribution, Revere was following standard eighteenth-century engraving practice, but Pelham's charge that Revere had committed an act of dishonor, self-interest, and theft, "as if you had plundered me on the highway," could not be taken lightly by a Freemason and patriot who had pledged himself to the ideals of honor, benevolence, and virtue. Was Revere guilty of stealing Pelham's engraving so he could profit from the patriotic enthusiasm following the Boston Massacre, or did he believe he was legitimately using his skill as an engraver to advance the cause of liberty? Possibly Revere shared his profits with Pelham, although he never recorded any financial arrangement with the aggrieved artist. He also never indicated that he thought his actions were dishonorable. His apparent silence in the face of Pelham's defamation of his character would not, however, be repeated. In the future, Revere would meet attacks on his honor as a businessman or a patriot quickly, vigorously, and sometimes abrasively through letters, petitions, and newspaper articles.[17]

In the aftermath of the Boston Massacre, Revere had to use all of his skills as an artisan, engraver, and entrepreneur to support his wife and five children, while temporarily setting aside his hopes of rising in the world. On April 16 Edes and Gill advertised another of Revere's prints, this one showing the landing of the hated British troops in Boston in 1768. Revere copied an original drawing by Christian Remick, adding the seemingly humble but politically barbed dedication to the earl of Hillsborough for his "well Plan'd Expedition, formed for supporting ye dignity of Britain and chastising ye insolence of America." He also engraved the frontispiece and 116 pages of William Billings's *New England Psalm-Singer.* Instead of making silver coffeepots for Epes Sargent and Robert Hooper, he returned to dentistry, flattering himself that his two years of experience, "in which Time he has fixt some Hundreds of Teeth," enabled him to "fix them as well as any Surgeon-Dentist who ever came from London." As an artisan and later as a manufacturer, Revere was always proud to advertise the practicality and superiority of his products, especially as they compared with English manufactures. His teeth were "not only an Ornament but of real Use in Speaking and Eating," and he also would clean teeth, waiting on "any Gentleman or Lady at their Lodgings." In December he had entered into a business arrangement with Edes and Gill, buying paper, primers, almanacs, and books from them, which he sold on commission.[18]

Samuel Adams hoped nonimportation would unite all elements of colonial society in a restoration of the Puritan values of piety, simplicity, and the sacrifice of private interest to the public good, but strains within the nonimportation movement showed that the patriot cause was often riding on a fragile coalition. One month after the Boston Massacre, Bostonians received the news that the Townshend duties were repealed, with the exception of the duty on tea. John Rowe, who had been charged with violating the nonimportation agreement in April 1769, attended a merchants' meeting on April 26, 1770, which voted to continue nonimportation, and noted his disapproval of "much of the Proceedings—think them too severe." Rowe's economic self-interest was only part of the reason for his opposition to continued nonimportation. Rowe was further distressed by the changing composition of the patriot cause. Moderate merchants were losing influence to William Molineux, whom Rowe denigrated as the "first Leader of Dirty Matters," and other agitators with radical ideas about liberty and equality.[19]

Popular leaders Samuel Adams, William Molineux, and Dr. Thomas Young had opened up the genteel merchants' meetings, populated by the likes of John Rowe, Edward Payne, and Thomas Boylston, to artisans and men of even lower social status. Dr. Young, who had brought his freethinking religious views and dislike of men of wealth and power from Albany, New York, to Boston in 1766, placed his hopes for revolution on the same artisans and laborers that Rowe shrank from as boorish, uneducated rabble-rousers. In May 1770, in the face of reports that Boston's merchants were deserting the nonimportation movement, Young wrote excitedly of the spirit of patriotism among Boston's artisans and tradesmen: "Never were the body of a people more knowing and less corrupt. Many common tradesmen in this town display the wisdom and eloquence of Athenian Senators."[20]

Young later described one of those artisans, Paul Revere, as "my worthy friend," of whom "No man of his Rank and Opportunities in life, deserves better of the Community. Steady, vigorous, sensible, and persevering." John Rowe was less impressed by Revere, whom he denigrated as one of the "Principal Actors" who "abused" the customs commissioners Henry Hulton and Benjamin Hallowell as they emerged from a public dinner at the concert hall on May 27, 1773.[21]

Rowe's disapproval of Paul Revere's growing influence in patriot circles was probably also a result of their Masonic differences. John Rowe was not only a long-standing member of two of Boston's most elite Modern lodges—the First Lodge and Master's Lodge—but, on November 23, 1768, he was installed as Provincial Grand Master of North America. Rowe obviously maintained the opinion of his predecessor, Jeremiah Gridley, that Ancient Masons were not entitled to Masonic legitimacy, for one week after Rowe's installation, St. Andrew's Lodge voted to consider petitioning the Grand Lodge of Scotland for a Grand Master of Ancient Masons. In the eyes of John Rowe, Paul Revere did not merit respect or social legitimacy either as a member of the Ancient and Honorable Society of Freemasons or as a "Principal Actor" in Boston's Revolutionary organizations.[22]

In spite of the tensions created by the nonimportation movement, the Sons of Liberty tried to sustain patriotic fervor in 1770 with their annual festival on August 14, informing "the Sons and Friends of Liberty" that they could buy tickets from several individuals, including Paul Revere. In September Dr. Young had high hopes for the nonimportation movement, writing Hugh Hughes that he had never seen "so fine an appearance of a fair firm and rational harmony in this Town since I have had the honor of being an inhabitant of it." He scoffed at reports of the British government "sending for the heads of the faction, of laying our towns in ashes, of subduing our republican spirits, and such puerile Bombast." Such attempts to make us "hewers of wood and drawers of water" would end in failure, Young observed, for "ten or twenty millions are not to be bridled mounted and gored by such a new market jockey as lately have jaded the nation." Twelve years after Dr. Young's letter to Hughes, Revere echoed Young's enthusiasm and used remarkably similar language to describe the causes of the American Revolution. Revere, too, drew upon Joshua 9:21 to indict the British government for wanting to make its American subjects "hewers of wood and drawers of water." Dr. Young, a self-taught student of Latin, Greek, French, and German who used science and reason to write about medicine and politics, and Paul Revere, an artisan with a common-school education who voiced his political ideas in cartoons and a handful of letters, both turned to the Old Testament to express their shared political ideology.[23]

Dr. Young may have been inspired by his residence among Boston's tradesmen, "those worthy members of society," but Paul Revere was equally exhilarated by his association with Young, Dr. Warren, James Otis, and the Adamses and his exposure to Enlightenment philosophy. Benjamin Franklin made plans to exchange the printer's trade for the life of a gentleman through reading books and forming a "club for mutual improvement," where ambitious young artisans discussed morals, politics, and natural philosophy, and by attracting a series of influential patrons who provided valuable business and political contacts. Paul Revere never achieved Franklin's financial success, which would have allowed him to retire from business and devote himself to "Philosophical Studies and Amusements." For Revere, the excitement of Enlightenment ideas about liberty and the natural rights of man came, not from reading Locke, Rousseau, Montesquieu, or Voltaire at his leisure, but through association with men whose superior education or ability to write allowed them to convey those ideas in newspapers, pamphlets, and political meetings. Revere may have been impressed by Dr. Young's flair for language or James Otis's superior command of the classics, but when they all dined at Liberty Tree in 1769 or met at other political gatherings, he must have been equally impressed that, despite the difference in their social rank, they were all Sons of Liberty.[24]

In the fall and winter of 1770, the patriot cause seemed to be losing support. Boston merchants voted to end nonimportation on October 11, 1770, an action that Harbottle Dorr blamed on "the perfidious Yorkers in conjunction with some here." Dorr credited the subscribers with adhering to the agreement "Religiously" but added: "It is suppos'd Ministerial Artifice first Induced the Yorkers to break it!" At the end of October, Captain Thomas Preston informed General Thomas Gage of "the complete victory obtained over the knaves and foolish villains of Boston"—referring to his acquittal in the Boston Massacre trial. William Palfrey attributed Preston's acquittal on October 30, 1770, not to his attorneys, John Adams and Josiah Quincy, but to a biased jury. Palfrey singled out the merchant Philip Dumaresq, later a Revere customer, who "repeatedly declared . . . that he believed Captain Preston to be as innocent as the Child unborn," and that "he would never convict him if he sat to all eternity." On December 5, nine months to the day after the "Horrid Massacre," Privates Kilroy and Montgomery were found guilty of manslaughter, but the six other defendants were acquitted. Samuel Adams, writing as Vindex in the *Boston Gazette,* tried to keep the public's focus on the Boston Massacre, but Thomas Hutchinson was confident that patriotic spirit was subsiding in the aftermath of the Massacre verdicts. Then, on December 31, 1770, Bostonians learned that their government had appointed Hutchinson as "Captain General and Governor in Chief of Massachusetts," Hutchinson's brother-in-law Andrew Oliver as lieutenant governor, and Thomas Flucker as secretary of the province. Harbottle Dorr thought they "highly merit their Commissions from the Present Infamous Ministry, for they have been faithful Drudges in their Service, and against their Country."[25]

With the end of nonimportation and the conclusion of the Massacre trials, Revere could now concentrate on events in his Masonic, family, and business life. On November 30, 1770, his brethren rewarded Revere's ten years of devoted service to Freemasonry by electing him Master of St. Andrew's Lodge for the following year. His seventh child, Elizabeth, was born on December 5, 1770, the same day that the jury reached its verdict in the soldiers' Boston Massacre trial. At his shop "opposite Dr. Clark's," Revere worked steadily, engraving prints for newspaper advertisements and almanacs, making buckles and buttons, and taking an occasional large order for more elegant dinnerware. He stopped advertising his dentistry skills after August 20, 1770, and his income from the goldsmith's trade rose to £59 in 1771, thanks in part to the patronage of Tory customers John

Joy, Thomas Amory, and Peter Johonnot, who placed orders for silver canns, "a silver Scoloped Tureen ladle," and teaspoons. He continued engraving plates for the patriot publishers Edes and Gills and began engraving plates for Isaiah Thomas, fellow Mason, Son of Liberty, and publisher of the *Massachusetts Spy.* He also accepted engraving orders from Ezekiel Russell, the publisher of the pro-government newspaper *The Censor.* As always, his Masonic brothers and fellow North End Caucus members placed their regular orders for knee and shoe buckles, teaspoons, and sugar tongs.[26]

Between 1771 and 1773 Revere restored the customer base that had contributed to his success in the early 1760s: the combination of fellow artisans with their small but frequent orders and ship's captains and merchants with their larger orders for teapots, coffeepots, and silverware. He made buttons and buckles and did mending for Gibbons Bouve, a housewright, and Thomas Emmons, a blockmaker and Masonic brother; silver tankards and teapots for Captain Joseph Hudson and Captain John Riordan; and silver coffeepots and church cups for merchants John Andrew and Zacariah Johonnot. He made buckles and did mending for Edward Proctor and produced a variety of items and did mending for Asa Stoddard. Despite his standing as a Son of Liberty and member of the North End Caucus, Revere continued to separate politics and business. He produced engravings for the patriot newspaper the *Boston Gazette,* and he made a silver cream pot and a child's silver spoon for the patriot Josiah Quincy Jr. During the same period, the Tory doctors Samuel Danforth and Philip Godfrid Kast patronized Revere for a variety of buckles, buttons, spoons, and, in Dr. Kast's case, a set of surgeon's instruments. Nor did Revere hesitate to make a "pair of silver cupps" in 1772 for the merchant Philip Dumaresq, one of the chief villains in Captain Preston's acquittal.[27]

The collapse of the nonimportation movement had taken much of the enthusiasm out of the patriot cause, and Governor Thomas Hutchinson succeeded in drawing moderate merchants to the side of government. Ezekiel Goldthwait, a merchant who had been involved in the protests against the Townshend Acts, deserted to the governor's side in 1771, defeating Samuel Adams for the office of registrar of deeds. The mercurial James Otis supported Hutchinson's right to convene the Massachusetts General Court outside Boston, an issue of great contention between the governor and the General Court in 1770–71. John Adams, suffering from physical and mental exhaustion, retired to Braintree after the legislative session of 1770–71, turning over his seat to Otis and not returning to politics until 1773. Dr. Benjamin Church, member of the North End Caucus and leading patriot, secretly defected to the side of government, providing Governor Hutchinson with information on patriot activities. By the end of 1772, John Hancock broke with Samuel Adams and became a political moderate and temporary ally of Governor Hutchinson.[28]

During these supposedly quiet years between the partial repeal of the Towns-hend duties in the spring of 1770 and the passage of the Tea Act in May 1773, Samuel Adams, Dr. Thomas Young, and the other leaders tried to keep patriotic spirit alive with their articles in the *Boston Gazette*. Starting in 1771, they found a more effective way of reviving the spirit of liberty. The annual observance of the Boston Massacre on March 5 became the most sacred holiday in the patriots' calendar, replacing the anniversary of the Stamp Act protest on August 14 and the repeal of the Stamp Act on March 18.[29]

On the first anniversary, Dr. Thomas Young and Paul Revere used their respec-tive talents to commemorate the danger of tyranny. Dr. Young delivered an ora-tion at the Factory Hall, while Paul Revere displayed "a very striking Exhibition" from the windows of his North Square home. In the first window, he showed the ghost of poor Christopher Seider surrounded by weeping friends while he tried in vain to stop the blood issuing from his mortal wound. Underneath a "monumental obelisk" with a bust of Seider and the names of the victims of the Boston Mas-sacre, Revere wrote: "Seider's pale Ghost fresh-bleeding stands / And vengeance for his Death demands." In the second window he portrayed the soldiers firing on the people during the Boston Massacre. Over this scene of the dead and wounded with "Blood running in streams from their Wounds," Revere wrote "FOUL PLAY." Finally, in the third window, Revere depicted a woman "representing America," carrying in her hand a staff affixed with the liberty cap. She rested one foot on the head of a grenadier "lying prostrate grasping a serpent.—Her Finger pointing to the Tragedy." The *Boston Gazette* reported that the tableau was "so well executed" that the "many Thousands" of spectators "were struck with solemn Silence, and their Countenances covered with a Melancholy Gloom." Church bells tolled between 9 and 10 P.M., "when the Exhibition was withdrawn, and the People retired to their respective Habitations."[30]

In addition to his political cartoons and tableaux, Revere signed petitions to demonstrate his patriotic commitment and to arouse his fellow citizens. On March 2, 1772, he was one of fifty-two men who petitioned the selectmen of Boston to hold a town meeting to ratify a committee decision choosing Dr. Joseph Warren as the Boston Massacre orator that year. The petitioners, including four of Revere's Hichborn cousins, Harbottle Dorr, and several members of the North End Caucus, urged the necessity of commemorating the Massacre "to impress upon our minds the ruinous tendency of standing Armies being placed in free and populous Cities; and the necessity of such noble exertions in all future times . . . whereby the designs of the Conspirators against the publick Liberty may be still frustrated." On June 2, 1772, Revere was the first of forty-five men to sign a petition to the selectmen protesting the encampment of the Fourteenth Regiment on Boston Common. They asked the selectmen to call a town meeting to deal with the matter at once, "for we shall not like to see again, our Streets Stained with the Blood of our Brothers." In the earlier petition, which contained the names of more socially or politically prominent men like Peter Chardon, Esq., William Phillips, Henry Bass, and Edes and Gill of the *Boston Gazette,* Revere's name was thirty-fifth out of fifty-two petitioners. But in the second petition Revere's name was first on a list that included several members of the North End Caucus, including his Masonic brother Edward Proctor; Nathaniel Barber, who had displayed the Liberty Bowl at his insurance office; and Isaac White, a candlemaker with a shop "opposite Salutation Tavern." On this roll of artisans and retailers, Revere signed his name boldly with a flourish worthy of John Hancock.[31]

Revere's activities in the years following the Boston Massacre were evidence of his growing political enlightenment and his worthwhile contributions to the patriot cause, but they still did not allow him entry into the leadership ranks of Boston's Revolution. While the Adamses, Dr. Warren, and Dr. Young planned political strategy that would be implemented by the likes of Paul Revere, Revere found another arena where his leadership abilities were recognized. His election as Master of St. Andrew's Lodge on November 30, 1770, was acknowledgment by his brethren of his virtue and merit as a Freemason and as a man. His duties were to preside over meetings and "maintain the honor and dignity of the Lodge." The position endowed Revere with the highest level of authority and dignity that he could achieve within the ranks of a Masonic lodge. Between 1770 and 1773 he also served as Senior Grand Deacon of his Grand Lodge. On April 24, 1770, the members of Tyrian Lodge in Gloucester, the first lodge chartered by the Massachusetts Grand Lodge, thanked Revere "for the Zeal and Activity he has shewn and exerted in the Establishment of this Lodge" and for "using his influence and Interest for Obtaining the Warrant with so much Expedition."[32]

For most of the first half of 1772, politics receded into the background as the Boston town meeting dealt with the routine business of voting on schoolmasters' salaries, inspecting the account of the granary, and considering whether to "make sale of the Street Dirt." On May 20 politics returned to the town meeting over the issue of royal salaries for the governor and judges of the Superior Court. In February and March 1771 Harbottle Dorr had been alarmed by newspaper reports that the governor of New York was receiving a royal salary and that a similar arrangement would be made for the governor, lieutenant governor, and secretary of Massachusetts. The idea of a ruler independent of the people was "a Terrible Stroke," as Dorr wrote in the margin of his copy of the *Boston Gazette.* The town meeting shared Dorr's opinion, instructing their representatives to the General Court that "Power without a Check is Tyranny," creating "a Master instead of a Governor" and "a Slave instead of a Subject." By the time the town meeting convened on October 28, 1772, rumors of royal salaries for the governor and judges had been confirmed. This intolerable step, in the words of Dr. Thomas Young, would revitalize the patriot cause by rousing not only the people but men pre-

viously considered "friends" to government. Although it would take time to educate the people to defend their liberties, Young assured Hugh Hughes that the
people of Massachusetts would not "relinquish one iota of our just claims" until
they had "regained every punctilio of our ravished rights and privileges," even if
the struggle lasted for "the remainder of the current century."[33]

Both the friends of government and the friends of liberty believed that the
source of salaries created ties of interest and dependence that would influence the
judgment of royal officials. Governor Hutchinson defended royal salaries as a
means of maintaining the government's equilibrium by freeing the executive
branch from becoming a tool of the legislative branch. At the town meeting of
November 2, 1772, Samuel Adams moved that a Committee of Correspondence be
appointed "to state the Rights of the Colonists . . . as Men, as Christians, and as
Subjects." Adams and Dr. Joseph Warren, the principal authors of a pamphlet of
rights and grievances presented to the Boston town meeting on November 20 and
then circulated to several other towns, maintained that it was precisely the assembly's control of the governor's salary that preserved equilibrium. A royal salary for
the governor would weaken "the ancient connection between him and this people." Their "slavery" would be complete when judges, "the men on whose opinions and decisions our properties liberties and lives, in a great measure depend,"
received salaries from the Crown. The town of Plymouth was one of many that
agreed with Adams and Warren that Crown salaries would complete "the System
of Despotism by exposing the Lives and Properties of this great People" to men
who were "dependent . . . upon those who distinguish, and separate their interest
from ours."[34]

The twenty-one men whom the Boston town meeting appointed to the Boston
Committee of Correspondence on November 2, 1772, reflected the town's belief in
choosing the right men to enlighten their fellow citizens. Eight months before the
establishment of the Boston Committee of Correspondence, the Braintree town
meeting voted to have an oration at their next meeting "on some branch of
government . . . by some person of a liberal education." The man they chose to
instill public spirit and "a just sense of our invaluable rights and privileges" was
John Adams. Likewise, the Boston town meeting chose men of property, liberal
education, extensive political experience, and proven credentials as "friends" of
the people to sit on the Boston Committee of Correspondence. The North End
Caucus contributed nine members, but they were not Paul Revere, goldsmith;
Adam Colson, leather dresser; or Gibbens Sharp, shipwright. They were Samuel
Adams, Dr. Joseph Warren, Dr. Benjamin Church, Dr. Thomas Young, William
Molineux, the merchants William Dennie and Nathaniel Appleton, Nathaniel
Barber, and the printer Joseph Greenleaf, Esq., for whom Revere contributed
several engravings for his *Royal American Magazine* in 1774. James Otis and Josiah
Quincy also contributed their political experience and rhetorical skills to the

Boston Committee of Correspondence. One-third of the members were Harvard graduates, and their connections extended throughout Boston's political institutions, churches, Masonic lodges, fire companies, and clubs.[35]

On October 27, 1772, the day before the Boston town meeting convened, James Otis and John Adams met behind closed doors at Edes' and Gill's *Boston Gazette* to discuss what course of action to take against royal salaries for provincial officials. Before these two lawyers, political leaders, and men of liberal education withdrew to discuss this weighty matter, Otis turned to three of his fellow Sons of Liberty to guard the door: "You Mr. Edes, You John Gill and you Paul Revere, can you stand there Three Minutes." His Masonic brethren, by repeatedly electing Revere to office throughout the Revolutionary period, accorded him the greatest respect for his knowledge, judgment, and leadership. In the coming years, Samuel and John Adams, Dr. Joseph Warren, and Dr. Thomas Young would depend on the patriot-silversmith as a trusted though subordinate associate who could gather and deliver intelligence and mobilize Boston's mechanics in defense of their rights. But for now, Revere, who had proudly affixed his name to patriot petitions just a few months earlier, was abruptly reminded of his inferior social status. In the eyes of James Otis, classically educated lawyer, orator, and author of *Dissertation on Letters, and the Principles of Harmony, in Poetic and Prosaic Composition* (1760), Paul Revere was no more than a sturdy sergeant-at-arms, capable only of barring the door while "the better sort" planned his future.[36]

CHAPTER SIX

"MR. REVERE WILL GIVE YOU THE NEWS"

PAUL REVERE'S role as master goldsmith seemed to take precedence over his activities as a Son of Liberty in the first months of 1773. Throughout January, February, and March he filled a steady stream of orders, including two large orders for silver spoons from Epes Sargent Jr., son of one of Gloucester's wealthiest merchant families and Master of Tyrian Lodge, which Revere had helped establish in 1770. The patronage of the Tories Eliphalet Pond, Esq., Dr. Samuel Danforth, and Dr. Phillip Kast also helped Revere more than double his income from the previous year. On September 2 Revere made a silver service for the Tory Dr. William Paine of Worcester, consisting of a coffeepot, teapot, tea tongs, tankard, and pairs of silver canns, butter boats, and porringers, as well as a cream pot, twelve large spoons, eighteen teaspoons, four salt spoons, and a wooden box. Whether Revere's income came from Tory doctors or the patriot publishers Edes and Gill, all of it was necessary to support his wife and seven children, ranging in age from their teens to the infant Isanna, born on December 15, 1772.[1]

Although business took up much of Revere's time, he also became entangled in a complicated dispute between William Burbeck and St. Andrew's Lodge of Freemasons. On March 5, 1773, on the same day that Dr. Benjamin Church delivered an oration "in commemoration of the Bloody Tragedy of the fifth March 1770," the Master, Warden, and a "number of Brethren of St. Andrew's" informed the Massachusetts Grand Lodge that they had been deprived of their charter by Burbeck, a former Master of the lodge, and asked for a dispensation until they could obtain a copy of the charter from the Grand Lodge of Scotland. Burbeck had been a key figure in a series of transactions connected to the purchase of the Green Dragon Tavern as the meeting place of St. Andrew's Lodge on March 31, 1764. On February 18, 1768, the eight lodge members who had originally purchased the Green Dragon conveyed the property to Burbeck. Seven other members of St. Andrew's Lodge were to reimburse Burbeck with interest within ten years, after which Burbeck would convey the property to yet another group of seven lodge members, including Paul Revere. In April 1771 Burbeck took the lodge charter into his possession, and in July 1772 Revere was a member of a committee ordered to "warn Mr. Burdick out this House" for refusing to surrender the charter. Perhaps Burbeck was using the lodge charter as a bargaining chip to ensure that his lodge brothers would repay him. But one Masonic historian believes that Burbeck's actions were motivated more by his concern over the impact of Paul Revere's political zeal on the future of St. Andrew's Lodge.[2]

Burbeck's identity as a moderate Son of Liberty had been established when he prepared the fireworks to celebrate the repeal of the Stamp Act in 1766 and joined Paul Revere at the Liberty Tree dinner on August 14, 1769. However, he was also an artillery expert who continued to serve the Crown as ordnance storekeeper at Castle William, where he hid the charter of St. Andrew's Lodge under the protection of the Castle's guns. Possibly Burbeck feared that Revere, who had already played a prominent role in the founding of the Massachusetts Grand Lodge in 1769, would use his rabid patriotism and anti-British ardor to encourage the members of St. Andrew's Lodge to sever their ties with the Grand Lodge of Scotland. Revere won this battle with Burbeck on May 13, 1773, when the Massachusetts Grand Lodge voted to suspend Burbeck for his actions. But Burbeck would have his victories in the days ahead, and the issue of St. Andrew's relationship with the Grand Lodge of Scotland would resurface after the Revolution.[3]

Readers of the *Boston Gazette* received an advance warning of the next political crisis on March 29, 1773, when the patriot newspaper published an extract of a "Letter from a Gentleman of London, December 24, 1772," on the "East India Business." Parliamentary efforts to assist the struggling East India Company by helping it sell seventeen million pounds of surplus tea culminated in the Tea Act of May 10, 1773, which allowed the company a remission of all duties on tea sold to the colonies and the direct sale of its tea to colonial agents. Colonial response to the economic and constitutional threats of the Tea Act did not fully emerge until the fall of 1773, but as early as March, the *Boston Gazette* alerted its readers to the danger of "ASIATIC WEALTH" that had "overwhelm'd every free constitution upon which it has hitherto been turned." A "Gentleman of London" lamented the "fall of British Liberty" but was consoled by its rise in America, which would, "like a young Phoenix . . . rise full plumed and glorious from her mother's ashes."[4]

During this next phase of the patriot struggle, Revere faced a personal crisis. Sara Orne Revere, his thirty-seven-year-old wife, died on May 3, 1773, five months after the birth of their eighth child. Revere and Dr. Joseph Warren, his brother Mason and brother Son of Liberty, now shared an additional bond, as Dr. Warren had suffered the death of his twenty-six-year-old wife, Elizabeth, one week earlier. Sara Revere was buried at the Old Granary Burying Ground, surrounded by her husband's family. There are no existing portraits or letters that illuminate her personality or her relationship with her husband, but surely Sara's skillful management of the Revere household had allowed her husband to pursue his active life as an artisan, Mason, and Son of Liberty. He now had sole responsibility, aided by his aging mother and his oldest daughter, Deborah, for the care of his children, including baby Isanna, who followed her mother in death on September 19, 1773.[5]

Despite his loss, Revere returned to work a week after Sara's death, engraving hat bills and a dog's collar for Ezra Collins and making silver hooks and eyes for Nathaniel Balch. The next week, John Rowe observed that Revere attended a committee meeting on fixing Boston's street lamps. By May 27 he was back to being a Son of Liberty, joining William Molineux and William Dennie in haranguing two customs commissioners outside the concert hall, as Rowe noted with disapproval. On the same day, the Massachusetts House of Representatives formed a Committee of Correspondence to communicate with its sister colonies. Within a month, there would be a new political controversy to report.[6]

On June 15, 1773, the Massachusetts House, prompted by Samuel Adams, published copies of letters written between 1768 and 1771 by Thomas Hutchinson and four of his relatives and friends to Thomas Whately, former secretary to the treasury under the Grenville ministry and the hated "compiler of the Stamp Act." Benjamin Franklin sent the letters to Thomas Cushing, speaker of the Massachusetts House, in the hope that political harmony might be restored if the colonists could see that the present crisis was due to the machinations of a few "very mischievous men" who misled king and Parliament about colonial affairs. The patriot press and public alike warmed to Franklin's "scapegoat theory," viciously condemning Hutchinson as a "pack horse of tyranny" who misrepresented his countrymen as disobedient subjects whose dependence on the mother country could be maintained only by "an abridgment of what are called English liberties." Mobs burned Hutchinson in effigy in Boston, New York, and Philadelphia; Hutchinson Street became Pearl Street; and the town of Hutchinson, Massachusetts, renamed itself Barre, in honor of Colonel Isaac Barre, the parliamentary defender of colonial liberty during the Stamp Act crisis. Franklin was wrong, however, in thinking that Anglo-American relations could be repaired. By October, Bostonians vowed to resist all "extorters" of the "slavish" Tea Act, including Lord North, "that detestable schemer," and the tea consignees, who included Governor Hutchinson's sons Thomas Jr. and Elisha.[7]

Patriots in New York and Philadelphia voiced their opposition to the Tea Act first, asking their fellow citizens to "secure your native Country from the deadly

Stroke now aimed in your persons against her." In Boston the North End Caucus sprang into action on October 23, 1773, when Paul Revere and the other members voted to "oppose the vending any Tea, sent by the East India Company . . . with our lives and fortunes." On the same day, Revere, his Masonic brother John Lowell, and Abiel Ruddock were voted a committee "to correspond with any Committee chosen in any part of the Town" and to call the North End Caucus together "at any time they think necessary" to deal with the tea crisis. October proved to be a very busy month for Revere, as he filled several orders for silver and engraving and began to exercise more leadership in the North End Caucus. Still, he found time to court twenty-seven-year-old Rachel Walker, whom he married on October 10, 1773. His courtship technique included a love poem he composed on the back of a bill:

> Take three fourths of a Paine that makes Traitors confess (Rac)
> With three parts of a place which the Wicked don't Bless (Hell)
> Joyne four sevenths of an Exercise which shop-keepers use (Walk)
> And what Bad men do, when they good actions refuse (Er)
> These four added together with great care and Art
> Will point out the Fair One nearest my Heart.[8]

Rachel Walker Revere took immediate responsibility for her new home and her husband's six surviving children, while her husband devoted himself to politics and the assumption of a new role as messenger of the American Revolution.

The North End Caucus continued to lead Boston's opposition to the Tea Act on November 2, when they chose a committee to contact the Boston Committee of Correspondence and appointed Drs. Thomas Young, Joseph Warren, and Benjamin Church to a committee demanding the resignation of the tea consignees. The latter refused the demand of both the North End Caucus and the inhabitants of Boston who met in a town meeting on November 5 that they resign their commissions. On November 5 the Boston town meeting, with John Hancock as moderator, proclaimed "That the disposal of their own property is the inherent right of freemen" and resolved that the town would take "all means in their Power, to prevent the Sale of the Teas exported by the East India Company." On November 17 "a Number of People" took matters into their own hands by gathering before the home of Richard Clarke, one of the tea consignees, and giving "several huzzas, whereupon a Gun was discharged upon them by a person in the house, which so enraged them that they broke his windows." To prevent a replay of the uncontrolled violence of the Stamp Act riots in 1765, Boston's patriot leaders knew that they would have to exert more control over the people, whether assembled in the North End Caucus, town meeting, or in the streets.[9]

On November 22 Dr. Joseph Warren was appointed to a subcommittee of the

Boston Committee of Correspondence that drew up a circular letter to Massachusetts towns urging their countrymen to resist the Tea Act before all their manufactures and land could be taxed "to support the extravagance and vice of wretches, whose vileness ought to banish them from the society of men." Then, on November 28, Warren wrote a letter to the towns announcing the arrival of the tea and a meeting to be held the next day at Faneuil Hall to discuss "what steps are to be immediately taken in order effectually to prevent the impending evil." Boston's patriots had a deadline to meet, for if the tea ship *Dartmouth* did not clear customs by midnight on December 16, the Crown could seize the ship and sell its cargo at auction. The patriots would then have to directly oppose royal authority.[10]

The thousands of people who assembled at Faneuil Hall at 9 A.M. on Monday, November 29, "to make a united and forceful Resistance to this last, worst and most destructive measure of Administration" were not attending a legal town meeting but a gathering of "the People" from Boston and surrounding towns. The throng, perhaps numbering five thousand, forced the relocation of the meeting to the Old South Meeting House, where the people resolved that the tea should be returned to England without payment of its duty. Before adjourning, the meeting chose Captain Edward Proctor of St. Andrew's Lodge and the North End Caucus to lead a watch of twenty-five men to protect the tea ship *Dartmouth*. Their task was not only to prevent mob violence but also to prevent Francis Rotch, the twenty-three-year-old son of the *Dartmouth*'s owner, or the tea consignees from unloading the tea. Five members of the volunteer watch besides Edward Proctor were Dr. Warren's lodge brothers from St. Andrew's: Paul Revere, Revere's cousin Robert Hichborn, Stephen Bruce, who was married to Revere's cousin Isanna, Thomas Chase, and Thomas Knox. Revere and Chase were also members of the North End Caucus, as were Henry Bass, James Foster Condy, Benjamin Edes, Moses Grant, and John Winthrop. A second watch was chosen on November 30, led by Ezekiel Cheever of the North End Caucus and including Adam Colson and Thomas Urann of St. Andrew's Lodge and the North End Caucus, Samuel Peck of St. Andrew's, and Thomas Tileston of the North End Caucus.[11]

The tea consignees, who were ordered to appear before the people on Tuesday, November 30, stated their position in a letter to Selectman John Scollay. It was "out of their Power" to send back the tea, but they agreed to store it until they received instructions from the East India Company. Sheriff Stephen Greenleaf then read a proclamation from Governor Hutchinson ordering the meeting to disperse, an order met with "a confused Noise and a general Hissing." The efforts of the artist John Singleton Copley to act as a mediator between the tea consignees, one of whom was Richard Clarke, his father-in-law, and the assembled people failed when the consignees stood by their answer to Selectman Scollay and refused to appear at the meeting. The meeting ended with the appointment of six persons "who are used to horses" to be ready to alarm the country towns if attempts were made to land the tea. Paul Revere, who would later gain fame for his abilities as a horseman and messenger, was not one of the six riders chosen.[12]

The tea agents remained at Castle William, where their obstinacy made them "infinitely more obnoxious to their countrymen than even the stamp-masters were," while the tea remained aboard the ships at Griffin's Wharf. Boston's patriots rallied support for their stand in Massachusetts and her sister colonies while the Boston Committee of Correspondence continued to press Francis Rotch and the captains of the tea ships to return their cargo to England before the customs' deadline passed. The merchant John Andrews informed his brother-in-law William Barrell of Philadelphia that William Palfrey "sets off Express for New York and Philadelphia . . . to communicate ye transactions of the town respecting the tea." Andrews reported that the country towns unanimously joined Boston in opposing the landing of the tea. Patriotic spirit was so strong that it was difficult to purchase a pair of pistols in Boston "as they are all bought up, with a full determination to repel force with force."[13]

The tea crisis dominated the lives of most Bostonians, including Paul Revere. Low attendance forced St. Andrew's Lodge to adjourn its meeting of November 30 because the matter of the tea consignees "took up the Brethrens Time." Revere was one of the many absent members, although he did attend a Grand Lodge meeting on December 3. After making a knee buckle for Edward Proctor on November 14 and a silver teapot for Captain John Riordan on November 18, both of whom were members of the volunteer watch aboard the tea ships, Revere did not take another order until December 14, when he made shoe buckles and six silver teaspoons for Nathan Phillips. On December 15 he engraved a head for Isaiah Thomas's *Essex Gazette* and mended an earring for Captain Francis Tree, his final orders for the year. The next evening, St. Andrew's Lodge adjourned its meeting "on account of the few Members Present." Paul Revere was among the absentees on December 16, the same day that Francis Rotch faced his final deadline on shipping the tea back to England.[14]

Over five thousand citizens of Boston and surrounding towns gathered at the Old South Meeting House on Thursday, December 16, to wait for Francis Rotch to answer their demand. They waited until "the candles were light in the house" when Rotch returned from Milton with Governor Hutchinson's refusal to issue a clearance pass for the *Dartmouth*. Upon receiving the unhappy news, Samuel Adams said there was "nothing further to be done—that they had now done all they could for the salvation of their Country and that he should go Home, set down and make himself as easy as he could."[15]

Within ten or fifteen minutes of Rotch's arrival, the narrator of the "Proceedings of Ye Body Respecting the Tea" heard "an hideous Yelling in the Street . . . as of an Hundred People, some imitating the Powaws of Indians and others the Whistle of a Boatswain." "An Impartial Observer" reported "the Savages" repaired to the tea ships, where they "applied themselves to the destruction of this commodity in earnest" and destroyed 342 chests of tea in two hours, "and not a single ounce of Tea was suffered to be purloined or carried off."[16]

The "brave and resolute men" who destroyed the tea hid their identities with war paint and vows of silence. In 1835 an "aged Bostonian" identified fifty-eight participants in the Boston Tea Party, and additional names have surfaced from family tradition. The author of the "Rallying Song of the Tea Party at the Green Dragon" claimed "Our Warren's there, and bold Revere," although it seems unlikely that such a prominent patriot leader as Dr. Warren was at Griffin's Wharf wielding a hatchet or flinging tea into Boston Harbor. Dr. Warren could, however, select appropriate men from the ranks of St. Andrew's Lodge or the North End Caucus. The Green Dragon Tavern, where St. Andrew's Lodge had held its meetings since 1764, was also the site of North End Caucus meetings since November 2, 1773. Masonic tradition relates that on December 16, the absent lodge brothers of St. Andrew's were meeting in a downstairs room of the Green Dragon in their capacity as members of the North End Caucus. Dr. Warren knew that he could rely on Paul Revere, Thomas Urann, Adam Colson, Edward Proctor, Thomas Chase, and Stephen Bruce to serve as "Chiefs" supervising the "Mohawks" at Griffin's Wharf. As Freemasons and members of the North End Caucus, they were used to deferring to Warren's leadership. But as master artisans, mariners, shopkeepers, and Masonic officers, they were also used to giving orders and maintaining discipline among apprentices, employees, and subordinate lodge brothers.[17]

If Revere's participation in the Boston Tea Party was shrouded in secrecy, the inauguration of his celebrated career as a courier on December 17, 1773, was not. John Boyle, Samuel Adams, and the *Boston Gazette* were among the contemporary diarists who reported the ride Revere made to New York with, as Boyle called it, "the Glorious Intelligence" of the Tea Party. The *Boston Gazette* congratulated Revere, identified only as "the Express that went from hence the Friday Afternoon after the Destruction of the Tea," for delivering the news "in a shorter Time than could be expected at this Season of the Year." He arrived in New York on Tuesday night, December 21, where another courier forwarded the news to Philadelphia, and he returned to Boston on Monday, December 27, with encouraging news. As the *Gazette* reported, the inhabitants of New York "one and all" declared that they would either send back the tea ships or destroy the tea, and that they "highly extolled the Bostonians for what the Indians had done here." Philadelphians greeted the news of the Tea Party with "the ringing of bells, and every sign of joy and universal approbation."[18]

One week after returning from New York, Revere resumed his diversified and successful business. In the next year, during which he earned almost £121, his orders included engraving a dog's collar for his friend Edward Proctor, mending "some kind of case" for Dr. Samuel Danforth, making silver cream pots and canns for Captain John Riordan, and charging John Joy for "cleaning your teeth and one pot Dentfrice." But the bulk of his work in 1774 was for engraving: cane heads for his former Clark's Wharf neighbor Isaac Greenwood and his friend Joseph Pierce Palmer, hat bills for Deacon William Boardman, crests and letters on forty-two dishes and plates for fellow goldsmith John Coburn, and, above all, copperplates to print maps and illustrations for books and magazines. On May 4 he engraved a plate for a map of East Florida for Captain Bernard Romans, and on July 9 he engraved another plate for "part of a map of Florida." On May 4 he also took an order from Henry Knox on behalf of the Tory printer James Rivington of New York, for whom he engraved a map and copied illustrations for a new edition of *Captain Cook's Voyage.*[19]

In January 1774 Revere's friend Isaiah Thomas, the publisher of the radical patriot newspaper the *Massachusetts Spy,* published the first issue of a new publication: the *Royal American Magazine.* This effort was aimed at a genteel, literary audience and contained text drawn largely from English magazines and "elegant Engravings" by Paul Revere. From January 1774 to the magazine's final issue in March 1775, Revere's work for Thomas and Joseph Greenleaf, who bought the *Royal American Magazine* in June 1774, provided a good source of income and enhanced his reputation as a patriot and an artisan. His engravings of John Hancock on the frontispiece of the March 1774 issue and Samuel Adams in the April 1774 issue allowed him to display some artistic skill, as they were both original designs drawn from Copley's portraits. "The able Doctor, or America Swallowing the Bitter Draught," "America in Distress," and his other political cartoons, although copied from English magazines, were an important contribution to the rhetoric of the American Revolution.[20]

On March 7, 1774, two days after John Hancock delivered the fourth annual Boston Massacre oration at the Old South Meeting House, the *Boston Gazette* reported the arrival of the brig *Fortune,* which included "that *baneful, detested, dutied Article* TEA" among its cargo. The publishers of the *Gazette,* who anxiously waited for "the Sachems" to "extricate us out of this *fresh* Difficulty," did not have to wait long. Immediately after receiving the news of the arrival of the tea, "His Majesty OKNOOKORTUNKOGOG King of the Narragansett Tribe" summoned his council "at the Great Swamp by the River Jordan," where they "did Advise and consent to the immediate Destruction thereof." Harbottle Dorr claimed that the destroyers of the twenty-eight chests of tea "Personated Indians as they did on the 16th of December." Paul Revere may have been one of the "brave fellows," for he described the incident with characteristic patriotic bravado in a letter to John Lamb, a New York Son of Liberty whom he had met in the course of his work as a courier between Massachusetts and her sister colonies: "You have no doubt heard the particulars relating to the last twenty-eight chests of Tea, it was disposed of in the same manner as I informed you of the other, and should five hundred more come, it will go the same way."[21]

In a diary entry of March 12, 1774, John Adams proclaimed: "There is so much of a Republican Spirit, among the People . . . that they never would submit to Tyrants or oppressive Projects." This spirit, Adams wrote, "spreads like a Contagion, into all the other Colonies." As part of their plan for reinforcing colonial unity, Boston's patriots welcomed a proposal of William Goddard, a printer in Philadelphia and Baltimore, for an independent colonial postal system. Goddard's plan was endorsed by the Boston Committee of Correspondence, the *Boston Gazette,* and Paul Revere, who wrote John Lamb that he was "highly pleased" by the idea of an independent postal system, calling it "one of the greatest strokes that our Enemies have mett with (except the late affairs of the Tea) since the year 1768."[22]

While John Adams and Paul Revere were elated by the spread of republican spirit and colonial unity, the British ministry, Parliament, and London newspapers were equally convinced that a policy of coercion toward Massachusetts would extinguish the colonial zeal for liberty. In a speech to Parliament, Lord North confidently endorsed a firm response to the Boston Tea Party: "Convince your colonies that you are able, and not afraid to control them, and, depend upon it, obedience will be the result of your deliberations." Beginning with the Boston Port Act, passed on March 31, 1774, Parliament passed a series of Coercive Acts that the colonists assailed as the "Intolerable Acts." The Boston Port Act would close the port of Boston on June 1 until the inhabitants of Boston made restitution to the East India Company for the destruction of its tea. Under the Massachusetts Government Act, after August 1, 1774, the Massachusetts Council would be appointed by the Crown and not chosen by the House of Representatives, and town meetings could not be called without the governor's approval. The Administration of Justice Act allowed the governor of Massachusetts to have soldiers or civil officers accused of capital offenses committed in the line of duty tried in another colony or Great Britain if he felt that a fair trial could not be held in Massachusetts. The Quartering Act of June 2, 1774, empowered colonial governors to quarter troops in any barn, uninhabited house, or building. The Quebec Act, although not technically one of the Coercive Acts, was condemned by the colonists for allowing the continuation of "popish" government in Quebec, including the lack of a representative assembly and trial by jury.[23]

The news of the Boston Port Act and the arrival, on May 13, 1774, of General Thomas Gage, commander-in-chief of British forces in North America and the new governor of Massachusetts, was greeted, not by the obedience that Lord North had predicted, but by outrage. John Boyle thundered: "By this cruel edict . . . Thousands of our Inhabitants will be involved in one common undistinguished Ruin!" John Andrews was indignant that "we must acknowledge and ask forgiveness for all past offenses, whether we have been guilty or no . . . and acknowledge the right of Parliament to d——n us whenever they please." If they capitulated to the demands of Parliament, the consequence would be a people "entirely dependent on the will of an arbitrary minister, who'd sacrifice the Kingdom to gratify a cursed revenge." Committees of Correspondence from Boston and seven surrounding towns met on May 12 and unanimously voted that it "is not in the power of language" to express the "Injustice and cruelty of this stroke, aimed seemingly at the Town of Boston but through them at all America." The next day, they sent for "Mr. Paul Riviere" to carry the news of the Boston Port Act "to the Southern Provinces"[24]

Revere left Boston on Saturday, May 14, armed with a proposal for a colonial ban on all British importations and broadside copies of the Boston Port Act, decorated with black borders, a skull and crossbones, and the liberty cap. Over the next two weeks, Revere was more than a messenger silently conveying letters between the Boston Committee of Correspondence and the "Southern Colonies." He was "our worthy fellow Citizen, Mr. Paul Revere," whose proven patriotism and valuable assistance to Boston's patriot leaders made him a trusted representative of Boston's Revolutionary movement. Revere could be relied upon to provide accurate information and informed political judgment both about events in Boston and the degree of support for his native town outside Massachusetts. On May 18 his "Affectionate Friend, Samuel Adams" updated Revere on political developments in Boston, apprising him that Newburyport merchants had "resolved nobly" to suspend all foreign commerce and that the Salem Committee of Correspondence was meeting to discuss similar action. The *Boston Gazette* reported overwhelming support for Boston at a Philadelphia meeting, where "it was noticed to Mr. Revere" that John Dickinson "spoke longer and with more Life and Energy than ever he had done on any former Occasion." In the coming months, Revere would become an essential link between the Boston Committee of Correspondence and the Continental Congress in Philadelphia. John Adams, attending Congress in October 1774, wrote his former law clerk William Tudor that "Mr. Revere will give you all the News" about transactions in Congress. His role as the "Express from Boston" moved Revere ever closer to the center of history, heightened his patriotic zeal, and advanced his rank in the patriot cause.[25]

Revere's news of the resolution of Rhode Island, Connecticut, New York, and Philadelphia "to stand by us to the last extremity" encouraged the patriots who met in town meeting and the Boston Committee of Correspondence to resist this latest stroke of tyranny, although not all Boston's citizens agreed with their stance. On May 30, in fact, 123 Boston merchants and other supporters of royal government, including several of Revere's customers, signed a petition supporting departing Governor Thomas Hutchinson and promising to pay for the destroyed tea. The same day, the Boston town meeting rejected the motion of merchants who recommended submission to the Boston Port Act and instead approved a draft proposal in favor of a policy of nonimportation. On June 5 the Boston Committee of Correspondence proposed a "Solemn League and Covenant," a community-wide pledge of total nonimportation and nonconsumption of British and West Indian goods after October 1. On June 28 the Boston town meeting rejected "by a vast majority" a motion of Boston merchants to censure and annihilate the Boston Committee of Correspondence for exceeding its authority and instead "approved the honest zeal of the committee of correspondence." Samuel Adams, a prime mover behind the Solemn League and Covenant, was also victorious on June 17, when the Massachusetts House of Representatives approved his resolution for a Continental Congress to meet on September 1, 1774.[26]

After the excitement of carrying the news of the Boston Port Act to Philadelphia and being treated as an authority on political affairs, it must have been a letdown to return to the ordinary tasks of mending buckles, engraving prints, and making spoons and porringers. But political events in the summer and fall of 1774 soon interfered with the resumption of his normal routine of business and attendance at Masonic meetings. Throughout the summer of 1774, Revere's Masonic brother Thomas Newell recorded the arrival of British troops and ships to surround Boston and wagonloads of grain and sheep from "worthy friends" and "sympathising brethren" in Massachusetts and Connecticut towns "for the benefit of the poor of this distressed town." On July 19 the Boston town meeting chose Revere to serve on a committee proposing members for a Committee on Ways and Means. The committee, whose members included Revere's lodge brothers Thomas Crafts, Edward Proctor, and Dr. Joseph Warren, along with Samuel Adams, Josiah Quincy, and John Rowe, would receive and distribute all donations for the "Employment or Relief" of the inhabitants of Boston. On August 30 Revere and twenty-one other men refused to serve as grand jurors under Chief Justice Peter Oliver. In a petition, they expressed their disapproval of Oliver, who had been impeached by the Massachusetts General Court in February for accepting a royal salary, and Parliament's more recent acts "of establishing the most compleat System of Despotism in this Province."[27]

General Gage's dispatch of over two hundred troops on September 1 to seize gunpowder stores at Quarry-Hill in Charlestown and two fieldpieces at Cambridge led to rumors that Gage had more hostile intentions, including the arrest of members of the Massachusetts House who refused to recognize his authority. A "concourse" of people from Middlesex County descended upon Cambridge on September 1 and 2, "determined by some means to give a check to a power which so openly threatened their destruction." The thousands of incensed patriots who gathered in Cambridge forced the mandamus councillors Thomas Oliver, Samuel Danforth, and Joseph Lee to resign their commissions. On September 4 Paul Revere excitedly wrote John Lamb that "the Spirit of Liberty never was higher than at present." He exulted over "some late movements of our friends in the Country," the resignations of "our new fangled Councellors," and the inability of His Majesty's judges to "git a Jury that will act with them." He assured Lamb: "in short, the Tories are giving way every where in our Province."[28]

Determined that Massachusetts should prepare plans for its defense and self-government, Dr. Joseph Warren was instrumental in organizing a meeting of over seventy delegates from nineteen Massachusetts towns who met in Dedham on September 6 and Milton on September 9. In the "Suffolk Resolves," drafted by Dr. Warren, the delegates pledged their allegiance to George III but strenuously condemned the Coercive Acts and General Gage's actions since becoming governor. They recommended the establishment of a Provincial Congress, the refusal of tax collectors to make payments to province or county treasurers "untill the Civil Government . . . is placed upon a Constitutional Foundation" or until ordered by the Provincial Congress, the election of militia officers "who have evidenced themselves the inflexible Friends to the Rights of the People" and would "acquaint themselves with the Art of War as soon as possible," and a policy of commercial nonintercourse with Great Britain and the West Indies "untill our Rights are fully resolved." They vowed that if their leaders, whom Harbottle Dorr named as "Hancock, Adams, etc.," were apprehended, they would imprison "every Servant of the present tyrannical and unconstitutional Government" until their leaders were freed. In the event that "our Enemies" made "any sudden Manoeuvers" requiring the assistance of "our Brethren in the Country," the Committee of Correspondence would dispatch couriers to the "several Towns in the Vicinity."[29]

Revere's business and Masonic activities played a secondary role to his work as a courier in September and October, beginning when he carried "the spirited and patriotick" Suffolk Resolves, which "were read with great applause" and unanimously passed by the Continental Congress, as Samuel Adams informed Dr. Charles Chauncy.[30] He returned to Boston on Friday evening, September 23, but he was on the road again on September 30 with additional intelligence for his patriotic brethren in New York and Philadelphia. In New York, Revere brought the news that Boston's carpenters and masons had stopped erecting barracks for the king's troops once they learned "it was contrary to the sentiments of their countrymen." He also delivered a handbill proclaiming that "although impoverished and distressed," Boston "is not yet subjugated and enslaved." On October 14 the Continental Congress approved a Declaration and Resolves, which upheld their colonial rights and liberties as Englishmen and denied Parliament's power to legislate for the colonies, and on October 18 Congress adopted the Continental Association, a policy of commercial nonintercourse with Great Britain until colonial grievances were redressed. On December 7 the Boston Town Meeting chose Paul Revere as one of the Committee of 63 to enforce the Continental Association.[31]

From the fall of 1774 to the spring of 1775, the Massachusetts Provincial Congress made preparations for self-defense and self-government, including the creation of a Committee of Safety to organize and arm the provincial militia companies.[32] Paul Revere helped implement the policies of his more learned colleagues in the Massachusetts Provincial Congress and the Boston Committee of Correspondence as a courier and member of an intelligence network that he and "upwards of thirty, cheifly mechanics," formed in the fall of 1774. Throughout this period, Revere and his fellow mechanics, who held secret meetings at the Green Dragon Tavern, gathered together "for the purpose of watching the Movements of the British Soldiers, and gaining every intelegence of the movements of the Tories."[33] On December 13, 1774, six days after Rachel Revere gave birth to their first son, Joshua, Revere assumed his now familiar role as a courier by riding to Portsmouth, New Hampshire, with news that two regiments of British troops were coming to take possession of Fort William and Mary. Revere's timely intelligence allowed the patriots of Portsmouth to collect four hundred men, who stormed the fort and carried off one hundred barrels of the king's gunpowder. In late January 1775 he "went express" to a meeting of the New Hampshire Provincial Congress in Exeter, his final ride before his most famous assignment on April 18–19, 1775.[34]

By now, Revere's reputation as an express rider and intelligence agent extended from Boston to New York, Philadelphia, and even London. Revere's cousin John Rivoire, the harbormaster and receiver general of customs in Guernsey, wrote to Revere that he had seen Revere described as "Express from Congress of Boston to Philadelphia" in London newspapers in November 1774. On April 18, 1775, an anonymous Tory writer who compiled a generally unflattering list of the Committee of 63, probably for inclusion in a London newspaper, identified Revere as a silversmith and "Ambassador from the Committee of Correspondence of Boston to the Congress of Philadelphia." On March 1, 1775, Revere and five other leaders of the self-created mechanics' intelligence committee notified John Lamb of the failure of Colonel Leslie and the Sixty-Fourth Regiment to capture munitions from the patriots of Salem on Sunday, February 26. The mechanics also mentioned that three persons, possibly including Revere, were detained at Castle Island from Saturday, February 25, to Monday, February 27, to prevent intelligence of Colonel Leslie's mission from reaching Marblehead and Salem. Revere and his colleagues promised to send Lamb weekly intelligence of events in the "metropolis and province."[35]

In the winter and spring of 1775, both General Gage and Massachusetts patriots prepared for confrontation. In February Gage ordered Captain Brown of the Fifty-Second Regiment and Ensign De Berniere of the Tenth Regiment on a scouting mission through Suffolk and Worcester Counties, "taking a sketch of the country as you pass," noting whether there were places that "strike you as proper for encampments," and the availability of "Provisions, Forage, Straw, etc." Although Brown and De Berniere disguised themselves "like countrymen, in brown clothes and reddish handkerchiefs round our necks," patriots from Watertown to Worcester were not fooled, including a servant at Mr. Brewer's Tavern in Watertown, who told the officers' servant "she knew our errant was to take a plan of the country." Throughout March and April, the Massachusetts Provincial Congress warned "the People" not "to relax in their preparations to defend themselves" and prepared rules and regulations for a Massachusetts Army. From November 2, 1774, to April 1, 1775, the Committee of Safety procured provisions and munitions. On April 1 the Committee met at Concord, where they voted that munitions stores at Concord and other sites not be removed without their orders. Meanwhile, Paul Revere and his fellow mechanics "frequently took Turns, two and two, to Watch the Soldiers, By patroling the Streets all night." On Saturday night, April 15, about midnight, the mechanics observed that "the Boats belonging to the Transports were all launched, and carried under the Sterns of the Men of War," and "likewise . . . that the Grenadiers and light Infantry were all taken off duty." As Revere noted with understatement: "From these movements, we expected something serious was [to] be transacted."[36]

On April 15, 1775, General Gage received orders from the earl of Dartmouth that all cannon, small arms, and military stores be "seized and secreted" and that "the persons of such as . . . have committed themselves in acts of treason and rebellion, should be arrested and imprisoned." The subsequent activities of the regiments under Gage's command aroused the suspicions not only of Paul Revere and his intelligence committee but of most of Boston's inhabitants, who "conjectured that some secret expedition was on foot." Dr. Joseph Warren sent Revere to Lexington on Sunday, April 16, to alert John Hancock and Samuel Adams, who had been attending meetings of the Massachusetts Provincial Congress in Concord, of the likelihood of a British expedition, the object of which was either their seizure or the seizure of munitions in Concord. Word was forwarded to Concord to hide the munitions, although Revere did not record whether he carried the news himself.[37] On his return, Revere stopped in Charlestown, where he "agreed with a Col. Conant, and some other Gentlemen, that if the British went out by Water, we would shew two Lanthorns in the North Church Steeple; and if by Land, one, as a Signal; for we were apprehensive it would be difficult to Cross the Charles River, or git over Boston neck."[38]

In his poem "Paul Revere's Ride," Henry Wadsworth Longfellow erred in describing Revere as merely the observer rather than the arranger of the lantern signals ("One, if by land, and two, if by sea; / And I on the opposite shore will be . . ."). Nor was the ride quite the impulsive dash through the countryside by a lone "apostle of liberty." Instead, it was a carefully planned and executed intelligence assignment involving Revere, an experienced courier and spy, and several other individuals who played their roles equally well. But if Longfellow took liberties with details for dramatic reasons, the real "Midnight Ride of Paul Revere" had plenty of its own moments of drama, danger, and excitement.[39]

On Tuesday evening, April 18, 1775, Dr. Warren received word from several sources that British soldiers were marching to Boston Common, "where was a number of Boats to receive them." About ten o'clock, Dr. Warren "Sent in great haste" for Revere "and beged that I would imediately Set off for Lexington" to warn John Hancock and Samuel Adams of the movements of the soldiers. Revere, after learning that Warren had already sent another express, William Dawes, by a longer route over Boston Neck, "called upon a friend" to hang the prearranged lantern signals from Christ Church. In his letter to Jeremy Belknap, Revere poetically recalled the scene as two friends rowed him across the Charles River to Charlestown, past the British warship *Somerset:* "It was then young flood, the Ship was winding, and the moon was rising."[40]

In Charlestown, Colonel Conant "and several others" told Revere they had seen the lantern signals, and Richard Devens of the Committee of Safety informed him that he had observed nine or ten British officers "all well mounted, and armed" on the road to Concord. Revere set off for Lexington about eleven o'clock, riding "a very good Horse" borrowed from Deacon Larkin of Charlestown. He had "almost got over" Charlestown Common when two British officers spotted him. Revere "turned my horse short, about, and rid upon a full Gallop" toward Medford with one of the officers in pursuit. He "got clear" of the officer, who got stuck in a clay pond, awakened the captain of the Medford Minutemen, and "alarmed almost every House, till I got to Lexington."[41]

Around midnight, Revere arrived at the parsonage of Reverend Jonas Clark, where Hancock and Adams were staying, only to find Sergeant William Munroe of the Lexington Militia barring his entrance. In a deposition written fifty years later, Munroe stated that in the early evening of April 18, Solomon Brown of Lexington, returning from market in Boston, informed him that he had seen nine British officers on the road. Munroe, supposing the officers "had some design upon Hancock and Adams," assembled at Reverend Clark's with a guard of eight men. When Revere requested admittance to speak to Hancock and Adams, Munroe told him the family "had just retired" and requested "that they might not be disturbed by any noise about the house." According to Munroe, Revere retorted: "Noise! You'll have noise enough before long. The regulars are coming out."[42] Munroe admitted Revere, who told Hancock and Adams "my errand." When William Dawes arrived about a half hour later, he and Revere had carried out their original assignment from Dr. Warren. Nonetheless, the two riders "refreshid our selves" and decided to set off for Concord, "to secure the Stores, &c. there." On the road, Revere and Dawes were overtaken by young Dr. Samuel Prescott of Concord, "whom we found to be a high Son of Liberty." After learning of their plan to alarm the inhabitants from Lexington to Concord, Prescott offered to help, saying that "the people between that and Concord knew him, and would give the more credit to what we said."[43]

About halfway between Lexington and Concord, a patrol of six British officers intercepted the three riders. Four of the officers, "with thier pistols in their hands," rode up to Revere, saying: "G—d d—n you stop. If you go an Inch further, you are a dead Man." Dr. Prescott jumped his horse over a low stone wall and got to Concord, a fact confirmed by Revere and other witnesses, including Reverend William Emerson of Concord, who noted the arrival of Prescott with his news by the "ringing of the bell" between one and two o'clock in the morning. According to Dawes family tradition, William Dawes eluded capture by leading the two soldiers who pursued him to a nearby farmhouse, where he shouted: "Halloo, my boys, I've got two of 'em." The soldiers retreated, and Dawes turned back toward Lexington.[44]

Revere's depositions on his ride, probably written within a month of the event, provide ample testimony of the coolness and ingenuity that had long made him a highly regarded subordinate officer to Dr. Warren and the other Revolutionary leaders. When he told the officer in charge that his name was Revere, the officer responded: "what said he Paul Revere." When the obviously well-known Revere said yes, the other officers "abused much." Revere then boldly bluffed his way out of the situation by telling the officers that they "would miss their Aim," that "I had alarmed the country all the way up, that their Boats, were catch'd a ground, and I should have 500 men their soon." When Major Mitchell of the Fifth Regiment threatened to "blow my brains out" for lying, Revere replied rather cheekily: "I esteemed my self a Man of truth, that he had stopped me on the high way . . . I knew not by what right; I would tell him the truth; I was not afraid." Thoroughly alarmed by Revere's "news," the officers headed for Lexington with Revere and four other men they had stopped earlier in the evening. They released Revere within sight of the Lexington Meeting House, after ordering him to exchange his borrowed horse with the tired horse of a British sergeant.[45]

While Captain John Parker and approximately seventy militiamen nervously assembled on Lexington Common at dawn to await the arrival of seven hundred British regulars, Paul Revere escorted John Hancock and Samuel Adams out of Lexington before the troops arrived and returned to Buckman's Tavern with Hancock's clerk to retrieve the patriot leader's trunk containing important political papers. From a chamber window, Revere saw the arrival of "the Ministeral Troops," and as he passed through the militia, he heard their commanding officer instruct the men to "Lett the troops pass by, and don't molest them, with out The[y] being first." Revere heard the report of a gun, "and saw the smoake in front of the Troops," who "imeaditly gave a great shout, ran a few paces, and then the whole fired." Revere had just witnessed the opening of the Revolutionary War and completed a ride that would, in the long run, catapult him into the pages of history and folklore. But in the short run, his ride marked the high point of his role at the center of history. Henceforth, he would play a much more secondary and, for him, disappointing role in the American Revolution.[46]

CHAPTER SEVEN

"AM OBLIGED TO BE CONTENTED
IN THIS STATE'S SERVICE"

P AUL REVERE claimed that he stayed at Lexington only long enough to
hear the first shots fired, after which he and John Hancock's clerk "made off"
with Hancock's trunk. The Reverend William Gordon, minister of the Third
Church in Roxbury, who rode to Concord to gather firsthand testimony on the
events of April 19, 1775, apparently interviewed Revere, repeating details contained
in Revere's depositions, but he went on to paint a much more exciting picture of
Revere's whereabouts after the first shots at Lexington: "The bullets flying thick
about him, and he having nothing to defend himself with, ran into a wood, where
he halted, and heard the firing for about a quarter of an hour." A letter from
Wethersfield, Connecticut, to "a Gentleman in New York," dated April 23, 1775,
provided a more final, if inaccurate, conclusion to Revere's ride, claiming that one
of the expresses from Boston "had the good fortune to arrive" while "the other
(Mr. Revere) is missing, supposed to be waylaid and slain." Revere did not record
his activities for the rest of that historic day of April 19, 1775, noting only that on
the following day he met with Dr. Joseph Warren in Cambridge, where "he
engaged me as a Messenger" for the Committee of Safety, "which gave me an
opportunity of being frequently with them." Certainly, much of the conversation
must have concerned what took place after Revere left Lexington green.[1]

The performance of neither the provincial nor the regular soldiers at Lexington
and Concord would gain them a place in the annals of military history. Still, the
proficient performance of Paul Revere and the patriot intelligence network and
the spirited if somewhat uncoordinated counterattack of provincial soldiers who
forced the regulars from Concord's North Bridge and relentlessly harassed them
on their retreat to Boston exceeded the performance of the British regulars under

Lieutenant Colonel Francis Smith. Revere had eliminated General Gage's element of surprise on April 16 when he carried the warning of a supposed expedition to Concord, which set the townspeople to moving the military stores to safety. Boston merchant John Andrews and the anonymous author of a letter "to a Gentleman in New York" boasted of the success of "the men appointed to alarm the country" on April 18–19, who "got over by stealth as early as the troops and took their different routes." Revere also unnerved the officers who intercepted him with his bluff that "I had alarmed the country all the way up . . . and I should have 500 men their soon," to the point that his claim was repeated in accounts written by Lieutenant William Sutherland of the Thirty-Eighth Regiment, by Major John Pitcairn, second-in-command of the British expedition, and by General Gage. In summing up the day's events, Lieutenant John Barker of the King's Own Regiment described a British expedition plagued by delay and numerous errors in military judgment. The grenadiers and light infantry, who had left Boston between 10 and 11 P.M., remained "halted in a dirty road" until 2 A.M. "waiting for provisions." By then, Revere, Dawes, and Dr. Prescott had alerted John Hancock, Samuel Adams, militiamen, and countrypeople on their respective routes, and Captain John Parker had assembled 130 militiamen at Lexington green to await the arrival of British troops, already fatigued by their long journey and apprehensive about facing 500 men in arms.[2]

Captain Parker dismissed his men at 2 A.M. after waiting an hour at Lexington green for the king's troops. When a detachment of five companies under Major John Pitcairn of the Royal Marines finally arrived in Lexington around 5 A.M., Captain Parker was able to muster only about seventy men who lived nearby or had remained at Buckman's Tavern. In a deposition to the Massachusetts Provincial Congress, Parker made it clear that his men, who had been ordered not to "meddle or make with said regular troops," were dispersing when the regulars opened fire. Depositions from members of Parker's company and spectators at Lexington green echoed Parker's description of British regulars "rushing furiously," firing upon and killing "eight of our party, without receiving any provocation therefor from us." Not surprisingly, General Gage, Major Pitcairn, and Lieutenant Barker charged that the provincials fired first against royal soldiers, who had been ordered not to attack them. However, the British officers united in their descriptions of an unsoldierly response by the king's troops, firing "without any order or regularity." Indeed, "the men were so wild," Barker wrote, "they cou'd hear no orders." Paul Revere had probably already left Lexington by the time Lieutenant Colonel Smith finally arrived with the rest of his forces to restore order to the ranks and lead them on to Concord.[3]

According to General Gage's account, Lieutenant Colonel Smith and his troops did not reach Concord until about nine o'clock, an extraordinarily slow pace. By then, Colonel James Barrett, commander of the Concord militia and superintendent of the town's military stores, had organized the roughly four hundred militiamen from Concord and surrounding towns and directed the removal of the stores. Lieutenant Colonel Smith and Major Pitcairn remained with the grenadiers on the east side of the Concord River searching for munitions, while seven light infantry companies under Captain Parsons further divided, leaving just three companies of British troops at the North Bridge under Captain Laurie, while the rest of the forces searched for military stores at Colonel Barrett's farm, located two miles beyond the bridge. The one hundred men under Captain Laurie were outnumbered and in poor position on the far side of the North Bridge, with the river behind them and a narrow footbridge their only means of retreat. Laurie sent to Lieutenant Colonel Smith for reinforcements and finally maneuvered his men into proper position on the near side of the bridge, which, in Lieutenant Barker's words, "he ought to have done at first, and then he wou'd have had time to make a good disposition." Although Captain Laurie gave no order to fire, Lieutenant Barker admitted that "the fire soon began from a dropping shot on our side." Captain Isaac Davis and Private Abner Hosmer, both of the Acton company, fell dead. Immediately, Major John Buttrick ordered the provincials to return fire: "Fire, fellow soldiers, for God's sake, fire!" The return fire killed three regulars and forced the British light infantrymen from the North Bridge. Only when they were halfway between the bridge and the center of Concord did the retreating British forces meet up with Lieutenant Colonel Smith and the grenadiers.[4]

The provincial soldiers "roused with Zeal for the Liberties of their Country" did not follow up their victory by taking military measures to pursue the retreating regulars, but their inaction was matched by Lieutenant Colonel Smith, who lingered in Concord for at least an hour after the skirmish at the North Bridge. By the time the regulars finally left Concord around noon, news of events at Lexington green had spread to towns throughout Middlesex, Suffolk, and Norfolk Counties. On their retreat to Boston, the regulars would be opposed by perhaps as many as 3,600 citizen-soldiers from over forty Massachusetts towns. Lieutenant Barker described the "critical situation" of the regulars as they marched from Concord to Lexington: "the Country was an amazing strong one, full of Hills, Woods, Stone Walls, etc. which the Rebels did not fail to take advantage of, for they were all lined with People who kept an incessant fire upon us."[5]

The second confrontation at Lexington green on April 19 brought better results for the provincial soldiers, with "their numbers increasing from all parts," while the regulars were losing numbers from "deaths, wounds, and fatigue." The regulars were saved from total disaster by the Right Honourable Hugh, Earl Percy, who arrived in Lexington between 2:00 and 2:30 P.M. with one thousand men and two fieldpieces. As soon as "the Rebels" saw the reinforcements and "tasted the field-pieces," in the words of Lieutenant Barker, "they retired." Credited by both Barker and historians for bringing a cool-headed leadership that had been sorely lacking in the British expedition thus far, Percy's last-minute rescue was the result of yet another outrageous British blunder.[6]

Before retiring on April 18, General Gage had left orders for Percy's brigade to assemble under arms at 4 A.M. Not until an express arrived with Lieutenant Colonel Smith's request for reinforcements at 5 A.M. on April 19 did Gage learn that Percy, who was not at home when Gage's orders arrived, had never received the orders. Percy's brigade was further delayed because the order to assemble the marines was mistakenly addressed to Major Pitcairn, who had marched the previous evening with the forces under Smith. Had Percy's brigade left Boston at four o'clock instead of nine o'clock, they would certainly have affected the outcome at Concord.[7]

At 3:45 P.M., Percy gave the order to begin the march back to Boston. For the next fifteen miles, according to General Gage's account, the regulars were assaulted by "a heavy fire on them from all sides, from walls, fences, houses, trees, barns, etc." For "a few trifling stores," Lieutenant Barker scoffed, the exhausted soldiers had marched "about fifty miles . . . through an Enemy's Country," arriving in Charlestown between 7 and 8 P.M. It was an end to an expedition "which from beginning to end was as ill plann'd and ill executed as it was possible to be." For the next year, General Gage controlled only the town of Boston and the Tories who acknowledged his authority. Thousands of Bostonians, including the Reveres, fled to Watertown or other country towns until Boston could be freed. The Grand Lodge of Massachusetts did not meet again until December 1776, and Paul Revere did not work as a goldsmith for the next five years. Instead, he was "in the government's service," as courier, engraver, gunpowder expert, and citizen-soldier in the Massachusetts militia.[8]

When Revere met with Dr. Warren and the Committee of Safety in Cambridge on April 20, there was much work to be done. Warren, who had left Boston at dawn on April 19 to ride to Lexington, spent the remainder of that day with William Heath, a member of the Committee of Safety and a colonel in the Massachusetts militia, trying to organize the sundry militia companies into a unified military force to attack the regulars as they retreated to Boston. With John and Samuel Adams and John Hancock in Philadelphia as Massachusetts delegates to the Continental Congress, Dr. Warren, in his dual roles as chairman of the Committee of Safety and president of the Massachusetts Provincial Congress, almost single-handedly directed military and civil affairs in the aftermath of the skirmishes at Lexington and Concord. He raised an army from masses of patriotic but undisciplined soldiers streaming in from the countryside and neighboring colonies, planned military strategy, organized intelligence networks, and worked to create a government, all the while concerned that Massachusetts proceed on a sound constitutional basis. Communication was essential to Warren's plans, and Paul Revere resumed his accustomed role as a courier on April 20. In November the Committee of Safety sent him to the Continental Congress in Philadelphia to inform the Massachusetts delegation of "the general state of things here, the movements of our land and naval forces, particularly an account of the several prizes made." Revere's work as a paid courier was necessary not only to the cause of liberty but to the support of his family.[9]

The first task for Warren and his colleagues was to publicize the patriot version of events on April 19, 1775, "a day to be remembered by all Americans . . . in which the Troops of Britain, unprovoked, shed the blood of sundry of the loyal Americans Subjects of the British King." Meeting in Concord on April 22, the Massachusetts Provincial Congress appointed a committee under the direction of Richard Devens to take depositions, "from which a full account of the transactions of the Troops under General Gage" could be collected and sent to England. Their account arrived in England on May 28, nearly two weeks before General Gage's account. On May 22 the Massachusetts Provincial Congress voted to print *A Narrative of the Excursion and Ravages of the King's Troops Under the Command of General Gage on the Nineteenth of April 1775, Together with the Depositions Taken by Congress To Support the Truth of It.*[10]

The depositions published in the *Narrative of the Excursion and Ravages of the King's Troops* were collected between April 20 and May 19, 1775. Since Revere's earliest accounts of his ride are in the form of a draft and corrected deposition, undoubtedly he prepared them for the Massachusetts Provincial Congress. Congress did not publish Revere's deposition, however, probably because he did not provide explicit testimony that the regulars fired first. Instead, the committee members relied on more pertinent testimony from members of the Lexington militia and townspeople, including Elijah Sanderson, one of four men in the custody of the British officers when they captured Revere. Sanderson claimed to have heard a British officer say, "Damn them we will have them," followed by the regulars shouting, running, and firing on the Lexington militia company, "which did not fire a gun before the regulars discharged on them."[11]

At the same time that Dr. Warren was overseeing the patriot propaganda effort, he was also trying to establish an army of 30,000 New England men, 13,600 from Massachusetts, "for the maintenance of the most invaluable rights of human nature, and the immediate defence of this Colony." From headquarters in Watertown on April 24, 1775, the Massachusetts Provincial Congress appointed a member from each county to recommend to the Committee of Safety men "such as are most suitable for officers in the Army now raising." General Gage and his army remained in Boston protected by fortifications on Boston Neck and the cannons of Admiral Graves's fleet, awaiting the arrival of reinforcements. If the British fortified Dorchester Heights and the Charlestown peninsula, their position would be almost invincible. Massachusetts would need experts in the military sciences of engineering and artillery in order to execute a successful siege of Boston. On

April 26 the Massachusetts Provincial Congress chose two veteran engineer-artillerists, Richard Gridley and William Burbeck, to organize "the defence of the rights and liberties of the American continent." For joining the American cause, the Provincial Congress rewarded Gridley, a half-pay officer in the British Army, and Burbeck, who left his post in charge of ordnance stores at Castle Island, with yearly salaries of £170 and £150, respectively. Gridley would also receive an annual pension of £123 and Burbeck, £97.6.8 per year, provisions that were not offered to any other officers.[12]

The desire to prove his patriotism on the battlefield and to obtain the honor and status that came with an officer's rank may have led Revere to hope for a commission in Gridley's artillery regiment. He did not, however, receive a commission in Gridley's regiment or in any other Continental regiment. If patriotic spirit, long service in the cause of liberty, and the respect of Boston's Revolutionary leaders were the only qualifications for a military commission, then Paul Revere had as good a claim as anyone. But when Richard Gridley, William Burbeck, and the members of the Massachusetts Provincial Congress and the Continental Congress pondered the criteria for choosing officers for the American Army, they concluded that an applicant's credentials as a Son of Liberty or a virtuous member of his community were not enough to win an officer's commission. The choice of qualified officers forced all the individuals involved in the decision-making process to question the ideals of republican society. They had to weigh their belief in virtue and merit as the only qualifications for leadership positions in a republican society against a lingering belief that leadership was best exercised by men who were previously accorded deference because of their wealth, education, and social position. The men who chose officers for the Continental Army believed, by and large, that an officer should be a gentleman, and Paul Revere most assuredly did not meet that criterion.[13]

Richard Gridley, appointed chief engineer with the rank of colonel, had extensive experience as a military engineer dating back to 1745, when he constructed the batteries that led to the surrender of the French fortress at Louisburg. His exemplary service with the artillery corps during Wolfe's defeat of Montcalm at the Plains of Abraham in 1759 had earned him a British officer's pension of half-pay for life. In civilian life, Gridley was a surveyor, civil engineer, member of Master's Lodge of Freemasons, and younger brother of Jeremiah Gridley, late attorney general of Massachusetts and Grand Master of Masons in North America.[14]

The process of procuring cannon and ammunition, organizing a company of ordnance storekeepers and artificers, enlisting men, and choosing suitable officers was a troublesome process involving Gridley, the Committee of Safety, and the Massachusetts Provincial Congress. On July 3, 1775, an exasperated Gridley complained that his judgment in the choice of officers "is of little weight" with the Provincial Congress. In the face of their continued interference, Gridley threatened to resign if he "must have persons transposed and imposed upon me without consulting me."[15]

Military experience and competence were factors as Gridley and William Burbeck, his second-in-command, debated the fitness of subordinate officers with members of the Committee of Safety and the Massachusetts Provincial Congress, but so, too, were nepotism, patronage, and concerns about the necessary social and educational skills required for military command. Gridley's sons Scarborough and Samuel were appointed major and captain in the regiment, respectively, and Burbeck's son Henry, who ended a distinguished military career as a brigadier general in the United States Army Artillerists, began his career as lieutenant in his father's regiment.[16]

Unlike most of the men who became officers in Gridley's regiment, Paul Revere had seen no military action during his brief wartime service in the French and Indian War, nor had he acquired expertise in artillery and engineering through membership in Boston's volunteer artillery companies or through individual study. In contrast, David Mason, appointed a major in the regiment on May 19, 1775, was a second lieutenant in command of a battery of cannon at Fort William Henry in 1757 during the French and Indian War and, since 1754, a member of the Ancient and Honorable Artillery Company, America's oldest organization of citizen-soldiers. In April 1763 Mason formed an artillery company that became better known as Adino Paddock's Company, for the officer who succeeded Mason as captain. Paddock, a Tory who left Boston for Halifax and then England in 1776, ironically aided his former countrymen by training several future Continental artillerists, including William Perkins and John Popkin, also members of the Ancient and Honorable Artillery Company, and John Crane, all of whom began their military careers in Gridley's regiment. Crane, a participant in the Boston Tea Party who rose from captain in Gridley's regiment to colonel of the Third Continental Artillery, gained a reputation as an outstanding officer with "great resolution, courage, energy, yet cool in danger and with an extraordinarily keen vision that enabled him to aim his cannon with devastating effect." Clearly, these officers deserved their commissions on the basis of merit.[17]

Paul Revere's unexceptional service as one of Gridley's seven lieutenants during the Crown Point expedition was surely not a strong enough claim on Gridley's favor to earn him a field officer's commission. Revere and Gridley's connection as brother Masons was also weak, as Revere was an Ancient Mason and Gridley a Modern Mason. Divided by interpretations of Masonic ritual, Revere and Gridley were members of different lodges affiliated with separate Grand Lodges, each of which held individual Masonic festivals. Moving in distinct Masonic circles, Gridley had little chance to see whether Revere was a model Freemason, a man of honor and integrity, or how he exercised his leadership skills in the Massachusetts Grand Lodge. Moreover, Gridley's more elite social status as a Modern Mason might have led him to believe that as an Ancient Mason, Paul Revere lacked the social rank and gentility to be an officer, no matter how effectively he may have filled his Masonic offices.[18]

Revere's connection to his Masonic brother William Burbeck was of much longer duration than his relationship to Richard Gridley, but their clash over the charter of St. Andrew's Lodge back in 1772 and 1773 may have doomed any chance that Revere had for obtaining a military commission in Gridley's artillery regiment. His membership on the committee that had tried to expel Burbeck from St. Andrew's Lodge in July 1772 surely did not endear Revere to Burbeck. Beyond any personal animosity that may have existed between Revere and Burbeck, what may have really weakened Revere's claim to an officer's commission were some personality traits he exhibited during the Revolutionary period.[19]

Revere's boldness, courage, and zeal in the cause of liberty served him well when he engraved inflammatory political cartoons, dumped chests of tea in Boston Harbor, and outwitted the British officers who intercepted him on April 19, 1775. In selecting field officers, however, his contemporaries looked for these qualities to be matched by a certain coolness, reflectiveness, and ease in giving orders to subordinates. George Washington and John Adams gave long and careful consideration to the qualities they believed necessary for military leadership. Washington, product of the Virginia aristocracy, thought that the appropriate officer's temperament was generally found among "gentlemen of fortune and reputable families." Adams, who believed that education and training could create good officers, nonetheless favored candidates of more genteel background, including William Tudor, his law clerk; William Bant, a merchant and John Hancock's former clerk; Benjamin Hichborn, an attorney and Revere's cousin; and Henry Knox, a bookseller—all "Young Gentlemen of Education and Accomplishments, in civil life as well as good Soldiers." Revere may have demonstrated his leadership in St. Andrew's Lodge and the Massachusetts Grand Lodge and exhibited an admirable poise and ingenuity during his ride to Lexington, but were these accomplishments enough to compete with the candidates that Washington, Adams, and other civil and military leaders had in mind?[20]

If Revere had really wanted to serve his country as a soldier, he could have immediately volunteered after Lexington and Concord, as did David Mason, who joined Gridley's artillery regiment; Henry Knox, who prepared fortifications around Boston even before receiving an officer's commission; and Israel Putnam of Connecticut, a fifty-seven-year-old veteran of the French and Indian Wars who, like Cincinnatus, left his plow to race to Cambridge to offer his military services. But Revere did not volunteer for military service right away, nor did he explain why he did not. Perhaps he did not consider his ride to Lexington finished until he reported back to Dr. Warren. His experiences as both a Freemason and a Son of Liberty had taught him always to defer to his superiors, and on April 20

Dr. Warren needed him more as a courier than a soldier. Perhaps, too, his experiences during the French and Indian War made him reluctant to put on a soldier's uniform, at least not without a high-ranking officer's commission. As General Nathaniel Greene of Rhode Island learned, "mankind are apt to pay deference to station and not to merit," and the "flattering attentions" paid to an officer because of his rank could be appealing. Service in the artillery was more desirable still, for in the words of Revere's friend John Lamb, "Artillery companies in every country are always looked upon in a superior light." Until his ambition for the honor and social distinction that came with an officer's rank could be satisfied, Revere would have to be content with serving the public good by carrying out less glorious but equally important endeavors.[21]

While Revere worked as a courier for the Committee of Safety, his wife, Rachel, prepared the family for the move to Watertown, with only fifteen-year-old Paul Jr. remaining behind in Boston to look after the family's property. Mrs. Revere attempted to send a letter and £125 to her husband by way of Dr. Benjamin Church, who had stunned his fellow members of the Committee of Safety when he volunteered to go into Boston on Saturday, April 22. Years later, when Revere recorded his Revolutionary service to Dr. Jeremy Belknap of the Massachusetts Historical Society, he wrote that although Dr. Church "appeared to be a high son of Liberty . . . I never thought Him a man of Principle; and I doubted much in my own mind, wether He was a real Whig." Revere's suspicions about Church were borne out. He failed to turn over Mrs. Revere's letter or the much-needed money to her husband, and in October 1775 his traitorous communications with the enemy were uncovered. Mrs. Revere proved to be an ardent Daughter of Liberty herself, when she admonished her husband for applying to Captain Irvin for a pass to get the family out of Boston, writing, "I should rather confer fifty obligations on them than receive one from them." By May 20, when Revere began engraving plates to print currency for Massachusetts, he and his wife, six children, and his mother were all crowded into John Cook's house in Watertown, along with fellow lodgers Benjamin Edes and Mr. and Mrs. Henry Knox.[22]

During the period between May 1775 and January 1776, Revere engraved plates to print colony notes, notes for soldiers' pay, and bills of credit. Revere could legitimately take pride in his patriotic contributions as an engraver, for money was as necessary to independence as an army or a civil government, but engraving also had its financial rewards. The Massachusetts Provincial Congress paid Revere over £240 for engraving in 1775 and £81.16.8 on January 24, 1776, for printing an additional 100,000 bills of credit. Through his engraving ability, Revere generally succeeded in combining his private interest and the public good, with one exception.[23]

On July 1, 1775, the Massachusetts Provincial Congress rejected his bill in the amount of £72.6.8 for engraving plates and printing 14,500 impressions of colony notes, voting instead to pay him only £50. The suggestion that Revere had allowed self-interest to override the necessity of serving the public good should have been taken seriously by Revere. Honor and virtue, once the exclusive province of the gentry, were no longer only a means of ensuring a gentleman's superior social and economic position. They were the concerns of all republican citizens who hoped to establish a society free from the corruption of England. There is no evidence whether Revere thought he had acted dishonorably in this instance, but if he expected to be considered a model republican in the future, he would have to be as zealous about his honor as George Washington, whom John Adams lauded for accepting command of the Continental Army, "leaving his delicious retirement, his family and friends, sacrificing his ease, and hazarding all in the cause of his country!"[24]

Two major concerns of Dr. Warren and other Massachusetts political leaders in the spring and summer of 1775 were that the Continental Congress direct the establishment of a legitimate civil government in Massachusetts and control of the army now forming in Massachusetts. On May 16 Dr. Warren, writing that "the sword should, in all free States, be subservient to the civil powers," asked the Continental Congress to "favour us with your most explicit advice respecting the taking up and exercising the powers of civil Government." Warren was also concerned that as "the Army now collecting from different Colonies is for the general defence of the rights of America," the Continental Congress should undertake "the regulation and general direction of it." Elbridge Gerry, alarmed by displays of "high notions of Government" and self-importance in the army, urged the Massachusetts delegates to the Continental Congress to press for the appointment of a "regular General," preferably "the beloved Colonel Washington," to discipline the army. The Continental Congress finally gratified the wishes of the Massachusetts Provincial Congress on June 9, 1775, when they advised that Massachusetts replace its de facto single-chamber form of government by directing the inhabitants to elect representatives who, in turn, would elect counsellors. Together, this representative assembly and council would "exercise the powers of Government" until a royally appointed governor would consent to govern Massachusetts "according to its Charter." Then, on June 16, the Continental Congress appointed George Washington to command the Continental Army.[25]

The day before Washington's appointment, Dr. Joseph Warren and the Massachusetts Committee of Safety learned of General Gage's plan to fortify Dorchester Heights and Bunker Hill. From these positions, Gage's Army, reinforced by the arrival of additional troops and Generals Howe, Burgoyne, and Clinton in May, could destroy the American Army and control Boston and its harbor. On the evening of June 16, the Massachusetts Committee of Safety ordered a detachment of a thousand men under Colonel William Prescott to fortify Bunker Hill in Charlestown.[26]

Although the heights on Charlestown peninsula were usually called Bunker Hill, local residents distinguished between Bunker Hill, the higher elevation commanding all water and land approaches to Charlestown, and Breed's Hill, located some fifty feet below. Colonel Richard Gridley wisely advised fortifying Bunker Hill, but General Israel Putnam argued for erecting breastworks on Breed's Hill. The disagreement ended just before midnight, when a conference of officers chose Breed's Hill, where Colonel Prescott's men worked through the night erecting a redoubt and breastwork. Their decision was a tactical mistake that was matched by mistakes on the British side. Instead of following General Henry Clinton's recommendation that the British army, under the cover of Admiral Graves's ships and guns, attack the uncompleted American redoubt from the rear at daybreak on June 17, General William Howe launched a frontal assault at two o'clock in the afternoon. The American Army performed well, withstanding two assaults, before running out of gunpowder. By 5 P.M., the British had won the erroneously named "Battle of Bunker Hill," but at a cost of more than a thousand casualties. James Warren had the sad duty of informing the Continental Congress that among the American casualties were "Our most worthy friend and President, Dr. Warren," whose loss "we feel most sensibly."[27]

Upon learning of Dr. Joseph Warren's death at Bunker Hill, John Adams lamented to James Warren, now president of the Massachusetts Provincial Congress: "Our dear Warren has fallen, with Laurills on his Brows, as fresh and blooming, as ever graced an Hero." In an age when men patterned their behavior on heroic models, Warren exemplified this tradition by adopting the values of classical heroes and, in turn, serving as a model himself. To an audience who understood the meaning of his acts, he used classical names as pseudonyms for his political essays, donned a Roman toga to deliver the Boston Massacre oration, and, without waiting for the arrival of his major general's commission in the American Army, headed to Bunker Hill to serve as a volunteer. He sacrificed rank and privilege to serve his fellow citizens and died a martyr's death. He remained in the redoubt at Breed's Hill until the very end, when Colonel Prescott ordered a retreat. As he headed down the back of the hill, Dr. Warren received a fatal bullet to the skull. One year later, Paul Revere carried out the sorrowful duty of identifying Warren's body in its unmarked grave on the Bunker Hill battlefield by two false teeth he had made for his Masonic brother. Two years after Warren's death, Revere honored his friend, not with stirring words, but by naming his son Joseph Warren Revere.[28]

Dr. Warren's death ended a relationship that Paul Revere shared with none of Boston's other Revolutionary leaders. Dr. Thomas Young may have called Revere "my worthy friend" and Samuel Adams may have signed his letters "Your Affectionate Friend," but there was still a patronizing tone and degree of inequality in those "friendships" that recalled sixteenth- and seventeenth-century notions of friendship as a dependent, utilitarian, patronage association instead of the Enlightenment concept of friendship as a voluntary, affectionate association of equals. Young's complimentary reference to Revere carried a tinge of condescension when he added: "No man of his Rank and Opportunities in life, deserves better of the Community." Obstacles of breeding and education prevented more than temporary moments of affectionate friendship as when Revere dined at Liberty Tree with James Otis, John Hancock, Samuel and John Adams, and Dr. Thomas Young in August 1769. Yet those barriers to true friendship between Dr. Joseph Warren and Paul Revere were overcome by Warren's ease among men of all ranks and his genuine respect for Boston's artisans, many of whom he knew as patients or as members of St. Andrew's Lodge of Freemasons. Although Revere deferred to the younger Warren's superiority as a political strategist, essayist, and orator, Warren acknowledged Revere's leadership abilities over subordinate Masons and Boston mechanics. Moreover, as Ancient Masons, Revere and Warren believed that worldly wealth and social distinctions mattered less than honor, integrity, and virtue—qualities that were not the exclusive possession of gentlemen.[29]

While Revere engraved plates and printed currency for Massachusetts during the summer of 1775, General Washington settled into his headquarters in a Cambridge mansion formerly occupied by the Tory merchant John Vassall and began the monumental task of organizing the Continental Army. Soon after his arrival in Cambridge on July 3, Washington praised the American entrenchments erected by Colonel Gridley, Lieutenant Colonel Rufus Putnam, and Henry Knox, who, despite his marriage to the daughter of the royal secretary of Massachusetts, volunteered his services as artillerist-engineer to General Artemas Ward immediately after the skirmishes at Lexington and Concord. Knox, whose interest in military matters dated to his youth, had developed his understanding of the military sciences through membership in the Boston Grenadier Corps beginning in 1772 and through independent study. On May 16, 1775, the Committee of Safety recommended that Knox "be applied to for supplying the Colony Army with Military Books." His pleasing personality and genuine merit earned him the respect of influential men, including General Washington and Major General Charles Lee, who "expressed the greatest pleasure and surprise" at the "situation and utility" of the works he erected at Roxbury. Washington was less impressed with the quality of the Massachusetts troops, dominated by "boys, deserters, and negroes," and their officers, who "have by no means corresponded with the judgment and wishes of either the civil or military." By the end of the year, Henry Knox would become a central figure in Washington's plans to strengthen the officer corps of the Continental Army.[30]

In this first year of the American Revolution, Paul Revere had not yet shown the engineering skill of Henry Knox or the bravery of Dr. Joseph Warren, nor did he possess the educational and civil accomplishments that might have impressed

George Washington or John Adams to recommend him above all others for a Continental officer's commission. Even his cousin Benjamin Hichborn overcame suspicions that he was a Tory by volunteering to carry letters from John Adams to Boston, during which he was captured and held aboard a British ship for two months, only to make a daring escape to tell his tale to the patriot leaders.[31]

Finally, in November 1775, Revere made a military contribution when the Massachusetts Provincial Congress sent him to Philadelphia to learn the art of manufacturing gunpowder from Oswell Eve. Robert Morris, Pennsylvania delegate to the Continental Congress, gave Revere a letter of introduction assuring Eve that a gunpowder mill in New England "cannot in the least degree affect your manufacture" and asking that he "Chearfully and from Public Spirited Motives" assist Revere. Eve, however, allowed Revere only a brief tour, nor did he provide him with a plan of the gunpowder mill. Elbridge Gerry wrote to Samuel Adams that Revere told him that Eve "was so selfish as to refuse" to give him a plan "without a reward of one hundred half-johannes." Fortunately, Revere's powers of observation, along with a plan of a gunpowder mill that Samuel Adams had obtained from "a gentleman in the Colony of New York," were sufficient for him to help design a gunpowder mill in Stoughton, which was in operation by May 1776.[32] With General Washington intent on reorganizing his army by reenlisting only the best officers from New England, perhaps now Paul Revere might find an opening in the Continental Artillery Regiment.[33]

Among the issues discussed in October, when Washington met with delegates from the Continental Congress, including Benjamin Franklin, and representatives from the New England governments were the "very unhappy disputes" in the artillery regiment, where Colonial Gridley "is become very obnoxious to that corps." On August 9, 1775, James Warren had attributed the problems in the regiment to Gridley, who "is grown old" and is "much governed by a son of his, who vainly supposed he had a right to the second place in the regiment." Whether this involved Scarborough Gridley, who as a major would be in line for promotion to lieutenant colonel, or Samuel is unclear, but both men were at the center of dissension in the regiment. On September 24 Scarborough Gridley was dismissed from the Massachusetts service for being "deficient in his duty" at Bunker Hill, although he was partially excused "on account of his inexperience and youth, and the great confusion which attended that day's transactions." On October 11 a court-martial tried Captain Samuel Gridley for "backwardness in the execution of his duty . . . and negligence in the care and discipline of his camp" but dismissed the complaint "as malicious, vexatious and groundless." The continuation of "irreconcilable differences" in the regiment convinced the conference committee to dismiss Colonel Gridley "in some honourable way." On November 17 the Continental Congress announced Gridley's retirement "on account of his advanced age" and the unanimous choice of Henry Knox as the new colonel of the Continental

Artillery Regiment. Congress compensated Gridley by appointing him chief engineer with half-pay for life.[34]

Henry Knox's supporters included Lieutenant Colonel William Burbeck and Major David Mason, both of whom remained in the reorganized artillery regiment; General Washington, who on November 16 had ordered Knox to Fort Ticonderoga to bring back to Boston the British ordnance captured by Ethan Allen in May; and John Adams, who, prompted by "a sincere opinion of your Merit and Qualifications," had championed Knox's candidacy, informing him on November 11 that "I believe you will very soon be provided for according to your Wishes." Adams especially placed a high premium on Knox's judgment of the character and qualifications of candidates for artillery and engineering commands from Massachusetts. Like Adams, Knox regretted "that few men of Genius, Spirit, and solid judgment are high up in the list of Colonels from that State." For a lieutenant colonel's commission in the artillery, Knox had in mind "a man of reading" with "certain principles of inflexible honor and sentiment, and a proportion of judgment with his genius." On these grounds, Knox dismissed David Mason, already promoted to lieutenant colonel on May 25, 1776, as "but so so" and characterized Major John Crane as "an exceedingly fine spirited fellow" who would have been an excellent candidate "were his education equal to his station." Revere was on friendly terms with both Knox and Adams and both men could vouch for his patriotic spirit, but did he possess the contemplative mind and sound judgment that they sought in an officer?[35]

In early December 1775 John Adams supported Thomas Crafts Jr., Paul Revere's friend and Masonic brother, for lieutenant colonel and George Trott for one of two major's commissions in the Knox regiment. They were "excellent officers, very modest, civil, sensible, and of prodigious Merit as well as Suffering in the American cause." The Continental Congress forwarded their names to General Washington so that he could "inquire into their characters and abilities," and Adams promised to "kick and bounce like fury" if Congress neglected his friends. However, Crafts and Trott had the audacity to refuse commissions. An exasperated Washington, who had already had his fill of New England officers, whom he labeled as "the most aggressive levellers among Americans," informed Congress that Crafts's "ambition was not fully gratified by the offer made him of a Majority." In a rambling, obsequious letter, whose misspellings and mangled syntax betrayed his lack of gentility, Crafts thanked Adams for his "sincere friendship," but he explained that he could not accept "under such humiliating circumstances" of serving with "so low and mean a person" as Major David Mason or Major John Crane, "a good Officer and worthy Man But Last June he was only a Sergant in the Company whereof I was Captain-Lieutenant." On February 18, 1776, Adams assured Crafts that "it was the Wish of your Friends here" that he and Trott "should have all those Rewards from your Country which you can desire." Adams added that it was "still their earnest Desire" that Crafts and Paul Revere "be provided for," but "it is not in their Power to affect it, and whether it ever will be is uncertain."[36]

John and Samuel Adams and James Warren all professed their sincere desire to help their "deserving" friends obtain Continental commissions, but as Samuel Adams explained, now that Congress had created a Continental Army, there were fewer opening for New England men "who were well worthy of Notice." John Adams suggested that political squabbling had already led to the removal of the Colonel David Brewer of the Ninth Massachusetts Regiment, "an experienced and a brave officer," who was dismissed from the service for making false returns to the Committee of Supplies and for employing men in his regiment "in labour on his farm." Congress would be paying close attention to candidates from New England, and with so many experienced officers and gentlemen of proven leadership abilities to recommend, the Adamses and James Warren could not be expected to place Paul Revere's name at the top of their list.[37]

Revere's bitter disappointment at failing to obtain a Continental Army commission was temporarily offset by the British evacuation of Boston on March 17, 1776. When Henry Knox arrived from Fort Ticonderoga with his "noble train of artillery" in January 1776, Washington finally had the artillery to carry out his plan to occupy Dorchester Heights. Lieutenant Colonel Rufus Putnam solved the problem of erecting earthworks in frozen ground by proposing the use of breastworks made of preassembled timber frames that could be filled with bales of hay, bundles of sticks, and baskets of earth. Colonel Gridley laid out the works on March 4 and, to the astonishment of both General Howe and Lieutenant John Barker of the King's Own Regiment, the "rebels" completed two strong redoubts on Dorchester Heights by the next morning. Lieutenant Barker noted in his journal that on March 6, a council of war voted "to quit the Town." On Sunday morning, March 17, 1776, General Howe and the nearly seven thousand troops under his command evacuated Boston forever. Soon, the Reveres would return to North Square, where Paul Revere would once again balance his private life with service to the state.[38]

Lieutenant Colonel William Burbeck refused to accompany General Washington and the Continental Army when they moved south to New York, claiming he felt bound by his contract with Massachusetts to remain in the state. He may have felt more bound to the salary for life that Massachusetts had guaranteed him. Washington did not approve of or accept Burbeck's explanation, and on May 25, 1776, the Continental Congress dismissed him from the army. Paul Revere accepted an appointment as major of a regiment to fortify the town and harbor of Boston on April 10, 1776. On May 9 he was chosen major in the state artillery regiment commanded by his friend Lieutenant Colonel Thomas Crafts Jr. when George Trott "declined to serve." He was promoted to lieutenant colonel on November 27, 1776, and used the military title to the end of his life.[39]

Despite the habit of deference to authority instilled in Revere by Masonic teaching and social convention and the force of republican rhetoric stressing the citizen's duty to sacrifice his private interest to the public good, Revere could not conceal his disappointment in being overlooked for a Continental commission. He had served the patriot cause long and well, but he seems to have discovered both the limits of his "friendships" with Boston's Revolutionary leaders and the limits of social mobility in his society. On April 5, 1777, he wrote John Lamb that he had expected "before this to have been in the Continental Army, but do assure you, I have never been taken notice off [sic] by those whom I thought my friends, am obliged to be contented in this State's Service." Lamb, who had lost an eye and been captured at Quebec in December 1775, had recently been promoted to colonel of the Second Continental Artillery and would soon receive additional wounds at Compo Hill, where the Continental Army harassed the British on their retreat from Danbury, Connecticut. Relegated to secondary status as a militia officer, with few prospects of military glory ahead, Revere saluted and perhaps envied his Revolutionary comrade Lamb when he wrote: "I wish you a successful Campaign. Victory and laurels to you—that you may long remain the scourge of Tyrants is the Sincere Wish of your Friend and Humble Servant."[40]

CHAPTER EIGHT

NO LAURELS ON HIS BROW

W HEN THE REVERES returned to their North Square home in the spring of 1776, they found a town and its people changed by the events of the past year. Their home, occupied by Paul Jr., and Revere's shop, which he had rented to Tory silversmith Isaac Clemens, were probably spared the damages experienced by so many of Boston's absent property owners, among them Doctor Samuel Cooper, who witnessed "Marks of Rapine and Plunder everywhere" and found his own "desolate empty House" so stripped of furniture and linens that he could not immediately move in. North Square no longer looked the same without the Old North Meeting House, pulled down by order of General Howe to provide firewood and room for the drilling of British troops. Liberty Tree, that powerful symbol of the patriot cause, had also ended up as firewood, and the Old West Church, where Dr. Mayhew had thundered his warning to unjust rulers so many years ago, had lost its steeple. Old South, scene of the Boston Tea Party meeting and Boston Massacre orations, had suffered the greatest indignities of all when the Light-Horse Seventeenth Regiment commandeered the church for use as a riding school. Timothy Newell, who had remained in Boston during the British occupation, described the damage inflicted by the soldiers: "The Pulpit, pews and seats, all cut to pieces and carried off in the most savage manner" except for Deacon Hubbard's "beautiful carved pew," which was "made a hog stye."[1]

The Reveres were back in North Square, but so many familiar faces were gone from Boston. Eleven hundred Tories had left with General Howe, among them Revere's customers Philip Dumaresq, Foster Hutchinson, Peter Johonnot, and William McAlpine. Dr. Warren was gone forever, and Dr. Young had removed to Philadelphia, where he, Thomas Paine, author of the pamphlet *Common Sense,* and other radical republicans worked toward creating a new frame of government for Pennsylvania that implemented their ideas of political and social equality. At the Continental Congress in Philadelphia, John and Samuel Adams were defining their vision of a republican society and creating an army and a government. The action had shifted from Boston to Philadelphia, but Paul Revere, who only the year before had been called the "Ambassador from the Committee of Correspondence of Boston to the Congress of Philadelphia," was now a minor actor in this next phase of the Revolutionary drama.[2]

On March 29, 1776, less than two weeks after the British evacuation and after an absence of nearly eleven months, Bostonians held their annual town meeting at the Old Brick Meetinghouse. Ezekiel Price, clerk of the Court of Common Pleas in Suffolk County, thought it "really a very pleasant sight . . . to see so many of my worthy fellow-citizens meet together in that now ravaged, plundered town." While Dr. Young and the Adamses discussed independence and republicanism in Philadelphia, Revere and the citizens of Massachusetts dealt with the less lofty issues of restoring town government, repairing the damage inflicted by the departing enemy, and fortifying Boston from future attack.[3]

General George Washington reported to Congress that the British had destroyed buildings and fortifications at Castle Island, abandoning "a great Number of Cannon," most of which they tried to render "entirely useless" by breaking off the trunnions or spiking them. Washington ordered a brigade to march for New York on March 28 and would set off himself on April 4, leaving only a few Continental regiments "to protect the Continental stores and to assist in fortifying the town and harbour." The town meeting appointed Revere, Colonel Thomas Crafts, and Colonel Thomas Marshall to ask Washington to leave behind four cannon belonging to Boston, and as a major in Colonel Josiah Whitney's state regiment, Revere helped "repair and raise such fortifications on Castle Island as may be found necessary."[4]

The town meeting also appointed Revere as a fire ward on March 29 and, on May 1, 1776, to a more important post on the Committee of Correspondence, Safety, and Inspection. The committee was to "communicate . . . any matters of importance to the Public," inspect inhabitants on suspicion of violating the resolves of the Continental Congress, and "make known to the General Court or Council all gross breaches of trust in any Officers or Servants of this Colony." Seeking individuals "whose Principles are known to be friendly to the Rights and Liberties of America," the town meeting chose John Hancock and several other members of the merchant elite as well as Paul Revere and several of his fellow master artisans and small merchants from the North End Caucus. Revere was also appointed to a subcommittee to collect the names "of all Persons who have in any manner acted against or opposed the Rights and Liberties of this country."[5]

On June 13 Revere's son John was born, and Major Paul Revere launched his military career as part of a combined expedition of Continental and militia troops to dislodge British ships from Nantasket Harbor. According to an anonymous account written by an officer in Revere's regiment, Revere arrived at Nantasket to discover that there were no breastworks on the island and "not one hundred men to support us." Finding "the enemies vessels all busy" and "having no boats proper to unload," Revere and his men used a flat-bottomed boat to attempt to unload their artillery. The boat, "which was intirely insufficient for so great a weight," filled with water when they loaded it with a heavy cannon, and they "did not recover it till low water." Despite this embarrassment, they landed a fieldpiece and another heavy cannon on shore in time to give the enemy "a grand salute" and get "rid of a Nest of scoundrels" who had blocked the harbor for two years. The Nantasket expedition, with all its moments of misadventure and ineptitude, fore-shadowed the rest of Paul Revere's inglorious military career.[6]

While Major Revere carried out the details of defending his countrymen by collecting and repairing cannon and monitoring the activities of the remaining Tories, men in and out of Congress set the course for the future of the American republic. In the fall of 1774 Thomas Paine, a former staymaker and unsuccessful tax collector, brought his disaffection with English government and society to Philadelphia, where he found a more congenial setting for his utopian views. In January 1776, when he anonymously published *Common Sense,* Paine did not call for the restoration of the celebrated rights and liberties of Englishmen or pay allegiance, as James Otis had in 1764, to "the grandeur of the British constitution." Instead, he called the king "the Royal Brute of Great Britain" and the constitution "the base remains of two ancient tyrannies. . . . The remains of monarchical tyranny in the person of the king. . . . The remains of aristocratical tyranny in the person of the peers." He exhorted Americans "to begin the world over again" as "the asylum for the persecuted lovers of civil and religious liberty from every part of Europe," by establishing annual assemblies with more equal representation, a written constitution, and "securing freedom and property to all men."[7]

On July 3, 1776, John Adams wrote to his wife: "Had a Declaration of Indepen-dency been made seven Months ago, it would have been attended with many great and glorious Effects." Yet, perhaps the delay was beneficial because "the Hopes of Reconciliation . . . have been gradually and at last totally extinguished" and time given for the people "to consider the great Question of Independence and to ripen their Judgments, dissipate their Fears, and allure their Hopes, by discussing it in News Papers and Pamphletts, by debating it, in Assemblies . . . as well as in private Conversations, so that the whole People . . . have now adopted it, as their own Act."[8]

On July 4, 1776, the Continental Congress adopted the Declaration of Inde-pendence, in which Thomas Jefferson outlined America's grounds for indepen-dence by listing the king's train of abuses against his subjects and proclaiming "that all men are created equal, that they are endowed by their Creator with certain unalienable Rights, that among these are Life, Liberty and the pursuit of Happiness." Abigail Adams was among "the Multitude" in Boston who heard Colonel Thomas Crafts read the Declaration of Independence from the balcony of the State House on July 18. After the reading of the proclamation, the crowd cheered, bells rang, cannons were fired, "and every face appear'd joyfull." Later, as Mrs. Adams described events to her husband, "the kings arms were taken down from the State House and every vestage of him from every place in which it appear'd and burnt in King Street. Thus ends royall Authority in this State, and all the people shall say Amen."[9]

By the time Colonel Crafts read the Declaration of Independence, the Revolutionary theater of war had moved from Boston to New York, and General Washington was "almost morally certain, that no attempts will be made on the Massachusetts Bay." If there should be attacks, Washington was confident that the militia was "more than competent to all the purposes of defensive War." In Boston, Paul Revere and the men of the Massachusetts Artillery Regiment prepared for a battle that was unlikely to occur, while John Boyle recorded the progress of offensive war in New York and New Jersey. After the British defeated the patriots at Long Island on August 27, took possession of New York on September 15, forced an American retreat from White Plains on October 28, and captured Fort Washington on November 16, General Washington and the Continental Army finally ended the year successfully near dawn on December 26 with a surprise attack on the largely Hessian forces stationed at the British garrison at Trenton. Washington followed up his triumph at Trenton one week later with another victory at Princeton. He settled into his winter quarters at Morristown, New Jersey, having restored confidence in the patriot cause.[10]

While Colonel Henry Knox earned a promotion to brigadier general on December 17, 1776, and received Washington's thanks in public orders for his exemplary service at Trenton along with laurels for the performance of his regiment at Princeton, Paul Revere, now a lieutenant colonel in the Massachusetts Artillery Regiment, shuttled back and forth between lackluster military duty at Castle Island and the resumption of his civilian life. He and Rachel had three more children between April 1777 and July 1782—Joseph Warren, Lucy, and Harriet. He also had ample time to attend town meetings (where he was reelected fire ward in 1777, 1778, and 1779) as well as Masonic festivals. The honor and recognition that Revere hoped he would receive as an officer in the Massachusetts Artillery Regiment came instead in the more familiar settings of St. Andrew's Lodge and the Massachusetts Grand Lodge. His Masonic brothers continued to show their respect for his leadership abilities by choosing him Master of St. Andrew's Lodge in 1778, 1779, 1781, and 1782 and by electing him to office in the Grand Lodge every year between 1777 and 1785, including a term as Deputy Grand Master from December 1783 to June 1785.[11]

Revere was still engraving plates to print state currency in September 1776, but by early 1777 Massachusetts was also relying on him for expertise in the art of casting cannon. On December 11, 1776, the Massachusetts Board of War met with Louis de Maresquelle, a recently arrived thirty-four-year-old French engineer, to consult about locations for a furnace to cast cannon. The Board of War selected Maresquelle and Colonel Hugh Orr to direct the operation of the new state furnace at Bridgewater, asking Orr to consult with Colonel Revere "upon the best method of casting brass cannon." Although Revere had never cast a cannon, the members of the board must have had confidence in his goldsmith's familiarity with metals, his artillery officer's knowledge of cannon, and his cleverness and desire to learn new skills. On February 28, 1777, the board ordered Revere to Bridgewater "for a Quantity of Tyre Iron and Cart Boxes for Carriages" and "to inquire how Mon. Maresquelle and Orr go on in Casting Brass and Iron Cannon." One month later, Revere reported that he had proved four cannon cast at Bridgewater, "three of which stood the proof and the other burst."[12]

Ever since the Committee of Correspondence, Safety, and Inspection had appointed him to its subcommittee on Tories in May 1776, Revere had taken the assignment of monitoring Tory activity very seriously. News of Tory involvement in the British burning of Danbury, Connecticut, on April 27, 1777, raised questions in the Boston town meeting about whether stricter measures should be taken against Boston's Tories. The Test Act of May 1, 1776, merely required every male over sixteen years of age to declare his loyalty to the American cause or be subject to the penalties of giving up all "arms, ammunition, and warlike equipment," the right of voting or holding office, and, in the case of ministers and schoolmasters, their salaries.[13]

Reverend John Eliot of the New North Church contemptuously described the Boston town meeting of May 17, 1777, where Colonel Thomas Crafts, "seconded by the great Paul Revere," motioned "to know the minds of the people" concerning "some more effectual way of expelling the Tories." The town meeting selected Paul Revere, Thomas Crafts, Deacon Caleb Davis, Colonel Isaac Sears, and John Winthrop Jr. to "wait upon" a member of the Massachusetts Council "and desire that the Persons voted by the Town to be inimical persons to these States, be immediately apprehended and confined." Reverend Eliot's only satisfaction over the meeting of May 17, which he compared to "the affair of the witches at Salem" with "everyone naming his neighbor," came from hearing a member of the House say he was going to nominate Crafts and Revere to the committee on Tories "and prove them enemies to ye country by their opposition to the General Court, from whom they held yr. military commissions." Despite the efforts of Revere and his associates, the government of Massachusetts did not order a wholesale imprison-ment or exile of Boston's Tories, who included Revere's customer Dr. Phillip Kast and his customer and Masonic brother Dr. Samuel Danforth. However, in June 1777 the Board of War voted that Reverend Doctor Mather Byles of the Hollis Street Church "be confined to his own House" with a sentry posted "to suffer no person to enter except his own Family and Kindred without a permit from the Board."[14]

Paul Revere's outspoken public stance against the Tories demonstrated not only his patriotism and devotion to republican principles but also an attempt to play a more prominent role in political affairs. Revere's presumption that he had the requisite social status or leadership skills to pass judgment on influential matters caused an indignant Reverend John Eliot to sputter and rage in a letter to his friend Reverend Jeremy Belknap: "O tempora, O mores, is at present the universal cant. Paul Revere haranguing in town meeting, the commandant of every particular company, the gentleman in his domestic circle, and every drab-bling dishclout politician, however various their opinions, have all some kind of observation to make upon the times."[15]

Since "the unhappy maneuvre" at Danbury, Connecticut, Eliot complained to Belknap, the people were "refreshed with resentment against the Tories." What Eliot feared more than any danger from Tories was who would "draw the line between Whig and Tory." In Boston "the most respectable triumvirate—Thomas Crafts, Paul Revere, and Harbottle Dorr"—had stepped forward to assume that authority. "The like jewels are not so precious," wrote Eliot, "but they may be found all over the province." Reverend Eliot, along with many other educated, wealthy, or genteel men, dreaded the dangerous democratic tendencies that had been unleashed by the republican revolution. Moderate, respectable men of affairs in the community were losing political and social control to men who previ-ously knew their place: the master goldsmith Paul Revere, the painter/japanner Thomas Crafts, and the ironmonger Harbottle Dorr.[16]

One week after Revere's speech against the Tories in the town meeting, his mother died at age seventy-three "after a tedious confinement." Revere had lived with his mother all of his life, and she had helped raise his children. Deborah Revere's death must have affected her son deeply, yet Rachel Revere suffered a loss as well. With her husband frequently away from home because of his military obligations, she bore the burden of her mother-in-law's final illness and the loss of her help in caring for the children: Joseph Warren, born not quite a month before his grandmother's death; Joshua, who was nearly two-and-a-half; and three girls under the age of twelve. Now more than ever, Rachel Revere would have to rely on the help of her stepdaughters, nineteen-year-old Deborah and fifteen-year-old Sarah.[17]

Back in July 1776 Henry Jackson had written his friend Colonel Henry Knox that Colonel Crafts and his officers "make a very gentle Coar of Officers—and they have a fine Regiment of men." But by the summer of 1777 Colonel Crafts and Lieutenant Colonel Revere were having difficulty maintaining discipline and military readiness among troops subjected to a tedious routine of guard duty, artillery drill, and hailing vessels as they passed Castle Island, with only the occasional excitement of receiving prisoners. On July 3 Colonel Crafts, alarmed by reports of sentries "found sleeping in their Boxes and often sitting down," ordered that they "should be taught their Duty in the strictest rule of Disapline as much as if their was the fullest Expectation of an immediate Attack." On July 13 Crafts posted a daily schedule of defense preparations, reminding his men to be ready "to repell and Defeat the Enemy should they attemp to Invade this State."[18]

At first, Crafts and Revere were lenient in imposing sentences for drunkenness, desertion, and neglect of duty. On August 16, for example, Revere merely reprimanded Sergeant John Griffith for "neglect of duty" and "reduced to the ranks" Gunner Nathaniel Fowles for "leaving his Detachment at Castle Island without Liberty of the Commanding Officer." By August 17 Crafts had lost patience not only with the enlisted men but with officers who "have taken upon themselves to Judge of the Propriety, or impropriety of Orders." By voluntarily entering the army, Crafts reminded them, they had given up "their Right of Private Judgment, and are to look on themselves as machines, to obey Orders implicitly." Finally, on August 24 an exasperated Crafts was "at last obliged" to impose corporal punishment on John Gregory who, while drunk, had created a disturbance in the streets and wounded a sergeant with a knife. Crafts's only concession was to reduce Gregory's punishment from 127 lashes on his "Naked Back with a Catt of Nine Tails" to "fifty Stripes."[19]

The difficulties that Crafts and Revere endured in trying to uphold some semblance of military command surely added to their sense of resentment over their inferior status as militia officers. In June 1777 Crafts and Revere asked Samuel Adams to urge the Continental Congress to grant militia officers on active duty equality in precedence of rank and command with Continental officers. Adams assured Revere of his and John Adams's support, but he explained that they did not raise the issue because Congress would never "make the Alteration you wish for" until the regiment was taken into Continental service. Then, in a somewhat patronizing rebuke, Adams lectured his "Friend" Revere and "the Gentlemen of your Core," to cherish "above all feelings . . . those of the Virtuous Citizen." While recognizing "that the Ambition of the Soldier is laudable" and "at such a crisis as this, it will be necessary," Adams delivered a pointed sermon on the danger of excessive ambition and the duty of a republican citizen: "We are contending not for Glory, but for the Liberty, Safety, and Happiness of our Country. The Soldier should not lose the Sentiments of the Patriot, and the Pride of Military Rank, as well as civil Promotion should for ever give way to the Publick Good."[20]

Revere must have been offended by Adams's implication that he had allowed his desire for honor and recognition to get in the way of his duty as a republican citizen. After all, Revere fully shared Adams's concern with declining virtue, and he was quick to condemn ambition and the love of luxury in others. In Massachusetts, farmers and merchants leveled accusations of greed and self-interest at each other for allegedly overcharging for goods and fueling inflation. The General Court responded by passing acts fixing prices in January and June 1777. In August, Revere informed Adams of the persistence of greed and vice in Boston, where "we are over run with sharpers, and hawkers, forestallers and monopolizers, this Town is become the very sink of the United States." A year later, Adams regretted the continued presence of "Love of Gain" in Boston, writing to Samuel Phillips Savage: "He is the best Patriot who stems the Torrent of Vice, because that is the most destructive Enemy of his Country."[21]

For most of the summer of 1777, Revere resumed his mundane military duties while other men gained the glories of war. General John Burgoyne began the British advance from Canada toward Albany with an easy victory on July 6, when he took possession of "the several Forts" at Ticonderoga. But thereafter the tide of battle turned against Burgoyne, who planned to isolate New England by establishing a British line along the Hudson River and Lake Champlain from New York to Montreal. Lieutenant Colonel Barry St. Leger's plan to quickly capture Fort Stanwix on his way to join up with Burgoyne in Albany ended in failure when the patriots of the Mohawk Valley fought back in the bloody Battle of Oriskany on August 6. St. Leger abandoned the siege on August 23 when his Indian allies, frightened by reports of the impending arrival of American reinforcements, deserted him. Meanwhile, on August 16 General John Stark and nearly two thousand militiamen from New Hampshire, Vermont, and Massachusetts surprised a British detachment under Lieutenant Colonel Friedrich Baum searching for oxen, cattle, and horses near Bennington, Vermont, and "totally routed" the outnumbered enemy. Paul Revere's only connection with Stark's glorious victory was to lead a detachment of his regiment to Worcester in early September to take charge "of several hundred prisoners" captured at Bennington and escort them back to Boston.[22]

Finally, Revere had a chance to see military action when he and his regiment were ordered to march to Newport, Rhode Island, on September 27, 1777, to expel the British and prevent a possible attack on Boston, but the regiment returned home without ever engaging the enemy. Colonel Crafts nonetheless thanked his men "for their extraordinary military and soldier-like behaviour" and declared that he was "almost assured of Victory and Success by the Spirit and Willingness with which they turn'd out on Occasion when there was a probability . . . to attack the Enemy." John Boyle was less enthusiastic, complaining that "the 9000 Men lately raised . . . returned home without effecting any Thing" at a "public

Expense . . . computed at 3500 Dollars pr. day." While Revere and his regiment failed to gain honor on the battlefield, Continental and militia troops under General Horatio Gates forced the surrender of General Burgoyne and over five thousand of his troops at Saratoga on October 17. On December 18, 1777, when Bostonians observed a "Continental Thanksgiving" to commemorate "the Signal Success of the American Arms the year past," they honored Benedict Arnold, Horatio Gates, Daniel Morgan, and the other heroes of the two Battles of Free-man's Farm, not Paul Revere and the thousands of men of the abortive Newport campaign.[23]

Back in Boston, Revere and his regiment had little to celebrate besides the news of France's formal recognition of American independence in December 1777 and the conclusion of a Franco-American alliance on February 6, 1778.[24] The cost of patriotism and virtue for Paul Revere and the officers and men of Colonel Crafts's regiment was thus far a high one. They had yet to earn any laurels for their performance in battle, and they were continually reminded of their inferior status compared to Continental troops when they received insufficient clothing allow-ances and wages.

In September 1777 Colonel Crafts asked the Board of War to "Furnish him with two pieces of blue Broad Cloth" for his officers, who were "almost destitute of Cloathing," and on March 30, 1778, Lieutenant Colonel Revere and several of his fellow officers, complaining about the high price of clothing, asked the council and House of Representatives for the "same Indulgence the Continental Officers have . . . of Drawing a few necessarys out of the State Stores—paying the same prices as they do." The House of Representatives granted the petition in April, but several officers petitioned the council and House again in January 1779 because they had yet to receive their full clothing allowance. On October 8 Captains William Todd, Phillip Marett, and Turner Phillips protested to the House that the officers and men "have not Wages sufficient to keep them in shoes." By that time, Captain Jonathan Edes, Captain Lieutenant John Meinzies, and Lieutenant Daniel Ingersoll had all asked to be discharged because of prolonged financial deprivation. Edes, who expressed his willingness "to turn out voluntarily for the Defence of his Country," asked for a discharge after two years' service, "finding that his Wages are so small as not to enable him to purchase the necessaries of life for the Support of himself and Family, and will not allow him to appear with that Decency becoming an Officer of his Rank."[25]

On March 1, 1778, General William Heath, the Continental Army commander of the eastern district, extended Revere's command at Castle Island to Governor's and Long Islands, "relying on your zeal and abilities" to assure "that no measures will be omitted which your own Honor and the safety of your Country require." Revere's "zeal and abilities" were divided between military preparations and as-sisting Colonel Crafts in using the "burch rod" and cat-o'-nine-tails to correct the increasingly unmilitary behavior of members of their regiment. On July 2, in hopes that "the Troops will learn from this example," the members of the regiment witnessed the execution of Thomas Harrison, a soldier in another regiment, shot to death for desertion. When Revere received orders on July 27 to march to Providence to join the second Newport expedition, he must have welcomed the chance to exchange the demands of keeping order over his dispirited and disorderly regiment for the chance to test his courage and leadership abilities in battle.[26]

In his artillery brigade orders of August 11, 1778, Major General John Sullivan of the Continental Army expressed his confidence in "the Officers Volunteers and soldiers who have with so much alacrity repaired to this place, to give their assistance in extirpating the British Tyrants from their Country." Major General John Hancock, General Solomon Lovell, Colonel Peleg Wadsworth, Colonel Thomas Crafts, and Lieutenant Colonel Paul Revere of the Massachusetts Militia joined Major General Nathaniel Greene, Brigadier General John Glover, Colonel Henry Jackson, and Colonel John Crane of the Continental Army. Volunteers included Revere's cousin Colonel Benjamin Hichborn of the Boston Independent Company, and the Marquis de Lafayette, "a young Nobleman of Rank and Fortune," whom Samuel Adams lauded for leaving "the Pleasure and Enjoyment of Domestick Life" in his native France, "voluntarily exposing himself to the Hardships of War . . . not in *his own,* but a foreign Country, in the glorious Cause of Freedom."[27]

Revere was "in high health and spirits" when he wrote Rachel, his "dear Girl," from Rhode Island in August 1778. He described the destruction in the "Garden of America" inflicted by "those Brittish savages" and Colonel Crafts's "severe mortification" at having to serve under Colonel Crane, who had served under him in Paddock's Artillery Company. Although he found it "very irksome to be seperated from *her,* whom I so tenderly love, and from my little lambs," Revere knew "were I at home I should want to be here." He hoped "the affair will soon be settled," but as he was writing, the effects of what Revere termed "the most severe N. East Storm I ever knew" were dooming the chances of American victory.[28]

The violent storm of August 12–13 delayed the arrival of the American expedition in Newport and also damaged both the French and English fleets, which were maneuvering into battle positions. From August 17 to 24, Revere was busy erecting and repairing artillery batteries while the American Army awaited the return of the French fleet under Count D'Estaing and dreaded the arrival of British reinforcements. The *Boston Gazette* commended Colonel Henry Jackson's regiment, which "behav'd to admiration, as did every one else," and General Lovell, who "did himself Honor by his coolness." On August 24 General Sullivan could not "help lamenting, the sudden and unexpected departure of the French fleet," whose commander had decided to return to Boston for repairs, but Sullivan still had faith in "the spirit and ardor of Americans . . . unless the enemy should receive a strong reinforcement." The reappearance of Lord Howe and the British fleet off Rhode Island, the impending arrival of British reinforcements under General Clinton, the continued absence of the French fleet, and the "great numbers of Volunteers" not willing to extend their service persuaded General Sullivan to give up the siege. Once again, Paul Revere was denied the chance to earn the glories of war.[29]

After Newport, the only excitement in Revere's military life at Castle Island occurred in January 1779, when he stopped the British ship *Minerva* and seized ten firearms and other merchandise that he deemed to be contraband. William Dunlop, commander of *Minerva*, protested that his ship was protected by a flag of truce while journeying from Halifax to Boston and New York carrying 114 American prisoners of war to be exchanged for an equal number of British prisoners. On March 27 a jury in the Maritime Court ruled that the goods in question were British property "not under protection and ought to be confiscated," with one-third of the proceeds to be paid to Revere and the men on duty when *Minerva* was seized and two-thirds to "the Government and people of this State."[30]

The problems that had afflicted the Massachusetts Artillery Regiment almost from its inception proved to be insurmountable. From June 1778 to January 1779, the House of Representatives appointed several committees to address grievances and make general inquiries into "the present State of Colonel Crafts' Regiment and report what is proper to be done." On February 10, 1779, Crafts, Revere, and Captain William Todd, on behalf of the officers and enlisted men of their regiment, reviewed their distressing situation for the council and House of Representatives. They had repeatedly failed to receive promised allowances, and their wages were in the form of currency so depreciated that "Those of us who have family's" could not afford to purchase wood, but "we are oblig'd to pay our full proportion of Taxes." The petitioners presumed "Your Honors will be sensible we labor under all the disadvantages of the Continental Battalions" and asked for "the same advantages . . . as your Wisdom may think just and equitable."[31]

By February 1779 the regiment had too many officers for its depleted ranks, thinned by desertion, discharges, and the luring away of potential recruits by the excitement and financial reward of Continental service or duty aboard a privateer.[32] On February 25 a committee of the Massachusetts House recommended reducing the regiment to three companies. The following day Colonel Crafts and "a Number of others," including Captain William Todd, Captain Winthrop Gray, and Lieutenant John Marston, petitioned the council for a settlement and offered their resignations. Lieutenant Colonel Paul Revere, who was in Newbury on unexplained business at the time, did not sign the petition, and on March 1, 1779, the House requested the council to retain Revere as commander of the reorganized state artillery regiment. Revere's acceptance of the command could be

interpreted as a virtuous act by a patriot willing to endure the continuing priva-
tions of military service to serve the public good, but to his detractors, Revere's
acceptance was proof of his unseemly ambition for status and power.[33]

Revere later said that his command of the regiment was beset with difficulties
from the beginning: "Because I accepted the command . . . and did all in my
power, to hinder the men from deserting; And because I would not give up my
Commission, in the same way the other officers did, some of them propagated,
every falsehood, Malice could invent in an underhanded way." One of those
resentful officers, in Revere's opinion, was Captain William Todd, who, shortly
after Revere took command, accused Revere of drawing rations at Castle Island
"for thirty men, more than I had there." Todd and Captain Winthrop Gray filed a
complaint against Revere, who appeared before the council, but as Revere stated,
"they never produced a single Article against me." Gray would not be a problem
for much longer, as the council accepted his resignation, but William Todd would
be a greater nemesis when he and Revere met a few months later in the disastrous
Penobscot expedition.[34]

In addition to his problems with Todd and Gray, Revere continued to be
plagued with desertion in his regiment, asking the council "to put an effectual
stop, to such proceedings, For it is in vain for us to Recruit men if the Marine
Officers may take them from us." Accordingly, on March 29, 1779, the council
ordered the Continental frigates *Providence* and *Boston* to give up deserters from
Revere's regiment and directed Revere "not to permit either of the aforesaid Ships
to pass the Castle until the Commanders . . . have delivered the men." When the
Providence did not give up all the deserters Revere knew were aboard, Revere "was
obliged to fire at, and bring her too," and he requested that the council issue
similar orders for the recovery of several of his men aboard the sloop *Providence*.
Revere's actions were not welcomed, either by his deserters or by the commanders
of the Continental vessels, one of whom would oppose him in a war council
during the Penobscot expedition.[35]

Revere continued his aggressive command at Castle Island through the spring
and summer of 1779. On April 20, 1779, Francis Gray, a sutler at Castle Island,
complained to the House of Representatives that "for the convenience of his
Business . . . he purchased a certain moveable Wooden Shop," and "that Paul
Revere, Esq., now in Possession of it, refuses to deliver it." Apparently, Revere
thought that the public good would better be served if the state, rather than Gray,
owned the shop, and the House agreed. On June 25 the House appointed a committee "to repair to Castle-Island" and consult with Revere and Gray to value the
sutler's shop and "examine if it will be for the benefit of this State to purchase it."[36]

On the same day that the council appointed a committee to meet with Revere
and Gray at Castle Island, the Massachusetts General Court began organizing a
combined military and naval expedition to expel British troops under the com-

mand of Brigadier General Francis McLean from the Magabagaduce, or Baga-duce, Peninsula (now Castine) in Penobscot Bay, Maine. The British hoped to establish a province for the settlement of Loyalists, a military post to secure communications between Halifax and New York free from the harassment of American privateers, and a position from which to launch operations against New England. Commodore Dudley Saltonstall of the Continental Navy was given command of a fleet of nineteen armed vessels, including three Continental vessels, twelve privateers, the entire Massachusetts Navy, and twenty-one transports to land roughly nine hundred Massachusetts militiamen, reduced from the original goal of fifteen hundred, on Magabagaduce Peninsula. General Solomon Lovell and his second-in-command, Brigadier General Peleg Wadsworth, both of whom had served with Paul Revere in the second Newport expedition, were in charge of the land troops, and Revere was given command of the artillery. Finally, Revere would have a chance to prove his bravery in battle and to earn the consequent honors of war. This massive amphibious operation involved the largest naval force of the Revolutionary War. Its success required "the greatest harmony" between the navy and army and a force of more than nine hundred militiamen, of whom Revere declared "one third of them were boys and old men." Neither criterion for success was present, and the result was, in Revere's words, "our unfortunate expedition to Penobscot."[37]

The American fleet arrived in Penobscot Bay on July 25, 1779, and the next day the marines, aided by General Wadsworth's division, took Nautilus Island. In the early morning of July 28, General Lovell landed three divisions, including Paul Revere and his corps, on Magabagaduce Peninsula. Despite heavy casualties, the four hundred marines and militiamen managed to ascend a one-hundred-foot precipice to move within six hundred rods of the enemy's Fort George after a "smart conflict." In Revere's opinion, "this was the only time in which we might have subdued the enemy had there been a plan laid; for the ships to have attacked the enemy's ships, and we to have marched on to the fort and stormed it. . . . Had we finally come off victorious, this would have been called, the bravest action since the war commenced."[38]

William Todd, late but not lamented member of Revere's artillery regiment, served as one of General Solomon Lovell's brigade majors on the Penobscot expedition. Major Todd had his own explanation for the failure of the American forces to capture Fort George, chiefly "the Backwardness of some of the principle Officers." One of the two officers Todd singled out was Lieutenant Colonel Paul Revere, who, he charged, "did not land his men agreeable to the Generals direction nor in any time to tender any assistance." Todd continued his charge of military ineptitude against Revere, claiming: "Neither was he dexterous after he had landed for the Army had forced the Enemy and gained the Height before Colonel Revere marched from the Beach."[39]

Revere's high hopes for his military career dissipated as the Penobscot campaign degenerated into a protracted dispute among its officers over the continuance and direction of the siege. From July 29 to August 14, General Lovell waited in vain for naval support from Commodore Saltonstall. Without that support, Lovell believed that he was "not in a Situation with his present Force to Storm." In councils of war on August 7 and 13, Lieutenant Colonel Revere voted with the minority to end the siege. From the beginning, Revere expressed doubt that the Penobscot expedition had a sufficient number of troops to take the British fort, and on August 7 he also voiced his concern that "field officers can not lead men in open field against the enemy." In short, as Revere later stated: "It always was my sentiment, that if we could not Dislodge the Enemy in seven days, we ought to Quit the ground, for Where the Enemy has the command of the Sea, we ought not to have risqued so much as we did."[40]

Finally, on August 13 Commodore Saltonstall agreed to participate in a land-and-sea assault on the British fort, but it was too late. The arrival of Sir George Collier and a British relief squadron of seven ships on August 13, coupled with Saltonstall's reluctance to attack the British fleet and Lovell's lack of confidence in his undisciplined troops, forced the Americans to give up the siege the next day. In the chaotic retreat that followed, five hundred Americans were killed or taken prisoner, the entire Massachusetts Navy was lost, at a cost of £1,739,175, and the character and conduct of Lieutenant Colonel Paul Revere raised troubling questions. Brigadier General Peleg Wadsworth ordered Revere to give up his boat in order to evacuate the crew of a schooner drifting toward the enemy. According to Wadsworth, Revere replied that the general "had no right to command either him or the Boat and gave orders to the contrary." To Wadsworth's astonishment, Revere's reason for refusing to give up the boat was because "he had all his private baggage at stake," prompting Wadsworth to ask Revere "whether he was there to take care of his private baggage or to serve the state." If the accounts of Revere's military performance by Major Todd, General Wadsworth, and others were accurate, then Lieutenant Colonel Paul Revere would be forced to defend "what is more dearer to me than life. my character" against multiple charges of insubordination, neglect of duty, and, worst of all, "unsoldierlike behavior tending to cowardice."[41]

Revere returned from Maine on August 26 and resumed his command at Castle Island until September 6, when the Massachusetts Council ordered him to resign to await charges brought against him by Thomas Jenners Carnes, a captain of Marines in the Penobscot expedition. Carnes, who ironically had voted with Revere on August 7 to discontinue the siege and on August 13 to evacuate, alleged that Revere was so frequently absent from duty that "the Captain of the Fleet was oblige to gett his Cannon on Shoar," and both General Wadsworth and General Lovell asked after him "several times." Carnes also denigrated Revere's ability as an artillery officer, stating: "I said then I thought it impossible that a Colonel of Artillery should make of such bad shot, and know no more about artillery." The most devastating attack on Revere's honor, courage, and ability came, however, from his old enemy, Major William Todd. Todd blamed the loss of the ordnance brig during the retreat on Revere's derelict command and claimed that Revere so infrequently attended the "General's Marque" that General Lovell said "he was surprized at Colonel Revere's inattention to his duty." Todd also testified that General Wadsworth vowed "that if the siege continued seven years, if it was possible to avoid it, he should not ask him [Revere] to take any command."[42]

Revere counterattacked with a rigorous cross-examination of the witnesses against him, citing supporting testimony from other witnesses and portraying William Todd as an untrustworthy witness, motivated solely by revenge against Revere. Revere admitted not attending General Lovell's meetings "so often as other Officers" because of his dislike of Todd, but General Lovell, under questioning by Revere, admitted that Revere met with him often outside the formal meetings. Under questioning by Revere's accuser Captain Carnes, Wadsworth denied that either he or General Lovell had sworn never to give Revere another command, testifying that he had "no recollection of the sort, or even that it was in my mind." In refuting charges that he was often derelict in his duties, Revere cited testimony from several officers who portrayed him as a diligent officer, including his cousin Acting Lieutenant Phillip Marett; James Brown, commander of the brig *Samuel;* and Captain Peleg Nichols. As to his alleged cowardice, Revere responded: "I never was in any Sharp Action, nor was any of the Artillery; but in what little I was, no one has dared to say I flinched. My Officers all swear, that when ever there was an alarm, I was one of the first in the Battery: I think that no mark of Cowardice."[43]

Despite his strong defense against charges of dereliction of duty and cowardice, Revere had a much shakier defense against charges of insubordination. At the request of Thomas Carnes, Gilbert Speakman testified that during the retreat of August 14, General Lovell sent Major Todd to order Revere and his men to "get some Cannon" from Hacker's Island. Revere allegedly took out a paper, which Speakman "took to be the orders from this Council," and said his orders were to be under Lovell's command during the Penobscot expedition, "and as the Siege was rais'd, he considered the expedition at an end, and therefore did not consider himself any longer under General Lovell's Command." Revere acknowledged coming home without orders, but he maintained that in the panicked retreat he could find neither General Lovell nor General Wadsworth, and he stood by his defense: "Surely no man will say, that the Expedition was not discontinued, when all the Shipping was either taken, or Burnt, the Artillery and Ordnance Stores, all destroyed. I then looked upon it that I was to do, what I thought right, Accordingly, I ordered . . . my men to Boston by the shortest route."[44]

Revere was most vulnerable on the charge of disobeying an order from General Peleg Wadsworth during the retreat from Penobscot Bay. Questioning the order of a superior officer was a serious breach of military discipline, and Revere's apparent concern over his private possessions at the expense of serving the state damaged his reputation for patriotism and republican virtue. Revere's explanation was indeed the weakest part of his defense. He conceded that he did initially refuse General Wadsworth's order to give up his boat with all his baggage on board but "afterwards ordered her to go." Later, Wadsworth went to get another boat, and "we parted good friends."[45]

In their report on October 7, 1779, the committee of inquiry concluded that the "Principal failure" of the Penobscot expedition was "the want of proper Spirit and Energy on the part of the Commodore." The committee lauded both General Lovell, who "acted with proper courage and spirit," and General Wadsworth, who, "throughout the whole expedition . . . conducted with great activity, courage, coolness and prudence." Unfortunately for Revere, as he noted in a petition to the council the next day, he "finds to his great detriment, that said committee have neither condemned or acquitted him." Revere was more disappointed with the conclusion of a second committee of inquiry on November 16, 1779, that found him culpable for "disputing the orders of Brigadier-General Wadsworth" and ruled that his leaving Penobscot River with his men "without particular orders from his Superior Officer" was "not wholly justifiable."[46]

From the beginning of his ordeal, Revere believed that he was the victim of a "deep laid" plan. He confided in General William Heath that he had "reason to think" that William Todd and Lieutenant John Marston, another disgruntled former member of his regiment who served as General Lovell's secretary at Penobscot, "wrote up things to my disadvantage which happened to arrive just before the news of our defeat." Revere also accused John Hancock, appointed to a committee to fortify Castle Island while Revere was at Penobscot, of spreading stories about the poor condition of Castle Island and Revere's inept command. He believed that his old nemesis William Burbeck had "urged him [Hancock] on" and that Ned Greene, secretary to the committee employing volunteers at Castle Island, in order "to git me from the Castle," persuaded Thomas Carnes "to enter a complaint against me."[47]

As early as September 9, 1779, before the convening of the first committee of inquiry, Revere invoked his right to be tried by a court-martial under Continental Army regulations, preferably under the direction of an artillery officer who would understand his duties. Colonel Israel Keith, former aide-de-camp to General Heath, sympathized with Revere's plight, writing: "the indelicacy with which Colonel Revere was treated by the Council in the manner of his arrest would have disgraced a sergeant in the army of General Washington." It would take Revere more than three years of petitioning for a court-martial to clear his name, all the while laboring under "every disgrace that the malice of my enemies can invent" and "maintaining a Family of twelve . . . out of remains of what I have earned by twenty years hard labour."[48]

On February 19, 1782, Revere was completely vindicated when a court-martial accepted the defense he had offered against charges of disobeying General Wadsworth and leaving without orders from a superior officer. The court ruled that "Lieutenant-Colonel Revere be acquitted with equal Honor as the other Officers in the same Expedition." He still had to defend his honor, however, in a nasty newspaper exchange with his chief accusers, William Todd and Thomas Carnes. Todd and Carnes repeated their charges against Revere and cast still more aspersions on his character. On April 8 Todd contended that Revere's "absolute harangue when holding a council always overpowered those more mildly disposed." He blamed Revere's "blistering rhetoric" and "false conceit of his superior genius" as "one of the causes of delay" in their war councils. Carnes, who denied being hired to bring charges against Revere, alleged that Revere called at his home "to require satisfaction." Undermining Revere's pose as an officer and a gentleman, Carnes concluded: "fighting is not a science that gentlemen, no more than myself is fond of." Revere responded with the same defense that had convinced the court-martial to acquit him, and he had the satisfaction of having the final word on April 15, when the newspaper war with Todd and Carnes ended.[49]

Although Revere was thoroughly shaken by the attack on his integrity, bravery, and patriotism in the aftermath of the Penobscot expedition, his vindication seems to have given him more energy and confidence in the future. He may have missed his chance to attain the glories of war by failing to obtain a Continental Army officer's commission, and he certainly failed to earn glory as commander of the Massachusetts Artillery during the Penobscot expedition. Within the decade, however, he would make up for those failures by acquiring honor and recognition as Paul Revere, Esq., respected artisan, merchant, manufacturer, and worthy citizen of the new republic.

CHAPTER NINE

PAUL REVERE, ESQ.

WITH A LARGE FAMILY to support, Paul Revere could not afford to wait for peace or a court-martial to clear his name before resuming business. On February 6, 1779, he engraved "sundrys" for Robert Pope for fifteen shillings "hard money," and in August 1780 he made "two child's shoe clasps," four silver cups, a thimble, and other items for Epes Sargent; a pair of stone buttons, a silver shoe buckle, and six teaspoons for Dr. Phillip Godfrid Kast; and a silver watch for Stephen Metcalf. In October 1781 Revere wrote Cousin Mathias Rivoire that he was "in middling circumstances and very well off for a Tradesman," but the resumption of the goldsmith's trade was not part of his original plan: "I did intend to have gone wholly into trade, but the principal part of my Interest, I lent to Government, which I have not been able to draw out, so must content myself, till I can do better."[1]

By 1780 Revere was taking steps to exchange the artisan's workbench for the merchant's account books by accepting payment for his silver in imported merchandise. In August he sent cocoa to Phillip Marett to be sold in Spain in exchange for "such articles" as Marett thought "will answer your ends." In October Epes Sargent paid for his order with indigo, silk handkerchiefs, plated spoons, and a "chest of English goods sold Captain John Hinckley," and in June 1781 Captain Mungo Mackay paid by cash and "Freight on some goods from France."[2]

Busy as he was reestablishing his silver business and going "into trade," Revere found time to renew his correspondence with his cousin John Rivoire in Guernsey and begin a new correspondence with a second cousin, Mathias Rivoire of Sainte Foye, France. He and Mathias traded genealogical information on the French and American branches of their family, while he and cousin John waged a spirited debate on Anglo-American politics. John Rivoire, harbormaster and receiver general for customs on Guernsey, seems to have reopened the correspondence in hopes of initiating a business relationship with his American cousin. On January 28, 1781, Rivoire began the first of a series of letters urging renunciation of the Franco-American alliance and reconciliation between England and America. He wished that the Americans "could open their eyes in time before it is too late to repent the dangerous Alliance they have made with the French" and accept Parliament's offer to repeal its acts and "leave it as it was in the Year 1763." Then, America could join "hand in hand" with England and "attack the Gold and Silver Mines in the Spanish Dominions in South America." John Rivoire never changed his opinion of the French as "the Vermin of Europe" or abandoned his hope for union between England and America, which would of course "reap great benefits" for the duty-free island of Guernsey.[3]

John Rivoire's letter of January 1781 compelled Revere to write a lengthy and passionate exposition of his political views to his "Dear Cousin" on July 1, 1782. He explained that Americans once held low opinions of the French nation, which "arose from our connection with Brittain," but now that the connection was broken, "we can see with more impartial eyes" that the French are "a brave, humane, generous, and polite Nation." In response to his cousin's belief that the war with Britain was "against all laws human and divine," Revere wrote: "You do not use all the candour which I am sure you are master of else you have not looked into the merits of the quarrel." Revere then enlightened his cousin with a stream of invective directed against the British nation that explained why he believed Americans would never consent to be part of the British Empire again. Parliament's claim that it had the right to tax and legislate for the colonists was a denial of "the birth right of an Englishman, not to be taxed without the consent of himself, or Representative." He reminded his cousin of America's patience in trying to redress its grievances and of Britain's response: "America took every method in her power by petitioning and etc. to remain subject to Brittain, but . . . the British King and ministers did not want colonies of *free men* they wanted Colonies of *Slaves*—Like the fable of the Woman and Hen by grasping at too much they will loose all."[4]

In a passage resembling Thomas Jefferson's indictment of the king and Parliament in the Declaration of Independence, Revere accused England of hiring foreign troops to "massacre us," setting Indians "on helpless women and children," and encouraging Negro servants "to assassinate their Masters." Revere's denunciation, however, bore none of Jefferson's restraint when he wrote: "They . . . ravished our wives and daughters—they have murdered our old men in cool blood . . . confined the men whom they have taken prisoners in loathsome ships and gaols till they have died by inches. I do assure you the name of an Englishman is as odious to an American as that of a Turk or a Savage." Revere ended his tirade by inviting his cousin to come to America, where "you may enjoy all the liberty here, which the human mind so earnestly craves after." He concluded: "I am not rich, but I am in good circumstances and if you will come here, you shall not want—while I have a shilling, you shall have a part."[5]

In his letter to John Rivoire, Revere also wrote: "I now follow my business again of a Goldsmith, and trade a little." The goldsmith's trade, which Revere was so anxious to abandon, proved to be the means of funding his subsequent success-ful businesses and laying the foundation for his social mobility. The goldsmith shop was in full operation by 1781, and Revere continued to make buckles, fine dinnerware, and Masonic items; mend and clean a variety of silver items for family, friends, and longtime customers; and cater to a clientele ranging from artisans to the mercantile and political elite. But his post-Revolutionary gold-smith business was no simple resumption of his old trade. A majority of the customers who patronized Revere after the Revolution were new, and so too were the objects he made for them. Revere adapted to changes in style, embraced technological advances, and set up new business alliances that earned him a degree of independence lacking in his pre-Revolutionary business. Revere would have to carry on the goldsmith's trade far longer than he wished, but after the Revolution he became less of a mechanic and more of an entrepreneur whose efficient man-agement of his goldsmith shop freed him to undertake new business ventures and to attain the rising economic and social status they brought.[6]

The signing of peace between England and America on September 3, 1783, cre-ated a new country anxious to proclaim a new cultural identity. Throughout the Revolutionary era, patriot orators and essayists had adopted the names of heroes of classical Greece and Rome, and Americans in the 1780s continued to find inspiration in antiquity. In painting, architecture, and decorative arts, Americans exchanged the excesses of the rococo style for the simplicity and restraint of the neoclassical style. Although the post-Revolutionary Revere is more often praised for his technological and entrepreneurial skills than for his aesthetic ability, he produced many exceptional pieces of neoclassical silver for the rising merchants and political leaders who were replacing the old Tory elite in post-Revolutionary Massachusetts.[7] Revere offered several versions of the neoclassical teapot, a stun-ning variety of spoons for their dinner tables, and a multitude of canns and goblets for Nathaniel Tracy, Moses Michael Hayes, Elias Hasket Derby, Perez Morton, and other elites, eager to display their wealth and assert their superior status in a society where the fluid social structure often made elite status fragile and fleeting.[8]

After the war, Revere took command of the marketplace by concentrating less on producing the wide variety of custom-made items that characterized his early business and more on designing standard forms that could be produced by his journeymen and apprentices. Beginning in the early 1780s, he reduced the amount of hand labor in his craft by experimenting with the use of sheet silver in his

7. The two silver salt spoons from an original set of eight made in 1796 are examples of the elegant dinnerware that Revere designed for the merchant and political elite in post-Revolutionary Boston. Courtesy, Paul Revere Memorial Association. Gift of Amory Goddard in loving memory of his mother and father.

cylindrical teapots. By 1785 he had acquired his own plating mill for the production of sheet silver. Further experimentation led him to develop several different seaming techniques for sheet silver that required less training and experience and could be competently executed by his workmen.[9]

Revere turned over much of the mending and less skilled work to his oldest son, Paul Revere Jr., who was in partnership with his father by August 1783. Paul Jr., whose apprenticeship was interrupted by the war, made spoons, buckles, thimbles, and an occasional soup ladle and handled most of the mending orders, leaving the design and execution of more artistic work to his father. Slowly—more slowly than he probably desired—Revere was removing himself from the artisan's world of brawny arms, broken fingernails, and leather aprons. Freed from much of the menial labor of the goldsmith's trade, the post-Revolutionary Revere functioned simultaneously as an artist producing elegant flatware, teaware, and coffee urns for Boston's most genteel citizens and an innovative and independent businessman who used technology and marketing skills to create new demands for his services.[10]

Revere's ability to renew prewar business relationships with fellow artisans and initiate new long-term associations with artisans after the Revolution stabilized his business and reduced his dependence on custom-made orders for the merchant elite. He continued to make teapots, salvers, punch bowls, porringers, and tankards for his fellow silversmith Stephen Emmery. He began engraving and printing clock and watch labels for Simon and Aaron Willard in 1781. He engraved and printed an extraordinary number of hat bills for Deacon William Boardman, a pre-Revolutionary customer who revived his business association with Revere in August 1783, and William Williams, who became a regular customer in 1792. From 1786 to 1793 Revere's mastery of the production of silverplate allowed him to manufacture a nearly endless supply of silver-plated saddle parts and harness fittings for the saddlers John Dyer, Zachariah Hicks, John Winnick, and Edward Cole.[11]

Not all of Revere's ambitious plans succeeded in the early 1780s. By 1782 he had entered into a partnership with Simon Willard in the manufacture and sale of Willard's patented clock jacks, but the attempt to transform himself from a mere mechanic who engraved clock labels for Willard into a budding merchant/manufacturer failed. By February 1785 Willard, who had already received advances of one hundred pounds from Revere, tried to reassure his apprehensive partner that there was "no risk" in their venture and that he could "make fifty dollars every week provided I could go on." Despite Willard's confidence, Revere did not recoup his investment. He was still trying to sell Willard's clock jacks in 1787, when John Blagge of New York wrote: "I am sorry to inform you that the Jacks remain unsold."[12]

In the early 1780s, as Revere improved his goldsmith business, he also became a merchant. In January 1783, while a state of war still existed between England and the United States, he received a shipment of English manufactured goods aboard the *Rosamond*. On June 30, 1783, he contacted the exiled Boston Tory Frederick William Geyer to act as his agent in London, asking Geyer to send goods that "may be fashionable, tho at the same time, I should not prefer the extreems of fashion; as a medium will best answer here." By September 1783 Revere had expanded his goldsmith's shop into "a large Store of hardware directly opposite where Liberty Tree Stood." He sold his own shoe and knee buckles and other stock items; "a great variety in the Ironmongery, Cutlery, and Plated Wares"; clock, watchmakers, goldsmith's, and jeweler's tools; as well as Willard's "Patent Clock-Jacks," imported brass candlesticks, bird cages, playing cards, stationery, looking glasses, and Irish linens. In newspaper advertisements, he also informed the public that he continued to carry on his goldsmith's business "where may be had at a short Notice any Vessel from a Thimble to a Tea Urn made in the newest Taste and finished in the neatest Manner."[13]

From 1783 to 1788 artisans, merchants and political elites, Hichborn relations, friends, and Masonic brothers bought everything from hardware to ivory combs and brushes and Barcelona handkerchiefs at Revere's store. Some of Revere's hardware customers, like Perez Morton, were also his best silver customers. Morton, a member of St. Andrew's Lodge and the North End Caucus, bought locks, screws, and hinges in 1784 and 1785, and he also ordered silver clasps, mugs, spoons, a cream pot, porringer, and "slop bowl" from Revere in the 1780s and 1790s. Revere provided various tools, including a frame saw, bench vise, and files for the clockmaker Simon Willard and nails for his son-in-law Amos Lincoln, a housewright. Cousin Benjamin Hichborn was the steadiest hardware customer among the Hichborn clan, purchasing an assortment of nails, hinges, locks, candlesticks, sconces, and knives.[14]

Revere's Masonic life was as active as his business life. During the Revolutionary War, he had served several terms as Master of St. Andrew's Lodge and filled several offices in the Massachusetts Grand Lodge, but he discovered that independence affected Freemasonry as much as it affected his business. Dr. Joseph Warren's death at Bunker Hill had left members of the Massachusetts Grand Lodge concerned about the legitimacy of a Grand Lodge without a Grand Master. Accordingly, the Massachusetts Grand Lodge summoned all the Masters and Wardens under its jurisdiction to a special meeting to elect a new Grand Master. On March 8, 1777, with only eleven members present, and only one a Master of a lodge, the Massachusetts Grand Lodge chose Joseph Webb as their new Grand Master. The question of whether they had exceeded their authority in electing a Grand Master would not be debated for another five years, but in the meantime, Paul Revere and his Masonic brethren considered the future of Freemasonry in the United States.[15]

On September 22, 1780, the Massachusetts Grand Lodge appointed Paul Revere, Joseph Webb, William Palfrey, Perez Morton, John Lowell, Colonel Edward Proctor, and James Jackson to write an address on Masonry "to all Masons in the Thirteen United States." One of the issues under consideration was the appointment of a national Grand Master, an idea suggested by Continental Army officers of the American Union Lodge in Morristown, New Jersey, in 1779. How American Masons would deal with the division between Ancient and Modern Masons and how much authority a national Grand Master would have over each Grand Lodge remained unanswered. On January 12, 1781, Perez Morton moved that the Massachusetts Grand Lodge chose a Grand Master General, an idea rejected by both St. Andrew's Lodge and the Massachusetts Grand Lodge. The Grand Lodge moved to delay such troublesome questions about the future of American Freemasonry "until a GENERAL PEACE, shall happily take place thro' the CONTINENT."[16]

On December 6, 1782, Paul Revere, Perez Morton, John Warren, James Avery, and John Juteau delivered a report on the actions of the Massachusetts Grand Lodge in choosing Joseph Webb as Grand Master back in 1777. With the exception of Brother Juteau, who dissented, the committee concluded that the commission granted to Dr. Warren by the Grand Lodge of Scotland had "died with him," and if the Massachusetts Grand Lodge had not appointed a successor, they would have seen "the Brethren . . . dispersed, the Pennyless go unassisted, the Craft Languish and Ancient Masonry be extinct in this Part [of the] World." Since "the Political Head of this Country" had destroyed "All connection and correspondence" between its American subjects and "the Country from which the Grand Lodge originally derived its commissioned Authority," the brethren of the Massachusetts Grand Lodge had acted legitimately under the Masonic principle "inculcating on its professors submission to the commands of the Civil Authority of the Country they reside in." The committee also determined that henceforth the Massachusetts Grand Lodge of Ancient Masons should be "free and independent in its Government and Official Authority of any other Grand Lodge, or Grand Master in the Universe."[17]

On December 16, 1782, by a vote of thirty to nineteen, the brethren of St. Andrew's Lodge, including William Burbeck, who succeeded Revere as Master of the lodge in 1782, voted to retain their allegiance to the Grand Lodge of Scotland. Animosity between Burbeck and Revere may have been a factor in the decision of the Massachusetts Grand Lodge not to appoint Revere to a committee to confer with St. Andrew's Lodge about its decision. Burbeck and four other committee members from St. Andrew's Lodge called the Grand Lodge's declaration of independence "inconsistent with the principles of Masonry, necessary to be observed for the good of the Craft." The members of St. Andrew's Lodge voted to continue to pay dues and be represented at the Massachusetts Grand Lodge and to reconsider the issue when the war was over.[18]

Peace did not change the minds of the majority of the members of St. Andrew's Lodge. On January 22, 1784, thirty members of the lodge voted to remain with the Grand Lodge of Scotland, while Paul Revere and twenty-two others voted for St. Andrew's membership in an independent Massachusetts Grand Lodge. The rupture of St. Andrew's Lodge was acrimonious, with Revere and his "agrieved Brethren" filing a lawsuit to recover their part of the stock of the lodge. The lawsuit was settled out of court, and Revere and his associates formed a new St. Andrew's Lodge under the jurisdiction of the Massachusetts Grand Lodge. In September 1784 Revere's lodge changed its name to Rising States Lodge, and between 1784 and 1793 Revere was elected to several terms as Master or Treasurer of his new lodge. Revere tried to restore harmony among his Masonic brethren when he served as president of a Masonic convention in Charlestown in May 1785, but the brethren of St. Andrew's Lodge still refused to join the Massachusetts Grand Lodge. On behalf of St. Andrew's Lodge, James Carter and Elisha Sigourney stated the belief that they were bound by their charter from the Grand Lodge of Scotland "which we deem sacred—these obligations once broken, this faith once destroy'd, we should conceive ourselves unworthy of confidence either as men or masons."[19]

The decision to retain allegiance to the Grand Lodge of Scotland or the Massachusetts Grand Lodge raised conflicting interpretations of Masonic principle that divided friends, neighbors, and former Revolutionary associates. Was Revere correct in his interpretation of Masonic principles that the war had severed ties between St. Andrew's Lodge and the Grand Lodge of Scotland and that allegiance was due solely to the Massachusetts Grand Lodge, or had he allowed his hostility toward all things British to override his sacred obligation to the Grand Lodge of Scotland?[20] John Boit of the North End Caucus voted with Revere, but North End Caucus members Gibbons Bouve, Asa Stoddard, John Symmes, and Thomas Urann voted with the majority of St. Andrew's Lodge to remain under the jurisdiction of the Grand Lodge of Scotland. Others who opposed Revere included Samuel Barrett, his neighbor and loyal customer; Manasseh Marston, a friend and neighbor; and James Graham, a customer. Those who sided with Revere generally were more recent members of St. Andrew's Lodge, who may have lacked the strong emotional ties to the lodge of long-standing members, or men with some connection to Paul Revere: Robert Hichborn, his cousin; Amos Lincoln, his son-in-law; Joseph Dunkerly, a miniature painter who rented Revere's North Square home; and Captain Nathaniel Fellows, a business associate.[21]

On February 26, 1784, Bostonians celebrated the ratification of the peace treaty between the United States and Great Britain with "the ringing of bells and discharge of cannon" and a procession from the State House to the Old South Meeting House. But peace did not necessarily bring either harmony, as Revere and his Masonic brethren had learned, or prosperity. Peace did bring a flood of

British goods into American markets that depleted merchants and consumers of cash and the imposition of prohibitive British trade regulations on American commerce. The decade of the 1780s was one of both optimism and apprehension for Revere and his fellow citizens as they anticipated the prosperity and social mobility that they hoped peace would bring, feared that they lacked the virtue necessary to sustain their republican revolution, and argued over their visions for the New Republic.[22]

Paul Revere, Samuel Adams, and John Adams were among the many Americans who lamented the love of gain, the loss of virtue, and the replacement of the commonwealth ideal with the development of divisive interest groups in their society. Conveniently forgetting the divisions within the patriot cause during the nonimportation movement, they preferred to remember an idyllic and harmonious union of merchants, artisans, farmers, and their families sacrificing their private interests to the public good in their fight against British tyranny. Their hopes for the reforming power and unifying force of republicanism now seemed misplaced as they surveyed a society rent by social, economic, and geographic divisions and, above all, by self-interest. In Massachusetts, merchants opposed farmers, moderates opposed reformers, and the eastern and western parts of the state clashed over the issues of political representation, monetary policy, and just how democratic their government and society should be.[23]

In 1778 the Massachusetts Legislature tried to create a compromise constitution that would reconcile opposing ideals for republican government in Massachusetts. Under the constitution approved by the legislature on February 28, 1778, all adult, white males could vote for representatives, but property qualifications were imposed on voters for governor, lieutenant governor, and senators. The constitution acceded to western demands on representation and eastern demands for a bicameral legislature but denied the governor veto power. Moderates thought the new state government was too weak, and reformers objected that the constitution should have been drafted in a separate convention elected by the people, not one created by the legislature it was meant to control. The voters, given no provisions to amend the constitution, soundly defeated it by a vote of 9,972 to 2,083 in October 1778.[24]

John Adams returned to Massachusetts as a delegate to the independently elected constitutional convention in September 1779 after a year as commissioner to France. He applied his reading in European and English political and legal thought and his observations on government and human nature gleaned from his experience in state and national politics to the creation of a more suitable state constitution. Like Theophilus Parsons, a young Essex County lawyer who had outlined his plan for the Massachusetts state government in May 1778, Adams believed that society was composed of different interests that should have a separate place in government. He proposed a bicameral legislature to balance the popular and aristocratic interests and a strong governor, chosen by the legislature and with veto power, to act as a disinterested mediator. If he and his colleagues could set up a government that would guarantee the security and liberty of its citizens and balance and restrain the various interest groups in their society, then they could revive the corporate ideal that Adams believed had existed during the Imperial Crisis.[25]

The final draft of the constitution, ratified on October 25, 1780, allowed the people, not the legislature, to elect the governor and weakened the governor's power by allowing the legislature to override his veto. Overall, however, the Massachusetts constitution expressed the political philosophy of John Adams and eastern mercantile interests. The governor still held veto power and wide appointive powers, including the appointment of judges on the basis of tenure for good behavior. The constitution also imposed a property qualification on voters and on candidates for governor, lieutenant governor, senators, and representatives. Reformers from western Massachusetts were victorious in gaining equal representation for every town having 150 ratable polls, a bill of rights assuring each citizen "the security of his person and property," and recognition of the people's sovereign power to create a constitution. The *Boston Gazette* approved the people's choice of John Hancock, Esq. to sit in the governor's chair, where "his Abilities and disinterested Zeal for the security and wealth of this and the other United States, may be more conspicuously and effectually displayed."[26]

The type of government that John Adams and Theophilus Parsons envisioned conformed to principles that fit Paul Revere's view of republicanism. Central to their prescription for the well-governed republic was the belief in an organic society that acknowledged the strengths and weaknesses of its constituent members and the need for balanced government to restrain the different and sometimes competing interests in society. In his writings, Parsons maintained that aristocratic and democratic segments of society both had something to contribute to government. Among "gentlemen of education, fortune, and leisure," society would find "the largest number of men, possessed of wisdom, learning, and firmness and consistency of character," while the people had "the greatest share of political honesty, probity, and a regard to the interest of the whole." In a properly constituted legislature, any "crude and hasty determinations of the house" would be "revised and controuled" by the more educated and thoughtful men of property in the Senate. Likewise, the ambition and "disregard to civil liberty" that might exist in the Senate would be frustrated by the rash but virtuous members of the House. The proper role for the people was to "look on, and observe the conduct of their servants, and continue or withdraw their favor annually, according to their merit or demerit."[27]

Deference to those of superior skill, education, and breeding was a principle instilled in Revere both as an apprentice artisan and as an Entered Apprentice in

St. Andrew's Lodge. He, in turn, expected deference from his apprentices, journeymen, and subordinate Masons. In the North End Caucus, Revere was, at first, content merely "to look on, and observe the conduct" of James Otis, the Adamses, and Dr. Warren, much as he had quietly learned his father's trade and Masonic principles. As he grew more enlightened about republican principles, largely through his association with more educated members of his society, Revere gradually took on more responsibility in the patriot cause and enjoyed the distinction that increasing responsibility conferred on him. Yet, throughout his life, he continued to try to balance, not always successfully, his ambition and desire for fame with his respect for the principles of hierarchy and deference. When he considered himself worthy to assume a more prominent leadership role in church and local politics in the late 1780s and 1790s, it was not as the mere mechanic "haranguing in town meeting" who had so horrified Reverend John Eliot back in 1777, but as Paul Revere, Esq., hardware merchant, foundry owner, and a man of property and substance in the community.[28]

Independence also stirred discussions about the nature of local government in the American republic, with citizens in several towns debating the merits of incorporation. In June 1784 Bostonians were in an uproar over a proposal to incorporate Boston, replacing the venerable town meeting with a mayor, council, and aldermen. Joseph Barrell, a prominent merchant, recommended incorporation as an efficient and economical mode of government. "An American," writing in the *Massachusetts Centinel,* reviewed the history of cities to deny that incorporation "will increase the powers of the great and rich, while it demolishes the influence of the middling class of people." Indeed, corporations "have contributed more towards delivering mankind from slavery than every other institution in civil society." "An American" closed his argument by suggesting that incorporation would improve "the low state of commerce in this state."[29]

In May, Samuel Adams had defended the town meeting, warning that incorporation might "be instrumental to the introduction of aristocracy, a government of all others . . . the worst." Adams also cited history, reminding his audience that a similar desire for change in the Greek and Roman republics had been the avenue by which aristocracy had entered. When the Boston town meeting convened on June 17, Faneuil Hall resounded with cries of "No corporation!" "No Mayor and Aldermen!" and "No Innovations!" shouted mainly by the mechanics of the town, who were "Possessed of an idea that the plan was fraught with latent evil." In describing the experience of "seeing *democracy* exhibited in perfection," the Reverend Jeremy Belknap wrote: "the shew of hands put me in mind of Milton's description of the flaming swords drawn and flourished in Pandemonium." The "tradesmen and other inferior orders" who were so distasteful to Belknap defeated incorporation "by a great majority," and efforts to revive incorporation in the fall and winter of 1785 met a similar fate. Whether Paul Revere opposed incorporation with the mechanics from whose ranks he sprang or supported the idea with the merchants and "better sort" whose ranks he was trying to enter is unknown. He was uncharacteristically silent during this transitional period in his life, when he was both a mechanic and aspiring merchant. When he did take a stand, in January 1792, it was with a surer sense of his place in the social structure.[30]

In his quest to become a merchant, Revere was continually frustrated by an inadequate source of currency to satisfy his British creditors. In September 1783 Frederick William Geyer wrote Revere that the Continental security that he had sent as payment was "no security" to him. In November an embarrassed Revere explained that "the most of what I possessed was in Government hands," which "I could not sell out without a very great loss." He expected to sell his securities at their full value in the near future, but in the meantime he sent Geyer 340 Spanish milled dollars and 4 silver ingots in payment. Revere had similar problems with other London merchants who refused to accept his bills of credit. On December 9, 1784, he paid John Sampson, a London jeweler who supplied him with jewelry and clock parts, with 23^1/$_2$ guineas, 105 Spanish milled dollars, 2 British silver ingots, a gold repeating watch, and 58,000 flat-seam needles, some of which he had tried to unload a year earlier on Captain Peter Cunningham, complaining "they are of no use here, our sail makers never use them." Revere hoped that the opening of the Massachusetts bank in July 1784 would end the "great Stagnation of Money" and revive business, but in April 1786 he complained to Geyer that business was still "extremely dull owing to the Scarcity of money."[31]

By the spring of 1785 the pages of the *Massachusetts Centinel* were filled with complaints over "the dangerous consequences of our commerce with Britain." British mercantile houses were sending agents to America instead of selling through American merchants, destroying American virtue and American manufactures by flooding the domestic market with "gewgaws and trifles" and articles "as were formerly *made* . . . in this country," and draining America of "our circulating medium, which is our greatest resource." On April 13, 1785, "Joyce, Jr." urged "the Freemen of this Commonwealth, particularly the ancient Supporters of the Publick Good, the TRADESMEN OF BOSTON," to "exterminate the Viper that is knawing at our vitals" by warning British agents and factors "to leave this hallowed land." Two days later, a group of "Gentlemen Concerned in Trade" formed a committee to draft resolutions dealing with "the present state of affairs." The members of the committee were John Hancock, who had declined to run for reelection as governor in 1785; state representatives Samuel A. Otis, Samuel Breck, and Caleb Davis; and the merchants Samuel Barrett, Samuel Breck, Edward Payne, Jonathan T. Austin, John Coffin Jones, and Thomas Russell. Paul Revere, the newly established hardware merchant, did not possess either the wealth or gentility to sit alongside Boston's merchant elite.[32]

The primary concern of the merchants who presented their resolutions before the town at Faneuil Hall on Saturday, April 16, was to protect their control over Boston's import trade. The committee resolved to draft a petition to the Confederation Congress "representing the embarrassments under which the trade now labours," urge merchants in the other states to ask their legislatures to grant Congress more control over trade, and not to have any intercourse with British factors or those who did business with them. Aside from a weak endorsement to "encourage all in our power, the manufactures and produce of this country," the meeting did not take any explicit action to protect the interests of Boston mechanics and, in fact, rejected a motion for higher import duties made by mechanics at the meeting.[33]

The mechanics, who were more concerned about protecting their manufactures than in whether competing British articles were sold by British or American agents, organized their own association on April 21 at the Green Dragon Tavern and drafted resolutions four days later. They asked the General Court for a prohibition or duty on imports, pledged to "withhold all commercial connection" with British factors, promised "a mutual correspondence" with the committee of merchants and traders, and proposed the creation of a committee of delegates representing "each branch of business." Noticeably absent from this committee or the Association of Tradesmen and Manufacturers it created was Paul Revere, heretofore considered a leader among Boston's artisans.[34]

Why Revere did not join Benjamin Austin Jr., owner of a ropewalk, member of a prominent merchant family, and brother and partner of Jonathan T. Austin of the Committee of Merchants and Traders, and his fellow Sons of Liberty Sarson Belcher and Gibbens Sharp in the Association of Tradesmen and Manufacturers is a mystery whose roots may lie in a combination of reasons. Revere had not yet reconciled his dual and sometimes conflicting identities as mechanic and merchant. As a mechanic, he should have supported measures to promote American manufactures, but as a merchant, he was guilty of importing the very "gewgaws," "ballooneries," and "trifles" that were supposedly depleting Americans of their money and their virtue. Perhaps, too, he did not want to risk his position as a leader among Boston's artisans and a recent entrant into the merchant's ranks by competing for leadership with Benjamin Austin Jr., who had the social status and personality to eclipse Revere's claim on the allegiance of his brother artisans. He may also have calculated that deference to the mercantile and political elite, which had thus far enabled him to maintain a flourishing and diversified business, was the best means of assuring his continued economic success and social mobility.[35]

John Hancock's careful cultivation of his image as a patriot and friend to the people earned him four consecutive gubernatorial victories. But men engaged in commerce reviled Hancock as a demagogue and poor administrator whose financial policies had nearly depleted the state's treasury and undermined public credit. They preferred James Bowdoin, whom "Philo-Civis" lauded as "an example of prudence, of temperance, of industry and republican manners for our imitation . . . a gentleman of the fairest reputation, of the strictest honour . . . of incorruptible integrity, and unquestioned abilities." After several defeats, Bowdoin became governor in 1785. Hancock resigned on January 29 of that year, leaving Lieutenant Governor Thomas Cushing to face Bowdoin in the election. Votes given to a third candidate, General Benjamin Lincoln, threw the election into the legislature, where the Senate decided in favor of Bowdoin.[36]

Paul Revere's enmity toward Hancock for maligning his reputation as commander of Castle Island in 1779 and his desire for an improved financial climate for his business pursuits were reasons to support James Bowdoin for governor. Revere did not ally himself either with the Committee of Merchants and Traders or with the Committee of Tradesmen and Manufacturers by signing their respective addresses of congratulation to Governor Bowdoin. However, he may have conveyed his belief in the need for stronger government and his support for Bowdoin to Thomas Wadsworth, a Boston friend then living in South Carolina, who wrote: "When your laws are made agreeable to your Constitution and executed with vigor then will your Government appear in dignity abroad harmony and peace with you at home. . . . If Mr. Bowdoin is chose and accepts I think he will help to make your Government more respectable."[37]

Governor Bowdoin proved to be a friend to both merchants and manufacturers in general and to Paul Revere in particular. In his inaugural address, Bowdoin recommended that a convention of delegates from all the states revise the Articles of Confederation to grant Congress more power to regulate trade. He supported efforts by the Association of Tradesmen and Manufacturers to improve their financial situation, which included a petition to the General Court requesting tariff legislation, although he did not endorse specific proposals. Paul Revere was a direct beneficiary of Governor Bowdoin's belief that the government should take an active role in encouraging manufacturing when, on February 8, 1786, Bowdoin recommended that the Senate and House grant "Paul Revere, Esq. of Boston, and John Noyes of Watertown, gentleman" a fifteen-year exclusive privilege of manufacturing iron by "the new invented steam engine."[38]

Revere's decision not to ally himself with the Association of Tradesmen and Manufacturers proved to be wise. Within a year of its formation, the organization dissolved, possibly over an internal political dispute. Beginning in March 1786, Benjamin Austin Jr., writing as Honestus, launched a series of attacks on the legal profession in the *Independent Chronicle*. Austin advocated the abolition of "the Pernicious Practice of the Law" and its replacement with a simplified legal system of arbitration. Debt-ridden farmers in western Massachusetts shared Austin's contempt for lawyers, but Boston lawyers and merchants were horrified by Austin's seeming assault on law and order. Boston's mechanics apparently did not wholeheartedly support Austin's plan either, or else they would have used their numbers to convince the town meeting to instruct Boston's representatives to vote for an investigation of the legal profession. The Association of Tradesmen and Manufacturers seems to have vanished shortly after its last publicly announced meeting on March 27. By his silence, Revere had disassociated himself from any connection to Benjamin Austin Jr. and the democratic anarchy that Austin's opponents believed Austin was advocating.[39]

Fears of disorder and declining virtue became reality in the summer of 1786, when citizens in western Massachusetts, unable to gain legislative action on their requests for debt relief, organized town and county conventions to air their grievances and used armed force to close courts in several western counties. Delegates from fifty towns in Hampshire County who convened on August 22, 1786, attributed the "many grievances and unnecessary burdens now lying upon the people" to several factors, including an inequitable system of taxation and representation, the existence of the Senate, courts of common pleas and general sessions of the peace, "the present method of practice of the attornies at law," and "the General Court sitting in the town of *Boston.*" Among their recommendations were a call for the towns to instruct their representatives "to use their influence in the next General Court" to gain a publication of paper money that would be legal tender in all payment and a revision of the state constitution. Armed insurgents led by Captain Daniel Shays, a Revolutionary War officer, shut down civil courts, tried to prevent the Supreme Judicial Court from trying criminal prosecutions for debt in Springfield, and threatened the Springfield arsenal.[40]

In the town meeting, in an address to Governor Bowdoin, and in newspaper articles, Bostonians voiced their disapproval of the methods of Shays and his followers and pledged "to co-operate in support of constitutional government." Paul Revere's cousin Benjamin Hichborn led a volunteer cavalry unit that captured Job Shattuck and other Shaysite leaders and brought them to Boston. Revere's name was not among the subscribers who loaned money to the state to supply forces under General Benjamin Lincoln that suppressed the rebellion in February 1787. But he expressed his support for their patriotic actions by making a bowl to be presented to General William Shepard "for his Ability and Zeal in quelling Shays' Rebellion."[41]

Discussing Shays's Rebellion with George Washington, Henry Knox wrote that "the commotions of Massachusetts have wrought prodigious changes in the minds of men in that state respecting the Powers of Government." In the aftermath of the rebellion, "every body" now favored strengthening government or there would be "no security for liberty or property." To Stephen Higginson, Knox wrote that he hoped events in Massachusetts would have a positive effect on delegates meeting in Philadelphia in May 1787 to strengthen the Articles of Confederation. The "great men" meeting in convention might "induce the adoption of some energetic plan, in the prosecution of which we might rise to national dignity and happiness." Fear of the excesses of democracy was a powerful motive to strengthen the national government, but so too was the hope that a stronger government would improve economic prospects, not only for merchants and speculators, but for artisans as well.[42]

The Constitution of the United States of America that thirty-nine of the forty-two delegates still at the convention approved on September 17, 1787, far exceeded the original goal of amending the powers of the Confederation. Largely the handiwork of James Madison of Virginia, the Constitution replaced a confederation of independent republics with a powerful national government that Madison hoped would provide "a republican remedy for the diseases most incident to republican government." Responding to critics like James Winthrop, who argued that "no extensive empire can be governed upon republican principles, and that such a government will degenerate to a despotism." Madison countered that it was precisely an extended republic that would offer the best protection against factionalism: "Extend the sphere and you take in a greater variety of parties and interests; and you make it less probable that a majority of the whole will have a common motive to invade the rights of other citizens."[43]

Madison, Alexander Hamilton, and other Federalists, as supporters of the Constitution came to be known, hoped that the new national government would attract refined, educated men who could be relied upon to make decisions in the best interests of the people. These "men of sense and property," as a writer in the *Connecticut Courant* called them, would provide a vast improvement over the quality of government that existed on the state level, where the people had difficulty in determining the public good, "beset as they continually are by the wiles of parasites and sycophants, by the snares of the ambitious, the avaricious, the desperate, by the artifices of men who possess their confidence more than they deserve it."[44]

Echoing Theophilus Parsons, Madison believed that the Senate would be composed of enlightened men of national character whose aristocratic "usurpations," if they occurred, would be checked by the House of Representatives, who, "with the people on their side, will at all times be able to bring back the Constitution to its primitive form and principles." This was no aristocratic despotism, but representative democracy, in which ultimate sovereignty rested with the people who delegated their powers to three separate branches of government. Separation of powers would protect the people by preventing any branch of government from "drawing all powers into its impetuous vortex."[45]

Although Shays's Rebellion strengthened the Federalist cause in Massachusetts, it also galvanized Anti-Federalists, who gained support from voter backlash against the repressive measures used to suppress the rebellion. John Hancock, the man "most likely to restore peace and contentment," decisively defeated James Bowdoin in the gubernatorial election of 1787. When the Constitutional Convention convened in Massachusetts in January 1788, the Anti-Federalists were in the majority. Among the delegates, Samuel Adams did not favor ratification, and John Hancock remained silent as usual until he could gauge popular opinion. Boston's mechanics, "near four hundred" of whom convened at the Green Dragon Tavern on January 7, 1788, enthusiastically adopted resolutions in support of the Constitution. Benjamin Austin Jr., now an Anti-Federalist leader, no longer spoke for Boston's mechanics. Their new leaders were John Lucas, a master baker and officeholder in town and state government; Benjamin Russell, publisher of the *Massachusetts Centinel;* and Paul Revere.[46]

Boston's mechanics unanimously adopted the resolutions drafted by Lucas, Russell, and Revere, which supported "the proposed frame of government" as one that was "well calculated to secure the liberties, protect the property, and guard the rights of the citizens of America." Economic self-interest was a strong motivating factor for the mechanics, who believed that if the Constitution was adopted, "trade and navigation will revive and increase, employ and subsistence will be afforded to many of our townsmen, who are now suffering from want of the necessaries of life; that it will promote industry and morality; render us respectable as a nation; and procure us all the blessings to which we are entitled from the natural wealth of our country, our capacity for improvement, from our industry, our freedom and independence."[47]

Economic well-being was the obvious reason for mechanics to support the Constitution, but there were other reasons. According to the opening statement of their "Proceedings," Revere and his brother mechanics convened to refute false rumors that "the democratick part of the community, viz, the Tradesmen of the seaports, and OUR BRETHREN the Yeomen of the Country" opposed the Constitution. In defense of their honor and patriotism, Boston's "Tradesmen and Mechanicks" reminded their fellow citizens that they had "always manifested their attachment to the principles of the Revolution—with steadiness and perseverance they pursued the prize of Independence—that object obtained, they have patiently though anxiously, waited for the blessings of good government."[48]

Revere's support for the Constitution was not only a vote for his future economic well-being but an opportunity to stand publicly with the eminent Federalist leaders in his society who shared his hopes for the future along with his abiding concern over the self-interest and lack of honor that were infesting the republic. In July 1783, for example, he was disturbed that the Suffolk County Court of the General Sessions of the Peace would even consider awarding a retailer's license to a "scoundrel" like Benjamin Bussey "in opposition to my friend Lewis of Dedham." In 1778, with fifty dollars borrowed from his grandfather, Bussey, a twenty-six-year-old Revolutionary War veteran, formed a partnership with a Prussian goldsmith who, within a year, supposedly made Bussey master of a trade that Revere learned only after several years' apprenticeship with his father. By 1792

Bussey had moved from Dedham to Boston, where his success as a merchant and property owner enabled him to retire from business in 1806.[49] When cousin John Rivoire suggested that Revere was trying to unjustly claim the estate of a relative in Philadelphia, a highly insulted Revere defended his "Honor and Honesty" by denying that he ever expected "to receive, one single Farthing by the death of any relation." Rather, "it has allways been my lot and I desire to be thankful it has been in my power to help others."[50] In the New Republic, Revere, whose honor had come under such scathing attack because of the Penobscot expedition, would work hard to prove that he was a model republican citizen who stood in stark contrast to men like Benjamin Bussey, scoundrels, upstarts, and, worst of all, Democrats.

By the narrow margin of 187 to 168, Massachusetts in February 1788 became the sixth state to ratify the Constitution.[51] How large a role Boston mechanics played in bringing Samuel Adams and John Hancock over to their side is debatable, but they proudly proclaimed their "approbation" of the Constitution in a parade celebrating ratification on February 9, 1788.[52] Paul Revere and the other members of the Committee of Tradesmen rode in a sleigh drawn by four horses behind a grand procession of blacksmiths, shipwrights, coopers, and other representatives of Boston's sundry trades, along with "The Ship Federal Constitution on runners drawn by thirteen horses."[53]

Paul Revere had reemerged as a leader of Boston's artisans. By November 1788 he had also broadened the boundaries of the mechanic's craft by opening an iron foundry in the North End. At his goldsmith shop he was fashioning exquisite luxury items that were helping his countrymen rise to a new level of social refinement, and at his foundry he was producing useful goods that lessened his countrymen's dependence on imported manufactures. From 1788 to 1800 the congregation of the New Brick Church relied on "Colonel Revere's" judgment on numerous committees. In October 1789 his townsmen chose "Paul Revere, Esq." to serve on a committee to join the selectmen in expressing "their affection and respect for President Washington, and the sense they have of the honor, done them by his Visit to this Metropolis." Revere had succeeded in erasing the humiliation of the Penobscot expedition, and he looked confidently to the future under the wise and benevolent administration of George Washington. However, political harmony would prove to be a more elusive goal as Americans continued to debate, more hotly than ever, the meaning of republicanism.[54]

CHAPTER TEN

A TRUE REPUBLICAN

T HE UNITY OF BOSTON'S artisans in support of the Constitution in 1788 dissolved little more than a year later. In the lieutenant governor's election of 1789, artisans divided their votes between Benjamin Lincoln, the Federalist candidate, and Samuel Adams, the victorious candidate, who ran as a moderate "friend of the people." In December, Fisher Ames, "a *firm decided* FEDERALIST," carried Boston by a narrow margin in his congressional victory over Samuel Adams. Followers of both candidates sought the backing of Boston's artisans, who once again split their vote. In the spring of 1789 the Federalist Paul Revere and the Anti-Federalist Benjamin Austin Jr. joined forces in the revived Association of Trademen and Manufacturers in hopes of organizing artisans throughout the country to gain congressional protection for domestic manufactures, but their alliance was brief. On May 6 the association voted to petition Congress for protective tariff legislation, but Paul Revere never signed the petition, and the association seems to have broken up soon after.[1]

To discuss the "artisan community" or a "mechanic ideology" obscures the differences in status, wealth, occupation, and ideology among artisans in Revolutionary and post-Revolutionary America. Dr. Joseph Warren and Samuel Adams knew that Ebenezer McIntosh and the mob of artisans and mariners who demolished Lieutenant Governor Thomas Hutchinson's mansion in 1765 or the rowdy journeymen ropemakers and apprentices involved in the Boston Massacre were a different breed from Paul Revere and the master artisans of the North End Caucus. In 1788 Boston artisans were momentarily united by pride in their identity as producers of useful goods for their fellow citizens, remembrance of their "attachment to the principles of the Revolution," and faith in the proposed national government as a means of assuring their economic and social mobility. Soon, however, Paul Revere would discover that his interpretation of republican principles—especially as they applied to artisans—clashed with that of Benjamin Austin Jr.[2]

As a Federalist, Revere deferred to the rule of the wise or wellborn because their principles and policies seemed best designed to secure the stability and progress of American society and advance his own interests and aspirations. In his reports on public credit, the Bank of the United States, and manufacturing, Secretary of the Treasury Alexander Hamilton proposed to put the United States on a sound financial footing and promote economic expansion. In 1790 and 1791 Congress ratified Hamilton's plan for the federal government to fund and assume the state debts and his proposal for a Bank of the United States. The new bonds issued by the federal government and the notes issued by the Bank of the United States were a readily available but stable circulating currency that encouraged business expansion. Hamilton's Report on Manufactures, if implemented, would have boosted domestic manufacturing through the use of protective tariffs and bounties for new industries. For Revere, whose business plans in the late 1780s were stymied by a shortage of an adequate circulating medium, and whose hopes for the future rested on his new role as a manufacturer of cast iron, brass, and copper products, Hamiltonian policies were clearly to his advantage.[3]

Yet, Revere's affiliation with the Federalists was more than blind submission to the judgment of his betters or calculated self-interest in which he bowed and scraped before his social superiors in return for their favors. When he deferred to the leaders of his society, Revere also did so out of "a courteous regard or respect" for men who shared his ideals. Intimately tied to Revere's esteem for men of superior educational and social status who sacrificed private interest to the common good was his desire to emulate such men. When Revere sacrificed his business to carry intelligence to New York and Philadelphia in 1774, he could consider himself as virtuous a patriot as Dr. Warren, who neglected his financial affairs in order to serve the common good. When he emulated Federalist leaders in his thoughts, words, and deeds, he received tangible rewards of government patronage and respect that elevated his status in Boston, but he also added to his self-esteem by identifying with such worthy republicans.[4]

Revere's high expectations for the United States under the Federalists also included hopes for his own economic opportunity and social mobility as the recipient of a federal office. In 1789 Representative Fisher Ames assured Revere: "I am no stranger to your services and zeal on the side of liberty, and in my mind, that sort of merit will greatly support the claims of the candidate who can plead it." However, Ames cautioned that "the number of expectants will be considerable, and many have merit and powerful patronage." Samuel Allyne Otis, secretary of the Senate, sent Revere his "good wishes" and recommended the Revenue

Department as the best place to seek an appointment. In 1791 Ames discouraged Revere's hope of becoming director of the National Mint, writing: "However your own ingenuity might qualify you for it, the circumstances will not much encourage the hope of an appointment." Ames suggested that Revere focus on the Excise Department, concluding, "I need not tell you how fully I confide in your integrity, industry and public spirit." Revere took Ames's advice and wrote to President Washington seeking a position in the Excise Department. Since he could not "claim the honor of such a personal acquaintance with your Excellency, as, will furnish you with sufficient information of my character," Revere referred the president to Henry Knox, Benjamin Lincoln, Fisher Ames, and Elbridge Gerry.[5]

Revere failed in his quest for federal appointment in the Washington administration, but in 1798, despite his business success, he still hungered for the prestige conferred by federal office when he sought appointment as director of a proposed national cannon foundry. In response to his inquiries, Representative Harrison Gray Otis replied that Revere's character "must be well known" to President Adams, "and I know of no person whose pretentions on all accounts are superior to yours." The national foundry was never built, and the Jeffersonian Revolution ended Revere's chances of ever receiving a patronage appointment. If Revere met the republican ideals of virtue and merit as the criteria for federal appointment, why, then, did he fail to receive a position?[6]

Both Presidents George Washington and John Adams did indeed believe that virtue and merit were essential qualifications for federal officeholders. But they also had clearly defined conceptions of what kind of men were most likely to possess those qualifications. Their ideal candidates were men of proven patriotism, integrity, wisdom, and experience who had already exhibited those qualities either as Continental Army officers, officerholders in the Confederation or state governments, or men of wealth and education used to exercising authority. Although Revere's patriotism, virtue, and merit during and after the Revolution were unquestioned (with the exception of his performance in the Penobscot expedition), he lacked the Continental Army or government experience of Alexander Hamilton, Henry Knox, Benjamin Lincoln, or his old friend John Lamb, all of whom received appointments in the Washington administration. Nor could he compete for the office of director of the Mint with David Rittenhouse, who had superior credentials as a scientist and mathematician, not to mention the powerful patronage of Secretary of State Thomas Jefferson.[7]

Revere had the endorsement of his congressman, Fisher Ames, one factor favoring appointment in the Washington administration, but he might have had more success if either Henry Knox or Benjamin Lincoln, whom he listed in his letter to President Washington, had championed his cause. Knox's papers overflow with entreaties from office seekers like William Rickard of North Carolina, who turned to Knox because of "your well known confidential intimacy with the

President," and Benjamin Lincoln, who sought Knox's help in procuring a federal judgeship for John Lowell because "You *have* I know *very much the ear of the President."* Revere's cousin Benjamin Hichborn solicited Knox to obtain an appointment in Marblehead for "my worthy Friend and Nephew Major Fosdick." Knox might have been especially helpful in recommending Revere for a position in the Boston customs office because of "the Intimacy and Friendship" between Knox and Benjamin Lincoln, the newly appointed collector of customs for the Port of Boston.[8]

Revere's relationship with Knox had always been cordial and would continue to be during Knox's tenure as secretary of war, when Revere was awarded several government contracts to produce cannons, but there is no evidence that Knox helped Revere try to obtain a federal appointment. Yet, even if Revere had asked for Knox's patronage, Revere possessed neither the degree of friendship nor the claim of Revolutionary war experience of three other supplicants for Knox's favor: Benjamin Lincoln, Benjamin Hichborn, and Henry Jackson. Nor did he have the requisite gentility that Knox thought was as critical for a federal officeholder as it had been for a Continental Army officer. Certainly, Revere could not compare with John Coffin Jones, Esq., a "merchant of eminence in Boston," for whom Knox wrote a letter of introduction to Thomas Jefferson: "His abilities, his honor, and his liberal Fortune unite to render him a valuable member of our republic, and as such I flatter myself he will receive the countenance of your Excellency."[9]

In advising Revere on seeking office, Fisher Ames inquired: "But how do you stand with General Lincoln? his good word would go far." Lincoln, whose friendship with Washington and Knox undoubtedly helped him earn the collector's post in Boston, seems to have had significant influence over filling subordinate positions in his department. On August 16, 1789, he wrote Washington that he had been "fortunate enough to procure a number of very respectable characters to fill the lower offices so that the department is now arranged agreeably to my wishes."[10] With no existing correspondence between Revere and Lincoln, evidence of their relationship and Lincoln's role in Revere's unsuccessful pursuit of federal office is elusive. However, Lincoln had never been a customer of Revere's until just before the gubernatorial election of 1785, when he placed several orders for silver and hardware, perhaps in hopes of gaining Revere's vote. Lincoln did not patronize Revere again until 1803, when he ordered a bell. Did Lincoln suspect that Revere preferred James Bowdoin as governor in 1785, and did that knowledge influence his decision to overlook Revere for a revenue position?[11]

Revere was denied the honor of a federal appointment as he had been denied the honor of a Continental officer's commission. But in 1791, when his chances for appointment seemed slim, Revere should have been consoled by reflecting on his children's progress. Several of the older children had married and made him a grandfather. In 1781 Deborah, his oldest child, had married the housewright Amos

Lincoln, whose character Revere knew well from their joint participation in the Boston Tea Party, Lincoln's service under Revere in the Massachusetts State Artillery Regiment, and his membership in St. Andrew's and Rising States Lodge. In 1788 Frances had married her father's former apprentice Thomas Stevens Eayres, and they and their young son would soon move to Worcester to establish their home and business. Paul Jr. was married with two children and taking on more responsibility for the goldsmith shop.[12]

The children of Revere's second marriage, who benefited from their father's improved economic status after the Revolution, seemed destined for still brighter prospects. In 1783 and 1784 Joshua and Joseph Warren Revere entered Boston Latin, to be followed by John, the youngest child, in 1798. The younger sons, especially John, reached a level of distinction in literary, scientific, political, and social circles that their father never attained. The older daughters were raised to become artisans' wives, but Revere saw to it that Harriet and Maria, the younger girls, received an education to prepare them for a different life.[13]

Despite dividing his time between the foundry and goldsmith shop, Revere continued to find artistic inspiration and economic success in the goldsmith's trade. Imported pattern books from Sheffield, England, inspired designs for several objects, many of which graced the tables of Boston's merchant elite. The design for his elegant silver pitchers, three of which he made for his own use, came from ceramic earthenware pitchers imported from Liverpool, England, in the 1790s and early 1800s. In 1786 Elias Hasket Derby's ship the *Grand Turk* returned from China with the first Chinese porcelain, which soon was in demand by wealthy Americans and whose design Revere incorporated in his silver bowls. In 1795 Derby asked Revere to make eight copies of silver beakers designed by the Parisian silversmith Denis Colombier in 1789. Revere's success could be measured by the continued patronage of his society's elites and by the special commissions he executed, including a tea set for Edmund Hartt for his "Ability, Zeal and Fidelity" in constructing the frigate *Boston* in 1799 and a silver urn he made in 1800 in honor of Captain Gamaliel Bradford of the Ship *Industry* for his "Gallant defense . . . when Attacked by four French Privateers in the Streights of Gibralter." Revere also displayed his economic success and increasing social refinement when he began making luxury items for himself in the middle to late 1780s.[14]

Revere could not afford to dwell on his disappointment in failing to receive a federal patronage position because his newest business required all his energy and attention. In 1787 he began building a foundry on Lynn Street in the North End on land owned by his cousin Benjamin Hichborn. With financial assistance from his cousins Benjamin and Samuel Hichborn plus cash withdrawals from his goldsmith shop, the foundry was in full operation by November 1788. Revere produced "Cast Bells and Brass Cannon of all Sizes, and all kinds of Composition Work, Manufacture Sheets, Bolts, Spikes, Nails, &c. from Malleable Copper and Cold

8. In 1799 a number of "citizens of Boston" commissioned Revere to make a silver tea service for Edmund Hartt, constructor of the frigate *Boston,* for his "Ability, Zeal and Fidelity in the completion of that Ornament of the AMERICAN NAVY." Courtesy, Museum of Fine Arts, Boston. Gift of James Longley.

Rolled." Revere's foundry earned him not only profits but a national reputation as an expert in metallurgy.[15]

Revere's interest in opening a foundry could be seen simply as a logical extension of his goldsmith's expertise in metals and his artillery officer's familiarity with ordnance. But it was also part of a quest by mechanics to assert their identities as model republican citizens. In the bustling American economy of the 1790s and early 1800s, "the celebration of commerce" seemed to be eroding the communal bonds of virtue and benevolence thought necessary to preserve a republic. As a merchant, Revere had sold imported luxury objects that some of his countrymen believed deprived Americans of their money, virtue, and independence from England. But at his foundry, he produced window weights, firebacks, stoves, nails, and a host of other utilitarian objects that improved the lives and livelihoods of his fellow citizens. Not only were the bells he began manufacturing in 1792 for churches, schoolhouses, and ships functional and decorative, but they also freed Americans from their slavery to English manufactures. The ordnance and ship fittings he began producing in 1794 contributed to the strength of the United States government and the safety of its citizens. Thus, Revere could enjoy the profits of his labor, confident in the knowledge that he was also serving the public good.[16]

In the social confusion of the 1790s, when, as Jeremy Belknap complained to Ebenezer Hazard, "We have had a great bluster here about *liberty and equality,*"

9. With financial assistance from two cousins and cash withdrawals from his successful goldsmith shop, Paul Revere opened a foundry in Boston's North End. His trade card, engraved by Thomas Clarke, c. 1796–1803, advertises the products manufactured by Paul Revere and Son. Courtesy, Paul Revere Memorial Association.

Revere's new role as a manufacturer accorded him a social and intellectual superiority that was becoming elusive in an age of equality. As "a specimen [of] how far our tradesmen are advanced in this science [of liberty and equality]," Belknap related the story of "one of our six per cent fortune-makers," formerly a tailor, who was stopped on Long Wharf by a blacksmith demanding payment of an outstanding debt. The "ci-devant tailor" scolded the blacksmith for dunning him in public, to which the blacksmith, "in the true style of equality, replied, 'Come, come, citizen pricklouse, do not give yourself such airs as these! It was but t' other day that you was glad to measure my a—— for a pair of breeches.'" As an iron founder, a trade requiring both scientific knowledge and mechanical skill, Revere could distinguish himself from every common laborer, blacksmith, or "citizen pricklouse" clamoring for social equality and respectability.[17]

Perhaps Revere fancied that his accomplishments as a metallurgist put him on a par with the educated men of his society who pursued the study of mathematics, astronomy, and natural history. While the members of the American Academy of Arts and Sciences in Boston digested Benjamin Lincoln's essays on the climate and soil of Massachusetts and the members of the American Philosophical Society in Philadelphia listened to Thomas Jefferson deliver a paper on paleontology, Paul Revere kept a journal and commonplace book, where he jotted down the composition of gunpowder, "A Speedy way to find the Time of flight for any proposed Range at 45 Degrees," "Observations on Sulphur or Brimstone," and "receipes" for artificial fireworks and signal rockets. To improve his knowledge of chemistry, he read Watson's *Chemical Essays* and consulted experts like Dr. Letsome of England, whom he asked to send him ore samples from Cornwall or Devon, "by which I shall be able to distinguish the different Ores by comparing them" and to test ore samples for him, "for I doubt my ability in Chimistree."[18]

The national recognition he earned for his skill in manufacturing ordnance and ship fittings gave Revere the honor denied him on the battlefield and in the Washington and Adams administrations. His clients included the United States government; the governments of Massachusetts, Rhode Island, and South Carolina; plus merchants and shipbuilders. In June 1795 Lieutenant Colonel Stephen Rochefontaine, a French engineer and Revolutionary War veteran now with the United States Army Corps of Artillerists, asked Revere to help a Frenchman who had developed a new method of casting iron guns. "I am so well acquainted with your fondness of scientific discoveries," Rochefontaine wrote, "that I am persuaded that it is enough to point out the Gentleman who may be useful in enlarging the knowledge of this country to be certain you will afford him all sort of assistance, and meet him with a hearty welcome."[19]

On October 21, 1797, "a very numerous and brilliant collection of citizens" in Boston witnessed the launch of the United States frigate *Constitution,* built at Edmund Hartt's shipyard with bolts, spikes, and other ship fittings supplied by Paul Revere. The success of his work on the *Constitution* spurred Revere to solicit Navy Secretary Benjamin Stoddard for more government contracts. Hearing that Stoddard had advised the committee building another frigate in Boston in 1798 "not to send abroad for any thing they can git manufactured in this Country," Revere declared that he could make old or new copper into bolts, spikes, staples, nails "or any thing that is wanted in ship building. . . . I supplied the Constitution with Dovetails, Staples, Nails, etc."[20]

His achievements in metallurgy gave Revere a confidence bordering on arrogance. In 1790 he respectfully, and almost obsequiously, wrote to Richard Watson, bishop of Llandaff, and author of the "invaluable Chemical Essays," to correct an error in the text referring to the coining of pewter money by the American Congress. Within a few years, however, Revere was boasting about his development of a method of melting copper, making it malleable, and drawing it into bolts and spikes that resulted in improved strength and superiority over conventional cast bolts. In October 1795 he advised Jacob Sheafe, the naval agent at Portsmouth, New Hampshire, that it would be a mistake to cast copper bolts to a smaller size "for when that metal is cast in sand, it looses a very great deal of its malleability." Instead, he proposed the use of his drawn copper bolts, which "retain their malleability and are as tough as Iron." Later, in response to an inquiry about the strength and malleability of his drawn copper, Revere replied: "I will risque my reputation, that you shall take one of those bolts and place it across two blocks of Iron and strike it with a large Black smith Sledge, backwards and forwards, three hundred times, before you can break them." In January 1799, when Sheafe had the audacity to complain about the quality of his copper spikes, Revere retorted that the workmen who drove the same spikes on the frigate that Edmund Hartt was building in Boston "told me they were equal to the English ones, And what is more, no man but my Self in the four New England States can melt the Copper, and draw it in to Spikes but my Self."[21]

In 1792 Revere volunteered to recast the bell for his church. Aaron Hobart of Abington was one of the few American bell founders at a time when most bells were ordered from England. Revere learned the rudiments of his new trade from a son and an employee of Hobart. Bell casting required extensive scientific knowledge of metals, mastery of acoustics and construction techniques to assure the proper tone for bells of various sizes, and practical knowledge of bell ringing. Reverend William Bentley of Salem visited Revere's foundry in August 1792 and "saw the preparation" for the casting of the New Brick Church bell, "the *first attempt in the Town of Boston.*" In his diary, Bentley recorded the results of Revere's first try at bell casting one month later: "The sound is not clear and prolonged, from the lips to the crown shrill." Revere apparently improved because Revere and Son manufactured nearly four hundred bells between 1792 and 1828.[22]

In bell casting, as in the manufacture of ordnance and ship fittings, Revere took an inordinate pride in his work that sometimes caused him to interpret customers' complaints as attacks on his honor. In 1802 Benjamin Heywood, Samuel Flagg, and Abel Stowell, members of a church committee that purchased a bell in Worcester, complained that Revere's bell "cannot be heard at a proper distance." In reply to their "obliging and Candid Letter of June 29," Revere condescendingly remarked: "The Various Causes assigned among the ignorant 'conjectures' are natural. . . . My ideas of the Philosophy [of sound] would take me more time to explain, than your patience would admit of." Messrs. Heywood, Flagg, and Stowell did not appreciate Revere's lecture on the theory of sound and responded that they assumed they were addressing a person who "would consider his honour and integrity as a faithful workman engaged to make his work acceptable to his employers, at least so far, as to examine into any defects complained of . . . and instead of meeting our letter with a sneer, would have pointed out some method of removing our complaints." On August 30 Revere addressed what he perceived as an attack on his honor in Heywood, Flagg, and Stowell's "very extraordinary letter" of August 25: "You are the first persons who ever charged me with deceiving them, or with want of Honour, or Integrity in business, and I despise the man who would charge me with either." In a calmer tone, he reminded them that they had ample opportunity to "have disputed the sound" of the bell when they heard it at his furnace. He claimed that their complaint was the first Revere and Son had ever received, and he closed with another lecture on the theory of sound and a reminder of the terms of payment.[23]

Revere's rising status in the business community was accompanied by growing respect from friends and strangers who turned to him for his sound advice and his favors. Dr. Silvester Gardiner, an exiled Boston Tory living in Poole, England, in 1785, offered to sell his Boston house to Revere and "to render you or any of my old friends in Boston every Service in my Power, altho we should not as you say agree in Politicks; that ought not to make any difference between gentlemen of liberal sentiments." Thomas Wadsworth, "Banished . . . from Civil Society" in Edge Hill, South Carolina, begged Revere to write "and tell those affairs you think I wish to know." In July 1785 the slave owner Wadsworth responded to Revere's apparent antislavery views, writing: "Suppose you will ask where it will put my Slaves I answer I have nothing to say on that subject now only they are black and therefore ought aright to be Slaves but don't ask me any more of these questions." Possibly Revere influenced Wadsworth, who, "induced from Motives of Humanity," freed his slaves and placed them under the care of the Society of Friends by the terms of his will in 1799. In 1798 Susanna Cox asked Revere to recommend her son to Stephen Higginson, agent for the ship *Herald:* "I doubt not from the goodness of your Heart you will encourage the ambition of a youth who wishes to number himself with the patriotic few."[24]

Reverend Thomas Shreve, an Episcopal clergyman, formerly of Boston but living in Parrsboro, Nova Scotia, in 1789, relied on Revere's friendship and discretion in a very delicate matter. Shreve's wife had given birth to a child while staying with the Reveres in Boston. The child was fathered by another man, and Shreve wanted Revere to "collect every circumstance of this poor unfortunate woman's conduct . . . as to enable me to sue a Divorce." Shreve asked Revere for his wife's delivery date, the name of "the Vile character she last lived with," and any other details that would assist "in preventing my and my children's ruin." Although Mrs. Shreve complained to her husband "that she had been used very ill by Colonel Revere," Shreve assured Revere, "I hope I shall not be troubled with her falsehood."[25]

Of all the individuals who valued Revere's qualities as a friend, benefactor, and model republican, Thomas and Ann Ramsden were perhaps the most frequent and grateful recipients of Revere's benevolence. Over a period of nearly eight years, Captain Thomas Ramsden, a merchant whose business had taken him from Boston to Paris, asked Paul Revere for a variety of favors, confident that he could depend on his old friend's integrity, business acumen, and disinterested friendship. In December 1796 Ramsden asked Revere to try to reform his prodigal nephew and "bring back this youth from any slips he has made." Ramsden continued: "Instill into him my amiable friend those principles of integrity and honor befitting a man and instruct him in those rights appertaining to the same. Make Vanish if possible only Ideas he may have adopted contrary to a *true Republican*. In Short my Dear Friend make him *think* as you do and I ask no more for he will then be what I want him."[26]

One year later, Ramsden and his wife needed Revere's help in extricating Ramsden from ruin. Before leaving Boston, Ramsden had left books, business papers, and household possessions in the care of his clerk, Thomas Woodhead. He had also left Woodhead a blank power of attorney with instructions to fill in the name of Harrison Gray Otis, John Page, or Paul Revere. Like Ramsden's nephew, Woodhead had succumbed to the temptations of vice. He had left his residence with the Reveres to live with a "Vile woman" whom Revere claimed was "his ruin" and "got connected with a Set of Men who took every advantage of Him." In 1797 Woodhead died with nearly $30,000 in demands on his estate. A few years earlier, Woodhead had written in his name and the name of Captain Ramsden's dissolute nephew, Thomas, on Ramsden's power of attorney, which, if upheld, could make Captain Ramsden liable for Woodhead's debts. Over the next several years, Revere, armed with a power of attorney from Ramsden, worked tirelessly to straighten out Ramsden's affairs. He gave Ramsden legal advice, sent a trunk of the Ramsdens' belonging to Mrs. Ramsden in England, did his best to collect debts owed to his friend, and tried to sell some of the Ramsdens' land in Vermont.[27]

Ann Ramsden thanked Revere for his "very *true* friendship, at a season, when no human being stepped forth, to stemm the torrent of villainy which appeared against us" and for his "kind attention in writing so frequently upon our concerns." Writing from Paris in 1801, Thomas Ramsden hoped that "it will one day be in my power" to make returns on the debt he owed Revere. Ramsden appreciated Revere's advice on business and political affairs and his work on his behalf. Most of all, Ramsden looked forward to seeing and talking to Revere after a long absence: "What pleasure I should feel in telling you old stories of Europe and listening to your instructive remarks and observations."[28]

The decade of the 1790s was one of incessant activity for Revere. In addition to his businesses, he became heavily involved in civic affairs. He served on several town meeting committees, including one to repeal laws against the theater in 1792; as Suffolk County coroner from 1796 to 1801; and as president of the Boston Board of Health from 1799 to 1801. He was a founder of the Massachusetts Mutual Fire Insurance Company in 1798 and a member of the Massachusetts Humane Society and the Charitable Fire Society. He continually worked to enlarge and refine his views through a course of self-education, subscribing to the *Federal Orrery, Massachusetts Magazine,* and the Boston Library Society.[29]

All of Revere's activities in his public and private life were part of a larger goal to practice the principles of true republicanism. He kept a vigilant and often critical eye on business and political developments, and as his correspondence reveals, he was disturbed by evidence of moral decline in his society. Revere eventually found a comfortable and respectable position in his society but only against a background of political disharmony and competing visions of republican society that divided family, friends, and economic and social institutions.[30]

Revere's faith in the Constitution as the best means to secure the future of republican society had already separated him from his New York friends and fellow Sons of Liberty John Lamb and Hugh Hughes, leaders in New York's strong Anti-Federalist organization. By 1792 James Madison and Thomas Jefferson were troubled by Hamilton's policies on federal funding and assumption of the states' debts and a charter for the Bank of the United States. Then, the French Revolution expanded into a European war between England, the great enemy of the American Republic, and France, America's war-time ally and sister republic. For the rest of the decade, Federalists and Republicans, as those opposed to Federalist "corruption" called themselves, battled over economic and foreign policy but most of all over their social vision for sustaining the republican revolution. By choosing to support the Federalist Party, Paul Revere committed himself to an image of the ideal society that separated him from those who had once shared his ideals: fellow artisans, former Sons of Liberty, brother Masons, and cousin Benjamin Hichborn.[31]

On December 30, 1791, the Boston town meeting appointed a committee of twenty-five citizens, including several prominent merchants and political leaders and the artisan leaders Paul Revere, John Lucas, and Benjamin Austin Jr. to report on the divisive issue of whether to change the form of town government. Proponents of more efficient town government advocated a town council, composed of the selectmen and representatives chosen annually by the people, to take over the legislative functions of the town meeting. A "Correspondent" in the *Independent Chronicle*, speaking in opposition, warned that "No wise man, nor any wise community, will ever put their most important concerns unnecessarily into the care of others." "A Mechanick and Friend to the Principles of '75" exhorted his "Brother Mechanicks": "Arouse! Shake off your Enchantment, and retain your Liberties!" by voting against the changes in town government and consigning the plan "to those regions where all is darkness and night eternal." On January 19, 1792, one of those "Brother Mechanicks," Paul Revere, defended the committee's report in favor of abolishing the town meeting. The chief opponents of the plan were Perez Morton, Revere's customer, fellow member of the North End Caucus, and former Masonic brother at St. Andrew's Lodge; and Benjamin Austin Jr., strenuous defender of democratic republicanism.[32]

In his speech, Revere outlined a vision of republicanism that clashed with that of Benjamin Austin Jr. He listed several problems that the town meeting was incapable of handling: The poor had been "greatly wronged" by the forestalling of firewood, mechanics "suffered greatly" by competition from "badly made" and underpriced "Country wares," streets "were always broken up," and "the Laws in their present State" were too inefficient to control the migration of "Negroes . . . Vagrants, etc." into Boston. Revere's main argument for replacing the town meeting with a town council was that the proposed council was modeled on the republican principles of representation that he admired in the federal and state governments. Such a government where *Virtue and patriotism* are the only guide . . . that lead to place and office," where town council elections would be based on "numbers, and not property," and where a Bill of Rights protected the people from unjust laws was the best system to "Remedy the Evils without infringeing or abridging the Liberties of this People." Where Benjamin Austin Jr. upheld democracy as the solution to the problems of his society, Paul Revere saw democracy as the problem and republican representation as the solution. Austin, however, prevailed on January 26, when Boston voters defeated the reform proposal by a vote of 701 to 517. In the future, both men would consider themselves spokesmen for Boston's artisans, but their definitions of "artisan republicanism" were radically different.[33]

On January 25, 1793, Bostonians held a celebration in honor of the French Revolution, but as Reverend William Bentley observed on March 25, the "melancholy news" of the beheading of King Louis XVI was "regretted most sincerely by all thinking people." By their actions, Bentley believed "the french loose much of their influence upon the hearts of the Americans by this event." Benjamin Austin remained an ardent supporter of the French Republic through his articles in the *Independent Chronicle* and as an organizer of Boston's Constitutional Society, one of the many "Democratic Societies" established to support the French Republic and to protect "the spirit of freedom and equality as eclipsed by the pride of wealth and the arrogance of power" in the American Republic. But Massachusetts Federalists lost their initial enthusiasm because of the growing radicalism and violence in France; French Ambassador Edmund Genet's bold attempt to enlist American privateers in the French cause, in violation of President Washington's neutrality policy; and the fear that the self-created "Democratic Societies" modeled on the Jacobin Club of Paris would unleash similar forces of anarchy in the United States.[34]

In January 1794 James Madison proposed that Congress increase duties on shipping and merchandise from countries that had no commercial treaties with the United States. The target of Madison's legislation was Great Britain, and it was part of his and Thomas Jefferson's vision of constructing a truly republican political economy to replace Alexander Hamilton's slavish imitation of England. Madison and Jefferson hoped to revive American virtue by encouraging commercial agriculture and household manufactures and by a foreign policy that would draw America closer to her sister republic in France. In February 1794 Benjamin Austin Jr. urged his fellow citizens assembled in the Boston town meeting to sanction Madison's legislation. Once again, Boston artisans would have to choose between rival political ideologies.[35]

The proponents of Madison's trade resolutions included Benjamin Austin Jr. and Perez Morton, both of whom had opposed Revere on the issue of abolishing the Boston town meeting in 1792; Dr. Charles Jarvis, whom Revere had lauded as "this Consistent Republican" for his eloquent defense of the reform of town government; and Thomas Crafts, Revere's brother Son of Liberty and longtime Masonic brother at St. Andrew's Lodge. They hoped that merchants and mechanics would stand behind the legislation as a means of ensuring a favorable balance of trade and promoting domestic manufactures. Benjamin Russell allowed the pages of his *Columbian Centinel,* formerly the *Massachusetts Centinel,* to be used as a forum from which opponents of Madison's proposal could rally Boston artisans to join merchants in maintaining cordial relations with Great Britain as the best means to protect their interests. After initially approving the trade resolutions, the Boston town meeting decided it was "inexpedient . . . to declare any opinion . . . but rather to leave the whole subject to Congress." "A Citizen" heartily endorsed the decision, predicting "that when the merchants and mechanic professions have time to deliberate, they will see their best interest, and pursue them."[36]

While Benjamin Austin Jr. used the *Independent Chronicle* and Benjamin Russell used the *Columbian Centinel* to debate the merits of the French Revolution, Madison's trade resolutions, and John Jay's treaty with England, Paul Revere had already concluded that it was in the artisans' "best interest" to affiliate with the Federalist Party. In light of his political differences with Benjamin Austin, Revere probably relished J. S. J. Gardiner's withering description of Austin as "lank Honestus with his lanthorn jaws," whose writings were "a hodge-podge of lies, slander and nonsense." Perhaps he felt a twinge of remorse that Dr. Charles Jarvis, whom he had once admired, was now a leader of a party whose members dared to call themselves Republicans, when it was so obvious to Revere that they were subverting republican principles. Although politics now separated him from Thomas Crafts, it still must have been difficult for Revere to see his old friend ridiculed as "Great Justice Crafts, great Faction's sapient son,/Who holds of sense a gill, of zeal a ton." Regardless of the respect he may have had toward Dr. Jarvis or the lingering friendship he felt toward Thomas Crafts, Paul Revere could not shake the fear of the social disorder that he and other Federalists attributed to the "Jacobins" or "Democrats." That fear was surely a factor when Paul Revere, Benjamin Russell, and other master mechanics and manufacturers decided to create a permanent association to further their interests—an association whose members did not include Benjamin Austin Jr., artisan leader and Democrat.[37]

On December 31, 1794, an unsigned notice in the *Columbian Centinel* invited "the Tradesmen, Mechanics, and Manufacturers of this town and vicinity, who keep apprentices" to meet at the Green Dragon Tavern "for the purpose of consulting on measures for petitioning the General Court, to revise and amend the Law respecting apprentices." The traditional story is that the author of the unsigned notice was Henry Purkitt, a prosperous cooper and Freemason, and that Paul Revere was insulted that he, one of Boston's most prominent mechanics, was not consulted. The error was quickly rectified at the first meeting, when Revere was appointed to chair the committee charged with drafting a petition to the General Court. Henceforth, Paul Revere would take a leading role in the establishment of the Boston Mechanic Association and serve as its first president, from 1795 to 1798. In their constitution, the members proclaimed their pride in their collective identity as ideal republican citizens who would continue to use the "mechanic powers" that "have ameliorated the condition of its citizens." But the membership requirements and the original impetus for establishing their organization ensured that the Boston Mechanic Association would not speak for all mechanics.[38]

Revere's experience with David Moseley, an incorrigible apprentice, had given him sufficient evidence of moral decline in his society and the consequent need for master mechanics and manufacturers to reassert the principles of virtue, order, and deference. In 1772 Moseley ran away to sea, and Revere recovered his apprentice only after suing the mariner who had "seduced" Moseley to leave. In light of Moseley's subsequent behavior, Revere may have wished he had never sued for Moseley's return. In 1776 Moseley married Revere's sister Elizabeth, who was several years older than her husband, and thereafter legal records and Revere's cash and memoranda books attest to Moseley's profligate spending, alcoholism, and general bad character.[39]

The members of the Boston Mechanic Association were among the community's wealthier master mechanics and manufacturers, persons "of good moral character," and men who had fulfilled their contracts as apprentices and wanted to make sure that apprentices continued to defer to their masters. Although the association was ostensibly nonpartisan, Federalists dominated its ranks. Early members included Revere's customer Zachariah Hicks, a saddler and a "firm and undeviating disciple of Washington and Adams"; David Cobb, an edge-tool maker and "a sturdy Federalist"; and John Bray, a culler and packer of fish and a Federalist who lost a patronage post under General Benjamin Lincoln when Lincoln was succeeded by a Democratic-Republican. Other members included Revere's son and sons-in-law, Paul Revere Jr. and Amos and Jedediah Lincoln; and his customers Edmund Hartt, builder of the frigate *Constitution,* and the hatters Thomas Stoddard Boardman and William Williams. Federalists or not, these were hard-working, successful, self-made men who shared Revere's belief that journeymen and apprentices must continue to observe the principles of virtue, order, and deference that had led to their masters' success.[40]

Neither the mercantile community nor the General Court supported the association's request for a charter of incorporation, despite their members' wealth, respectability, and Federalist credentials. None of the twenty "principal merchants" whom Benjamin Russell, Paul Revere, and Edward Tuckerman solicited as allies in their cause responded, although at least six of the merchants were Revere's customers, business associates, or brother Masons. The General Court, which readily granted the association's request for legislation tightening a master's control over apprentices, rejected requests for incorporation five times before finally granting a charter in 1806. Both Benjamin Russell, who led the fight for incorporation, and Joseph T. Buckingham, the chronicler of the organization's early history, believed that the mercantile and political elite, who may have shared the Federalist beliefs of the organization's leadership, feared that the establishment of an independent mechanics' interest threatened their political and social dominance. Russell blamed "avaricious and narrow-minded men" who saw in the Boston Mechanic Association "a combination of sordid Tradesmen, associated to impose on the publick, and to extract exorbitant prices for labour and fabricks." In their January 15, 1799, petition to the General Court, the association also attributed the failure of their earlier attempt to secure a charter to "the state of political parties in our country," when "associations of almost every description were considered as *rallying points* of sedition."[41]

When Paul Revere turned down another term as president in 1798, the association was in a state of decline, plagued by an inability to retain old members or attract new ones. Without a firm legal status, the association could carry out few of its goals, including arbitration of disputes among members, financial assistance to needy members, and loans to encourage mechanical inventions. Revere's decision to step down as president may have been influenced by the dramatic increase in demand for cannon from his foundry as a result of the Quasi-War with France. But he may also have been frustrated by the inability of the Boston Mechanic Association to represent "artisan republicanism" when artisans were divided by occupational interests, economic status, and politics.[42]

Boston artisans recovered some of their unity in January 1800, when they marched in a procession honoring the memory of the recently deceased George Washington. The role of the mechanic association in organizing the artisans' parade and other tributes to Washington revived membership, and a new constitution that emphasized the organization's charitable functions and prohibited political discussions may have placated critics. Paul Revere remained a member of the association until his death, but after 1799 he played almost no leadership role except on May 2, 1806, when he was chosen moderator of the first meeting of the newly incorporated Massachusetts Charitable Mechanic Association. The renamed organization relaxed its rules on apprenticeship and relinquished its original goal of mediating disputes between members or between members and the public. It was now a less threatening benevolent organization devoted to the education and assistance of its members and the advancement of American manufactures. If Revere was disappointed that the Massachusetts Charitable Mechanic Association had abandoned some of its lofty goals, he could nonetheless take some comfort in the fact that the organization vowed to practice the principles of benevolence and enlightenment that he held dear.[43]

Freemasonry offered Revere a more encouraging opportunity to promote and protect the republican principles of honor, benevolence, harmony, and social order that seemed in danger in the 1790s. Amid the partisan strife of the day, Freemasons called upon all men of virtue, regardless of rank, religion, or party, to unite in brotherly love and practice ideals that would strengthen the republic. In March 1792 Revere's efforts to restore harmony among Freemasons and prepare Freemasonry to spread republican principles resulted in the creation of a new Grand Lodge uniting the Ancient Masons of the Massachusetts Grand Lodge and the Modern Masons of St. John's Grand Lodge. On December 8, 1794, after John Warren declined the office, Paul Revere was chosen Grand Master of the Massachusetts Grand Lodge and served for three years, the maximum term allowed. On July 4, 1795, Grand Master Paul Revere addressed an assembly of his Masonic brethren, Governor Samuel Adams, distinguished guests, and fellow citizens at the dedication of the new State House, designed by Charles Bulfinch and built by Revere's son-in-law and Masonic brother Amos Lincoln: "Worshipfull Brethren. I congratulate you on this auspicious day:—When the Arts and Sciences are establishing themselves in our happy country, a Country distinguished from the rest of the World, by being a Government of Laws, where Liberty has found a safe and secure abode, and where her sons are determined to support and protect her."[44]

Revere's final address as Grand Master reflected his happiness over the spread of Freemasonry "to every part of the Globe" and his pride over his role in doubling the number of lodges under his jurisdiction. But his concern with the conduct of subordinate lodges and the quality of Masonic candidates, expressed in his final speech and in several actions taken during his term as Grand Master, suggest that Freemasonry was not immune from the political disputes of the day. By November 1795 Reverend William Bentley complained: "The business of our Lodge cannot be transacted without the narrow prejudices of private life." Although Revere, a firm Federalist, and Bentley, an equally staunch Republican, never let political differences affect their friendship, their Masonic brethren in the years following Revere's term as Grand Master seem to have forgotten that brotherly love must override all differences of opinion.[45]

Suspicions that Republicans were taking over Freemasonry began with the election of Josiah Bartlett to succeed Paul Revere as Grand Master in 1797. Bartlett had held no posts under Revere, and during his term seven of the eight lodges he chartered were in Republican towns. In September 1798 the *Columbian Centinel* reported that "the *Masons* have been charged to have installed two Right Worshipful *Democrats*" at the Meridian Lodge in Watertown. The "virulence of invective," as Reverend Bentley called it, reached a frenzy between 1798 and 1799, when Reverend Jedediah Morse of Charlestown, an orthodox Calvinist and Federalist, and Bentley, a liberal Unitarian and Republican, waged a rhetorical war over Morse's attempt to link Bentley and other American Masons with the Bavarian Illuminati as part of a worldwide conspiracy against liberty and religion. Massachusetts Masons restored harmony and revived their patriotic image on February 11, 1800, when 1,600 of them—Federalists and Republicans—marched in a procession honoring the memory of George Washington, their late president and Masonic brother. After the procession, William Bentley and Paul Revere, separated by politics but united by Masonic love, dined together.[46]

The political disharmony of the late 1790s was distressing to Revere, but it did not distract him from his goal of acquiring prosperity and respectability and serving the public good. On March 11, 1800, he informed Representative Harrison Gray Otis that "after a great many tryals and very considerable expense," he had perfected the technique of melting copper and hammering it hot. Revere hoped that Otis could secure congressional sanction for his plan to have the federal government send him copper ore from Maryland and New Jersey and pay his expenses so "I would build Furnaces and endeavour to make myself Master of the Business." On January 17, 1801, Revere contemplated the possibility that the federal government might be turned over from the Federalist John Adams to the Republican Thomas Jefferson. How that would affect Revere's business and his life was as yet unknown, but as he commented to Harrison Gray Otis, "What a dreadful change in Politicks."[47]

CHAPTER ELEVEN

"IN MY LAST STAGE, HOW BLEST AM I, TO FIND CONTENT AND PLENTY BY"

I N 1798 PAUL REVERE, respected businessman and citizen, received the additional honor of historical recognition when he provided some "facts, and Anecdotes, prior to the Battle of Lexington, which I do not remember to have seen in any history of the American Revolution" to Jeremy Belknap, the corresponding secretary of the Massachusetts Historical Society. Revere signed both his name and the signature "A Son of Liberty of the year 1775," with the instruction "do not print my name," but Belknap was sufficiently impressed by his narrative to publish it in the society's *Collections* in 1798 under the heading "A Letter from Col. Revere to the Corresponding Secretary." Belknap omitted Revere's grandiose introduction and his account of his activities as a courier before April 1775, but he kept Revere's self-congratulatory statement that he was offering a unique perspective "of some matters, of which no person but my self have documents, or knowledge," including observations on the conduct and character of the traitorous Dr. Benjamin Church. With the publication of Revere's letter, Belknap acknowledged that the historical contributions of Paul Revere were as worthy of veneration as those of Samuel Adams, John Adams, or John Hancock.[1]

Political events in 1798 brought temporary political prosperity to President John Adams and more lasting economic prosperity to Paul Revere. The publication of the XYZ Papers in April 1798 detailed the French government's request for a bribe from American envoys before opening negotiations over grievances arising from France's seizure of American vessels and confiscation of their cargoes. In the ensuing atmosphere of patriotism and war hysteria, Congress revoked all treaties with France, appropriated money for the completion of frigates first authorized in 1794, and approved a system of harbor defenses, a provisional army of 10,000 men to be raised at the president's request, and a tripling in size of the regular army. Petitions of support for the president streamed in from around the country, including one from the Massachusetts General Court on June 7, 1798, that pledged "to support every measure" of the federal government "to protect the commerce and preserve the Independence of our country" and another from the Massachusetts Grand Lodge, whose members put aside their prohibition of political discussions within "this ancient Fraternity" to join their fellow citizens in support of the president "when the illiberal attacks of a foreign Enthusiast, aided by the unfounded prejudices of his followers, are tending to embarrass the public mind."[2]

The Quasi-War with France in 1798 more than doubled ordnance production at Revere's foundry over the previous year, allowing Revere to earn profits and make a patriotic contribution to his country's defense. Defense preparations also created a demand for copper sheathing to protect the hulls of the United States Navy's vessels just as Great Britain restricted copper exportation in order to meet its own wartime demands. An American entrepreneur who could produce sheet copper comparable to English manufactures could make an immense profit, but it was a risky enterprise. A copper mill required a significant investment of money for equipment and an equally significant investment of time in mastering the technique of rolling copper into sheets. Paul Revere was not the first American to attempt such an undertaking, but he was the first to succeed.[3]

At the age of sixty-five, Revere launched his most daring business venture. In February 1800 he informed Secretary of the Navy Benjamin Stoddard that he had already manufactured over 23,000 weight of copper bolts and spikes for the United States Navy and merchants in Boston and Salem, and he was confident that "if government will provide oar and expenses," he would build a furnace and "make my self Master of the business." In May, Revere visited Stoddard in Philadelphia, where naval constructor Joshua Humphreys promised to send him some Maryland ore for a trial smelting. Revere smelted and refined the copper ore and rolled it into sheets using a silversmithing mill, and on January 17, 1801, he announced his readiness to manufacture sheet copper for the United States government. He bought land on the east branch of the Neponset River in Canton, Massachusetts, for six thousand dollars from Messrs. Robbins, Leonard, and Kinsley. Previously the site of the Revolutionary gunpowder mill he helped design in 1776, Revere's copper mill was more recently part of Leonard and Kinsley's ironworks. On January 13, 1801, Revere asked Eben Lee to buy rolls for his copper rolling mill at a mill in Maidenhead, England, and engage in some industrial espionage: "If you can git into the Works I wish you to observe their works and how they heat their Copper." All that remained, as he wrote Stoddard, was for the government to keep its promise of advancing him $10,000 "to assist in procuring a mill and utensils for rolling copper . . . as building the above works will be a very great expense."[4]

In May 1800, while meeting with Secretary Stoddard and Joshua Humphreys in Philadelphia, Revere sat for a portrait by the French artist Charles Balthazar Julien Fevret de Saint-Memin. The man that Saint-Memin depicted, in his dress and demeanor, was a prosperous and dignified man of consequence in his community who had long ago discarded the plain, unbuttoned linen shirt and leather mechanic's vest that he wore when he sat for John Singleton Copley more than thirty years earlier. The Reveres had also outgrown their modest home in North Square. In the United States Direct Tax of 1798, Revere was listed as the owner and occupant of a three-story wooden dwelling on Clark's Court measuring 630 square feet with seventeen windows situated on 4,730 square feet of land with a barn 400 feet square, valued at $2,000. By 1800 Revere had sold his North Square home to John Hunting and bought the Newman Greenough house on the corner of Charter and the present Hanover Street in the North End. Although the three-story brick mansion house boasted a garden and trees, it certainly did not rival the grounds of the old Hutchinson mansion, but the Reveres filled their new home with fashionable furniture and Revere's stylish silver.[5]

While Paul Revere's fortunes were rising, John Adams's were falling. Despite his administration's favorable peace negotiations with France, Adams could not overcome the defection of the Hamiltonian wing of his party, which opposed his policy toward France; the disaffection of Federalists, who protested the imposition of taxes to support the provisional army; or Republican charges that he was responsible for the Alien and Sedition Acts and the nation's first political army. In the presidential election of 1800, Adams received sixty-five electoral votes to seventy-three votes each for Thomas Jefferson and Aaron Burr. On February 17, 1801, the House of Representatives gave the election to Thomas Jefferson.[6]

Dr. Nathaniel Ames, who had spent the past two years reviling the Federalists for the Alien and Sedition Acts, the Direct Tax of 1798, and the creation of "a standing army of mercenaries," welcomed in his diary the dawn of the nineteenth century and the election of Thomas Jefferson: "December 31, 1800. Here ends the 18th Century. The 19th begins with a fine clear morning wind at S. W.; and the political horizon affords as fine a prospect under Jefferson's administration, with returning harmony with France—with the irresistible propagation of the Rights of Man, the eradication of hierarchy, oppression, superstition and tyranny over the world."[7]

Federalists contemplating the country's future under Jefferson feared the consequences of what they considered to be the president's dangerous enthusiasm and his naïveté about men and politics. Fisher Ames did not share his brother Nathaniel's gleeful anticipation of the golden age of Jeffersonian republicanism. On April 16, 1802, Ames warned Theodore Dwight: "The next thing will be, as in France, anarchy: then Jacobinism, organized with energy enough to plunder and shed blood." Ames continued: "The only chance of safety lies in the revival of

10. When Paul Revere sat for his portrait by Charles Balthazar Julien Fevret de Saint-Memin (1770–1852) in Philadelphia c. 1800, he was transformed from the artisan that John Singleton Copley captured at his workbench to a prosperous entrepreneur about to open the country's first successful copper-rolling mill. Mezzotint of Revere engraved by Saint-Memin from his chalk drawing. Courtesy, Paul Revere Memorial Association. Gift of Miss Marion Cole.

the energy of the Federalists *who alone will or can preserve liberty, property, or Constitution.*"[8]

Paul Revere soon joined in the Federalist denunciation of the Republican party for destroying the Republican principles and institutions that the Federalists believed they had created. But in the spring of 1801 he was more worried that the Jefferson administration would not honor the previous administration's promise of support for his copper mill. When, in the spring of 1801, naval agent Stephen Higginson refused to advance Revere his loan without a new government order, Revere requested retiring Secretary of the Navy Benjamin Stoddard to issue the order, explaining, "I have plunged my self into a large debt." On April 21, 1801, Revere asked Attorney General Levi Lincoln, prominent Republican and brother of his sons-in-laws Amos and Jedediah Lincoln, to intercede on his behalf with Acting Secretary of the Navy Samuel Smith. When Smith claimed that no law authorized his department to lend money for the erection of copper works, Revere replied that it was "exceeding hard" that an individual should suffer "when he is exerting him self for the good of the Government." Finally, on June 29, 1801, after Revere had spent "at least $15,000" of his own money, the Navy Department agreed to advance him $10,000. On May 24, 1802, Revere apprised Secretary of the Navy Robert Smith that he had completed enough copper sheets to repay the $10,000 government loan.[9]

The lives of each of Revere's sons in the New Republic were affected by their birth order, the social status and profitability of each of their father's businesses, and individual circumstances. Paul Jr., who grew up as the son of a master gold-smith and whose apprenticeship with his father was interrupted by the Revolutionary War, had neither the educational nor the professional advantages of his younger half-brothers. Marriage at the age of twenty-two and a family of twelve children born over a twenty-year period brought a financial burden that impaired his ability to achieve economic independence from his father. In 1798 he, his wife, and seven children were living in a brick dwelling on Fleet Street owned by Perez Morton, and Paul Sr. often paid his oldest son's taxes and rent throughout his adulthood. Paul Revere Jr. followed in his father's footsteps as a goldsmith and bell founder, a Freemason, and a member of the Massachusetts Charitable Mechanic Association, but he never emerged from his father's formidable shadow. In 1801 Paul Jr. left Paul Revere and Sons to operate his own bell foundry while continuing to work as a goldsmith until 1806. When Paul Revere Jr. died of consumption on January 16, 1813, at the age of fifty-three, he had long ceased to be his father's business heir. That role went to his much younger half-brother, Joseph Warren Revere, who operated Revere and Son with his nephews, Thomas Stevens Eayres Jr. and Paul Revere III, the son of Paul Revere Jr.[10]

Joshua Revere, Paul and Rachel Revere's first child, had advantages that were unavailable to Paul Jr. Joshua did not attend a writing school in preparation for a mechanic's life. Instead, his father, who was making the transition from mechanic to merchant and manufacturer, sent him to Boston Latin. Whether Revere trained Joshua as a goldsmith is unknown, but he was associated with Revere and Son. Joshua Revere died on August 14, 1801, at the age of twenty-six, but he had already displayed attributes that might well have propelled him into the ranks of genteel society. In the words of his obituary writer in the *Columbian Centinel*: "It is but common justice to say, the deceased was a young gentleman, whose literary acquirements rendered him the instructive companion; whose native integrity made him the correct citizen; and whose spotless morals and amiable deportment, endeared him to all his acquaintance; and will embalm his memory."[11]

Of all Revere's sons, Joseph Warren Revere was the most intimately associated with his father's businesses, yet he managed to build an independent identity and reputation. Trained as a goldsmith by his father, Joseph Warren Revere became his father's partner in the foundry and copper mill in 1804. In 1804–5, he toured copper works in England, France, Holland, Denmark, and Sweden, sketching machinery, jotting down notes on production methods, and acquiring technological knowledge to improve Revere and Son's mastery of the copper business. Revere attributed much of the success of his foundry and copper mill to his son, and in 1811 he turned over the business to him. Joseph Warren Revere continued his father's and Dr. Joseph Warren's tradition of benevolence and public service. He was a Freemason, although he belonged to more fashionable lodges than Rising States, and a member of the Massachusetts Mechanic Association and Massachusetts Humane Society. After his father's death, he improved and expanded the business by merging with competitors and hiring outside experts like Frederick William Davis, a chemist who improved the efficiency of the copper refining process at the company's Point Shirley Works in Winthrop, Massachusetts. His business accomplishments and his marriage to Mary Robbins, daughter of Judge Edward Hutchinson Robbins and grandniece of Governor Thomas Hutchinson, brought Joseph Warren Revere wealth, political office, and entry into Boston's most genteel society.[12]

The profitability of Revere's post-Revolutionary businesses guaranteed that John Revere, the youngest child, would never have to make a silver teapot, cast a bell, or roll sheet copper. John Revere attended Boston Latin and the Independent School in Lexington. In 1807 he received a Bachelor of Arts degree from Harvard, where he studied with James Jackson, one of the most eminent physicians of the day, and in 1811 he received a medical degree from the University of Edinburgh. In the 1820s Dr. John Revere taught chemistry at the Maryland Institute and made valuable discoveries in applied chemistry, translated Magendie's *Summary of Physiology* and a collection of surgical essays by Baron Dominique Jean Larrey, chief surgeon to Napoleon, published several research articles, and served as coeditor of the *Maryland Medical Recorder* and vice president of the Medical Society of Maryland. His tenure as professor of the theory and practice of medicine at Jefferson Medical College in Philadelphia from 1831 to 1841 and at the medical school of the University of the City of New York (now New York University) from 1841 to his death in 1847 earned Dr. John Revere a reputation "as one of the best and most learned professors of medicine in the United States," according to the *Transactions of the American Medical Association* in 1850. A man of science, education, and devotion to humanity, Dr. John Revere exceeded all his father's unfulfilled aspirations to gentility.[13]

In August 1804 Paul Revere described the flourishing state of his business in a letter to his friend Thomas Ramsden: "I have spent for the last three years most of my time in the Country, where I have Mills for Rolling Sheets, and Bolts, Making

11. This pen-and-ink sketch, possibly by Paul Revere, depicts his copper mill and "dwelling house" in Canton, Massachusetts. Here, he carried on "a tolerable advantageous business" and enjoyed the charms of country life. Courtesy, Massachusetts Historical Society.

Spikes, etc. and every kind of copper fastning for Ships, it has got to be a tolerable advantageous business." While Joseph Warren Revere looked after the foundry in Boston, his father supervised the operation of the mill in Canton. After a gale on October 9, 1804, blew the roof off his foundry on Lynn Street, Revere combined the foundry and copper operations at his Canton mill, but he maintained a retail outlet in Boston. He and his family spent winters at their Charter Street home in Boston and summers in Canton.[14]

In their first three years of operation, Paul Revere and Son manufactured six thousand feet of copper sheathing for the dome of the Bulfinch State House, produced all the copper for the overhaul of the U.S.S. *Constitution,* and provided copper nails, bolts, spikes, and sheet copper for the United States Navy, shipbuilders, and merchants. In 1803 sales of sheet copper generated a gross revenue of $14,610.24. At their foundry, Revere and Son were equally busy, casting iron for the proprietors of the Charles River Bridge, ordnance for the state and federal government, and bells for ships, schoolhouses, and churches. Despite his complaints about the Jefferson administration's embargo policies in 1807–9, Revere and Son became a profitable business with customers in Massachusetts and also in New York, Baltimore, and Philadelphia.[15]

Throughout his operation of the Canton mill, Revere suffered from a shortage of raw copper or old sheet copper, the "rough materials" necessary for the manufacture of his products. In June 1803 he suggested to Navy Secretary Smith that "what is Stripped off Ships belonging to the Government, should be reserved to be worked over again" and that American ships in the Mediterranean stop at

Smyrna, where "copper is produced of the best sort," and buy copper to be brought back as ballast. He contacted firms and agents in Providence, New York, Philadelphia, and Leghorn, Italy, to scour the market for copper. In August 1803 he explained to Beck and Harvey of Philadelphia that he could not supply them with as large a quantity of bolts as they wanted because of the European war and consequent copper shortage unless they could "procure us Stock Old Copper of any kind, Old Stills, old Sheathing Copper; or any kind that has been worked."[16]

In 1807 Revere petitioned Congress for tariff legislation to encourage the domestic manufacture of copper by imposing a duty on imported sheet copper and removing the duty on old copper. Under the existing laws, as he complained to Secretary of the Treasury Albert Gallatin in April 1806, the collectors charged a duty on old copper, "which nearly amounts to a prohibition of that Article," and further injured the domestic production of sheet copper by charging no duty on competing new sheet copper from England. Revere bragged that Revere and Son "are the only persons in the United States" who had "accomplished the object" of manufacturing copper, "altho many have attempted it," and that they had "no doubt they can supply the whole quantity at present imported into the United States provided the government should give their support." Revere's cockiness and the appearance that he was seeking special privileges aroused the opposition of coppersmiths and braziers in Philadelphia and New York who feared that if Congress granted Revere's petition, it would reduce their supply of copper and damage their manufactures. On January 21, 1808, the Committee on Commerce and Manufactures of the United States Congress, influenced by the petitions of the coppersmiths and braziers, granted Revere's request that old copper be duty-free but refused to impose the duty on imported sheet copper.[17]

An abundant water supply was as necessary to Revere's mill as a steady copper supply. In October 1804 he sued Jonathan Leonard and Adam Kinsley, the iron manufacturers who had conveyed part of their property to him in 1801, for erecting dams that Revere believed "obstructed and diverted the water" from his copper mill to their ironworks. The Massachusetts Supreme Judicial Court unanimously ruled against Revere, and the wording of their decision suggested that they thought the suit was unwarranted. The court found no evidence of "interruption of the plaintiff's right" and stated that all he had to do was hoist the gates of the dam when he needed water for his slitting mill. He had "no right . . . to *command the defendants* to open the gates."[18]

Revere's dispute with Leonard and Kinsley did not end with their legal victory. In February 1808 Leonard and Kinsley petitioned the Canton selectmen to build a road through Revere's property, prompting a rather patronizing and imperious letter from Revere and Son to the selectmen. Confident of his status as a major taxpayer in Canton, Revere believed that the selectmen would not act on a petition "which prays that a Man's real estate which has cost at least $12,000 and where they have not land sufficient should have a Road made thro it; without informing the owners of it till within a few hours of the time they had set for viewing and laying it out." Surely, the selectmen would never grant the petition, "which will distress Industrious Men, Men who spend more real money in the Town of Canton, than any five men in it." He also charged that Leonard and Kinsley sought "to drive us from Canton, that they may purchase our Estate for less than nothing." Leonard and Kinsley did not ruin Revere, but the experience contributed to Revere's fear that dishonor and self-interest were becoming rampant in American society.[19]

As he entered a new century, Paul Revere was justifiably proud of the obstacles he had overcome to establish the first successful copper-rolling mill in the United States and hopeful about the economic future for himself and his family. He was less sanguine about broader social and political developments occurring during Jefferson's term of office. A letter he wrote in August 1804 to Thomas Ramsden briefly describing his "tolerable advantageous business" was largely a denunciation of political and social decline that he attributed to the Republicans. Repeating the sentiments of fellow Federalists John Adams, Fisher Ames, and Benjamin Lincoln, Revere condemned the French Revolution and, by implication, Republican support for France: "I was positively sure that *Liberty* and *Equality* in France, were mere names, and would only Serve to give France a Master, similar to the One She had before." He hoped "that this revolution will give greater stability to the Government . . . 'Tho I very much doubt it,—For man is an uneasy Animal."[20]

Thomas Ramsden had written to Revere asking for help in obtaining a position as American consul in Dunkerque. In his reply, Revere spoke as a true Federalist, indicting the "Democrats" for corrupting republicanism by introducing the pernicious practices of equality and partisanship: "I very much doubt my influence with the present Administration. My sentiments differ very widely from theirs in politicks;—My friend, You know I was allways a warm *Republican;* I allways deprecated Democracy; as much as I did Aristocracy; Our Government is now compleately Democratic; they turn every person out of office who are not, nor will be of their way of thinking, and acting." Revere's cousin Benjamin Hichborn "was of their party, and it was said he had great influence," but after a paralytic stroke the Democrats "found he could do but little for them" and replaced Hichborn's nephew, Nathaniel Fosdick, as collector for the Port of Portland "for no other reason but because he was not a Democrat." Despite his distaste for the Jefferson administration and his lack of political influence, Revere promised to do what he could for Ramsden by using his connection to Attorney General Levi Lincoln, with whom "I may possibly have some little influence . . . as two of his brothers married two of my daughters."[21]

Jefferson abolished internal taxes, reduced the size of government, and purchased the vast Louisiana Territory in 1803, all of which seemed to be fulfillments of his party's rhetoric to institute "a wise and frugal government," restore republican simplicity and virtue, and establish an agricultural empire for a nation of yeomen farmers, who were "the most valuable citizens" because "they are the most vigorous, the most independent, the most virtuous, and they are tied to their country and wedded to its liberty and interests by the most lasting bands." Through their adroit use of the party press, the Republicans issued an appealing rhetoric, calling for the abolition of Alexander Hamilton's corrupt Federalist political economy, which they charged favored the interests of merchants and speculators. The establishment of a Republican political economy would promote equality of opportunity for a nation of virtuous and independent citizens.[22]

By 1801 Republicans outnumbered Federalists 69 to 36 in the United States House of Representatives and 18 to 13 in the Senate. In the presidential election of 1804, Jefferson carried Massachusetts. Within the state, Massachusetts Republicans toppled the Federalists from power by capturing the legislature in 1806 and the governorship in 1807. In December 1807 Massachusetts Federalist Christopher Gore lamented the victory of the party of "demogogues, democrats, and disorganizers" and predicted the future state of affairs under the Republicans would be "as bad as Vice and Folly can make them." The near-hysteria of Federalist Party leaders as they pronounced the death of the republic might be dismissed as the rantings of disgruntled elites who were envious of the popularity of the Republicans and embittered by the expected loss of what they believed to be their legitimate role as leaders of their society. Yet, the professed ideals of the Republican Party, which on the surface might have seemed tailor-made for the socially ambitious Paul Revere, were as anathema to Revere as they were to Fisher Ames, Harrison Gray Otis, or Christopher Gore.[23]

By the time Jefferson assumed the presidency, the Republican Party had welcomed into its ranks ambitious, independent, hard-working mechanics and entrepreneurs, many of whom found their efforts at upward mobility stymied by a Federalist-dominated social structure. By encouraging the efforts of these men, as virtuous as Jefferson's beloved yeomen farmers, the Republicans would destroy the corrupt and enervating influence of Federalist economic policies, which favored the interests of merchants, speculators, "great landholders and monied men."[24]

In New York, tallow chandlers, shoemakers, hatters, tanners, and cartmen—men as proud of their mechanic's skills as Paul Revere—supported Republican candidates. George Warner, a sailmaker, James Cheetham, a former hatter turned editor and pamphleteer, and Matthew L. Davis, a printer who would become the object of Revere's wrath in 1803, gained prestige as members and leaders of Republican political organizations. New York's Republican mechanics represented their party's views, much like Paul Revere and the Federalist mechanics in Boston, in political meetings, Fourth of July oratory, speeches at the dedication of public buildings, newspaper essays, and pamphlets.[25]

In the Maine district of Massachusetts, the Republicans attracted a youthful population who had emigrated to the frontier region of New England in search of cheap land, religious freedom, and other opportunities not as easily available in more Federalist-dominated parts of the state. Henry Dearborn, who was as hungry for economic and social distinction as Paul Revere, found a variety of opportunities in Kennebec County, Maine, where he settled after his Continental Army service. He abandoned his pre-Revolutionary medical practice for more risky but potentially more profitable commercial ventures, including real estate, lumbering operations, and the ownership of a wharf, ferry, and store. Dearborn also abandoned the Federalists, who had appointed him United States marshall for the District of Maine in 1790 and whom he represented in Congress from 1794 to 1797. By the early 1800s Dearborn had helped transform Maine into a Republican stronghold, and he was rewarded for his efforts by appointment as Jefferson's secretary of war from 1801 to 1809, collector of the Port of Boston during the embargo crisis, and major general of the United States Army during "Mr. Madison's" War of 1812.[26]

For all the superficial resemblance between Paul Revere and the Republican mechanics and entrepreneurs, there were real and perceived differences that kept Revere wedded to the Federalist Party. Revere's superior economic status separated him from the tallow chandlers, hatters, and other lesser mechanics in New York's Republican Party and from the journeymen at his Canton mill. There is no evidence of an apprenticeship system or system of specialization at Revere's mill. Instead, the five to twelve workers that Revere employed between 1802 and 1809 were shifted from one area of production to another as needed. Revere's workers could not count on their employer's progression from apprentice to master mechanic but would most likely remain journeymen. But it was more than an economic gulf that separated Revere from the self-made men of the Republican Party and the workers at his mill. The division was the result of Revere's sense that the mechanic members of the Republican Party and his employees were not observing the Federalist ideals of hard work, temperance, and deference to authority that he thought were responsible for his own success. Those traits were certainly not exhibited by his workers, who had a remarkable record of tardiness, absenteeism, drunkenness, and rapid turnover. In 1803 Revere complained to Joshua Humphreys: "We are obliged to pick up *hands* as we can and as they begin to know something of the Business they leave us."[27] Revere's experiences as an employer and his observations on American society convinced him that his countrymen were being seduced by the Republican Party's ideas about equality and an innate benevolent nature of humans. Perhaps, too, he was also aware that his own ambition was a passion that must be tamed, and that only the Federalists could preserve republican virtue and social order.[28]

One of the central tenets of both Freemasonry and republicanism was benevolence, and Revere believed that the Republicans were neglecting this important societal bond.[29] When his son-in-law and former apprentice Thomas Stevens Eayres became mentally ill in the early 1790s, Revere moved his daughter and grandchildren into his home and sent his son-in-law to board in the country. After the death of Frances Revere Eayres in June 1799, Revere took responsibility for his grandchildren and for Eayres, whose relatives ignored Revere's repeated requests that they assume their family obligations. Revere seems to have been motivated not only out of duty to his late daughter and Eayres's deceased father, who was one of his Revolutionary associates, but out of benevolence toward a fellow human being. Although he complained about the cost of Eayres's care under Dr. Samuel Willard of Uxbridge, Revere did his best for his son-in-law, writing to Dr. Willard: "I highly approved of your putting him to work with your People, and I am sure your humanity will not suffer him to be pushed farther than he is able to bear. It was Dr. Danforth's Opinion, some years ago, that nothing but hard Labour, and Coarse living, could help him."[30]

On June 28, 1799, Matthew Livingston Davis of New York, Eayres's brother-in-law, claimed he was "willing to do all that I can [for Eayres], in justice to a young and increasing family." By 1802 Revere was tired of waiting for assistance and made more permanent arrangements for his son-in-law's care. He petitioned the Suffolk County Probate Court to declare Eayres *non compos mentis*, and the court appointed Revere's son-in-law Jedediah Lincoln as Eayres's guardian. Revere also discovered that Eayres's father had left his son a house, whose sale could provide sufficient funds for Eayres's care until Eayres's son was old enough to take responsibility. Revere fired off several irate letters to Eayres's family, most notably to Matthew Livingston Davis. When Davis, a member of the Tammany and Mechanics Society, organizer of the Society for Free Debate in 1798, Republican Fourth of July orator in 1800, and one of Aaron Burr's closest political lieutenants in the New York City election of 1800, complained about the tone of Revere's letters, Revere erupted in anger at Davis and the pretensions of the Republican Party: "Had your Brother received no more Friendly Actions from me, than He has from his Sisters and Brothers, he must now have been confined in one of the cells of the Alms House! (Philanthropy only profest, is too much like our modern profest Patriots)."[31]

Revere's unpleasant experience with the Eayres family did not deter him from practicing benevolence. Deborah Sampson Gannett, a Sharon neighbor, repeatedly received Revere's charity. At the age of twenty, Deborah Sampson had disguised herself as a man and enlisted in the Continental Army. As "Robert Shurtleff," she fought for over a year and a half until she was wounded and her sex revealed. After her honorable discharge from the army, she married a man whom Revere described as "a good sort of man, though of small force in business." In 1804 Revere supported Mrs. Gannett's request for a congressional pension by writing on her behalf to Secretary of War William Eustis, describing her as "a woman of handsome talents, good morals, a dutiful wife, and an affectionate parent . . . a small effeminate, and converseable woman whose education entitled her to a better situation in life." Deborah Sampson Gannett received her pension, but she continued to rely on Paul Revere as her benefactor. In 1806, when Mrs. Gannett asked Revere to loan her ten dollars for a "short time," she apologized "that after receiving ninety and nine good turns as it were—my circumstances require I should ask the hundredth."[32]

Benevolence, virtue, and integrity had always been essential to Freemasonry, but the necessity of those ideals may have assumed greater significance as Revere surveyed Jeffersonian America. On May 20, 1806, he congratulated Reverend George Richards of Portsmouth, New Hampshire, on his "pleasing Masonic discourse" at the consecration of a lodge in Portland. "I think every Mason who reads it," Revere commented, "must acknowledge that the precepts, and Sentiments it Contains, bespeaks the Christian, Mason, and the Man." Employing familiar Masonic phraseology concerning the fitness of Masonic candidates, Revere observed: "It is too much the practice of Lodges to admit the worthless and profane to polute our hallowed Temple; Caution and jealousy, with respect to Candidates, Cannot be too much impressed on all Lodges." Was this just a routine Masonic admonition, or was Revere worried that the democratic nonsense of the Republican Party had compromised Masonic standards?[33]

Federalist and Republican accusations that the other was destroying republicanism reached a new level of rhetorical and physical violence on August 4, 1806. On that day, Federalist attorney Thomas O. Selfridge shot and killed Charles Austin, the eighteen-year-old son of Benjamin Austin Jr., the venomous Republican "scribbler" who excoriated the Federalists in the *Independent Chronicle*. Selfridge's manslaughter trial was a political drama waged in the courtroom and the newspapers that affected the lives and reputations of several individuals involved in the case, including Paul Revere, foreman of the jury that acquitted Selfridge. The "unfortunate encounter" between Thomas Selfridge and Charles Austin, in Selfridge's words, "excited the prejudices, awakened the passions, and agitated the feelings of the community in a manner which has neither precedent nor parallel."[34]

The affair began with the Republican Fourth of July celebration in Boston. The attendance of the Tunisian ambassador drew an unexpected crowd, forcing Eager, a Republican tavern keeper who catered the banquet, to ask Benjamin Austin Jr., chairman of the Fourth of July committee, for more money. When Austin refused, Eager consulted attorney Thomas Selfridge. Upon learning that Austin was accusing Selfridge of encouraging Eager's lawsuit (i.e., of committing the unethical legal practice of barratry), Selfridge demanded satisfaction. Austin refused to issue a public retraction, and Selfridge posted him as "a coward, a liar, and a scoundrel" in the *Boston Gazette* on August 4. In the *Independent Chronicle* of the same day, Austin stated that he considered it "derogatory to enter into a news-paper controversy" with Selfridge "in reply to his insolent and false publication." After learning that Austin had made threats against him, Selfridge armed himself with pistols before walking down State Street to meet a client shortly after one o'clock on the afternoon of August 4. Soon after, Selfridge and young Austin met. Charles Austin struck Selfridge on the forehead with a large hickory cane, but he was no match for Selfridge's pistol.[35]

On December 2, 1806, after instructions from Federalist Chief Justice The-ophilus Parsons, the grand jury, whose foreman was Thomas Handasyd Perkins, prominent member of the Massachusetts Federalist Central Committee, charged Selfridge with manslaughter, not murder as the Republicans expected. Selfridge's trial opened on December 23 with Federalist Judge Isaac Parker presiding and Republican Attorney General James Sullivan prosecuting the case. The cream of the Federalist bar—Christopher Gore, Samuel Dexter, Harrison Gray Otis, and Fisher Ames—defended Selfridge on the grounds of a man's right to preserve both his life and his honor. On December 26, after deliberating for fifteen minutes, the jury, and its foreman, Paul Revere, returned a verdict of not guilty. Chief Justice Parsons and Selfridge were hung in effigy, and Selfridge went into temporary exile in Charleston, South Carolina, where he wrote a pamphlet defending not only his honor but "the integrity of jurors" and "the wisdom of the court" from "the audacious efforts of democracy."[36]

Paul Revere's honor came under fire in the *Independent Chronicle* beginning on March 16, 1807, when "An Enquirer" charged Revere with visiting Selfridge within days of his acquittal "and in the presence of a gentleman of undoubted veracity" telling Selfridge "that it was *fortunate* for him" that he had his trial in Suffolk County. On March 26, 1807, "An Enquirer" questioned Revere's "im-partiality and known candour" by referring to Revere's friendship with Selfridge, a charge that had some merit, since Revere had employed Selfridge to collect debts only six months before Selfridge killed Charles Austin. Two days later, under the headline "Falsehood Exposed," the *Columbian Centinel* defended Re-vere, who refused to "condescend to notice the scurrillity of a *Chronicle* scribbler," and charged "An Enquirer" with "uttering a *base and infamous falsehood*" against Revere: "Colonel Revere's character as an honest *Man*, a conscientious *Citizen*, and a *Patriot*, in the darkest hours of his country's adversity—and which the records of 1773, 4, and 5, and the Historical Societies files, will evince—is too solidly established, to be shaken by the breath of a common calumniator."[37]

The "gentleman of undoubted veracity" who was present during Revere's con-versation with Selfridge was Levi Dow, a Boston wharfinger, client and presumed friend of Selfridge, and a Democrat. On April 2, 1807, the *Independent Chronicle* published an affidavit from Dow, who pledged "the sacred honor of a MASON" as to the validity of his charges, along with affidavits from Revere's employees Asa Bird and Eleazer Morton. Bird testified that he heard Revere say that if he was on Selfridge's jury, he would clear Selfridge, "for he was a gentleman and ought to be cleared." Morton claimed that Revere "thought it likely" that he would be on Selfridge's jury, "and that he never should consent to hang him." In the same issue, the *Independent Chronicle* published Revere's reply from Canton, dated March 30, 1807, stating, "I declare the whole to be an infamous falsehood."[38]

The final attack came on May 18, 1807, when "An Enquirer" denounced Revere for violating the sanctity of the jury by forming an opinion on Selfridge's innocence before the trial began and for his relationship with Selfridge that led him to "visit with so much familiarity a man, on whose fate you had so recently decided." He also rebuked Revere, who acknowledged himself "a member of this respectable fraternity [Masons]," for not responding to Dow's affidavit with one of his own. Revere was sufficiently disturbed by the attacks on his honor to write to Selfridge, who replied with a letter and advised Revere to "make any use of it publicly to Mr. Gore." Selfridge of course supported Revere's claim of the absolute impartiality and integrity of the jurors. Fortunately, Revere did not have to publish Selfridge's letter to save his honor. Public attention was diverted to more weighty political events in the summer of 1807, chiefly former vice president Aaron Burr's conspiracy trial for his mysterious machinations in the American West and the assault of the British frigate *Leopard* on the American frigate *Chesapeake*.[39]

Revere emerged from the Selfridge case with an unshakable commitment to the Federalist Party and higher status within Federalist circles. In the aftermath of the *Leopard*'s firing on *Chesapeake* and seizure of four presumed deserters on June 22, 1807, during which three Americans were killed and eighteen wounded, moderate Federalists called a public meeting in Boston at which they united in protest with Republicans. Revere sided with conservative Federalists who chose a more measured response to the "British Outrage" against American honor. He was one of the "Vice-Presidents" who assisted Christopher Gore in presiding at the Federalists' annual Fourth of July dinner at Faneuil Hall. The "upwards of four hundred" gentlemen and their honored guests, former President John Adams and Robert Treat Paine, toasted Federalist heroes and said nothing at all about the *Chesapeake-Leopard* incident. Gore and his cohorts wrested control of the public response to the *Chesapeake* affair from the Republicans and moderate Federalists by calling a town meeting on July 16, at which they managed a strong Federalist presence among the voters and the resolutions committee, which passed tepid resolutions supporting the federal government's response to the *Chesapeake* incident.[40]

Revere's letters reflect the contempt of a Federalist for the various Embargo Acts passed during the Jefferson and Madison administrations, but they also exhibit his pragmatism as he contemplated the opportunities created by the vacillating policies. On July 20, 1807, he wrote to Joseph Carson of Philadelphia, "Any appearance of war with England enhance the price of copper." In March 1808 he wrote Carson that he had enough copper at the moment, "till we know for certain how our Government is going to lead us respecting the two great beligerant Powers." He did not let his disapproval of the embargo stop him from casting four brass cannon for a United States revenue cutter, one of the Jefferson administration's tools for enforcing the embargo, in November 1808. On March 6, 1809, Revere uttered his strongest words against the embargo while nonetheless taking advantage of its positive results: "The miserable conduct of our Rullers, in laying that cursed Embargo, had nearly deprived us of selling Copper for ships but as good sometimes comes out of Evil, and their being no chance of gitting copper . . . from England . . . we are supplying some Gentlemen in New York with upwards of 16,000 of sheet . . . to make two boilers for two Steam Boats."[41]

The "Gentlemen in New York" were Robert Fulton and Robert R. Livingston, who in 1807 designed and manufactured the *Clermont,* the first practical and financially successful steamboat. Revere and Son manufactured fifty-six plates of copper for Fulton and Livingston on March 31, 1809, the beginning of a long business relationship that helped Revere and Son survive the business stagnation created by the embargo. Revere's diversity of manufactures, from bells to ordnance to a variety of copper products, and his ability to find new markets for his products allowed him to weather any adverse effects of the embargo. He increased his payroll from six workers in 1808 to twelve workers in 1809, and on March 1, 1811, he transferred to his son business assets of slightly over $40,000 in real estate and stocks of manufactured and unmanufactured articles at the Canton mill.[42]

The relative tranquility of Revere's business life stood in sharp contrast to political turmoil on the state and national levels. On July 18, 1808, the Boston Board of Health appointed a committee to investigate the complaint of Captain Amos Binney "that in the execution of his duty . . . he had been calumniated and his veracity called in question, by Mr. Joseph W. Revere." Binney had prosecuted Revere and Son for a violation of an ordinance regulating the conveyance of wastewater on their Boston property. In his father's defense, Joseph Warren Revere denounced Binney's testimony as "an infamous falsehood." He maintained that Revere and Son had not violated any regulations and that Binney's prosecution "originated in party motives, and personal enmity to Colonel Paul Revere." Binney later became a shareholder in the Republican State National Bank of Massachusetts, but he denied any political malice toward Revere. The Board of Health upheld Binney and expressed their disapproval of Joseph Warren Revere's conduct, but on August 1, 1808, they found the premises of Paul Revere and Son "according to law."[43]

Revere's scorn for Republican political leaders grew with his advancing years, moving him to mock the opposition in letters and poetry. In a letter to his son

Joseph Warren, Revere described a ridiculous dinner attended by Republican Governor Elbridge Gerry, who "acts more like a Boy than a man." On July 16, 1810, the governor and lieutenant governor arrived at Squantum to dine with "the Bunker Hill self created Society." They found the company drawn up in two lines "at one end seated on a Rock was John Swift (the man of furor) representing an Indian Sachem." The governor and lieutenant governor marched through the lines with their hats off, "but the rain coming down so violently, they put their hats on eat a few clams, got into their Carriages and off they went. From this Specimen, Judge of your Rulers."[44]

Revere was just as disgusted with national politics. He hewed to the Federalist belief that Jefferson controlled the ineffectual, pro-French foreign policy of the Madison administration, putting his thoughts into poetry:

> What great and good men steers our National Ship;
> Ore *Shoals*, and thro' Rocks; how they make her to skip.
> Sage Jefferson is Captain; Brave Madison's mate,
> Both Sailors; both Soldiers; how happy our fate.
> Secretary Monroe's, a friend to Old France.
> He offer'd them money; was willing to dance.[45]

Freemasonry was also not immune from the contentious climate of the day, and for the second time Revere was a member of a lodge that dissolved in controversy. The ostensible reason that Rising States Lodge surrendered its charter on December 10, 1810, was the lodge's resentment at being displaced from their rank in the Massachusetts Grand Lodge when St. Andrew's Lodge was admitted into the Grand Lodge in 1809. However, on September 9, 1811, the Grand Lodge committee investigating Rising States reported that "discord and uneasiness" had existed in the lodge "for five years past," with members "generally at variance with each other" over several issues, including "the disappointment of certain characters in not being elected to the first offices of the Lodge." Revere, whose Masonic activity after 1800 was sporadic, was not an official member of Rising States Lodge when the members voted to dissolve, but he did accept his share in the division of the lodge's funds. The Grand Lodge condemned the "alarming and dangerous innovation" of dividing the funds instead of returning them to the Grand Lodge, but Revere was exonerated on June 8, 1812, when he proved to the Grand Lodge committee that all the money he received "had been faithfully applied to the relief of the distressed members of the Masonic family." Thus, Revere's Masonic career ended on a sad and inglorious note.[46]

Revere's retirement in 1811 allowed him to withdraw from the daily cares of business and the personal and political squabbles he experienced as a Federalist in the Jeffersonian Age. "Cantondale," his summer home whose charms he described in verse, provided a setting for a balanced life devoted to family, friends, exercise, the joys of nature, improving his mind, and reflecting on his philosophy of life:

> . . . In my last stage, how blest am I,
> To find Content and Plenty by?
> Just work enough to keep in health;
> I exercise prefer to Wealth.
> Within my Cot, I sit reclin'd;
> I soothe to peace my thoughtful mind;
> Receive my Friends, with kind embrace;
> Give them the best, with Chearful face.
> The double dealing Hypocrite,
> I try to shun, with all my might,
> The Knave, I hate; the cheat despise;
> The flatterer fly; but court the wise.
> The poor man's hope; the Widow's friend;
> The Orphan's guide; who often lend;
> Within my Cot, I'm pleased to find;
> Such men's congenial to my mind.[47]

The happiness of Revere's "last stage" was marred by the death of his son Paul, Jr. on January 16, 1813, followed five months later by the death of his beloved Rachel, at the age of sixty-eight, weeks after the completion of their portraits by Gilbert Stuart. He continued to "trudge on," a central tenet of the philosophy of life he formulated in "Cantondale," remaining physically and mentally active to the end. He subscribed to several Boston Federalist newspapers, which gave him an exhaustive but partisan view of the political events that led to "Mr. Madison's War," and he remained a subscriber to the Boston Library until March 1818. On September 8, 1814, the nearly eighty-year-old Revere was the first of 150 North End mechanics who signed a petition volunteering their labor to assist Governor Caleb Strong in strengthening Boston's defenses against possible British attack during the War of 1812. The mechanics' offer was accepted, and they built Fort Strong on Noddle's Island. He never lost his love of horses either, remaining a horseman until at least the age of eighty.[48]

When Paul Revere died in Boston on May 10, 1818, at the age of eighty-three, his contemporaries did not dwell on his ambition or the abrasiveness that some-times got the better of him. The passing of Colonel Revere was not the time to review the charges of self-interest and cowardice raised in the aftermath of the Penobscot expedition or his alleged partisanship during the Selfridge trial. In-stead, Revere's fellow citizens recalled a life "spent in active exertions in useful pursuits" and "in the performance of acts of disinterested benevolence or general

12. and 13. Joseph Warren Revere paid the artist Gilbert Stuart (1755–1828) $200 for the portraits of his parents on June 1, 1813. Rachel Revere died on June 26, but Paul Revere lived nearly another five years, honored by contemporaries for a life "spent in active exertions in useful pursuits." Courtesy, Museum of Fine Arts, Boston. Gift of Joseph W., William B., and Edward H. R. Revere.

utility." The author of his obituary celebrated Revere as a model citizen of the New Republic:

> Cool in thought, ardent in action, he was well adapted to form plans and to carry them into successful execution—both for the benefit of himself and the service of others. In the early scenes of our revolutionary drama . . . as well as at a later period of its progress, his country found him one of her most zealous and active of her sons. His ample property, which his industry and perseverance had enabled him to amass, was always at the service of indigent worth, and open to the solicitations of friendship or the claims of more intimate connexions. His opinions upon the vicissitudes of life, were always sound, and founded upon an accurate observation of nature and an extensive experience. His advice was, therefore, as valuable as it was readily proffered.[49]

Paul Revere would surely have appreciated the irony that Henry Wadsworth Longfellow, the architect of his fame as an American folk hero, was the grandson of Brigadier General Peleg Wadsworth, who had challenged Revere's patriotism and honor in the Penobscot expedition. Undoubtedly, he would have delighted in the effects of Longfellow's epic poem: the patriotic orators who mentioned him in the same breath as the Founding Fathers, the towns named after him, and the annual reenactment of his ride to Lexington. Such "posthumous panegyricks" would have more than fulfilled his desire for honor and recognition. But the man who struggled mightily, if not always successfully, to balance ambition and virtue, the benefits and obligations of republicanism, should have been equally gratified by his contemporary William Tudor's assessment of his life: "He was one of the most influential citizens of the town, and entirely in the confidence of the leading patriots. . . . Mr. Revere was through life an upright, useful, respectable citizen."[50]

NOTES

Introduction

1. *Life of Henry Wadsworth Longfellow with Extracts from His Journals and Correspondence,* ed. Samuel Longfellow (Boston, 1891), 2.401.

2. "Paul Revere's Ride," *The Poetical Works of Longfellow,* Cambridge ed. (Boston, 1975), 207–9.

3. The poet's intent was not to document the details of Paul Revere's ride, which had been accurately covered in such nineteenth-century texts as Richard Frothingham's *History of the Siege of Boston* (1849) and George Bancroft's *History of the United States* (1858). As both a literary scholar (professor of modern language and literature at Harvard from 1836 to 1854) and an American poet, Longfellow was more interested in creating a tradition of American epic poetry that would inspire both his fellow poets and the rest of his countrymen. On the nineteenth-century coverage of Paul Revere's ride see Richard Frothingham, *History of the Siege of Boston* (6th ed., 1903; reprint, New York, 1970), 58–60; Bancroft, *History of the United States,* 7.288–90. My interpretation of Longfellow is based on several years of research as a park ranger at Longfellow National Historic Site in Cambridge, Massachusetts. Secondary works on Longfellow include Edward Wagenknecht, *Henry Wadsworth Longfellow: Portrait of an American Humanist* (New York, 1966), and Newton Arvin, *Longfellow: His Life and Work* (Boston, 1962, 1963).

4. Definition of "virtue" in Gordon S. Wood, *The Creation of the American Republic, 1776–1787* (New York, 1969), 65–70.

5. *Webster's New Universal Unabridged Dictionary,* 2d ed., s.v. "ambition."

6. On the concepts of honor, fame, reputation, and ambition see Trevor Colbourn, ed., *Fame and the Founding Fathers: Essays by Douglass Adair* (New York, 1974), 3–26; Gordon S. Wood, *The Radicalism of the American Revolution* (New York, 1992), 39–41, 207–10.

7. Daniel T. Rodgers, "Republicanism: The Career of a Concept," *Journal of American History* 79 (June 1992): 11–38.

8. Captain Thomas Ramsden to Paul Revere, December 30, 1796, Revere Family Papers II, roll 4, Revere Papers, Massachusetts Historical Society (MHS); Elbridge Gerry to John Wendell, January 12, 1801, Washburn Autograph Collection, MHS. For a sampling of the voluminous literature on republicanism and its critics, in addition to the Rodgers essay noted above, see Robert E. Shalhope, "Toward a Republican Synthesis: The Emergence of an Understanding of Republicanism in American Historiography," *William and Mary Quarterly,* 3d ser., 29 (January 1972): 49–80; Shalhope, "Republicanism and Early American Historiography," *William and Mary Quarterly,* 3d ser., 39 (April 1982): 334–56; Joyce Appleby, "Liberalism and the American Revolution," *New England Quarterly* 49 (March 1976): 3–26; Appleby, "The Social Origins of American Revolutionary Ideology," *Journal of American History* 64 (March 1978): 935–58; Isaac Kramnick, "Republican Revisionism Revisited: Liberal and Classical Ideas in the New American Republic," *American Historical Review* 87 (June 1982): 629–64; James T. Kloppenberg, "Christianity, Republicanism, and Ethics in Early American Discourse," *Journal of American History* 74 (June 1987): 9–33.

9. Paul Revere to Thomas Ramsden, August 4, 1804, roll 2, Revere Papers (loose manuscripts, 1802–13).

10. Esther Forbes, *Paul Revere and the World He Lived In* (Boston, 1942), 3–17. Recent genealogical research does support the staunch Protestantism of Revere's French ancestors. See André J. Labatut and Pamela Labatut, "Paul Revere's Paternal Ancestry: The Rivoires: A Huguenot Family of Some Account," *New England Historical and Genealogical Register* 150 (July 1996): 277–98.

11. Gary Nash has described the terms "artisan community," "artisanal culture," and "artisan republicanism" as phrases "of convenience" that obscure differences within the "artisan community." On "artisan community" see Nash, "Artisans and Politics in Eighteenth-Century Philadelphia," in *The Craftsman in Early America,* ed. Ian M. Quimby (New York, 1984), 62–88. On "artisan republicanism" see Sean Wilentz, *Chants Democratic: New York City and the Rise of the Working Class, 1788–1850* (New York, 1984), chap. 2. Other sources on the importance of artisans in the Revolution and Early Republic include Carl Bridenbaugh, *The Colonial Craftsman* (New York, 1950); Charles S. Olton, *Artisans for Independence: Philadelphia Mechanics and the American Revolution* (Syracuse, N.Y., 1975); Eric Foner, *Tom Paine and Revolutionary America* (New York, 1976); Dirk Hoerder, "Boston Leaders and Boston Crowds, 1765–1776," in *The American Revolution: Explorations in the History of American Radicalism,* ed. Alfred F. Young (DeKalb, Ill., 1976), 233–71; Gary B. Nash, *The Urban Crucible* (Cambridge, Mass., 1979); Howard B. Rock, *Artisans of the New Republic: The Tradesmen of New York City in the Age of Jefferson* (New York, 1979); Alfred F. Young, "George Robert Twelves Hewes (1742–1840): A Boston Shoemaker and the Memory of the American Revolution," *William and Mary Quarterly,* 3d ser., 38 (October 1981): 561–623; Jackson Turner Main, *The Social Structure of Revolutionary America* (Princeton, N.J., 1965), 76–82, 132–35, 199. On defining a characteristic of the artisan community as a life "of productive labor" see Nash, "Artisans and Politics in Eighteenth-Century Philadelphia," 63.

12. On the influence of Freemasonry in eighteenth- and nineteenth-century America

see Steven C. Bullock, "The Ancient and Honorable Society: Freemasonry in America, 1730–1860" (Ph.D. diss., Brown University, 1986); Bullock, *Revolutionary Brotherhood: Freemasonry and the Transformation of the American Social Order* (Chapel Hill, N.C., 1996).

13. Revere's upward mobility began in the late 1780s, when he expanded his goldsmith business into a hardware store and began serving on church and town committees. As a Freemason since the early 1760s, he steadily rose through the ranks to become Grand Master of the Massachusetts Grand Lodge in 1794.

14. Longfellow, *Life of Henry Wadsworth Longfellow*, 2.39.

1. Clark's Wharf

1. Hichborn is also spelled "Hitchbourn." Revere was baptized a day after his birth—on December 22, 1734, "old style," or January 1, 1735, "new style." See *Report of the Record Commissioners: Boston Town Records* (hereafter *Boston Town Records*), 24.218; Thomas B. Wyman Jr., "Records of the New Brick Church," *New England Historical and Genealogical Register* 19 (July 1865): 235; Donald M. Nielsen, "The Revere Family," *New England Historical and Genealogical Register* 145 (October 1991): 292–96. The Reveres' residence is based on an advertisement in the *Weekly News Letter:* "Paul Revere Goldsmith, is Removed from Capt. Pitt's, at the Town Dock, to the North End over against Col. Hutchinson's," quoted in Elbridge Henry Goss, *The Life of Colonel Paul Revere* (Boston, 1891), 1.11–12. On the North End see Walter Muir Whitehill, *A Topographical History of Boston*, 2d ed. (Cambridge, Mass., 1968), 27.

2. Forbes, *Paul Revere*, 3–7; André J. Labatut, "Some New Information about the Ancestry of Paul Revere," *New England Historical and Genealogical Register* 143 (July 1989): 235–39; Labatut and Labatut, "Paul Revere's Paternal Ancestry," 277–98; Patrick M. Leehey, "Reconstructing Paul Revere: An Overview of His Ancestry, Life, and Work," in *Paul Revere—Artisan, Businessman, and Patriot: The Man behind the Myth* (Boston, 1988), 14–19.

3. On Boston Huguenots see Forbes, *Paul Revere*, 4–5; Charles C. Smith, "The French Protestants in Boston," in *Memorial History of Boston*, ed. Justin Winsor (Boston, 1881), 2.249–68. On Faneuil Hall see Whitehill, *Topographical History*, 41–42.

4. Forbes, *Paul Revere*, 10–11; Goss, *Life of Colonel Revere*, 1.9; Leehey, "Reconstructing Paul Revere," 19–21.

5. On French Huguenots in Boston see Smith, "French Protestants in Boston," 254–55; Samuel Adams Drake, *Old Landmarks and Historic Personages of Boston* (1900; reprint, Detroit, 1970), 63–64; Forbes, *Paul Revere*, 12. On the New Brick Church see Reverend Alexander McKenzie, D.D., "The Religious History of the Provincial Period," in *Memorial History of Boston*, ed. Winsor, 2.220–26 (quote on establishment of New North by seventeen "substantial mechanics" on 220–21); Chandler Robbins, *A History of the Second Church, or Old North in Boston, to Which Is Added a History of the New Brick Church* (Boston, 1852), 170–80; Henry Ware, *Two Discourses Containing the History of the Old North and New Brick Churches United as the Second Church in Boston* (Boston, 1821), 25–41, 54–55 (dissenters' objections quoted on 54); Forbes, *Paul Revere*, 30–31.

6. Subscribers included Governor William Burnet, the Honorable Jonathan Belcher,

Esq., the Honorable Samuel Sewall, Dr. Zabdiel Boylston, Thomas Hutchinson Jr., Oxenbridge Thacher, the Reverend Mr. Nathaniel Appleton of Cambridge, the Reverend Mr. Experience Mayhew of Chilmark, and Isaac Greenwood, M.A., Hollis Professor of the Mathematics at Harvard. See Samuel Mather, *The Life of the Very Reverend and Learned Cotton Mather* (1729), in Evans, *Early American Imprints,* no. 3188; Goss, *Life of Colonel Revere,* 1.10. The anglicization of Apollos Rivoire's name is discussed in Leehey, "Reconstructing Paul Revere," 20–21.

7. On the marriage of Revere's parents see Nielsen, "The Revere Family," 292. On the Hichborns see Leehey, "Reconstructing Paul Revere," 21–24. For various charges involving Thomas Dexter between 1631 and 1633, including a successful complaint of battery against John Endecott and charges of sedition and drunkenness, see Nathaniel B. Shurtleff, *Records of the Governor and Company of the Massachusetts Bay in New England* (Boston, 1853), 1.86, 97, 103, 108. Letter from Endecott to Winthrop quoted in Forbes, *Paul Revere,* 14.

8. The terms "goldsmith" and "silversmith" were used synonymously in the eighteenth century, although "goldsmith" was the more common term. As a master goldsmith, Revere worked primarily in silver, but he also made small gold items like sleeve buttons and rings. On terminology see Martha Gandy Fales, *Early American Silver* (New York, 1970), x.

9. Forbes, *Paul Revere,* 66; Clifford K. Shipton, *Sibley's Harvard Graduates* (Boston, 1933–75), 17.36–44, especially 36–40; Drake, *Old Landmarks,* 250, 293–94.

10. On artisans' homes see Carl Bridenbaugh, *Cities in the Wilderness: Urban Life in America, 1625–1742,* 3d ed. (New York, 1964), 308. On Revere's North Square home see Whitehill, *Topographical History,* 15; Forbes, *Paul Revere,* 162.

11. Descriptions of the Clark-Frankland and Hutchinson mansions appear in Whitehill, *Topographical History,* 27–28; Drake, *Old Landmarks,* 162–68; Edwin L. Bynner, "Topography and Landmarks of the Provincial Period," in *Memorial History,* ed. Winsor, 2.526; Bernard Bailyn, *The Ordeal of Thomas Hutchinson* (Cambridge, Mass., 1974), p. 10 n. 16 (on Hutchinson mansion). On artisans' furnishings see Bridenbaugh, *Cities in the Wilderness,* 412.

12. Arthur M. Schlesinger Sr., "The Aristocracy in Colonial America," *MHS Proceedings* 74 (1962), reprinted in *The Social Fabric: American Life from 1607 to the Civil War,* ed. John H. Cary and Julius Weinberg (Boston, 1978), 1.76–77; Jane Carson, *World Book Encyclopedia,* 1969 ed., s.v. "Colonial Life in America."

13. Jonathan L. Fairbanks et al., *Paul Revere's Boston, 1735–1818* (Boston, 1975), 77–93; Bridenbaugh, *Cities in the Wilderness,* 411–13, 428–31, 436–38, 454–56; Bridenbaugh, *Cities in Revolt: Urban Life in America, 1743–1776* (1955; reprint, New York, 1971), 156–70; Forbes, *Paul Revere,* 33–36; *Boston Newsletter,* December 6, 1733. The bell-ringing agreement signed by Paul Revere and six other boys is reproduced in *Paul Revere—Artisan, Businessman, and Patriot,* 149.

14. On colonial social structure and economy see Jack P. Greene, *Pursuits of Happiness: The Social Development of Modern British Colonies and the Formation of American Culture* (Chapel Hill, N.C., 1988), 186–89; Nash, *Urban Crucible,* 112–28. Defoe is quoted in Roy Porter, *English Society in Eighteenth Century* (New York, 1982), 64.

15. On Thomas Hancock see W. T. Baxter, *The House of Hancock: Business in Boston,*

1724–1775 (1945; reprint, New York, 1965), 3–10, 39–61, 95–107, 129–46; Arthur B. Tour-tellot, *Lexington and Concord: The Beginning of the War of the American Revolution* (New York, 1963), 59–60; Nash, *Urban Crucible,* 167–69; Marc Egnal, *A Mighty Empire: The Origins of the American Revolution* (Ithaca, N.Y., 1988), 36–40; Bridenbaugh, *Cities in Revolt,* 71; Forbes, *Paul Revere,* 35. On the importance of books and education in colonial society see Main, *The Social Structure of Revolutionary America,* 251–61; Daniel J. Boorstin, *The Americans: The Colonial Experience* (New York, 1958), 293–301.

16. Forbes, *Paul Revere,* 12, 30–31; Goss, *Life of Colonel Revere,* 1.17–18.

17. J. A. L. Lemay and P. M. Zall, eds., *Benjamin Franklin's Autobiography* (New York, 1986). Throughout this work, I have quoted Revere and others using their spelling, capi-talization, and punctuation. I leave it to readers to supply [*sic*] where modern usage differs.

18. Lemay and Zall, *Franklin's Autobiography,* 7–8; Bridenbaugh, *Cities in the Wilderness,* 411–12, 451–56; Bridenbaugh, *Cities in Revolt,* 70–71, 134–71.

19. On colonial social structure, especially in Pennsylvania, see James T. Lemon, *The Best Poor Man's Country: A Geographical Study of Early Southeastern Pennsylvania* (New York, 1972), 1–41, 51–56; Richard Hofstadter, *America at 1750: A Social Portrait* (New York, 1971), 131; Greene, *Pursuits of Happiness,* 170–206.

20. On education in England and colonial society see Boorstin, *Colonial Experience,* 171–78; Bridenbaugh, *Cities in the Wilderness,* 121–23, 281–83, 442–45; Main, *Social Structure of Revolutionary America,* 240–46; Bernard Bailyn, *Education in the Forming of American Society: Needs and Opportunities for Study* (Chapel Hill, N.C., 1960), 19. On the Hutchin-sons' role in establishing schools see Robert Francis Seybolt, *The Public Schools of Colonial Boston, 1635–1775* (1935; reprint, New York, 1969), 8, 67–68; Bailyn, *Ordeal of Thomas Hutchinson,* 10. On North Writing School see Forbes, *Paul Revere,* 28–29; Drake, *Old Landmarks,* 57.

21. John Adams to James Warren, May 12, 1776, in *Letters of Delegates to the Continental Congress,* 15 vols., ed. Paul H. Smith (Washington, D.C., 1976–88), 3.3, 660–62. On Bowdoin see *Sibley's Harvard Graduates,* 11.514–50.

22. On David Rittenhouse see Leonard D. White, *The Federalists: A Study in Admin-istrative History* (New York, 1956), 140. On Revere's efforts to become director of the Mint see Fisher Ames to Paul Revere, April 26, 1789, and January 24, 1791, roll 1, Revere Family Papers, MHS (loose manuscripts, 1746–1801). See also Bailyn, *Education in Forming of American Society,* 3–49; Boorstin, *Colonial Experience,* 171–205.

23. On Franklin see Lemay and Zall, *Franklin's Autobiography,* 47–49. On Knox see *Dictionary of American Biography* (New York, 1926–36, hereafter *DAB*), 10.475–77; White, *The Federalists,* 152–53; quote from Adams's autobiography in Francis S. Drake, *Life and Correspondence of Henry Knox* (Boston, 1873), 86; John Adams to Henry Knox, Novem-ber 11, 1775, in Henry Knox Papers, 1719–1825, Massachusetts Historical Society Microfilm (1960), reel 1; Revere to John Lamb, on unsuccessful quest for Continental Army commis-sion, April 5, 1777, Lamb Papers, New York Historical Society, quoted in Goss, *Life of Colonel Revere,* 1.280–81. On Rittenhouse see *DAB,* 8.630–32.

24. Revere to Brown and Benson (foundry in Providence, R.I.), November 3, 1788, requesting a copy of Watson's *Chemical Essays;* Revere to Reverend Richard Watson,

author of the essays, February 21, 1790, correcting an error in the book; Revere to Dr. Letsome, December 3, 1791, sending him a sample of tin for chemical analysis and promising to send additional mineral samples; all in Revere's Letterbook, 1783–1800, vol. 53, roll 14, Revere Papers, MHS. Examples of Revere's technical notes and experiments in Journal and Commonplace Book, 1777–1801, vol. 51, no. 1, and Memoranda Book, 1788–1795, vol. 51, no. 7, roll 14, Revere Papers, MHS. Quote on his successful experiments with copper in Revere to Harrison Gray Otis, March 11, 1800, roll 1, Revere Papers. On the concept that knowledge must be tested by observation and experimentation see Boorstin, *Colonial Experience,* 149–68.

25. Revere to John Rivoire, July 1, 1782 (letter addressed to "Dear Cousin," and the recipient is not identified, but in the letter Revere refers to John Rivoire's letter of January 28, 1781, in the Revere Papers, roll 1); subscriptions to the *Federal Orrery,* January–July 1795, and *Massachusetts Magazine,* October 1, 1795, and membership dues to the Boston Library Society, December 9, 1797, in roll 1, Revere Papers; subscriptions to the *Centinel, Repertory, Gazette,* and *Palladium* in Cash Books, 1811–18, vol. 33, roll 11, Revere Papers; Revere to Reverend George Richards, commenting on Richards's Masonic discourse, May 20, 1806, Letterbook, 1805–10, vol. 53, roll 14, Revere Papers.

26. On enrollment of Joshua, Joseph Warren, and John at Boston Latin see Henry F. Jenks, *Catalogue of the Boston Public Latin School, with an Historical Sketch* (Boston, 1886), 373. On John Revere see Forbes, *Paul Revere,* 403, 411, 441–42; Eugene F. Cordell, *Medical Annals of Maryland, 1799–1899* (Baltimore, 1903), 548; Howard A. Kelly and Walter L. Burrage, *Dictionary of American Medical Biography* (New York, 1928), 1828; *Transactions of the American Medical Association* (Philadelphia) 3 (1850): 460–61; Nielsen, "The Revere Family," 314; Elizabeth Grundy and Jayne E. Triber, "Paul Revere's Children: Coming of Age in the New Nation" (unpublished manuscript at the Paul Revere Memorial Association, Boston, 1983). On Maria and Harriet see receipt from William Turner to Paul Revere, April 1, 1798, and Maria Revere to her mother, Rachel, describing her curriculum, May 25, 1801, roll 1, Revere Papers; Grundy and Triber, "Paul Revere's Children." On curriculum of girls' schools see advertisements in *Columbian Centinel,* December 17, 1800, and April 24, 1802.

27. On apprenticeship see Bridenbaugh, *Cities in the Wilderness,* 46–48; Forbes, *Paul Revere,* 22. On Revere's customers and range of work see Revere's Waste Book and Memoranda, vol. 1 (1761–83), roll 5, Revere Papers, MHS. On the nature and process of the silversmith's craft see Fales, *Early American Silver,* 23–25, 115–16, 195–206.

28. For an insightful analysis of Revere's silver shop, including the range of his customers and work and a comparison of his pre- and post-Revolutionary business, see Deborah A. Federhen, "From Artisan to Entrepreneur: Paul Revere's Silver Shop Operation," in *Paul Revere—Artisan, Businessman, and Patriot,* 65–93. See also Fairbanks et al., *Paul Revere's Boston,* 27–57; Forbes, *Paul Revere,* 65–67. For customers' orders see Waste Book and Memoranda, vol. 1 (1761–83), roll 5, Revere Papers, e.g., Benjamin Greene's orders, March 12 and April 3, 1762; Captain Collings, June 3, 1762; Joshua Brackett's order for mending a pair of stone buttons, May 10, 1762; Nathaniel Hurd's order for mending a picture frame, June 22, 1763; Thomas Hichborn Sr.'s order for shoe and knee buckles, August 21 and October 7, 1763.

29. Main, *Social Structure of Revolutionary America,* 75–83, 275; Carl Bridenbaugh, *Colonial Craftsman,* 85; Federhen, "From Artisan to Entrepreneur," 65–75; Forbes, *Paul Revere,* 122–27; Revere's Waste Book and Memoranda, vol. 1 and vol. 2 (1783–97), roll 5, Revere Papers, MHS.

30. On social hierarchy see Main, *Social Structure of Revolutionary America,* chap. 6 ("Social Classes in the Revolutionary Era") and chap. 7 ("Contemporary Views of Class"); Wood, *Radicalism of the American Revolution,* 24–42 ("Patricians and Plebeians"). On the combination of skills and mixture of dependence and independence in silversmith's craft see Fales, *Early American Silver,* 115–32, 203–5; C. Louise Avery, *Early American Silver* (New York, 1930), 76–84, 213–17, 233; Kathryn G. Buhler, *Paul Revere, Goldsmith* (Boston, 1956), text under item 14 on variation in finials and handle tips on tankards. Andrew Oliver's order, September 14, 1764, in Waste Book and Memoranda, vol. 1, roll 5, Revere Papers.

31. Forbes, *Paul Revere,* 89–93; Drake, *Old Landmarks,* 149–50; Nash, *Urban Crucible,* 170–72, 260–62; Peter Shaw, *American Patriots and the Rituals of Revolution* (Cambridge, Mass., 1981), 195–99; Richard L. Bushman, *King and People in Provincial Massachusetts* (Chapel Hill, N.C., 1985), 14–25, 261–62.

32. *Boston Town Records* (1742–57), 14.57; Nash, *Urban Crucible,* 170–73; Egnal, *Mighty Empire,* 38–40; Bridenbaugh, *Cities in Revolt,* 59–60.

33. Nash, *Urban Crucible,* 172–73; *Boston Town Records,* 14.95–96.

34. Nash, *Urban Crucible,* 221–24; John Stetson Barry, *History of Massachusetts* (Boston, 1855–57), 2.159–62.

35. Lawrence Delbert Cress, *Citizens in Arms: The Army in American Society to the War of 1812* (Chapel Hill, N.C., 1982), 7–11, 25–33; Russell F. Weigley, *History of the United States Army,* 2d ed. (New York, 1980), 8–12; Jayne E. Triber, "Massachusetts and the Federal Garrison at Fort Independence, 1798–1815: The Propriety of a Standing Army in a Republic" (M.A. thesis, University of Massachusetts, Boston, 1985), 15–18. On description of the Knowles rioters, Thomas Hutchinson referred to the participation of "men of all orders," Boston town records described the role of "Persons of Mean and vile Condition," and in a letter to Josiah Willard, Governor William Shirley wrote that he was convinced that the mob had been "secretly Countenanc'd and encourag'd by some ill minded Inhabitants and Persons of Influence in the Town"; all quoted in Nash, *Urban Crucible,* 222–23 and n. 108.

36. On the banking controversy of 1740–41 see Nash, *Urban Crucible,* 212–14; Egnal, *Mighty Empire,* 34–37. On Hutchinson's bill of 1748 see Nash, *Urban Crucible,* 224–27.

37. On the anger against Hutchinson in 1748 see Nash, *Urban Crucible,* 224–27. For the traditional story that Revere attended Mayhew's sermons see Goss, *Life of Colonel Revere,* 1.17–18 (his source is a story by Thomas C. Amory in *Student and Schoolmate,* 1869); Forbes, *Paul Revere,* 33.

38. On Mayhew's theology see Egnal, *Mighty Empire,* 25–26; Sydney E. Ahlstrom, *A Religious History of the American People* (Garden City, N.Y., 1975), 1.426–36.

39. The date of Mayhew's speech was January 30, 1749, "old style" or 1750 under the "new style" calender. Jonathan Mayhew, *A Discourse Concerning Unlimited Submission and Non-Resistance to the Higher Powers: With Some Reflections on the Resistance Made to King*

Charles I And on the Anniversary of his Death, delivered January 30, 1749/1750, West Church Boston, Evans, *Early American Imprints,* no. 6549, 1, 20, 24, 41–44, 54.

2. An Artisan and a Freemason

1. Paul Revere to Mathias Rivoire, October 6, 1781 (date penciled in on manuscript), roll 1, Revere Family Papers, MHS; Forbes, *Paul Revere,* 39–41; Nielsen, "The Revere Family," 292.

2. Forbes, *Paul Revere,* 39–40; Nash, *Urban Crucible,* 224–27; Fred Anderson, *A People's Army: Massachusetts Soldiers and Society in the Seven Years' War* (Chapel Hill, N.C., 1984), 8, 26–39.

3. Anderson, *People's Army,* 6–12, 50; Derek McKay and H. M. Scott, *The Rise of the Great Powers, 1648–1715* (London, 1983), 177–200; Forbes, *Paul Revere,* 42–43.

4. Revere's reminiscences of service at Crown Point, fragment, second copy, April 27, 1816, roll 3, Revere Papers (loose manuscripts and undated materials, 1814–1964); Anderson, *People's Army,* 66–73, 211–12.

5. *Boston Town Records,* 14.280–81.

6. Anderson, *People's Army,* 38–39; Forbes, *Paul Revere,* 44.

7. Weigley, *History of the U.S. Army,* 4–7; Cress, *Citizens in Arms,* 9–18; Richard H. Kohn, *Eagle and Sword: The Federalists and the Creation of the Military Establishment in America, 1783–1802* (New York, 1975), 1–9; Barry, *History of Massachusetts,* 1.483–90; Triber, "Massachusetts and Fort Independence," 7–13.

8. Anderson, *People's Army,* 9, chap. 4; Lemay and Zall, *Franklin's Autobiography,* 114–20.

9. Anderson, *People's Army,* 11, 78–83.

10. Anderson, *People's Army,* 8–10, chap. 6.

11. Anderson, *People's Army,* 169–75 (General Winslow to William Shirley, August 2, 1756, quoted on 172).

12. On war developments during Revere's term of service see Anderson, *People's Army,* 12, 180. Revere and the other soldiers and officers in his company were the only artillerists in Massachusetts provincial service. They were members of an elite and unique company that was twice the size of an infantry company and whose members possessed a variety of specialized skills. The artillerist's sense of superiority was later expressed in letters of Revere's friend John Lamb, who sought an appointment as an artillery officer in 1775, "having made that branch of military science more particularly my study," and who later complained about having the artillery placed under the command of a regular regimental officer: "the Artillery in every service, are always considered as a distinct corps. . . . I conceive myself to be degraded by this new arrangement." See Anderson, *People's Army,* 50, on Gridley's artillery train, and John Lamb to the New York Congress, June 2 and August 28, 1775, in Peter Force, *American Archives* (Washington, D.C., 1837–53), 4th ser., vol., 2, p. 891 and vol. 3, p. 445 (henceforth 4.2.891 and 4.3.445, etc.).

13. On conflicting views of military service see Anderson, *People's Army,* 170–79, 194–95. Loudoun's views were expressed in a letter to the duke of Cumberland, August 29, 1756, in Anderson, *People's Army,* 177.

14. Revere's marriage to Sara Orne is recorded in Edward McGlenen, *Boston Marriages*

from 1700 to 1809 (1903; reprint, Boston, 1977), vol. 30 (1752–1809), 25. On marriage and children see Nielsen, "The Revere Family," 296–301. Revere charged his brother £9.19.0 for "board, sundrys out of shop, cash lent," etc., April 9, 1761, Waste Book and Memoranda, vol. 1 (1761–83), roll 5, Revere Papers. Tax deficiencies, rising poor relief, and other financial problems created by the war were noted in town meeting records for 1757, *Boston Town Records*, 14.296, 307. See also Forbes, *Paul Revere*, 55–56, 473–74.

15. Revere's taxes, 1758–62, roll 1, Revere Papers. On rising taxes and poor relief see Boston town meeting, May 15 and June 12, 1759, *Boston Town Records*, 16.24, 29; Nash, *Urban Crucible*, 241–42. John Burt, a master goldsmith who died in 1745, left an estate worth £6,460.4.9, of which his tools were valued at £238.7.6. For a list of tools in a well-equipped silversmith shop and inventory of Burt's estate see Fales, *Early American Silver*, 202–3, 232–33. On Paul Revere Sr.'s contributions to his son's success see Federhen, "From Artisan to Entrepreneur," 65. Advertisement for Benjamin Greene and Son, merchants, on Greene's Wharf, *Boston Evening Post*, April 24, 1769, in *Harbottle Dorr Collection of Annotated Massachusetts Newspapers, 1765–1776*, Massachusetts Historical Society Microfilm (1966, hereafter *Dorr Collection*), 2.483.

16. E.g., "cutting copper for hatt prints" (hat prints or hat bills were labels bearing the hatter's name that were affixed to the inside of hats) for William Hichborn, August 18, 1762; orders for Thomas Hichborn Jr. on May 2 and October 7, 1763; orders for Thomas Hichborn Sr. on June 12, August 21, and October 20, 1763; knee buckles for Joshua Brackett on May 8, 1761 and shoe buckles on February 12, 1763; a dozen turtle shell "Jackett" buttons and six teaspoons for Samuel Cochran on June 3 and 24, 1761; Revere's long-term relationship with Isaac Greenwood is evident in his notation on January 11, 1765: "This Day Settle With Mr. Isaac Greenwood and Passed Receipts"; all in Waste Book and Memoranda, vol. 1, roll 5, Revere Papers. Customer identifications in Thwing Index, MHS; Federhen, "From Artisan to Entrepreneur," 73–75; Forbes, *Paul Revere*, 55, 65–67, 125–26.

17. On economic success and social mobility of mariners see Main, *Social Structure of Revolutionary America*, 74, 89–90. Orders for William Tory, John Collings, and Barnabas Benney in Waste Book and Memoranda, vol. 1, roll 5, Revere Papers.

18. E.g., Revere made two small "scalop'd salvers" for Nathaniel Hurd on April 16, 1762, two "silver waiters" for Samuel Minott on August 16, 1762, and a pair of silver canns for John Avery on July 13, 1762, Waste Book and Memoranda, vol. 1 (1761–83), roll 5, Revere Papers. Coburn (Revere spells it "Coubourn"), Hurd, and Minott are listed in the Thwing Index, MHS. Definition of "repoussé" in Fales, *Early American Silver*, 302. On Revere's business relationships with other silversmiths see Janine E. Skerry, "The Revolutionary Revere: A Critical Assessment of the Silver of Paul Revere," in *Paul Revere—Artisan, Businessman, and Patriot*, 47; Federhen, "From Artisan to Entrepreneur," 73–74; Fairbanks et al., *Paul Revere's Boston*, 21. Skerry, in particular, notes that "considerable research remains to be done" on the business arrangements of eighteenth-century silversmiths.

19. On the status of Revere's business see Federhen, "From Artisan to Entrepreneur," 65–75; Skerry, "The Revolutionary Revere," 46; Forbes, *Paul Revere*, 65. On the importance of craftsmen in colonial society see Bridenbaugh, *Colonial Craftsman*, 126–27. On Revere's apprentices, in addition to his brother, see charges for boarding Samuel Butts on May 19, 1762, and Matthew Metcalf on September 8, 1762, in Waste Book and Memo-

randa, vol. 1, roll 5, Revere Papers. See also orders for Joshua Brackett, who bought a pair of stone buttons on May 10, 1762, and Robert Hichborn, who bought knee buckles on January 5, 1764, in Waste Book and Memoranda, vol. 1, roll 5, Revere Papers.

20. On the economic background of the period see Nash, *Urban Crucible*, 233–46; Egnal, *Mighty Empire*, 126–32. On artistic trends among the colonial aristocracy and Revere's expertise in the rococo style see Fairbanks et al., *Paul Revere's Boston*, 27–59; Skerry, "The Revolutionary Revere," 47–49; Avery, *Early American Silver*, 76–82, 88. Revere charged the sugar dish for Lucretia Chandler to the merchant Benjamin Greene on March 12, 1762 (the dish is engraved "B. Greene to L. Chandler"). He made a silver tankard for Thomas Greene on September 8, 1762, candlesticks for Zacariah Johonnot ("Johonot") on December 25, 1762, and a child's whistle for Foster Hutchinson on August 18, 1762; all in Waste Book and Memoranda, vol. 1, roll 5, Revere Papers. Customer identifications in Federhen, "From Artisan to Entrepreneur," 74–75; James H. Stark, *The Loyalists of Massachusetts and the Other Side of the American Revolution* (1910; reprint, Clifton, N.J., 1972), 125 (Benjamin Greene), 410 (Zacariah Johonnot), 133, 137, 410 (Foster Hutchinson).

21. On Revere's Masonic career see Edith J. Steblecki, *Paul Revere and Freemasonry* (Boston, 1985); Steblecki, "Fraternity, Philanthropy, and Revolution: Paul Revere and Freemasonry," in *Paul Revere—Artisan, Businessman, and Patriot*, 117–47. On membership of St. Andrew's Lodge and Masonic ideals see Bullock, *Revolutionary Brotherhood*, 91–94; Bullock, "The Ancient and Honorable Society," 43–51. For information on early Massachusetts Masons see Henry J. Parker, "Index to Early Masons, 1733–1800" ("Parker Index"), a handwritten ledger compiled in 1886, at the Grand Lodge of Massachusetts in Boston. Information on Revere is on 266–67.

22. Bullock, "The Ancient and Honorable Society," 12–57; Bullock, *Revolutionary Brotherhood*, 50–82, 85–98; Steblecki, "Fraternity, Philanthropy, and Revolution," 117–21.

23. Otis, Rowe, and the wine merchant Edmund Quincy Jr. were members of the First Lodge (later known as St. John's Lodge); the merchant Edmund Quincy Sr., Reverend Samuel Quincy, and Richard Gridley, whom Revere served under during the Crown Point expedition, were members of Master's Lodge; and Jeremiah Gridley, who became Grand Master of North America in 1755 and attorney general of Massachusetts in 1766, was a member of the Royal Exchange Lodge; information in "Parker Index," 140–41 (on Jeremiah and Richard Gridley), 238–39 (on Otis), 262–63 (on the Quincys). Additional information on Jeremiah Gridley appears in Hiller B. Zobel, *The Boston Massacre* (New York, 1970), 57.

24. List of members of St. Andrew's Lodge by occupation and residence, January 1762, in Ezra Palmer et al., *The Lodge of St. Andrew and the Massachusetts Grand Lodge Centennial Memorial* (Boston, 1870, hereafter *Centennial Memorial*), 241–42. Steven Bullock's analysis of the membership of St. Andrew's Lodge, 1752–75, finds that 28.3 percent were artisans, 3.3 percent were retailers, 36.7 percent were in the seagoing trades, 26.7 percent were merchants, and 4.2 percent were professionals, in *Revolutionary Brotherhood*, 91–94, especially table 2. See also Steblecki, "Fraternity, Philanthropy, and Revolution," 121; Steblecki, *Paul Revere and Freemasonry*, 11. Josiah Flagg, Paul Revere, and five other boys

signed a bell-ringing agreement with the wardens of Christ Church, c. 1750, in *Paul Revere—Artisan, Businessman, and Patriot,* 149.

25. Palmer, *Centennial Memorial,* 5–6, 34–35 (Charles W. Moore on early history of St. Andrew's Lodge), 92–93 (oration by Hamilton Willis); Earl W. Taylor, *Historical Sketch of the Grand Lodge of Massachusetts* (Boston, 1958), 5–6; Steblecki, "Fraternity, Philanthropy, and Revolution," 120.

26. On the dispute between Ancient and Modern Masons see Palmer, *Centennial Memorial,* 34–35, 92–93; Taylor, *Historical Sketch of the Grand Lodge of Massachusetts,* 4–6; Henry Wilson Coil, *A Comprehensive View of Freemasonry* (Richmond, Va., 1973), 109. For a summary of the social and economic differences between Ancient and Modern Masons, see Bullock, *Revolutionary Brotherhood,* tables 1, 3, and 4 on pp. 60 and 94. Merchants made up 66 percent of the membership of Boston's Modern Lodges compared with 26.7 percent of the Ancient Lodges, while artisans made up only 8.2 percent of the membership of the Modern Lodges compared with 28.3 percent of the Ancient Lodges. In 1771 the real estate holdings of Boston's Modern Masons were nearly twice the value of Ancient Masons. On the social differences between Ancient and Modern Masons, the appeal of Ancient Freemasonry for artisans anxious to acquire gentility, and the overall importance of Ancient Freemasonry in Revolutionary and Post-Revolutionary America see Bullock, *Revolutionary Brotherhood,* chaps. 3–4; Bullock, "The Revolutionary Transformation of American Freemasonry," *William and Mary Quarterly,* 3d ser., 47 (July 1990): 347–69. On occupations of members of St. Andrew's, January 1762, see *Centennial Memorial,* 241–42. On William Burbeck, a former member of the First Lodge of Boston, see Membership File, Boston, Massachusetts, Grand Lodge of Massachusetts A.F. & A.M., Samuel Crocker Lawrence Library, Boston.

27. Grand Master of Scotland to brethren of several lodges, disputing Grand Master Jeremiah Gridley's position that the charter of St. Andrew's was an infringement of his authority, June 4, 1762; the St. John's Grand Lodge vote condemning members of St. Andrew's as "Irregular Masons," January 27, 1766; St. John's reversal of its decision, April 10, 1766; all in *Proceedings in Masonry: St. John's Grand Lodge, 1733–1792, and Massachusetts Grand Lodge, 1769–1792* (Boston, 1895, hereafter *Grand Lodge Proceedings*), 90, 102, 105. On Gridley's legal career see John M. Murrin, "The Legal Transformation: The Bench and Bar of Eighteenth-Century Massachusetts," in *Colonial America: Essays in Politics and Social Development,* 3d ed., ed. Stanley N. Katz and John M. Murrin (New York, 1983), 551–52, 556–67.

28. To be admitted into a Masonic lodge, a man had to be proposed by a member and unanimously accepted by the lodge as a man of virtue. See Bullock, "The Ancient and Honorable Society," 54–57.

29. Steblecki, in "Fraternity, Philanthropy, and Revolution," 122, finds that a sampling of 309 of Revere's customers between 1761 and 1796 shows that approximately 146 were Masons. Federhen, "From Artisan to Entrepreneur," 74, claims that over a dozen names of Revere's lodge brothers are recorded in his first daybook (1761–83). I have identified twenty-six members of St. Andrew's Lodge among Revere's customers in his two waste books (1761–97). For an overview of the connection between Freemasonry and Revere's

business see Steblecki, "Fraternity, Philanthropy, and Revolution," 121–26. For a list of Masonic items made by Revere see Steblecki, *Paul Revere and Freemasonry,* appendix 5, 108–19. Orders for James Graham (Revere spells it "Grayham") and Richard Pulling on February 24, 1762, James Jackson on March 2, 1762, and George Stacy on March 5, 1762, are in Waste Book and Memoranda, vols. 1 and 2, roll 5, Revere Papers. Masonic identifications in *Centennial Memorial,* 227, 232 (on Samuel Barrett), 231 (James Graham and James Jackson), 232 (Captain Caleb Hopkins), 242 (Richard Pulling); "Parker Index," 16–17 (Samuel Barrett), 136–37 (James Graham). George Stacy is not in either of these sources, but Edith Steblecki found a record of him in the Grand Lodge files as a Newburyport merchant who joined St. John's Lodge in Newburyport sometime between 1781 and 1787. She found no record of him as a member of St. Andrew's or St. John's Lodges before 1781, but he did attend St. Andrew's Lodge as a visitor on April 11, 1765. See Steblecki, *Paul Revere and Freemasonry,* 114 n. 4. Additional information on Barrett and Hopkins in Thwing Index, MHS.

30. John Revere paid Dr. Samuel Danforth $77.50 for "medical attendance," in John Revere's Account as executor of Paul Revere's Will, roll 3, Revere Papers (loose manuscripts and undated material, 1814–1964). On May 27, 1780, Revere began renting his home to George DeFrance, and on July 19, 1784, he began renting to Joseph Dunkerly ("Dunkerley"), Waste Book and Memoranda, vol. 1, roll 5, Revere Papers. Masonic identifications are in *Centennial Memorial,* 233, 234, 236.

31. On Revere's Masonic offices see Steblecki, *Paul Revere and Freemasonry,* appendix 2, 102–4; "Parker Index," 266–67. Description of duties of Masonic officers in By-Laws of St. Andrew's Lodge, St. Andrew's File, Boston, Massachusetts, Grand Lodge of Massachusetts A.F. & A.M., Samuel Crocker Lawrence Library; Steblecki, *Paul Revere and Freemasonry,* 17–18. On the appeal of Ancient Masonry for artisans and men of middling rank and how Freemasonry opened up leadership opportunities for these men see Bullock, "Revolutionary Freemasonry," 363–69; "Ancient and Honorable Society," 85–101; Bullock, *Revolutionary Brotherhood,* 106–8.

32. Members of the North End Caucus listed in Alan Day and Katherine Day, "Another Look at the Boston Caucus," *Journal of American Studies* 5 (April 1971): 32–33; Goss, *Life of Colonel Revere,* vol. 2, appendix C, 635–36. On Masonic ideals see Bullock, "The Ancient and Honorable Society," 12–57, 85–101; Bullock, *Revolutionary Brotherhood,* 50–82, 85–98.

33. Besides Revere, the other members of both the North End Caucus and St. Andrew's Lodge were Thomas Chase, Adam Colson, William Hoskins, John Lowell, John Merritt, Edward Proctor, Asa Stoddard, Eben and John Symmes, Thomas Urann, and Dr. Joseph Warren. On the North End Caucus see Day and Day, "Another Look at the Boston Caucus," 32–33; Goss, *Life of Colonel Revere,* vol. 2, appendix C, 635–36. On St. Andrew's Lodge members see *Centennial Memorial* (alphabetical order), 232–36; "Parker Index" (in order listed above), 58, 68–69, 166–67, 206–7, 218–19, 258–59, 266–67, 298–99, 304–5, 320–21, 326–27. On the connection between Freemasonry and the American Revolution see Bullock, *Revolutionary Brotherhood,* 109–33 (on range of political opinion from patriot to Rowe's "cautious neutrality" to Tory); Neil L. York, "Freemasons and the American Revolution," *The Historian* 55 (Winter 1993): 315–30.

34. Anderson, *People's Army,* 14–21; John Boyle, *Boyle's Journal of Occurrences in Boston,*

1759–1778, New England Historical and Genealogical Register 84 (April 1930): 149 (October 16, 1759), 154 (September 26, 1760).

35. Bernard's arrival in Boston on August 2, 1760, was noted in *Boyle's Journal of Occurrences*, New England Historical and Genealogical Register 84 (April 1930): 154. Bernard's description of Boston is quoted in Bridenbaugh, *Cities in Revolt*, 193. His comments to the Board of Trade are quoted in Bushman, *King and People*, 122.

36. Nash, *Urban Crucible*, 274–75; Egnal, *Mighty Empire*, 46–47; Bushman, *King and People*, 14–15, 266.

37. On the importance of gentility as a qualification for a political leadership see Bushman, *King and People*, 14–25, 55–56, 86–87; Bullock, "The Ancient and Honorable Society," 115–16. On political background of period see G. B. Warden, *Boston, 1689–1776* (Boston, 1970), 49–151; Nash, *Urban Crucible*, 272–75. On quoted material see Shirley's comment on the "Mobbish Spirit" of the town meeting in a letter to the Lords of Trade, December 1, 1747, in Nash, *Urban Crucible*, 273; John Adams, "Novanglus," in Bernard Bailyn, *The Ideological Origins of the American Revolution* (Cambridge, Mass., 1967), 109–10; Mayhew, *A Discourse Concerning Unlimited Submission*, 24, 54.

38. Bushman, *King and People*, 162–63; Forbes, *Paul Revere*, 60–61; Nash, *Urban Crucible*, 275–76 (Adams's quote is on 276).

39. Nash, *Urban Crucible*, 275–76; Bailyn, *Ordeal of Thomas Hutchinson*, 47–56. Otis's quote on "fundamental principles of law" is in I. R. Christie, *Crisis of Empire: Great Britain and the American Colonies, 1754–1783* (New York, 1966), 37–38. The quote on "star-chamber tyranny" is in Egnal, *Mighty Empire*, 47.

40. Members of the North End Caucus in Day and Day, "Another Look at the Boston Caucus," 32–33; Goss, *Life of Colonel Revere*, vol. 2, appendix C, 635–36. On taverns and clubs in the North End see Forbes, *Paul Revere*, 112–14; Bridenbaugh, *Cities in Revolt*, 157–59; Drake, *Old Landmarks and Historic Personages*, 176.

41. Day and Day, "Another Look at the Boston Caucus," 19–42; G. B. Warden, "The Caucus and Democracy in Colonial Boston," *New England Quarterly* 43 (March 1970): 19–45; Warden, *Boston, 1689–1776*, 93–95, chap. 7; Nash, *Urban Crucible*, 85–87. Warden, in "The Caucus and Democracy in Colonial Boston," 21 n. 2, cites two eighteenth-century sources for the origins of the Boston Caucus in the 1720s: William Gordon, *History of the Rise, Progress, and Establishment of the Independence of the United States of America*, and Peter Oliver, *The Origins and Progress of the American Rebellion*.

42. Nash, *Urban Crucible*, 76–88.

43. Warden, "Caucus and Democracy in Colonial Boston," 28–45; Day and Day, "Another Look at the Boston Caucus," 29–35; Nash, *Urban Crucible*, 277–79; Hoerder, "Boston Leaders and Boston Crowds," 233–71.

44. See Waste Book and Memoranda, vol. 1, roll 5, Revere Papers. Revere's income varied widely between 1761 and 1775, and in some years it was so low it suggests that his records were incomplete. In addition, he rarely recorded his income from dentistry, a skill he began practicing in 1768. Conclusions about Revere's economic status must thus take into consideration his erratic bookkeeping. See Main, *Social Structure of Revolutionary America*, 70–82, for information on annual income for artisans and laborers, "not found (without food or lodging)." Income varied widely, and the figures cited are perhaps on the

higher end of the scale. Clearly, Revere's average yearly income as a master goldsmith separated him from the ranks of journeymen artisans and laborers. What is more interesting is how often Revere's income rose and fell dramatically in this period, which made his economic and social position unpredictable and at times precarious.

45. Bridenbaugh, *Colonial Craftsman*, 68; Fairbanks, *Paul Revere's Boston*, 20, 46–57; Fales, *Early American Silver*, 115–16.

46. Goss, *Life of Colonel Revere*, 2.667–68; Forbes, *Paul Revere*, 66–67.

47. The description of Revere as "cool in thought, ardent in action" is from his obituary in the *Boston Intelligencer and Evening Gazette*, May 16, 1818. The "Rallying Song of the Tea Party at the Green Dragon" is in Francis S. Drake, *Tea Leaves: Being a Collection of Letters and Documents Relating to the Shipment of Tea to the American Colonies in the Year 1773, by the East India Tea Company* (1884; reprint, Detroit, 1970), 176.

3. The Political Awakening of Paul Revere

1. Income is rounded to nearest pound. Barrett was a customer 1762–65, 1773; Hopkins in 1763–64, 1766, and 1767; Hill in 1761, 1763–66, 1768–69, 1772; Johonnot in 1762–63, 1765–66, 1773; Copley (listed as "Mr. John Copley") in 1763, 1765, and 1767; all in Waste Book and Memoranda, vol. 1, roll 5, Revere Family Papers, MHS. On Copley see Stark, *Loyalists of Massachusetts*, 216–18. On Revere's engravings see Forbes, *Paul Revere*, 105–7; Clarence S. Brigham, *Paul Revere's Engravings* (New York, 1969). On his Masonic offices see Steblecki, *Paul Revere and Freemasonry*, appendix 2, 103. In addition to Deborah Revere, Paul Revere Jr. was born on January 6, 1760, and Sarah Revere on January 3, 1762. See Nielsen, "The Revere Family," 299.

2. *Boyle's Journal of Occurrences*, May 24, 1763, *New England Historical and Genealogical Register* 84 (April 1930): 162; McKay and Scott, *Rise of the Great Powers, 1648–1815*, 197–200.

3. Egnal, *Mighty Empire*, 126–35; Nash, *Urban Crucible*, 246–47.

4. *Boyle's Journal of Occurrences*, *New England Historical and Genealogical Register* 84 (April 1930): 164. Harbottle Dorr claimed that the poem "Prognosticator, or the Vision" was about the failure of Nathaniel Wheelwright, in *Boston Gazette*, February 4, 1765, *Dorr Collection*, 1.17. For background on the postwar depression see Egnal, *Mighty Empire*, 129–39; Nash, *Urban Crucible*, 246–50.

5. In 1763 Copley ordered gold bracelets (Revere writes "bracletts"), gold and silver picture frames, and a gold picture case on January 7, January 8, February 7, February 18, and February 26. Greene's order is dated March 29. Thomas Hill ordered teaspoons on February 12 and the butter cups on August 12. In contrast to these larger orders, Revere made shoe buckles for Joshua Brackett on February 12, 1763, and mended buttons for Caleb Hopkins on March 24, 1763. He also allowed his Hichborn relations longer credit terms in 1763; all in Waste Book and Memoranda, vol. 1, roll 5, Revere Papers. See also Federhen, "From Artisan to Entrepreneur," 67–69.

6. Revere's waste book listed no business between February 2 and March 4, 1764. On February 6, 1764, the Boston selectmen noted Revere's refusal to remove his sick child from home and their order that "a Flag be put out" in front of the house. On February 20 Revere

promised the selectmen he would not go in and out of his infected house "contrary to Orders." The Reveres were still quarantined on March 1, 1764. On Revere's business see *Waste Book and Memoranda*, vol. 1, roll 5, Revere Papers. On the smallpox epidemic and its impact on the Revere family see *Boston Town Records*, 20.31–32, 40–41, 47; *Boyle's Journal of Occurrences*, February 26, 1764, *New England Historical and Genealogical Register* 84 (April 1930): 164.

7. Christie, *Crisis of Empire*, 45–54; Lawrence Henry Gipson, *The Coming of the American Revolution, 1763–1775* (New York, 1962), 55–68; Bushman, *King and People*, 149–54; Bailyn, *Ideological Origins of American Revolution*, 94–104; Jack P. Greene, ed., *Colonies to Nations: A Documentary History of the American Revolution* (1967; reprint, New York, 1975), 12–26.

8. In Greene, *Colonies to Nation*, 28–33.

9. Arthur Savage Jr. to Samuel Phillips Savage, February 8 and March 1, 1765, S. P. Savage II Papers, MHS.

10. Text of Stamp Act in Greene, *Colonies to Nation*, 42–43. On colonial reaction to the expected impact of the Stamp Act see Shaw, *American Patriots and the Rituals of Revolution*, 5–7; Christie, *Crisis of Empire*, 55–58.

11. On Revere's business affairs in 1765, including the notation that he was renting out part of his shop, see *Waste Book and Memoranda*, vol. 1, roll 5, Revere Papers. On customer identifications see *Centennial Memorial*, 231–36; "Parker Index," 114–15 (on Josiah Flagg); advertisement for Webb's shop in *Boston Gazette*, January 30, 1769, *Dorr Collection*, 2.383. The account of Flagg's debt to Revere of £204.9.6 is undated, but the debt included the cost of one-half of engraving copperplates for their singing book, published in 1765, in roll 3, Revere Papers. See also Revere and Flagg's advertisement for their psalmbook in *Boston Gazette and Country Journal*, January 21, 1765, *Dorr Collection*, 1.11. On attachment of Revere's estate see Suffolk County Supreme Judicial Court Files, case no. 86511, microfilm reel 275, courtesy of Judicial Archives, Massachusetts Archives. On depressed trade conditions see Egnal, *Mighty Empire*, 129–35; Nash, *Urban Crucible*, 292–300.

12. Biographical information on Harbottle Dorr in introduction to *Dorr Collection*, vol. 1; *New York Gazette*, June 6, 1765, reprinted in *Boston Evening Post*, June 24, 1765, *Dorr Collection*, 1.111, 114; Thomas Whately, "The Regulations Lately Made . . . ," in Greene, *Colonies to Nation*, 46–51. See also Gipson, *Coming of the Revolution*, 85–88 (Patrick Henry's quote on 87).

13. Bernard's quote in Gipson, *Coming of Revolution*, 88. On reaction to the Stamp Act in Boston newspapers in the summer of 1765 see *Dorr Collection*, vol. 1, e.g., *New York Gazette*, July 4, 1765, reprinted in *Boston Evening Post*, July 15, 1765, *Dorr Collection*, 1.123. On Dulany's "Considerations on the Propriety of Imposing Taxes on the British Colonies" see Greene, *Colonies to Nation*, 45–46, 51–59; Edmund S. Morgan and Helen M. Morgan, *The Stamp Act Crisis: Prologue to Revolution*, 2d ed. (New York, 1963), 99–119. On the colonial concept of liberty see Bailyn, *Ideological Origins of American Revolution*, 79–84.

14. On Sharp and Stoddard see Goss, *Life of Colonel Revere*, vol. 2, appendix C, 635–36; Day and Day, "Another Look at Boston Caucus," 32–33; Suffolk Probate Court Record Book, case no. 18463, vol. 84, p. 205, microfilm reel 34 (1784–86), Judicial Archives, Massachusetts Archives, on Asa Stoddard, who died intestate. On Dorr see biographical

information in introduction to *Dorr Collection*, vol. 1, and his shop advertisement, *Boston Gazette*, April 18, 1768, *Dorr Collection*, 2.80. Revere's will and inventory of his estate are in Suffolk Probate Court Record Book, case no. 25527, vol. 116, p. 246 (will, November 15, 1816, and codicil, March 14, 1818), and p. 315 (inventory and schedule of estate, June 18, 1818), microfilm reel 49, Judicial Archives, Massachusetts Archives, and in roll 3, Revere Papers. On the contrast in income and range of Revere's work in 1762 and 1765 see Waste Book and Memoranda, vol. 1, roll 5, Revere Papers. See also Bailyn, *Ideological Origins of American Revolution*, 94–104; Bushman, *King and People*, 194–98 (quote from *Boston Post-Boy and Advertiser*, August 26, 1765, on 194).

15. Morgan, *Stamp Act Crisis*, 265–79; Shaw, *American Patriots and Rituals of Revolution*, 26–33; Bailyn, *Ordeal of Thomas Hutchinson*, 64–69; Nash, *Urban Crucible*, 226, 273–81.

16. Morgan, *Stamp Act Crisis*, 159–61; Pauline Maier, *From Resistance to Revolution: Colonial Radicals and the Development of American Opposition to Britain, 1765–1776* (New York, 1974), 3–26, 307; Nash, *Urban Crucible*, 292–97. Note that McIntosh is also spelled "MacIntosh" and "Mackintosh."

17. Contemporary accounts of events in supplement to *Boston Gazette*, August 19, 1765, *Dorr Collection*, 1.166; *Boyle's Journal of Occurrences*, August 14, 1765, *New England Historical and Genealogical Register* 84 (April 1930): 169. The *Boston Gazette* of September 16, 1765, reported that the tree "upon which the Effigies of a Stamp Master was lately hung, was honour'd last Wednesday with the Name of, THE TREE OF LIBERTY," *Dorr Collection*, 1.193. Background information in Morgan, *Stamp Act Crisis*, 161–65; Shaw, *American Patriots and Rituals of Revolution*, 9–13; Nash, *Urban Crucible*, 292–97.

18. Morgan, *Stamp Act Crisis*, 166–67; Nash, *Urban Crucible*, 294; Shaw, *American Patriots and Rituals of Revolution*, 34.

19. *Boston Gazette*, September 2, 1765, *Dorr Collection*, 1.177; Edward Payne to unidentified recipient on the Stamp Act, September 1765, Ezekiel Price Papers, MHS; Morgan, *Stamp Act Crisis*, 167; Shaw, *American Patriots and Rituals of Revolution*, 35; Nash, *Urban Crucible*, 294–99.

20. On Avery's order and gap in Revere's business activity between August 1 and September 14, 1765, see Waste Book and Memoranda, vol. 1, roll 5, Revere Papers. On identifications see John Cary, *Joseph Warren: Physician, Politician, Patriot* (Urbana, Ill., 1961), 55 (Avery and Warren's Harvard affiliation); "Parker Index," 58, 72–73, 330 (Masonic identification of Chase, Crafts, and Welles); Day and Day, "Another Look at Boston Caucus," 32–33; Goss, *Life of Colonel Revere*, vol. 2, appendix C, 635–36 (North End Caucus members); Drake, *Tea Leaves*, 92–94 (list of Tea Party participants).

21. Revere was chosen clerk of the market, although he declined the post, on March 10, 1766, in *Boston Town Records*, 16.165. For the offices held by John Avery of the Loyal Nine, Thomas Chase of the Loyal Nine and the North End Caucus, Stephen Cleverly of the Loyal Nine, and Benjamin Edes of the Loyal Nine and the North End Caucus see Robert Francis Seybolt, *The Town Officials of Colonial Boston, 1634–1775* (Cambridge, Mass., 1939), 317 (on John Avery); 319, 321, 327, 332, 351, 357 (Thomas Chase); 320–21, 361 (Stephen Cleverly); 280, 290, 303, 308, 312, 315, 319 (Benjamin Edes). On the role of master artisans in colonial society, patrician attitudes toward the lower and middling classes, and the relationship between Revolutionary leaders and artisans see Bridenbaugh, *Colonial Crafts-*

man, 126–27, 143, 155–81; Wood, *Radicalism of the American Revolution*, 19–42; Hoerder, "Boston Leaders and Boston Crowds," 232–71.

22. On the economic background of the Stamp Act crisis see Nash, *Urban Crucible*, 292–300, 351. On the prestige of the goldsmith's craft and how it was culturally different from less skilled trades see Bridenbaugh, *Colonial Craftsman*, 68–75, 126–27; Fales, *Early American Silver*, 23–25, 115–25; Bullock, "Ancient and Honorable Society," 120–22; Bullock, *Revolutionary Brotherhood*, 85–98, 106–8.

23. On Masonic rituals and processions and their conveyance of "images of authority, gentility, and honor," see Bullock, *Revolutionary Brotherhood*, 52–56; Bullock, "Ancient and Honorable Society," 47. On Revere's Masonic offices and description of duties see Steblecki, *Paul Revere and Freemasonry*, appendix 2 and p. 17.

24. On petitioning see Bushman, *King and People*, 46–54. On the relationship between leaders and crowd see Hoerder, "Boston Leaders and Boston Crowds," 232–71. The circular letter from Massachusetts House of Representatives to assemblies of North America, inviting them to the Stamp Act Congress in New York, June 8, 1765, is in Morgan, *Stamp Act Crisis*, 139.

25. Text of Declaration of Stamp Act Congress and discussion in Morgan, *Stamp Act Crisis*, 142–54; *Boyle's Journal of Occurrences*, November 1, 1765, *New England Historical and Genealogical Register* 84 (April 1930): 170.

26. *Boston Gazette*, October 7, 1765, *Dorr Collection*, 1.216; *Boyle's Journal of Occurrences*, November 1, 1765, *New England Historical and Genealogical Register* 84 (April 1930): 170–71. On the celebration at the Royal Exchange Tavern on November 5 see *Boston Evening Post*, November 18, 1765, *Dorr Collection*, 1.273. See also Shaw, *American Patriots and Rituals of Revolution*, 179–80, 188–89; Hoerder, "Boston Leaders and Boston Crowds," 245.

27. *Boston Gazette*, November 25, December 9, December 23, 1765, *Dorr Collection*, 1.287, 296, 302. See also Nash, *Urban Crucible*, 299–300; Morgan, *Stamp Act Crisis*, 92–94.

28. Henry Bass to Samuel Phillips Savage, December 19, 1765, S. P. Savage Papers, vol. 2, 1751–1829, MHS; Morgan, *Stamp Act Crisis*, 234–40.

29. Maier, *From Resistance to Revolution*, 77–91; Morgan, *Stamp Act Crisis*, 240–44 (Bernard's comment to John Pownall, July 20, 1765, is on 241).

30. *Boston Gazette*, January 27, 1766, *Dorr Collection*, 1.328; Shaw, *American Patriots and Rituals of Revolution*, 181; Brigham, *Revere's Engravings*, 22–25.

31. *Boston Gazette*, February 24, March 31, April 7, May 6, 1766, *Dorr Collection*, 1.348, 372, 378, 396.

32. *Boston Gazette*, May 12, 19, 26, 1766, *Dorr Collection*, 1.408, 411–12, 415; Egnal, *Mighty Empire*, 154–56.

33. On Burbeck see Membership File, Grand Lodge of Massachusetts; "Extract of a Letter from General Henry Burbeck to Colonel Samuel Swett . . . March 18, 1848, on his father William Burbeck," *New England Historical and Genealogical Register* 12 (October 1858): 351–52. On the Stamp Act repeal celebration and Revere's participation see *Boyle's Journal of Occurrences*, May 19, 1766, *New England Historical and Genealogical Register* 84 (July 1930): 249; *Boston Gazette*, May 19 and May 26, 1766, *Dorr Collection*, 1.411, 415; Forbes, *Paul Revere*, 110–12; Brigham, *Revere's Engravings*, 26–31. The text of Declaratory Act appears in Greene, *Colonies to Nation*, 84–85.

34. Pitt's remarks, January 14, 1766, in Greene, *Colonies to Nation*, 68–72.

35. Shaw, *American Patriots and Rituals of Revolution*, 52–58; Morgan, *Stamp Act Crisis*, 327–37; Christie, *Crisis of Empire*, 59–61; Gipson, *Coming of the Revolution*, 106–7.

36. Morgan, *Stamp Act Crisis*, 347–52; Christie, *Crisis of Empire*, 61–65; Gipson, *Coming of the Revolution*, 108–15; Greene, *Colonies to Nation*, 65–66, 72–78.

37. *Boston Gazette*, May 6, 1766, *Dorr Collection*, 1.396; *Boston Town Records* (May 14, 1766), 16.182–84.

38. Nash, *Urban Crucible*, 351; "Proceedings of the North End Caucus," in Goss, *Life of Colonel Revere*, vol. 2, appendix C, 635–44.

39. Forbes, *Paul Revere*, 54; Cary, *Joseph Warren*, 55–59. To deepen his understanding of Freemasonry Revere became a Royal Arch Mason in 1769, which is discussed in chapter 4, and he was a subscriber to *Calcott's Candid Disquisition on the Principles and Practices of the Most Ancient and Honorable Society of Free and Accepted Masons* (1772), Evans, *Early American Imprints*, no. 12345.

40. A copy of the Copley portrait, with explanatory text, is in Fairbanks et al., *Paul Revere's Boston*, 18–19. For my analysis of the Copley portrait I have drawn on Forbes, *Paul Revere*, 109–10.

4. A Son of Liberty

1. Mary Revere, Revere's fourth child, was born on March 31, 1764, but died on April 20 or April 30, 1765, and Frances Revere, his fifth child, was born on February 19, 1766; in Nielsen, "The Revere Family," 299. On news of the Stamp Act's repeal, see *Boyle's Journal of Occurrences*, *New England Historical and Genealogical Register* 84 (July 1930): 249. On Revere's business see Waste Book and Memoranda, vol. 1, roll 5, Revere Family Papers, MHS. For information on Adam Colson see Palmer, *Centennial Memorial*, 232; "Parker Index," 68–69; Thwing Index, MHS; Drake, *Tea Leaves*. On the need for continued vigilance see the Boston town meeting's instructions to representatives in Massachusetts General Court, May 14, 1766, *Boston Town Records*, 16.182–84; *Boston Gazette*, May 6, 1766, *Dorr Collection*, 1.396.

2. The first article by "Paskalos" appeared in the *Gazette* on June 2, 1766, and others continued through May 4, 1767. "Paskalos" was succeeded by "A True Patriot," beginning February 29, 1768, in the *Gazette* and continuing through March 14, 1768. See *Dorr Collection*, 1.424, 642; 2.38, 44; Cary, *Joseph Warren*, 43–44, 60–68. On Mayhew's sermon on May 23, 1766, and death on July 9, 1766, see *Boyle's Journal of Occurrences*, *New England Historical and Genealogical Register* 84 (July 1930): 250; *Boston Gazette*, July 14, 1766, *Dorr Collection*, 1.451. See also Mayhew, *A Discourse Concerning Unlimited Submission*, 54.

3. For background and information on the Malcolm case see George G. Wolkins, "Daniel Malcolm and Writs of Assistance," *MHS Proceedings* 58 (October 1924): 5–84 (Sheafe and Hallowell depositions on 26–29, Greenleaf deposition on 34–39); Zobel, *Boston Massacre*, 51–57; Thomas C. Barrow, *Trade and Empire: The British Customs Service in Colonial America, 1660–1775* (Cambridge, Mass., 1967), 202–3, 213–26.

4. Depositions of Captain Daniel Malcolm, William Mackay, Nathaniel Barber, Caleb

Hopkins, and Paul Revere in Wolkins, "Daniel Malcolm and Writs of Assistance," 39–42, 43–45, 32–33, 50–51, 52.

5. Wolkins, "Daniel Malcolm and Writs of Assistance," 21–25, 73; Barrow, *Trade and Empire*, 202–3.

6. Waste Book and Memoranda, vol. 1, roll 5, Revere Papers. William Palfrey (Revere spells it "Palfry") became a member of St. Andrew's Lodge in 1761, and John Symmes joined in 1766; in Palmer, *Centennial Memorial*, 232, 233. On Palfrey see also Baxter, *House of Hancock*, 24; Maier, *From Resistance to Revolution*, 126, 164. On John Symmes see "Parker Index," 304–5; Thwing Index, MHS; Goss, *Life of Colonel Revere*, 2.635, 638; Federhen, "From Artisan to Entrepreneur," 74–75. On Gibbens Sharp ("Gibben Sharp" in Revere's waste book) see Day and Day, "Another Look at the Boston Caucus," 28, 32; Goss, *Life of Colonel Revere*, 2.635–37, 641–43. Marc Egnal describes "two subcycles" of depression in the colonial economy caused by postwar difficulties in the British economy. The first subcycle lasted from 1760 to 1766, with 1765 being the worst year and 1766 a time of "mild recovery." The second and more severe subcycle lasted from 1766 to 1770, reaching its lowest point in 1768. See Egnal, *Mighty Empire*, 126–38.

7. Barrow, *Trade and Empire*, 213–16 (Pitt's remarks on colonial events to Lord Shelburne, February 7, 1767, on 215); Greene, *Colonies to Nation*, 114–15.

8. Greene, *Colonies to Nation*, 114–19; Barrow, *Trade and Empire*, 213–26; Bushman, *King and People*, 165–69; *Boyle's Journal of Occurrences, New England Historical and Genealogical Register* 84 (July 1930): 253.

9. On response to the Townshend Act see Massachusetts circular letter in Greene, *Colonies to Nation*, 121, 134–36; Committee of Boston Merchants' Report, March 4, 1768, in Anne Rowe Cunningham, ed., *Letters and Diary of John Rowe, Boston Merchant* (1903; reprint, Ann Arbor, Mich., 1968), 153–55; Massachusetts House resolutions on nonimportation, February 26, 1768, in *Boston Gazette*, February 29, 1768, *Dorr Collection*, 2.34.

10. On nonimportation as an ideal republican solution see *Boston Gazette*, February 29, 1768, *Dorr Collection*, 2.34; Nash, *Urban Crucible*, 351–54; Stephen E. Patterson, *Political Parties in Revolutionary Massachusetts* (Madison, Wis., 1973), 63–66. On merchants' support for nonimportation and their economic motives see Cunningham, *Letters and Diary of John Rowe*, 152–55; merchants' draft petition against revenue acts, January 1767, in Ezekiel Price Papers, MHS; Cushing to DeBerdt, *Miscellaneous Bound Manuscripts*, MHS; Charles M. Andrews, "The Boston Merchants and the Non-Importation Movement," *Colonial Society of Massachusetts Publications* (hereafter *CSM Pubs.*) 19 (February 1917): 159–259, especially 168–80; Egnal, *Mighty Empire*, 138–39, 161–63.

11. *Boston Gazette*, May 9, 1768, *Dorr Collection*, 2.100; nonimportation agreement of July 31, 1769, cataloged under name of Harbottle Dorr, Ms. L, MHS. Ezra Collins was Revere's neighbor, customer, and Masonic lodge brother. Thomas Crafts and John Symmes were members of St. Andrew's Lodge. Symmes, John Boit, and Abiel Ruddock were members of the North End Caucus. On Collins see Forbes, *Paul Revere*, 273, 454. On the North End Caucus see Day and Day, "Another Look at the Boston Caucus," 29–33; Goss, *Life of Colonel Revere*, vol. 2, appendix C, 635–36. For Masonic information on Ezra Collins, Thomas Crafts, and John Symmes see Palmer, *Centennial Memorial*, 231–33; "Parker Index," 66–67, 72–73, 304–5.

12. *Boyle's Journal of Occurrences, New England Historical and Genealogical Register* 84 (July 1930): 253; *Boston Gazette*, February 22, 1768, *Dorr Collection*, 2.31. On the Board of Customs Commissioners see Barrow, *Trade and Empire*, 220–23. On colonial fears of the invasion of placemen and pensioners see Bailyn, *Ideological Origins of American Revolution*, 102–4.

13. Revere placed his first advertisement as a "dentist" in the *Boston Gazette* on September 5, 1768, *Dorr Collection*, 2.228. See also Waste Book and Memoranda, vol. 1, roll 5, Revere Papers.

14. Text of nonimportation agreement in *Boston Town Records*, 16.221. Revere's income in 1768 was £47.6.11, compared with £47.18.10 for 1767. On Revere's income and range of work in 1768 and 1769 see Waste Book and Memoranda, vol. 1, roll 5, Revere Papers. Revere refers to Edmund Quincy IV (1703–88) as "Edmund Quincy Tertius" or "the third" in his waste book, perhaps because Quincy's father (Edmund III) had died in 1738. On Edmund Quincy see *A Pride of Quincys: A Massachusetts Historical Society Picture Book* (Boston, 1969). On Tristram Dalton see Benjamin W. Labaree, *Patriots and Partisans: The Merchants of Newburyport, 1764–1815* (New York, 1975), 210–11. For Revere's dentistry advertisements see *Boston Gazette* and *Boston Evening-Post*, September 5, 12, 26, December 19, 1768; *Gazette*, October 10, 17, November 14, 28, December 26, 1768; and *Evening-Post*, January 16, 1769; all *Dorr Collection*, vol. 2, issues are contained between pages 228 and 364. On artisan support for nonimportation see Nash, *Urban Crucible*, 321, 354–59.

15. On the importance of artisans in the Revolutionary period and how the Revolution enhanced the status of artisans see Nash, "Artisans and Politics in Eighteenth-Century Philadelphia," 62–88; Nash, *Urban Crucible*, 321–25, 351–82; Olton, *Artisans for Independence*, 33–47; Hoerder, "Boston Leaders and the Boston Crowd." On the appeal of Freemasonry to artisans as a means of acquiring gentility see chapter 2. On the genteel attributes of honor and reputation see Wood, *Radicalism of the American Revolution*, 39–41, 207–10.

16. On Royall Tyler and quote from Tyler's *Conversation* see Shipton, *Sibley's Harvard Graduates*, 11.313–18. On Boston's caucuses and political clubs see Warden, "Caucus and Democracy in Boston," 28–34; Day and Day, "Another Look at the Boston Caucus," 29–33.

17. For membership and organization of North End Caucus see Day and Day, "Another Look at the Boston Caucus," 19–42; Goss, *Life of Colonel Revere*, vol. 2, appendix C, 635–44. On the concept of mobilization (the process of previously excluded people participating in public affairs) see Edward Countryman, *A People in Revolution: The American Revolution and Political Society in New York, 1760–1790* (New York, 1989), 132–34. The quote on electing proper representatives to General Court appears in *Boston Gazette*, April 27, 1767, *Dorr Collection*, 1.636. On the role of the Boston crowd see Hoerder, "Boston Leaders and Boston Crowds," 246–53.

18. Dorr's comment on Otis's election to the General Court, *Boston Gazette*, October 7, 1765, *Dorr Collection*, 1.217. On deference to leaders in the Revolution see Nash, *Urban Crucible*, 351–62; Hoerder, "Boston Leaders and Boston Crowds," 235–41; Wood, *Radicalism of the American Revolution*, 86–87. See also Otis, *The Rights of The British Colonies Asserted and Proved*, in Greene, *Colonies to Nation*, 30–31; Bailyn, *Ideological Origins of the American Revolution*, 94–143 ("The Logic of Rebellion").

19. Information on Gibbens Sharp, John Boit, Caleb Champney, and Adam Colson in Day and Day, "Another Look at Boston Caucus," 32–33; Goss, *Life of Colonel Revere,* vol. 2, appendix C, 635–44; Thwing Index, MHS; Palmer, *Lodge of St. Andrew,* 227–36. Inventory of Revere's estate, Suffolk Probate Court Record Book, case no. 25527, vol. 116, p. 315, microfilm reel 49, Judicial Archives, Massachusetts Archives, and roll 3, Revere Papers. On Revolutionary ideals see Wood, *Creation of the American Republic,* 46–74; Bailyn, *Ideological Origins of the American Revolution,* 301–19.

20. Dickinson's "Letters" appeared in colonial newspapers, including the *Boston Gazette,* between November 1767 and February 1768; reprinted in Greene, *Colonies to Nation,* 121–33. On ladies' linen manufacture and the popularity of "The Liberty Song" see the *Boston Gazette,* June 6, July 18, 1768, *Dorr Collection,* 2.134, 166. On Revere's engravings see Brigham, *Revere's Engravings;* order for Mein and Fleeming ("Fleming"), February 5, 1768, in Waste Book and Memoranda, vol. 1, roll 5, Revere Papers. See also John E. Alden, "John Mein: Scourge of Patriots," *CSM Pubs.* 34 (February 1941): 571–99.

21. *Boyle's Journal of Occurrences,* June 10, 1768, *New England Historical and Genealogical Register* 84 (July 1930): 255; *Boston Gazette,* June 20, 1768, *Dorr Collection,* 2.141; Molineux to Harrison, June 15, 1768, Sparks Manuscripts X, New England Papers, vol. 3, f. 1 (hereafter Sparks Mss. 10.3:1 etc.), by permission of the Houghton Library, Harvard University. On Bernard's and Hutchinson's reactions see Bailyn, *Ordeal of Thomas Hutchinson,* 121. On William Molineux see Nash, *Urban Crucible,* 333–37, 354–55. See also Egnal, *Mighty Empire,* 159.

22. *Boston Gazette,* July 18, 1768, *Dorr Collection,* 2.166; Hoerder, "Boston Leaders and Boston Crowds," 249–53.

23. Edes and Gill reported: "The reigning Toast in this Province is the Massachusetts 92," in the *Boston Gazette,* July 11, 1768, *Dorr Collection,* 2.163. Governor Bernard called Edes and Gill "the trumpeters of sedition" in a letter to Hillsborough, January 25, 1769, Sparks Mss. 10.3:17, by permission of the Houghton Library, Harvard University. John Rowe noted vote of Massachusetts General Court, June 30, 1768, and registered his disapproval of the seventeen yea votes, in Cunningham, *Letters and Diary of John Rowe,* 167. Description of the Liberty Bowl, which is at the Museum of Fine Arts in Boston, in Brigham, *Paul Revere's Engravings,* 36–37; Forbes, *Paul Revere,* 128–29; Goss, *Life of Colonel Revere,* 1.63–64.

24. On the connection between colonial opposition and Wilkes see Shaw, *American Patriots and Rituals of Revolution,* 58–68; George M. Elsey, ed., "John Wilkes and William Palfrey," *CSM Pubs.* 34 (February 1941): 411–28; Bailyn, *Ideological Origins of American Revolution,* 110–12 (quote by William Palfrey to Wilkes, February 21, 1769, on 112). The completion of the Liberty Bowl was reported in the *Boston Gazette,* August 8, 1768, *Dorr Collection,* 2.191.

25. Brigham, *Revere's Engravings,* 35–38; Forbes, *Paul Revere,* 129–30. Eliot's reminiscence from his commonplace book is recounted in the October 1832 sketch of Revere in the *New England Magazine,* 309; Brigham, *Revere's Engravings,* 36.

26. Paxton to Townshend, February 24 and May 18, 1768, *Miscellaneous Bound Manuscripts,* MHS. On the arrival of troops and the reactions of Bernard, Hutchinson, and Boston's patriots see *Boyle's Journal of Occurrences, New England Historical and Genealogical*

Register 84 (July 1930): 256–57; Bailyn, *Ordeal of Thomas Hutchinson,* 122–25 (on Bernard and Hutchinson); Nash, *Urban Crucible,* 360–62 (patriot reaction). Adams began the "Vindex" series in the *Gazette* on December 5, 1768, *Dorr Collection,* 2.311. For radical Whig arguments against standing armies and the importance to the patriot cause see Bailyn, *Ideological Origins of the American Revolution,* 34–36, 61–63. On Revere's wartime experience see chapter 2.

27. Quoted excerpts from the "Journal of the Times" in *Boston Evening-Post,* February 6 and January 30, 1769, *Dorr Collection,* 2.389, 386. See also excerpts in *Evening-Post,* December 12, 1768, January 2, 30, February 13, and March 6, 1769, *Dorr Collection,* 2.323, 343, 385, 397, 423.

28. On August 1, 1768, Boston merchants adopted stricter nonimportation resolutions to last from January 1, 1769, to January 1, 1770. See Andrews, "The Boston Merchants and the Non-Importation Movement," 204–6; Greene, *Colonies to Nation,* 146–47. Orders in Waste Book and Memoranda, vol. 1, roll 5, Revere Papers. On Sargent see Forbes, *Paul Revere,* 216. On Hooper, Cox, and Berry see Stark, *Loyalists of Massachusetts,* 125, 128, 137, 222–23.

29. Revere's Masonic offices are listed in Palmer, *Centennial Memorial,* 227; "Parker Index," 266–67; Steblecki, *Paul Revere and Freemasonry,* appendix 2, 103. For a detailed discussion of Revere's Masonic career in the 1760s see Steblecki, *Paul Revere and Freemasonry,* 18–19.

30. On the establishment of the Massachusetts Grand Lodge of Ancient Masons see Steblecki, *Paul Revere and Freemasonry,* 20–21; Palmer, *Centennial Memorial,* 31–32; Taylor, *Historical Sketch of the Grand Lodge of Massachusetts,* 6–7; *Grand Lodge Proceedings,* 1733–92, 226. Revere, Proctor, and Urann were all members of the North End Caucus. Thomas Crafts's contributions as a Son of Liberty included participation in the Boston Tea Party, and Caleb Hopkins commissioned the Liberty Bowl.

31. On the connection between Ancient Freemasonry and social mobility see the previous discussion in chapter 2. See also Wood, *Radicalism of the American Revolution,* 24–42 ("Patricians and Plebeians"), 189–95, 213–25.

32. For the list of participants and an account of the Liberty Tree dinner see "An Alphabetical List of the Sons of Liberty who dined at Liberty Tree, Dorchester, August 14, 1769," written in the hand of William Palfrey, *MHS Proceedings* 11 (August 1869): 140–42; John Adams's diary entry for August 14, 1769, in L. H. Butterfield, ed., *Diary and Autobiography of John Adams, 1755–1770,* vol. 1 (Cambridge, Mass., 1961), 341; *Boston Evening-Post,* August 21, 1769, *Dorr Collection,* 2.632.

33. On Bernard see account of his departure on August 1, 1769, in *Boyle's Journal of Occurrences, New England Historical and Genealogical Register* 84 (July 1930): 259; description of him as Hillsborough's "tool" and "that Enemy to American Liberty" in a letter from Dennys DeBerdt, Massachusetts colonial agent, to speaker of the Massachusetts House Thomas Cushing, June 1, 1769, in Albert Matthews, ed., "Letters of Dennys DeBerdt, 1757–1770," *CSM Pubs.* 13 (March 1911): 375. John Adams to Jonathan Sewell, February 1760, on common people and their enlightenment, and Adams's "Dissertation on the Feudal and Canon Law (1765)," quoted in Wood, *Radicalism of the American Revolution,* 27, 190, 191.

34. On the activities at Liberty Tree see John Adams's account in Butterfield, *Diary of John Adams*, 1.341; Zobel, *Boston Massacre*, 145. On Thomas Hichborn Sr. and Thomas Hichborn Jr. see Goss, *Life of Colonel Revere*, vol. 2, appendix C, 636–38 (North End Caucus members); *Boston Town Records*, 18.233 (members of the Committee of Correspondence, Safety, and Inspection). On participation of Stephen Bruce, Thomas Chase, Adam Colson, and Edward Proctor in the Boston Tea Party, see Drake, *Tea Leaves*, 92–93. Stephen Bruce's Masonic identification is in *Centennial Memorial*, 233; "Parker Index," 44–45. Chase, Colson, and Proctor have been previously identified. On Joshua Brackett see Forbes, *Paul Revere*, 67, 227. The quote about King George's "vile Bohea" is from "Rallying Song of the Tea Party at the Green Dragon," in Drake, *Tea Leaves*, 176.

35. Mein began publishing the manifests in his *Boston Chronicle* on August 17, 1769. William Palfrey defended Hancock in the *Boston Evening-Post*, August 28, 1769, and several other patriot merchants defended themselves on September 4 and 25, 1769, see *Dorr Collection*, 2.641, 653, 683; Alden, "John Mein: Scourge of Patriots," 586. On James Otis's brawl in the British Coffee House see *Boston Gazette*, September 11, 1769, *Dorr Collection*, 2.658; Zobel, *Boston Massacre*, 146–49.

36. Waste Book and Memoranda, vol. 1, roll 5, Revere Papers; *Boston Town Records*, 16.298; George Mason to Customs Collector Joseph Harrison, October 20, 1769, Sparks Mss., 10.3.40; on the attack on John Mein see Mein to Joseph Harrison, November 5, 1769, identifying leaders, Sparks Mss. 10.3:51, both by permission of the Houghton Library, Harvard University; Alden, "John Mein: Scourge of Patriots," 586–88; Zobel, *Boston Massacre*, 152–63; Palfrey, "An Alphabetical List of the Sons of Liberty who dined at Liberty Tree," 140–41 (for identification of Molineux, Davis, Dashwood, and Marshall as Revere's co-celebrants at Liberty Tree).

37. On Dorr see advertisement for his shop in the *Boston Gazette*, April 18, 1768, and introduction to newspaper collection, 1770–71, *Dorr Collection*, 2.80 and 3.1. On Revere's North Square home see deed, February 15, 1770, roll 1, Revere Papers; Forbes, *Paul Revere*, 162–64 (She claims that Revere also had a mortgage of £160), 458–59, 474; Whitehill, *Topographical History of Boston*, 15. On the connection between property and independence see Wood, *Radicalism of American Revolution*, 23, 178–79; Dickinson's Letter 12, in Greene, *Colonies to Nation*, 133.

38. On North Square see Forbes, *Paul Revere*, 164–68, and frontispiece for Price's 1769 map of Boston; Whitehill, *Topographical History of Boston*, 27–28. Harbottle Dorr identified Hutchinson as the object of attack in "Anecdotes for the Amusement of the Cabal," *Boston Gazette*, January 1, 1770, *Dorr Collection*, 3.3.

5. "My Worthy Friend Revere"

1. A letter from "The People," *Boston Gazette*, January 15, 1770, *Dorr Collection*, 3.18. On the nonimportation meeting of January 17, 1770, which Harbottle Dorr claimed was "the First Time the Inhabitants were Invited to join ye Merchants," see *Boston Gazette*, January 22, 1770, *Dorr Collection*, 3.23; "Journal of Transactions in Boston," January 18, 1770, and George Mason to Joseph Harrison, January 24, 1770, Sparks Mss. 10.3:56 and 10.3:63, by permission of the Houghton Library, Harvard University. Benjamin Greene was a

customer in 1762, 1772, and 1773, Waste Book and Memoranda, vol. 1, roll 5, Revere Family Papers, MHS. On the pressure to maintain nonimportation see Zobel, *Boston Massacre*, 164–72; Andrews, "Boston Merchants and Non-Importation," 221–31. On Josiah Quincy's disapproval of crowd action see Shaw, *American Patriots and Rituals of Revolution*, 160–62.

2. *Boston Gazette*, February 5, 1770, *Dorr Collection*, 3.31; Hoerder, "Boston Leaders and Boston Crowds," 258; Shaw, *American Patriots and Rituals of Revolution*, 193–95.

3. Location of incident in Forbes, *Paul Revere*, 173. On Richardson's character and description of events see William Palfrey to John Wilkes, March 5, 1770, in Elsey, "John Wilkes and William Palfrey," 416–17; Zobel, *Boston Massacre*, 54–55 (John Adams's characterization of Richardson on 55), 172–74.

4. Description of Richardson's unsuccessful attempt "to take down the pageantry" and what followed in *Boyle's Journal of Occurrences*, February 22, 1770, *New England Historical and Genealogical Register* 84 (July 1930): 262. Account of the "barbarous murder" of Christopher Seider in *Boston Gazette*, February 26, 1770, *Dorr Collection*, 3.50. On identifications of Thomas Knox, John Matchett, and Edward Proctor see Palfrey, "An Alphabetical List of the Sons of Liberty who dined at Liberty Tree," 140–41; Day and Day, "Another Look at the Boston Caucus," 30, 32; Goss, *Life of Colonel Revere*, vol. 2, appendix C, 635–36, 642–43; Palmer, *Centennial Memorial*, 233 (on Knox and Proctor); "Parker Index," 190–91 (Knox), 258–59 (Proctor). See also Zobel, *Boston Massacre*, 174–77 (Richardson's threat that he would "make it too hot for you before night" is on 174).

5. Contemporary accounts of the funeral of Seider (also spelled "Snider," "Snyder," and "Sneider") and actions of the Sons of Liberty appear in *Massachusetts Gazette and Boston Weekly News-Letter*, March 1, 1770, and *Boston Gazette*, March 5, 1770, *Dorr Collection*, 3.53, 56. On the political symbolism of the funeral see Shaw, *American Patriots and the Rituals of Revolution*, 194; Maier, *From Resistance to Revolution*, 194; Zobel, *Boston Massacre*, 178.

6. Revere produced engravings for Edes and Gill on January 10, March 9, and March 28, and he made a pair of stone buttons set in gold for John Joy on July 28; in Waste Book and Memoranda, vol. 1, roll 5, Revere Papers. References to Revere's other business activities are found in newspapers advertisements and other places in the Revere Papers, which will be discussed later in the chapter. The extraordinarily low income he recorded in his waste book suggests both a critical decline in Revere's business and careless bookkeeping, perhaps a result of the distraction of political events.

7. *Boston Gazette*, March 5, 1770, *Dorr Collection*, 3.56. On events leading to the Boston Massacre see depositions of Samuel Bostwick, deposition no. 23, March 19, 1770, and John Gray, deposition no. 9, March 22, 1770, in *A Short Narrative of the Horrid Massacre in Boston* (Boston, 1770), appendix, 13 and 6 (patriot account of the Boston Massacre with depositions gathered by a committee of James Bowdoin, Dr. Joseph Warren, and Samuel Pemberton, and published by Edes and Gill); *A Fair Account of the Late Unhappy Disturbance at Boston in New England* (London, 1770), 11 (Tory account of the Boston Massacre). See also Zobel, *Boston Massacre*, 182–83.

8. On the colonial belief about a conspiracy against liberty see Bailyn, *Ideological Origins of the American Revolution*, 144–59 ("A Note on Conspiracy"). On patriot accounts of the Boston Massacre see *Short Narrative*, 10–11, 16–17, 21 (review of events written by James

Bowdoin, Dr. Joseph Warren, and Samuel Pemberton). For the Tory version see *Fair Account,* 5–7, 12.

9. Compare patriot accounts of unruly soldiers in *Short Narrative,* 21, with Tory descriptions of armed citizens looking to attack soldiers in *Fair Account,* 14–16. On the description of Private White striking the apprentice Edward Garrick see William Tyler, deposition no. 24, March 21, 1770, and Edward Payne, deposition no. 56, March 21, 1770, *Short Narrative,* appendix, 13–14, 43–44. For opposing versions of the encounter between the grenadiers and townspeople see Henry Bass, deposition no. 25, March 16, 1770, *Short Narrative,* appendix, 14–15, and William Davies, deposition no. 99, March 13, 1770, *Fair Account,* appendix, 3. On the actions of the soldiers at Dock Square see Thomas Marshall, deposition no. 41, March 20, 1770, *Short Narrative,* appendix, 26–27. See also Zobel, *Boston Massacre,* 184–90.

10. Depositions of Nathaniel Fosdick, deposition no. 51, March 17, 1770, and Robert Patterson, deposition no. 69, March 20, 1770, *Short Narrative,* appendix, 36–37, 55–56. On the relationship between Revere and Fosdick see Waste Book and Memoranda, vol. 1, roll 5, Revere Papers; Goss, *Life of Colonel Revere,* 2.667–68; Forbes, *Paul Revere,* 66–67. On identification of Isaac Greenwood, Samuel Maverick's master, and his relationship with Revere see Waste Book and Memoranda, vol. 1, roll 5, Revere Papers; Thwing Index, MHS; Federhen, "From Artisan to Entrepreneur," 73–75; Forbes, *Paul Revere,* 125–26. See also Zobel, *Boston Massacre,* 175, 191–92.

11. Depositions of Nathaniel Fosdick, Henry Knox, and Richard Palmes in *Short Narrative,* appendix, 36–37, 42, 38–40. Preston to Major General Thomas Gage, March 19, 1770, in Randolph G. Adams, "New Light on the Boston Massacre," *American Antiquarian Society Proceedings* 47 (October 1937): 290–91.

12. *Short Narrative,* 11–12; Zobel, *Boston Massacre,* 182, 191, 192 (background on Gray, Kilroy, Caldwell, and Carr), 198–200 (account of events).

13. *Boyle's Journal of Occurrences,* March 5 and March 8, 1770, *New England Historical and Genealogical Register* 84 (July 1930): 264; John Rowe's diary entry, March 8, 1770, in Cunningham, *Letters and Diary of John Rowe,* 199; Zobel, *Boston Massacre,* 214–15.

14. On propaganda efforts see Zobel, *Boston Massacre,* 212–14. For a comparison of the depositions see *Fair Account,* especially 3–6, for the overwhelming number of officers and soldiers who offered testimony, and the appendix to *Short Narrative* for the range of patriot deponents, e.g., Samuel Atwood was from Wellfleet, Matthias King from Halifax, John Goddard from Brookline, William Wyat from Salem, Benjamin Frizel from Pownalborough, and George Coster from Bay of Bulls, Newfoundland, 21, 22, 25, 40, 48, 53.

15. "The BLOODY MASSACRE perpetrated in King Street" appeared at the top of Revere's engraving. See Forbes, *Paul Revere,* 152–53, 458, diagram of Massacre scene between 130 and 131; Zobel, *Boston Massacre,* 211.

16. *Boston Gazette,* March 12, 19, 26, 1770, Dorr Collection, 3.61, 65, 71. Under the date of March 9, 1770, Revere charged Edes and Gill for "Engraving 5 Coffings for Massacre," and on March 28, 1770, he charged them for "Printing 200 Impressions of Massacre," in Waste Book and Memoranda, vol. 1, roll 5, Revere Papers. On the Boston Massacre see Brigham, *Revere's Engravings,* 41–57.

17. *Boston Gazette,* April 2, 1770, *Dorr Collection,* 3.74. Clarence Brigham notes that Pelham's letter to Revere "did not come to light" until 1893, when Paul Leicester Ford published an article on the Copley-Pelham letters in the April edition of the *Atlantic Monthly.* Brigham also points out that since all of Pelham's letters were in rough draft form, "some sceptics" have doubted whether Pelham ever sent his letter to Revere. In any case, there is no recorded reply by Revere to Pelham. Esther Forbes claims that by October 4, 1774, Pelham and Revere had "settled matters between them" and that Revere was "handling" Pelham's engravings, but I found no such indication in Revere's Waste Book. On Revere and Pelham see Henry Pelham to Paul Revere, March 29, 1770, in Ford, *Copley-Pelham Letters, MHS Collections* 71 (1914): 83; E. Alfred Jones, *The Loyalists of Massachusetts: Their Memorials, Petitions, and Claims* (London, 1930), 231; Brigham, *Revere's Engravings,* 41–44; Forbes, *Paul Revere,* 153–56. On the importance of honor, virtue, and benevolence, see Bullock, "Ancient and Honorable Society," 43–101; Wood, *Radicalism of the American Revolution,* 103–6, 215–20.

18. On Revere's "View of Boston and the Landing of Troops in 1768" see *Boston Gazette,* April 16, 1770, *Dorr Collection,* 3.87; Brigham, *Revere's Engravings,* 58–64. William Billings dated the preface to the *New England Psalm-Singer* October 7, and Edes and Gills advertised it in the *Boston Gazette* on December 10, 1770, in Brigham, *Revere's Engravings,* 65–70. On dentistry see Revere's account with Edes and Gill, January 15, 1769–January 5, 1772, listing a charge for advertising his dentistry skills in the *Boston Gazette* on July 30, 1770, roll 1, Revere Papers, and his advertisement in the *Boston Gazette,* August 13, 1770, *Dorr Collection,* 3.196. On Revere's business relationship with Edes and Gill, see entry on December 20, 1770, where Revere recorded that he bought paper, probably for his engravings, and two dozen primers "bound and unbound," and, on April 22, 1772, "eight callendars, eight Ames and three Low's Almanacks, eight Church's History of King Phillip's War," with the notation "To Commissions of sale of 40 ditto," roll 1, Revere Papers.

19. On the range of ideologies and interests in the nonimportation movement and the Revolutionary cause in Boston see Nash, *Urban Crucible,* 339–62; Andrews, "The Boston Merchants and the Non-Importation Movement," 159–259. Rowe was accused of violating nonimportation by the "committee appointed by the merchants of boston to examine the importation of goods from Great Britain," April 27, 1769, in Ezeziel Price Papers, MHS. Biographical sketch of Rowe and his diary entry for April 26, 1770, registering his disapproval of Merchants' Meeting, in Cunningham, *Letters and Diary of John Rowe,* 5–8, 201. On Molineux see Rowe's diary entry, October 24, 1774, in Cunningham, *Letters and Diary of John Rowe,* 286–87; Nash, *Urban Crucible,* 333–37, 354–55.

20. Repeal of Townshend duties is reported in *Boston Gazette,* April 30, 1770, *Dorr Collection,* 3.104. On the original genteel membership of the Merchants' Committee and John Rowe's disapproval when the meetings were opened up to the town see his diary entries on March 1 and 4, 1768, compared with that of April 26, 1770, in Cunningham, *Letters and Diary of John Rowe,* 152–55, 201. On the split in nonimportation and patriot movements see Andrews, "Boston Merchants and the Non-Importation Movement," 232–59; Patterson, *Political Parties in Revolutionary Massachusetts,* 68–70; Nash, *Urban Crucible,* 356–57. Young to New York Son of Liberty Hugh Hughes, May 17, 1770, quoted

in Pauline Maier, *The Old Revolutionaries: Political Lives in the Age of Samuel Adams* (New York, 1982), 109.

21. On descriptions of Revere see Dr. Thomas Young to John Lamb of the New York Sons of Liberty, May 13, 1774, quoted in Isaac Q. Leake, *Memoir of the Life of General John Lamb* (Albany, N.Y., 1850), 85–86; John Rowe's diary entry in *Letters and Diary of John Rowe,* 245. Among the "several others" who were involved in the abuse directed at the customs commissioners, Rowe named William Molineux and William Dennie along with Paul Revere. Background on Dr. Thomas Young appears in Maier, *The Old Revolutionaries,* 101–38; Nash, *Urban Crucible,* 355–56.

22. On John Rowe's Masonic career see "Parker Index," 274–75; *Grand Lodge Proceedings,* 1733–92, 131, 148–61; Taylor, *Historical Sketch of The Grand Lodge of Massachusetts,* 3–5.

23. *Boston Gazette,* August 6, 1770, *Dorr Collection,* 3.191; Young to Hugh Hughes, September 15, 1770, *Miscellaneous Bound Manuscripts,* MHS; Revere to John Rivoire, July 1, 1782, roll 1, Revere Papers. On Young see Maier, *The Old Revolutionaries,* 126–38.

24. Young to John Lamb, June 19, 1774, quoted in Maier, *The Old Revolutionaries,* 120–21. On Franklin's "Junto" and his plans to retire from business at age forty-two to devote himself to "Philosophical Studies and Amusements" see Lemay and Zall, *Benjamin Franklin's Autobiography,* 47–49, 57, 100. On the Enlightenment ideas that shaped Revolutionary thought see Bailyn, *Ideological Origins of the American Revolution,* 26–30. See also David D. Hall, "The World of Print and Collective Mentality in Seventeenth-Century New England," in *Colonial America: Essays in Politics and Social Development,* ed. Stanley N. Katz and John M. Murrin, 3d ed. (New York, 1983), 162–76. Hall's comments on the artificial divisions between print and oral culture and the "collective mentality" of the seventeenth century have merit for a discussion of the eighteenth century as well.

25. On the end of nonimportation see Dorr's comment in margin of the *Boston Gazette,* October 15, 1770, *Dorr Collection,* 3.276; Andrews, "Boston Merchants and the Non-Importation Movement," 254. On the Boston Massacre trials and the political aftermath see Preston to Gage, October 31, 1770, in Adams, "New Light on the Boston Massacre," 338–40; Palfrey to John Wilkes, October 23, 30, 1770, in Elsey, "John Wilkes and William Palfrey," 425; *Boyle's Journal of Occurrences* 84 (July 1930): 267; *Boston Gazette,* December 31, 1770, and "Vindex" in the *Boston Gazette,* January 21, 1771, *Dorr Collection,* 3.345, 370–71; Zobel, *Boston Massacre,* 245–47, 294, and chap. 20 ("The Flame Subsides"). Revere made two silver cups for Dumaresq (he spells it "Dumaresque") on October 3, 1772, in Waste Book and Memoranda, vol. 1, roll 5, Revere Papers.

26. Revere was elected Master of St. Andrew's Lodge on November 30, 1770, in Steblecki, *Paul Revere and Freemasonry,* appendix 2, 103. Mary Revere was born on March 19, 1768, and Elizabeth Revere on December 5, 1770, in Nielsen, "The Revere Family," 300. Revere's last dentistry advertisement in 1770 was in the *Boston Gazette,* August 20, 1770, *Dorr Collection,* 3.204. On February 21, 1771, John Joy ordered silver canns for £13.4.0, and on December 3 Thomas Amory ordered a tureen ladle for £4.6.6 and Peter Johonnot ("Johonot") ordered twelve "large polished teaspoons" for £3.8.0. Revere engraved plates for Edes and Gill on April 3 and September 26, 1771, for Isaiah Thomas on March 12, and December 21, 1771, and, on December 21, 1771, he engraved three plates for

Ames' Almanac, published by Ezekiel Russell. Asa Stoddard (sometimes spelled "Stodder") of St. Andrew's Lodge and the North End Caucus ordered a variety of items from shoe and knee buckles to teaspoons and sugar tongs in 1771, paying, not in cash, but against orders drawn on other individuals; all in Waste Book and Memoranda, vol. 1, roll 5, Revere Papers. On Revere's Tory customers merchant/distiller Thomas Amory, distiller Peter Johonnot, merchant/housewright John Joy, and publisher Ezekiel Russell see Stark, *Loyalists of Massachusetts,* 125, 135, 137, 344–45, 410, 412, 454–54. On his relationship with Isaiah Thomas see Forbes, *Paul Revere,* 205–6.

27. Bouve ordered sugar tongs and buckles and had Revere mend some earrings, January 18, April 15, July 20, August 5, August 29, and December 1, 1772, and September 9, 1773. Emmons came to Revere for stone buttons and mending on September 12, 1772, and for silver knee buckles on July 14, 1773. Hudson ordered a silver tankard on February 11, 1773. Riordan placed several orders for knife handles, forks, spoons, knee buckles, a teapot, and "Cleaning, burnishing and mending a Coffee Pot" on October 2, October 16, and November 11, 1773. John Andrew ordered silver coffeepots on January 20 and April 15, 1772. Zacariah Johonnot ordered a silver "flaggon" with engraving on March 18, 1773. Revere made a knee buckle and did mending for Captain Edward Proctor on November 14, 1773, and made buckles, spoons, and a variety of other items, along with mending, for Asa Stoddard between 1771 and 1773. Revere produced engravings for Edes and Gill on January 20, 1771, September 15, 1772, February 11 and September 9, 1773. Josiah Quincy's order is dated October 2, 1773. Dr. Danforth ordered a silver vessel on October 2, 1772, a pair of silver shoe buckles and stone sleeve buttons on March 18, 1773, and stone buttons on August 10, 1773, and he had Revere mend a whistle and bells on August 2, 1773. Dr. Kast, a steady customer since the early 1760s, continued to come to Revere for spoons, buckles, buttons, and gold wire in 1771 and 1773 and for a set of surgeon's instruments on September 9, 1773. Dumaresq's order is dated October 3, 1772. All in Waste Book and Memoranda, vol. 1, roll 5, Revere Papers. On Emmons see Palmer, *Centennial Memorial,* 233; Thwing Index, MHS. On Riordan see Thwing Index, MHS. On Danforth, see *Boston Town Records,* 18.281; Thwing Index, MHS; Forbes, *Paul Revere,* 313, 444, 445. On Kast see Stark, *Loyalists of Massachusetts,* 131. On Dumaresq see Stark, *Loyalists of Massachusetts,* 125, 134, 137; Palfrey to John Wilkes, October 23, 30, 1770, in Elsey, "John Wilkes and William Palfrey," 425.

28. General background on the "quiet years" in Green, *Colonies to Nation,* 173–94; Patterson, *Political Parties in Revolutionary Massachusetts,* 70–73; Egnal, *Mighty Empire,* 248–69. On Ezekiel Goldthwait see Nash, *Urban Crucible,* 333, 352, 357. On John Adams see Shaw, *American Patriots and Rituals of Revolution,* 123–24.

29. On attempts to sustain the patriotic spirit, Harbottle Dorr identified several articles by Adams and Young in the *Boston Gazette,* e.g., Adams writing as Vindex on January 21, 1771, and as Candidus on October 7, 1771, and Young's essay on the Boston Massacre in the *Boston Evening Post,* February 11, 1771, *Dorr Collection,* 3.370–71, 576, 399. On patriot commemorations see Shaw, *American Patriots and Rituals of Revolution,* 104–5.

30. *Boston Gazette,* March 11, 1771, *Dorr Collection,* 3.417.

31. Petition to Selectmen of Boston, March 2, 1772, fMS Am1075, and June 2, 1772, fMS Am1075.1, by permission of the Houghton Library, Harvard University. Peter Chardon,

Esq., advertised for sale or lease "A Wood Wharf situated on Fish Street, with several Stores and Houses thereon . . . Also Part of a Dwelling House," *Boston Gazette,* November 18, 1771, and February 24, 1772, *Dorr Collection,* 3.611 and 4.34. Phillips was on the Merchants' Committee during the nonimportation movement, in Cunningham, *Letters and Diary of John Rowe,* 152–53. For Isaac White's advertisement see *Boston Gazette,* November 18, 1771, *Dorr Collection,* 3.611. The others have been previously identified.

32. Description of duties of the Master of a lodge in St. Andrew's File, Boston, Massachusetts, Grand Lodge of Massachusetts A.F. & A.M., Samuel Crocker Lawrence Library; Steblecki, "Fraternity, Philanthropy, and Revolution," 126. Steven Bullock describes the Master of a Masonic lodge as "an enlightened despot" in Bullock, *Revolutionary Brotherhood,* 65. Revere's offices in the Grand Lodge are listed in Steblecki, *Paul Revere and Freemasonry,* appendix 2, 103. On Revere's involvement with Tyrian Lodge see Records of Tyrian Lodge File, Boston, Massachusetts, Grand Lodge of Massachusetts A.F. & A.M., Samuel Crocker Lawrence Library; Brother James R. Pringle, address on history of Tyrian Lodge on the occasion of its 150th anniversary, *Grand Lodge Proceedings* (1920), 27–37. Revere also represented Tyrian Lodge at Grand Lodge meetings from 1770 to 1773, according to the *Grand Lodge Proceedings* for that period.

33. On the mundane matters of the Boston town meeting in early 1772 see *Boston Town Records* (1770–77), 18.62–82. On the issue of royal salaries see *Boston Gazette,* February 4 and March 11, 1771, *Dorr Collection,* 3.385, 418; Boston town meeting of May 20 and October 28, 1772, *Boston Town Records,* 18.83–86, 89–90; Dr. Thomas Young to Hugh Hughes, August 31, December 21, 1772, *Miscellaneous Bound Manuscripts,* MHS.

34. On the appointment of a Committee of Correspondence, their pamphlet of rights and grievances, and opposition to Crown salaries see *Boston Town Records,* 18.93–108; Plymouth Committee of Correspondence to Boston Committee of Correspondence, December 14, 1772, *Boston Committee of Correspondence Records* (Bancroft Collection), Manuscripts and Archives Division, The New York Public Library, Astor, Lenox and Tilden Foundations (photostat at the Massachusetts Historical Society, hereafter *BCC*), 1.22; Greene, *Colonies to Nation,* 178, 180; Bushman, *King to People,* 170–75.

35. Braintree town meeting, March 5, 1772, reported in the *Boston Gazette,* March 16, 1772, *Dorr Collection,* 3.45. On the membership of the Boston Committee of Correspondence, see *BCC,* 1.1–2; *Boston Town Records,* 18.93; Richard D. Brown, *Revolutionary Politics in Massachusetts: The Boston Committee of Correspondence and the Towns, 1772–1774* (Cambridge, Mass., 1970), xi, 59–64. Revere engraved plates for Joseph Greenleaf between July and December 1774; in Waste Book and Memoranda, vol. 1, roll 5, Revere Papers.

36. Butterfield, *Diary of John Adams,* 1.64–65. On James Otis see Shipton, *Sibley's Harvard Graduates,* 11.247–87.

6. "Mr. Revere Will Give You the News"

1. Revere's recorded income for 1773 was slightly over £154, compared with almost £66 for the previous year. Sargent ordered six large silver spoons on February 3 and twelve silver teaspoons on March 18. Pond, Danforth, and Kast ordered a variety of spoons, buckles, and buttons in February and March. Revere also engraved plates for Edes and Gill in

February and September 1773. Other orders placed by Danforth and Kast in 1773 were discussed in chapter 5. Dr. Paine's silver service was in commemoration of his marriage to Lois Orne, who was related to Revere's wife, Sara Orne Revere. See Waste Book and Memoranda, vol. 1, roll 5, Revere Family Papers, MHS. Information on Sargent is in James R. Pringle's address on the history of Tyrian Lodge on the occasion of the lodge's 150th anniversary, *Grand Lodge Proceedings* (1920), 27–33. On Eliphalet Pond see Stark, *Loyalists of Massachusetts*, 125. On Dr. William Paine see Forbes, *Paul Revere*, 474; Federhen, "From Artisan to Entrepreneur," 67–68; Stark, *Loyalists of Massachusetts*, 139, 385–87. On the Revere children see Nielsen, "The Revere Family," 298–301.

2. On Dr. Church's Boston Massacre oration see *Boyle's Journal of Occurrences*, March 5, 1773, *New England Historical and Genealogical Register* 84 (October 1930): 363. Neither the minutes of St. Andrew's Lodge nor the *Grand Lodge Proceedings* reveal Burbeck's motivations. On Burbeck's seizure of the charter of St. Andrew's Lodge and the complicated transactions involving ownership of their meeting place see *Grand Lodge Proceedings, 1733–92*, 247; Steblecki, *Paul Revere and Freemasonry*, 11–14.

3. On Burbeck's political motivation for secreting the St. Andrew's charter see oration by Hamilton Willis at centennial anniversary of St. Andrew's, November 29, 1856, in Palmer, *Centennial Memorial*, 120–22. On Burbeck see Membership File, Boston, Massachusetts, Grand Lodge of Massachusetts A.F. & A.M., Samuel Crocker Lawrence Library; biographical information in "Extract of a Letter from General Henry Burbeck to Colonel Samuel Swett . . . March 18, 1848, on his father William Burbeck," *New England Historical and Genealogical Register* 12 (October 1858): 351–52; Palfrey, "An Alphabetical List of the Sons of Liberty who dined at Liberty Tree," 140.

4. *Boston Gazette*, March 29, 1773, *Dorr Collection*, 4.265. On the Tea Act see Greene, *Colonies to Nation*, 196–200; Benjamin Woods Labaree, *The Boston Tea Party*, 2d ed. (Boston, 1979), 58–79.

5. *Boston Evening Post*, May 3, 1773, *Dorr Collection*, 4.284; Cary, *Joseph Warren*, 123; Nielsen, "The Revere Family," 298–301; Forbes, *Paul Revere*, 174–76, 473–74.

6. Orders for Ezra Collins (Revere spells it "Collings") and Nathaniel Balch were dated May 10, 1773, Waste Book and Memoranda, vol. 1, roll 5, Revere Papers. On Revere's attendance at a committee meeting on May 18 and abuse of the customs commissioners on May 27, 1773, see Cunningham, *Letters and Diary of John Rowe*, 244–45. On the formation of a Committee of Correspondence of the Massachusetts House see *Boston Gazette*, May 31, 1773, *Dorr Collection*, 4.298.

7. Franklin asked that the letters not be published, but once they were circulated beyond the confines of the Committee of Correspondence and other selected individuals, it became impossible to prevent publication. On the publication of the Hutchinson letters see the *Boston Gazette*, June 21, 1773 (announcing the Massachusetts House's resolutions on the Hutchinson letters), June 28, 1773 ("Lucius" attacked Hutchinson as "a pack horse of tyranny"), August 9, 1773 (condemning Hutchinson for his suggestion to abridge English liberties), *Dorr Collection*, 4.309, 316, 338; Bailyn, *Ordeal of Thomas Hutchinson*, 221–59; Shaw, *American Patriots and the Rituals of Revolution*, 39–41. "Lucius" is identified as William Phillips, whose election to the council had been vetoed by Hutchinson, in Bailyn, *Ordeal of Thomas Hutchinson*, 243. Harbottle Dorr identified North as "that detestable

schemer" in the *Boston Gazette*, October 18, 1773, *Dorr Collection*, 4.379. A letter from Philadelphia to a Boston merchant about resistance to the Tea Act promised that the tea consignees would be "as obnoxious as were the Commissioners of Stamps," *Boston Gazette*, October 18, 1773, *Dorr Collection*, 4.380.

8. On response to the Tea Act see *Boston Gazette*, October 25, 1773, *Dorr Collection*, 4.383; "Proceedings of the North End Caucus," in Goss, *Life of Colonel Revere*, vol. 2, appendix C, 641; Cary, *Joseph Warren*, 129; Labaree, *The Boston Tea Party*, 89–103. On John Lowell, who became a member of St. Andrew's Lodge in 1764, see Palmer, *Centennial Memorial*, 233. On Revere's business in October 1773 see Waste Book and Memoranda, vol. 1, roll 5, Revere Papers. On his courtship and marriage to Rachel Walker see Nielsen, "The Revere Family," 296; Forbes, *Paul Revere*, 178–79 (poem to Rachel Walker).

9. "Proceedings of the North End Caucus," in Goss, *Life of Colonel Revere*, vol. 2, appendix C, 641–43; report of the Boston town meeting of November 5 in *Boston Gazette*, November 8, 1773, *Dorr Collection*, 4.391; description of the crowd at Richard Clarke's house in *Boyle's Journal of Occurrences*, November 17, 1773, *New England Historical and Genealogical Register* 84 (October 1930): 368. On the contention that the North End Caucus took the lead in opposing the Tea Act see Day and Day, "Another Look at the Boston Caucus," 36–37; Cary, *Joseph Warren*, 130–31. On Boston's preparations to resist the landing of the tea see Labaree, *The Boston Tea Party*, 104–15.

10. *BCC*, 6.452–57 (quoted material on 455), 459; L. F. S. Upton, "Proceedings of Ye Body Respecting the Tea," *William and Mary Quarterly*, 3d ser., 22 (April 1965): 287–300. Upton identifies the author of this unsigned narrative as a "moderate Tory."

11. *Boston Gazette*, November 29, December 6, 1773, *Dorr Collection*, 4.403, 407; Upton, "Proceedings of Ye Body Respecting the Tea," 289–92; "Minutes of the Tea Meetings, 1773" (in handwriting identified as that of Town Clerk William Cooper), *MHS Proceedings* 20 (November 1882): 10–13; Labaree, *The Boston Tea Party*, 118–21. On members of St. Andrew's Lodge see Palmer, *Centennial Memorial*, 231–36, and "Parker Index," except for Samuel Peck, who was identified in Drake, *Tea Leaves*, 93, 140. On North End Caucus members see Goss, *Life of Colonel Revere*, vol. 2, appendix C, 635–36; Day and Day, "Another Look at the Boston Caucus," 32–33.

12. *Boston Gazette*, December 6, 1773, *Dorr Collection*, 4.407–8; "Proceedings of Ye Body Respecting the Tea," 292–96; Labaree, *The Boston Tea Party*, 122–25. Revere is not listed among the six express riders in "Minutes of the Tea Meetings," 13, although Esther Forbes said he was, in *Paul Revere*, 182–83.

13. *Boston Gazette*, December 13, 1773, *Dorr Collection*, 4.412; John Andrews to William Barrell, December 1, 1773, "Letters of John Andrews," *MHS Proceedings* 8 (1864–65): 324–25; Labaree, *The Boston Tea Party*, 126–38.

14. Meetings of November 30 and December 16, 1773, in Boston Tea Party File, Boston, Massachusetts, Grand Lodge of Massachusetts A.F. & A.M., Samuel Crocker Lawrence Library; *Grand Lodge Proceedings*, 1733–92, 250–51; Waste Book and Memoranda, vol. 1, roll 5, Revere Papers. On members of the watch aboard the tea ships see "Minutes of the Tea Meetings," 11, 13.

15. John Andrews to William Barrell, December 18, 1773, "Letters of John Andrews," 325–26; "Proceedings of Ye Body Respecting the Tea," 296–97.

16. "Proceedings of Ye Body Respecting the Tea," 298–99; "An Impartial Observer" in the *Boston Gazette,* December 20, 1773, *Dorr Collection,* 4.415; Labaree, *The Boston Tea Party,* 138–45.

17. The description of "brave and resolute men" is in the *Boston Gazette,* December 20, 1773, *Dorr Collection,* 4.416. The North End Caucus was holding meetings at the Green Dragon by November 2, 1773, according to minutes in Goss, *Life of Colonel Revere,* vol. 2, appendix C, 641. On the identity of members of the Boston Tea Party and connection to St. Andrew's Lodge and North End Caucus see Drake, *Tea Leaves,* 92–120, 124, 146, 168; Cary, *Joseph Warren,* 130–35; Boston Tea Party File, Boston, Massachusetts, Grand Lodge of Massachusetts A.F. & A.M., Samuel Crocker Lawrence Library; Robert Glenn Cole, "The Lodge of Saint Andrew: Headquarters of the Revolution" in *Masonic Gleanings: From American and Masonic History* (Chicago, 1954, 1956), 17–18, 20–22; Goss, *Life of Colonel Revere,* vol. 2, appendix C, 635–36; Labaree, *The Boston Tea Party,* 142–45.

18. *Boyle's Journal of Occurrences,* December 17 and 27, 1773, *New England Historical and Genealogical Register* 84 (October 1930): 371–72; Samuel Adams to Thomas Mifflin and George Clymer of Philadelphia and Philip Livingston and Samuel Broom of New York, December 17, 1773, noting that Paul Revere was "sent express" to carry the news about the destruction of the tea, *BCC,* 6.469; *Boston Gazette,* January 3, 1774, and *Boston Evening Post,* January 24, 1774, *Dorr Collection,* 4.426, 428; Forbes, *Paul Revere,* 197–200; Labaree, *The Boston Tea Party,* 152–55. Note that Boyle, Adams, and Forbes all claim Revere was sent to Philadelphia, but Revere, in his 1798 letter to Jeremy Belknap of the Massachusetts Historical Society, in which he recounted his services as a courier, said he was "imployed . . . to carry the Account of the Destruction of the Tea to New-York." The *Pennsylvania Chronicle,* dated December 20 to December 27, 1773, reported in news from New York, December 22, that "Last night an express arrived here from Boston" but did not report his arrival in Philadelphia. It seems likely that after Revere completed his brisk pace to New York, another messenger would have continued the trip to Philadelphia.

19. Orders for Proctor, May 4; Danforth, February 6; Riordan, January 22; Joy, March 5 ("Dentfrice" is Revere's spelling of dentifrice: "a powder, paste, or liquid for cleaning teeth"); Greenwood, January 5 and 22; Palmer, March 25; Boardman, February 6; and Coburn ("Couborn"), August 25. Those orders and orders for Romans and Rivington in Waste Book and Memoranda, vol. 1, roll 5, Revere Papers. On Revere's engraving for James Rivington see Rivington to Henry Knox, March 17 and April 8, 1774, Henry Knox Papers, 1719–1825, Massachusetts Historical Society Microfilm (1960), reel 1.

20. Revere listed engraving orders for Isaiah Thomas on February 6, March 5, April 11, July 6, and August 8, and for Greenleaf on September 10, November 7, and December 5. See Waste Book and Memoranda, vol. 1, roll 5, Revere Papers. The *Royal American* advertised that it was "Embellished with elegant Engravings" in the *Boston Gazette,* May 16, 1774, *Dorr Collection,* 4.498. Additional information is in Brigham, *Paul Revere's Engravings,* 79–92; Forbes. *Paul Revere,* 205–7.

21. On Hancock's Massacre oration see *Boyle's Journal of Occurrences,* March 5, 1774, *New England Historical and Genealogical Register* 84 (October 1930): 373. On the arrival and destruction of the tea see *Boston Gazette,* March 7, 14, 1774, *Dorr Collection,* 4.460, 462; Revere to John Lamb, March 28, 1774, John Lamb Papers, New York Historical Society,

quoted in Goss, *Life of Colonel Revere*, 1.136–37. The Boston Committee of Correspondence to Committees of Dorchester, Roxbury, Brookline, Newton, Cambridge, and Charlestown, March 7, 1774, reporting the arrival of a tea vessel; Boston Committee of Correspondence meeting, March 8, 1774, and Boston Committee of Correspondence to Sandwich, March 9, 1774, announcing the destruction of the tea, in *BCC*, 9.727–30. See also Labaree, *The Boston Tea Party*, 164–67.

22. Butterfield, *Diary of John Adams*, 2.92–93. On Goddard's plan for a postal system see Boston Committee of Correspondence meeting, March 15 and 17, 1774, *BCC*, 9.732–33; *Boston Gazette*, March 21, 1774, *Dorr Collection*, 4.467; Revere to John Lamb, March 28, 1774, in Goss, *Life of Colonel Revere*, 1.136–37; Labaree, *The Boston Tea Party*, 217; Brown, *Revolutionary Politics in Massachusetts*, 181–84.

23. Greene, *Colonies to Nation*, 202–11; Labaree, *The Boston Tea Party*, 170–93; Christie, *Crisis of Empire*, 82–89 (North's speech to Parliament quoted on 85).

24. *Boyle's Journal of Occurrences*, May 13, 1774, *New England Historical and Genealogical Register* 84 (October 1930): 374; John Andrews to William Barrell, May 18, 1774, "Letters of John Andrews," 327–28; *BCC*, 9.756–58.

25. Revere left Boston on May 14 and returned on May 28. On reports of his ride see the *Boston Gazette*, May 16, (calling him "our worthy fellow Citizen, Mr. Paul Revere") and May 30, 1774 ("it was noticed to Mr. Revere" that John Dickinson "spoke longer and with more Life and Energy than ever he had done"), *Dorr Collection*, 4.498, 505; *New York Gazette and Weekly Mercury*, May 23, 1774; "Diary of Mr. Thomas Newell of Boston, 1773–1774," *MHS Proceedings* 15 (October 1877): 352; Forbes, *Paul Revere*, 207–9. His return with letters from Committees of Correspondence in New York, Philadelphia, and New Haven was reported in the Boston Committee of Correspondence, May 28, 1774, *BCC*, 9.762. See also Samuel Adams to Paul Revere (addressed to him "in New York or Philadelphia"), May 18, 1774, roll 1, Revere Papers; Labaree, *The Boston Tea Party*, 219, 221, on support for trade suspension in Newburyport and Salem; John Adams to William Tudor, October 7, 1774, in Smith, *Letters of Delegates to Continental Congress*, 1.157. Adams also wrote his wife on October 7, 1774: "Mr. Revere will bring you the Doings of the Congress," in L. H. Butterfield, ed., *The Adams Family Correspondence* (Cambridge, Mass., 1963), 1.164–65.

26. Report of Revere's ride appears in *Essex Gazette*, May 30, 1774, quoted in Goss, *Life of Colonel Revere*, 1.146–47. On "The Address of the Merchants and Others of Boston to Governor Hutchinson, May 30, 1774" see the *Boston Gazette*, June 6, 1774, *Dorr Collection*, 4.511; Stark, *Loyalists of Massachusetts*, 125; Bailyn, *Ordeal of Thomas Hutchinson*, 273. The names of several of Revere customers, including George Brinley, John Coffin, Philip Dumaresq, Peter Johonnot, and John Joy, are on the petition. On continued resistance to the Coercive Acts, including the Solemn League and Covenant, see Lawrence S. Mayo, "The Spirit of Massachusetts," in Albert Bushnell Hart, *Commonwealth History of Massachusetts*, vols. 2–3 (1928–29; reprint, New York, 1966), 2.539–43; Brown, *Revolutionary Politics in Massachusetts*, 189–99; Patterson, *Political Parties in Revolutionary Massachusetts*, 80–86; Nash, *Urban Crucible*, 357–59; report of town meeting, June 27–28, 1774, in *Boston Gazette*, July 4, 1774, *Dorr Collection*, 4.525. On resolution for a Continental Congress see *Boston Evening Post*, June 20, 1774, *Dorr Collection*, 4.517; Mayo, "The Spirit of Massachusetts," 544–45.

27. See Waste Book and Memoranda, vol. 1, roll 5, Revere Papers for correlation between Revere's business and political life. Note Revere's absence from Grand Lodge meetings in June, September, and December 1774, *Grand Lodge Proceedings, 1733–92*, 254–56. On the arrival of regiments and provisions from towns in Massachusetts and Connecticut see "Diary of Thomas Newell," June 14, 15, July 1, 8, August 9, 13, 1774, *MHS Proceedings* 15: 353–56 (Newell noted his attendance at St. Andrew's Lodge on December 2, 1773, when he was chosen Junior Deacon, on p. 346). On Revere's appointment to the committee to choose a Committee on Ways and Means see Boston town meeting, July 19, 1774, *Boston Town Records*, 18.181–85. Petition of grand jurors, Massachusetts Superior Court, Suffolk County, August 30, 1774, in *Miscellaneous Bound Manuscripts*, MHS. The action of the grand jurors was also mentioned in "Diary of Thomas Newell," 357, and supplement to the *Boston Gazette*, September 5, 1774, *Dorr Collection*, 4.566. Oliver's impeachment was discussed in the *Boston Gazette*, February 14 and March 7, 1774, *Dorr Collection*, 4.449, 458.

28. *Boston Evening Post*, September 5, 1774, *Dorr Collection*, 4.563; *Letters and Diary of John Rowe*, 283–84; *Boyle's Journal of Occurrences, New England Historical and Genealogical Register* 84 (October 1930): 378–79; "Diary of Mr. Thomas Newell," 357; Revere to John Lamb, September 4, 1774, John Lamb Papers, New York Historical Society, quoted in Goss, *Life of Colonel Revere*, 1.150.

29. Text of the Suffolk Resolves in the *Boston Evening Post*, September 19, 1774, *Dorr Collection*, 4.576–77. See also Cary, *Joseph Warren*, 152–73.

30. For the gap in Revere's business between September 10 and November 7 see Waste Book and Memoranda, vol. 1, roll 5, Revere Papers. Revere also missed meetings of the Massachusetts Grand Lodge on September 2 and 7 as well as December 2, 1774, and March 3, 1775, although he was chosen Grand Treasurer on September 2, 1774; in *Grand Lodge Proceedings, 1733–92*, 255–57. On support of the Continental Congress for the Suffolk Resolves see Samuel Adams to Dr. Charles Chauncy, September 9, 1774, in Force, *American Archives*, 4.1.793; proceedings of the Continental Congress on the Suffolk Resolves in Force, *American Archives*, 4.1.901–16; Greene, *Colonies to Nation*, 242–43.

31. Revere's return to Boston from Philadelphia on September 23 is mentioned in the *Boston Gazette*, September 26, 1774, *Dorr Collection*, 4.583. John Andrews refers to both of Revere's rides to Congress in letters to William Barrell on September 24 and October 19, 1774, "Letters of John Andrews," 366, 378. The Boston Committee of Correspondence notes that "Mr. Paul Reviere be engaged to go Express to the Continental Congress" in its minutes for September 29, 1774, *BCC*, 11.856. A letter from New York, October 5, 1774, mentions Revere's arrival with news of the patriotic resolve in Boston, in Force, *American Archives*, 4.1.820–21. See also "Diary of Thomas Newell," October 17, 1774, 360. On the Declaration and Resolves of the First Continental Congress and the Continental Association see Greene, *Colonies to Nation*, 243–50; *Boston Town Records*, 18.205–7; John Andrews to William Barrell, December 7, 1774, "Letters of John Andrews," 389; Nash, *Urban Crucible*, 378.

32. Members of the Massachusetts General Court formed themselves into the Massachusetts Provincial Congress on October 7, 1774, in Salem when General Gage canceled a meeting of the General Court. See resolves of Massachusetts Provincial Congress in Force, *American Archives*, 4.1.830, 834, 838, 842, 843–45, 847; *Boston Evening Post*, Octo-

ber 10, 1774, and *Boston Gazette,* October 17, 1774, *Dorr Collection,* 4.591, 595; *Boyle's Journal of Occurrences,* October 26, 1774, *New England Historical and Genealogical Register* 84 (October 1930): 380; Patterson, *Political Parties in Revolutionary Massachusetts,* 109–114.

33. Revere to Jeremy Belknap, 1798, in which he reviewed his services as a courier, member of an intelligence network, and his ride of April 18–19, 1775, in *Paul Revere's Three Accounts of His Famous Ride* (Boston, 1976, hereafter *Three Accounts*).

34. Joshua Revere's birth on December 7, 1772, in Nielsen, "The Revere Family," 301. On Revere's ride and events in Portsmouth see Governor Wentworth of New Hampshire to General Gage, December 14, 1774; Captain Cochran, commander of Fort William and Mary, to Governor Wentworth, December 14, 1774; Extracts of Letters to Gentlemen in New York, December 16, 1774; all in Force, *American Archives,* 4.1.1041–43. Boston Committee of Correspondence minutes for December 16, 1774, also note that "Mr. Paul Riviere who was sent last Monday to Portsmouth Express—returned this Morning and Reported to the Committee," *BCC,* 11.870. On Revere's ride to Exeter see John Wentworth to Thomas Waldron, Portsmouth, January 27, 1775, quoted in Jeremy Belknap Papers, *MHS Collections,* 6th ser., 4 (1891): 73.

35. On Revere's reputation as express rider and intelligence agent see John Rivoire to Paul Revere, January 12, 1775, roll 1, Revere Papers; Tory list of the Committee of 63 in *MHS Proceedings* 12 (1898): 139–42 (information on Revere on 141). On the mechanics' intelligence committee see their letter to John Lamb of New York, March 1, 1775, in Leake, *Memoir of John Lamb,* 99–100. The five other mechanics beside Revere who signed the letter were Joseph Ward, a distiller; Revere's friend Joshua Brackett; and three other long-term associates in the patriot cause: Thomas Chase, Thomas Crafts Jr., and Benjamin Edes. On Leslie's expedition see also *Boyle's Journal of Occurrences,* February 26, 1775, *New England Historical and Genealogical Register* 85 (January 1931): 6–7; Forbes, *Paul Revere,* 226–29.

36. *Instructions of General Gage to Captain Brown and Ensign De Berniere,* February 22, 1775, and *Narrative of Ensign De Berniere,* in Force, *American Archives,* 4.1.1263–68; Minutes of Massachusetts Provincial Congress meetings in Concord, March 23, 30, and April 5 and letter from Congress to colonies of Connecticut, Rhode Island, and New York, April 10, 1775, Force, *American Archives,* 4.1.1344, 1345, 1350–55, 1364–66; Massachusetts Committee of Safety and Supplies minutes, November 2, 1774–April 1, 1775, Force, *American Archives,* 4.1.1365–70. On Revere's activities see Revere to Jeremy Belknap, 1798, in *Three Accounts.* Note that Revere's first deposition and a corrected copy, written almost immediately after his ride, focus exclusively on his ride of April 18–19, 1775. His letter to Belknap provides more background on his role as a courier and intelligence agent as well as details leading up to his "Midnight Ride."

37. Dartmouth's orders to Gage, April 15, 1775, and Extract of a Letter to a Gentleman near Philadelphia from Boston, April 20, 1775, in Force, *American Archives,* 4.2.336, 359–60. In his depositions, Revere claimed that the presumed object of the British expedition was either the arrest of Hancock and Adams or the seizure of munitions at Concord, and in his letter to Belknap, he listed the seizure of the patriot leaders as the primary goal. Based on information from an informant, possibly Dr. Benjamin Church, found in General Gage's papers, Allen French concluded that the seizure of munitions at Concord was the main

objective of Gage. See Revere's depositions, *Three Accounts;* Allen French, *General Gage's Informers: New Material upon Lexington and Concord* (1932; reprint, New York, 1968), 21; Tourtellot, *Lexington and Concord,* 77–79; Robert A. Gross, *The Minutemen and Their World* (New York, 1976), 115. David Hackett Fischer discusses evidence that Revere carried a warning of an impending expedition to Concord as early as Saturday, April 8, in *Paul Revere's Ride* (New York, 1994), 87, 385 n. 20. Clearly, a British expedition was no secret to the patriots.

38. Paul Revere to Jeremy Belknap, 1798, *Three Accounts.*

39. "Paul Revere's Ride," in *The Poetical Works of Longfellow,* 207–8. Longfellow called Revere "an apostle of liberty" in a letter to a Miss P., March 30, 1871, thanking her for the gift of a silver spoon made by Revere, in Longfellow, *Life of Henry Wadsworth Longfellow,* 3.171–72. On Revere's ride as an act of successful mobilization involving riders who spread the alarm through several counties see Fischer, *Paul Revere's Ride,* 138–48.

40. Quotes from Revere's depositions and letter to Belknap, *Three Accounts.* See also Tourtellot, *Lexington and Concord,* 85–94. Robert Newman, the sexton at Christ Church (better known today as the Old North Church), is generally credited with being the "friend" who hung the lanterns, but in 1876 John Lee Watson, a descendant of John Pulling, credited his ancestor with the deed, claiming that Revere was more likely to call upon Pulling, "an intimate friend" since boyhood, fellow member of the North End Caucus and other political committees, and vestryman at Christ Church. See Watson, "Paul Revere's Signal: The True Story of the Signal Lanterns in Christ Church, Boston," *Boston Daily Advertiser,* July 20, 1876, reprinted in *MHS Proceedings,* 15 (1876): 164–77.

41. Revere's account to Belknap has a few more details and embellishments than his earlier deposition, e.g., the mention of Colonel Conant and others seeing the lantern signals and the comments that Devens saw ten British officers, not nine as Revere wrote in the earlier depositions, and that the officer who chased him got stuck in a pond. In the depositions, Revere merely said that the officer, "finding He could not catch me, returned." See *Three Accounts.*

42. Rivalry between the towns of Lexington and Concord over which town deserved credit for being the site of the first battle of the American Revolution dates to September 2, 1824, when Samuel Hoar welcomed General Lafayette to Concord with the words that he stood on the ground "where the first forcible resistance" was raised against Britain. Sergeant William Munroe's deposition was one of several from participants and witnesses to events on April 18–19, 1775, gathered in 1825 by Elias Phinney in his *History of the Battle of Lexington on the Morning of the 19th of April 1775* (1825; reprint by the Society for the Preservation of Colonial Culture, 1968), Munroe's deposition, 33–35. In 1827 Concord published its version of events in Ezra Ripley, *History of the Fight at Concord on the 19th of April, 1775* (reprint by Society for the Preservation of Colonial Culture, 1968), information on Munroe, 10–11. See also David B. Little, *America's First Centennial Celebration* (Boston, 1974).

43. Revere's account to Belknap, 1798, *Three Accounts.*

44. In his 1775 depositions, Revere quoted the profanity of the British officers when they seized him. In the 1798 letter to Belknap he testified to Dr. Prescott's arrival in Concord; see *Three Accounts.* Reverend William Emerson's *Diary of April Nineteenth, 1775* is quoted

in Tourtellot, *Lexington and Concord*, 151, and in Gross, *The Minutemen and Their World*, 116, 118. The story of Dawes's actions in eluding capture is told in Henry Ware Holland, *William Dawes and His Ride with Paul Revere* (Boston, 1878), written by a great-grandson of Dawes. Henry Wadsworth Longfellow was aware of this book, writing to George Washington Greene on October 27, 1878, that Holland "convicts me of high historic crimes and misdemeanors. How they rode together, when one went over the Brighton bridge . . . and the other through Medford, does not very distinctly appear." See Longfellow, *Life of Henry Wadsworth Longfellow*, 3.292.

45. Revere's first deposition and corrected copy, 1775, in *Three Accounts;* deposition of Elijah Sanderson, one of the four men taken prisoner by the British before they seized Revere, corroborating Revere's account, in Phinney, *History of the Battle of Lexington*, 31–33.

46. Revere's depositions, 1775, *Three Accounts;* Tourtellot, *Lexington and Concord*, 110–11, 123–43; Phinney, *History of the Battle of Lexington*, 18–23.

7. "Am Obliged to Be Contented in This State's Service"

1. Revere's first two depositions end with his hearing the first shots; in his later account to Jeremy Belknap he added the detail about Hancock's trunk. In the Belknap letter he also wrote that he met with Dr. Warren in Cambridge on April 20; *Three Accounts.* On May 12, 1775, the Massachusetts Committee of Safety ordered that Reverend Gordon be given "free access" to prisoners at Lexington, Concord, and "elsewhere" to take depositions on events of April 19, Massachusetts Committee of Safety minutes, in Force, *American Archives*, 4.2.800. See "Reverend William Gordon of Roxbury to a gentleman in England, May 17, 1775," in Force, *American Archives*, 4.2.624–31; "Extract of a letter from Wethersfield, Connecticut to a Gentleman in New York, April 23, 1775," in Force, *American Archives*, 4.2.362; Allen French, *The Day of Concord and Lexington* (Boston, 1925), 64.

2. Details and analysis of the military performances at Lexington and Concord may be found in French, *Day of Concord and Lexington*, especially chaps. 7–12, 17–18, 20–33; Tourtellot, *Lexington and Concord*, chaps. 4–6; Fischer, *Paul Revere's Ride*, 188–201, 206–32, 245–60. For contemporary accounts see John Andrews to William Barrell, April 19, 1775, "Letters of John Andrews," 403–5; "Letter from Boston to a Gentleman in New York, April 19, 1775," in Force, *American Archives*, 4.2.359; Sutherland's and Pitcairn's accounts in French, *General Gage's Informers*, 44, 52; "A Circumstantial Account of an Attack, that happened on the 19th of April, 1775, on His Majesty's Troops, by a Number of People of the Province of Massachusetts Bay" ("General Gage's Account"), April 29, 1775, in Evans, *Early American Imprints*, no. 14192; diary of Lieutenant John Barker of the King's Own Regiment, in "A British Officer in Boston in 1775," pt. 1, *Atlantic Monthly* 34 (April 1877): 398.

3. On the patriot version of events at Lexington and Concord see *A Narrative of the Excursion and Ravages of the King's Troops Under the Command of General Gage on the Nineteenth of April 1775, Together with the Depositions Taken by Congress to Support the Truth of It* (May 22, 1775; reprint, New York, 1968). See Captain Parker's deposition, dated April 25, 1775, 3–4, and similar depositions from Elijah Sanderson, Simon Winship, and members of militia companies from Lexington, Lincoln, and Concord, 5, 6–7, 12. On the

British version see "General Gage's Account," based on information supplied by Lieutenant Colonel Smith, Major Pitcairn, and other officers who were present at Lexington and
Concord; Pitcairn's letter to Gage, April 26, 1775, containing details repeated in Gage's
account, in French, *General Gage's Informers*, 52–53; "A British Officer in Boston," 398–99.

4. The British version of events is in "General Gage's Account"; "Diary of a British
Officer," 398–401; Captain Walter Laurie to General Gage, April 26, 1775, in French,
General Gage's Informers, 95–98. On the American version see Ripley, *History of the Fight at
Concord*, 13–25. For an analysis of events at the North Bridge and especially of British
military errors see Tourtellot, *Lexington and Concord*, 149–65; French, *Day of Concord and
Lexington*, 161–65, 177–92.

5. Description of provincial soldiers in *Boyle's Journal of Occurrences* April 19, 1775, *New
England Historical and Genealogical Register* 85 (January 1931): 9; French, *Day of Concord
and Lexington*, 215–25; Tourtellot, *Lexington and Concord*, 165–81. See also Lieutenant
Barker's account in "Diary of a British Officer in Boston," 400.

6. "Diary of a British Officer in Boston," 400.

7. French, *Day of Concord and Lexington*, 226–39; Tourtellot, *Lexington and Concord*,
181–90.

8. On British accounts of their retreat to Charlestown see "General Gage's Account"
and "Diary of a British Officer in Boston," 400–401. Revere's last silver entry was on
April 1, 1775, with the next silver entry listed on August 31, 1780, in Waste Book and
Memoranda, vol. 1, roll 5, Revere Family Papers, MHS. See also *Grand Lodge Proceedings*,
1733–92, 258. On his government service between 1775 and 1780 see Revere to his cousin
Mathias Rivoire, October 6, 1781 (date penciled in on manuscript), roll 1, Revere Papers.

9. For background on events in this period see Cary, *Joseph Warren*, 185–204; Allen
French, *The First Year of the American Revolution* (1934; reprint, New York, 1968), 46–55,
126–37. Revere mentioned being "engaged . . . as a messenger" in his letter to Jeremy
Belknap in *Three Accounts*. See also resolve to pay Revere £10.4.0 on August 22, 1775, for
"riding for the Committee of Safety" and for printing currency, in *Acts and Resolves of
Massachusetts* (Boston, 1918), 19.66; James Warren to John Adams, November 14, 1775,
stating that "You will learn by Revere the general state of things here," in *Warren-Adams
Letters*, vol. 1:1743–77; vol. 2:1778–1814, Appendix, *MHS Collections* 72–73 (1917–25), 1.184;
similar letter from James Warren to Samuel Adams, November 12, 1775, *Warren-Adams
Letters*, 2.425; pass signed by James Otis on November 12, 1775, for Revere to ride express to
the Continental Congress, owned by the Paul Revere Memorial Association and printed
in *Paul Revere—Artisan, Businessman, and Patriot*, 178.

10. On the description of April 19, 1775, as "a day to be remembered by all Americans" see
Boyle's Journal of Occurrences, April 19, 1775, *New England Historical and Genealogical Register* 85 (January 1931): 8–11. On the appointment of a committee of the Massachusetts Provincial Congress to publicize the patriot version of events at Lexington and Concord see
"Proceedings of the Massachusetts Provincial Congress," April 22 and May 22, 1775, and a
letter dated "Whitehill, June 10, 1775," noting the arrival of accounts written by General
Gage and his subordinate officers. The Massachusetts Provincial Congress also forwarded
copies of material sent to England to the Continental Congress on May 3, 1775; all in Force,
American Archives, 4.2:765, 673–75, 945–46, 486–501. See also Cary, *Joseph Warren*, 191.

11. Sanderson, Solomon Brown, and Jonathan Loring, who had spotted a small party of British officers on the road to Lexington on the evening of April 18, volunteered to try to pursue the officers and report back to the citizens of Lexington. They testified on April 25, 1775, that they were stopped by a British patrol on April 18 at "about ten of the clock" and detained until two o'clock the next morning. Not until December 17, 1824, did Sanderson add that while he, Brown, and Loring were in custody, the British officers also held Paul Revere and a one-handed pedlar named Allen. In this later account, Sanderson repeated details mentioned in Revere's accounts. Depositions of Solomon Brown, Jonathan Loring, and Elijah Sanderson are in *A Narrative of the Excursion and Ravages of the King's Troops*, 5. Sanderson's later deposition is in Phinney, *History of the Battle of Lexington*, 31–33.

12. On Dr. Warren's efforts to organize an army see Warren to the Provincial Congress of New Hampshire, April 23, 1775, and "Proceedings of the Massachusetts Provincial Congress," April 24 and 26, 1775, in Force, *American Archives*, 4.2.377–78, 766, 768–69. See also Cary, *Joseph Warren*, 193; John Richard Alden, *The American Revolution, 1775–1783* (New York, 1962), 33–34; Aubrey Parkman, *Army Engineers in New England: The Military and Civil Work of the Corps of Engineers in New England, 1775–1975* (Waltham, Mass., 1978), 1–3. The generous pensions offered Gridley and Burbeck are discussed in French, *First Year of the American Revolution*, 73–74. On Gridley's and Burbeck's military background see Parkman, *Army Engineers in New England*, 1–3; "Extract of a Letter from General Henry Burbeck to Colonel Samuel Swett . . . March 18, 1848, on his father William Burbeck," *New England Historical and Genealogical Register* 12 (October 1858): 351–52. See also Colonel Gridley's recommendations for officers to the Massachusetts Committee of Safety, June 16, 1775, in Force, *American Archives*, 4.2.1354.

13. When Revere began seeking a Continental commission is difficult to ascertain. The first reference to his interest in a commission that I found was in a letter from John Adams to Thomas Crafts on February 18, 1776, in which Adams claimed that "it was the Wish of your Friends here" [in the Massachusetts delegation to the Continental Congress] that Thomas Crafts, George Trott, and Paul Revere "should have all those Rewards from your Country which you can desire [i.e., a Continental commission]." Since the process of choosing officers was a time-consuming one, involving letters of application, conversations about the qualifications of candidates, and the exchange of many letters among members of the Committee of Safety, Massachusetts Provincial Congress, and the Massachusetts delegation in the Continental Congress, it seems logical that Paul Revere had pressed his candidacy long before Adams wrote his letter in February 1776. Since Revere had served as an artillery lieutenant under Gridley in the Seven Years' War, it would also seem logical that he would seek an officer's commission under Gridley in 1775. See John Adams to Thomas Crafts Jr., February 18, 1776, in Smith, *Letters of Delegates to Continental Congress*, 3.273. On criteria for the choice of American officers see Victor Daniel Brooks, "American Officer Development in the Massachusetts Campaign, 1775–1776," *Historical Journal of Massachusetts* 12 (January 1984): 8–18; Sidney Kaplan, "Rank and Status among Massachusetts Continental Officers," *American Historical Review* 56 (January 1951): 318–26.

14. On Gridley's military, civilian, and Masonic background see Parkman, *Army Engineers in New England*, 1–3; Anderson, *People's Army*, 14–19, 50; "Parker Index," 140–41.

15. On the formation of Gridley's artillery regiment see Massachusetts Provincial Con-

gress to Gridley, May 10, 1775, directing him to recommend qualified officers to the Committee of Safety; Gridley to Committee of Safety, June 2, 1775, recommending establishment of ordnance storekeeper and company of artificers; Gridley to Committee of Safety, June 16, 1775, recommending officers to be commissioned by the Massachusetts Provincial Congress; Gridley to Massachusetts Provincial Congress, July 3, 1775; all in Force, *American Archives*, 4.2.797, 894, 1354, 1477–78. See also French, *First Year of the American Revolution*, 73–74.

16. All of the Burbeck sons served under their father. In addition to Henry, Joseph and Thomas were matrosses in the Gridley regiment while John served as an artillery captain under his father when William Burbeck resigned his Continental commission to return to state military service. On Scarborough Gridley see Francis B. Heitman, *Historical Register of Officers of the Continental Army during the War of the Revolution, April 1775 to December 1783* (1914; reprint, Baltimore, 1967), 14, 262; *Massachusetts Soldiers and Sailors of the Revolutionary War* (Boston, 1896–1908), 6.875. On Samuel Gridley see Heitman, *Historical Register*, 262; *Massachusetts Soldiers and Sailors*, 6.875; Oliver Ayer Roberts, *History of the Military Company of the Massachusetts, Now Called the Ancient and Honorable Artillery Company of Massachusetts, 1637–1888* (Boston, 1897), 2.128. For genealogical information on Gridley's sons see oration on Richard Gridley by Daniel T. V. Huntoon, *Memorial Services of Commemoration Day, Held in Canton, May 30, 1877 under the Auspices of Revere Encampment, Post 94, GAR* (Boston, 1877), notes on 15, 21. On Henry Burbeck see Heitman, *Historical Register*, 262. On the military service of Joseph, Thomas, and John Burbeck see *Massachusetts Soldiers and Sailors*, 6.817–18. For genealogical information on Burbeck's sons see Mary Kent (Davey) Babcock, "Christ Church, Boston, Records," *New England Historical and Genealogical Register* 100 (January 1946): 30, 32 (on Henry, Joseph, and John Burbeck) and (April 1946): 133 (on Thomas Burbeck).

17. On David Mason see Heitman, *Historical Register*, 14, 383; Nancy S. Voye, ed., *Massachusetts Officers in the French and Indian Wars, 1748–1763* (Boston, 1975), ref. no. 3671; Roberts, *Ancient and Honorable Artillery Company*, 2.68–70. On Adino Paddock see Roberts, *Ancient and Honorable Artillery Company*, 2.112–14. On William Perkins see Heitman, *Historical Register*, 15, 436; Roberts, *Ancient and Honorable Artillery Company*, 2.133; Bradford Adams Whittemore, *Memorials of the Massachusetts Society of the Cincinnati* (Boston, 1964), 464–65. On John Popkin see Heitman, *Historical Register*, 15, 446; Roberts, *Ancient and Honorable Artillery Company*, 2.140; Whittemore, *Massachusetts Society of the Cincinnati*, 489–90. On John Crane see Heitman, *Historical Register*, 15, 176; Whittemore, *Massachusetts Society of the Cincinnati*, 125–28 (quote on 125–26).

18. St. John's Grand Lodge (Modern Masons) and the Massachusetts Grand Lodge (Ancients) advertised their separate festivals of St. John the Baptist in Boston newspapers in the 1760s and 1770s.

19. On the Burbeck-Revere dispute see chapter 6.

20. On criteria for the choice of American officers see Brooks, "American Officer Development in the Massachusetts Campaign, 1775–1776," 8–18 (Washington's concept of an appropriate officer corps quoted on 10). On his choice for officers see John Adams to James Warren, July 23, 1775, in *Warren-Adams Letters*, 1.85–88. On Tudor see Smith, *Letters*

of Delegates to Continental Congress, 1.71. On Bant see Baxter, *House of Hancock,* 241, and advertisement for his shop on Dock Square in the *Boston Gazette,* October 28, 1771.

21. Mason marched to Medford with five hundred men after Lexington and Concord and immediately entered artillery service, in Roberts, *Ancient and Honorable Artillery Company,* 2.68–70. On Knox see Noah Brooks, *Henry Knox: A Soldier of the Revolution* (1900; reprint, New York, 1974), 30–31. On Putnam see French, *First Year of the American Revolution,* 83. On Cincinnatus as a model republican see Garry Wills, *Cincinnatus: George Washington and the Enlightenment* (Garden City, N.Y., 1984), 13–16, 20–23, 36–37. On the social distinction that came with military service see General Nathaniel Greene to Jacob Greene, Esq., June 28, 1775, in Force, *American Archives* 4.2.1126–27; John Lamb to New York Committee of Safety, July 17, 1775, quoted in French, *First Year of the American Revolution,* 388–89. On republicanism and virtue see Wood, *Creation of the American Republic,* 53–60, 65–70.

22. On Benjamin Church see Revere's letter to Belknap, 1798, in *Three Accounts;* General Washington to Continental Congress, enclosing documents relative to findings against Dr. Church, October 5, 1775, in Force, *American Archives,* 4.3.957–60; French, *General Gage's Informers,* 147–201; French, *First Year of the American Revolution,* 495–96. On Rachel Revere's zeal for liberty see Rachel Revere to Paul Revere, May 2, 1775, Revere Family Papers II, 1775–1964, roll 4, Revere Papers. A committee of the Massachusetts Provincial Congress met with Revere on May 20, 1775, to discuss his proposal "for an alteration in the value of the colony notes," in William Lincoln, ed., *Journals of the Provincial Congress of Massachusetts, 1774 and 1775* (Boston, 1838), 244–45. On July 8, 1775, the Massachusetts Provincial Congress paid twelve shillings to John Cook "for the use that Mr. Paul Revere made of his house whilst he was striking off the Colony notes," in Force, *American Archives,* 4.2.1497. See also Forbes, *Paul Revere,* 267–69, 271–77.

23. His engraving work for Massachusetts is noted in *Journals of the Provincial Congress of Massachusetts,* 244, 296, 369, 375, 437, 441, 467, 473 (May–July 1775); *Acts and Resolves of Massachusetts* (Boston, 1918), 19.66, 69, 110, 170, 229 (August 1775–January 1776). Esther Forbes, on p. 277 of *Paul Revere and the World He Lived In,* credits Revere with engraving plates to print Continental currency as well, but there is no mention of his name in the *Journals of the Continental Congress* for 1775 (Washington, D.C., 1905), nor does Brigham, on p. 239 of *Paul Revere's Engravings,* find any evidence that he engraved Continental currency. On importance of paper money see Cary, *Joseph Warren,* 200–201; French, *First Year of the American Revolution,* 172–74.

24. Revere's account was submitted to a committee of the Massachusetts Provincial Congress on June 22, the committee's report was not accepted on June 27, and on July 1 the Congress voted to pay Revere £50, in *Journals of Provincial Congress of Massachusetts,* 375, 437, 441; Force, *American Archives,* 4.2.1434, 1451, 1472, 1474. On honor, virtue, and republicanism see Wood, *Creation of the American Republic,* 107–18; Wood, *Radicalism of the American Revolution,* 39–41. See also John Adams to Elbridge Gerry, June 18, 1775, in Smith, *Letters of Delegates to Continental Congress,* 1.503–4.

25. Dr. Joseph Warren, president pro temp of the Massachusetts Provincial Congress, to Samuel Freeman, secretary pro temp of the Continental Congress, May 16, 1775; Gerry to

Massachusetts delegates, June 4, 1775; John Hancock, president of the Continental Congress, to Massachusetts Provincial Congress, June 10, 1775, on the formation of a new
government; Washington's appointment as commander-in-chief of the Continental Army,
June 16, 1775; all in Force, *American Archives*, 4.2.620–21, 905–6, 955, 1848. See also French,
First Year of the American Revolution, 134–42.

26. Arrival of British generals and soldiers on May 26, 1775, in *Boyle's Journal of Occurrences, New England Historical and Genealogical Register* 85 (January 1931): 16.

27. On the Battle of Bunker Hill see French, *The First Year of the American Revolution*,
chaps. 15–16; Parkman, *Army Engineers in New England*, 3–4; Alden, *The American Revolution*, 35–39; Cary, *Joseph Warren*, 218–21. On the death of Dr. Joseph Warren see James
Warren to the Continental Congress, June 20, 1775, in Force, *American Archives*, 4.2.1039–
40.

28. On Warren's death and Revere's role in identifying his body see John Adams to
James Warren, June 27, 1775, in Smith, *Letters to Delegates of Continental Congress*, 1.544–
46; Cary, *Joseph Warren*, 218–21; French, *First Year of the American Revolution*, 229–30;
Forbes, *Paul Revere*, 301–3, 464 n. 36. Joseph Warren Revere was born on April 30, 1777, in
Nielsen, "The Revere Family," 301. On hero worship in Revolutionary and Early National
period and on Dr. Warren's example see Wills, *Cincinnatus*, 109–32, 174.

29. Dr. Thomas Young to John Lamb, May 13, 1774, quoted in Leake, *Memoir of the Life
of General John Lamb*, 85–86; Samuel Adams to Paul Revere, May 18, 1774, roll 1, Revere
Papers. On the changing concept of friendship in the mid-eighteenth century see Wood,
Radicalism of the American Revolution, 57–64, 73–77; Frank Lambert, "Subscribing for
Profits and Piety: The Friendship of Benjamin Franklin and George Whitefield," *William
and Mary Quarterly*, 3d ser., 50 (July 1993): 529–48 (especially 544–45). Henry Wilson Coil
stresses that Ancient Masons "paid less heed than did their older rivals [Modern Masons]
to a man's worldly wealth and honor," in Coil, *A Comprehensive View of Freemasonry*, 108–
9. See also Cary, *Joseph Warren*, 23–25, 54–57.

30. The Committee of Safety ordered Timothy Austin to ready the Vassall house for
Washington's occupancy on July 8, 1775, in Force, *American Archives*, 4.2.1368. On the order
that Knox should supply military books see "Minutes of the Committee of Safety," *Revolution: Miscellaneous*, 1775–78, Massachusetts Archives Collection (hereafter MAC)
140.112, courtesy of Massachusetts Archives. On Knox and the admiration for his abilities
see Knox to his wife and brother, July 6, 1775 (referring to Washington's and Lee's approval
of his works at Roxbury), quoted in Brooks, *Henry Knox*, 32; Washington to the president
of Congress, July 10, 1775, mentioning the American entrenchments and the unfavorable
quality of Massachusetts troops and officers, in Force, *American Archives*, 4.2.1624–27;
Parkman, *Army Engineers in New England*, 4–5; *DAB*, 10.475–76; Brooks, *Henry Knox*,
30–37.

31. Benjamin Hichborn was captured in June 1775 and escaped in October from the British ship *Preston* in Boston Harbor, in *Sibley's Harvard Graduates* (Class of 1768), 17.36–38.

32. On the gunpowder mill see Orne, Azor, November 10, 1775, letter on behalf of
committee for erecting powder mills to Paul Revere, and Robert Morris to Oswell Eve,
November 21, 1775 (letter of introduction for Paul Revere), both in *Miscellaneous Bound
Manuscripts*, MHS; letters of introduction from Morris and John Dickinson in Smith,

Letters of Delegates to Continental Congress, 2.368; Elbridge Gerry to Samuel Adams, December 13, 1775, on Eve's self-interest, and Adams to Gerry, January 2, 1776, mentioning the plans he forwarded to Revere, in Force, *American Archives,* 4.4.255–56, 541–42; Samuel Adams to Paul Revere, December 23, 1775, enclosing plan for mill, roll 1, Revere Papers. Goss, *Life of Colonel Revere,* 2.392–400, and Forbes, *Paul Revere,* 290–92, credit Revere both with designing and with setting up the gunpowder mill, but Massachusetts records only name two other individuals in connection with the erection and operation of the mill. A committee of the Massachusetts House and Council met with Thomas Harling on January 19, 1776, to determine where the gunpowder mill should be erected, and on May 9, 1776, the Massachusetts Council appointed Thomas Crane "to carry on the manufacturing of Gunpowder in the Colony Mill at Stoughton." See *Revolution: Miscellaneous,* 1774–83, MAC 138.279; Force, *American Archives,* 4.4.1310; *Acts and Resolves of Massachusetts,* 19 (Boston, 1918), 173–74, 182, 200, 217, 399–400.

33. On the reorganization of the army see "Proceedings of Committee of Conference at the Camp at Cambridge," October 18–23, 1775 (including Continental Congress committee of Benjamin Franklin, Benjamin Harrison, and Thomas Lynch), and "Proceedings of Council of General Officers (Washington, Ward, Lee, Putnam, Thomas, Heath, Spencer, Sullivan, Greene, and Gates)," November 2, 1775, both in Force, *American Archives,* 4.3.1155–63, 1333–35; French, *First Year of the American Revolution,* chap. 31, especially 502–12.

34. Conference committee proceedings, October 23, 1775, on disputes in regiment and need to dismiss Gridley in "some honourable way," in Force, *American Archives,* 4.3.1162; James Warren to John Adams, August 9, 1775, on trouble in Gridley's regiment involving his son, in *Warren-Adams Letters,* 1.101; court-martial of Major Scarborough Gridley in "Memoir and Orderly Book of Colonel William Henshaw," *MHS Proceedings* 15 (October 1876): 158; court-martial of Captain Samuel Gridley, October 11, 1775, in Force, *American Archives,* 4.3.1049; announcement of Gridley's replacement by Henry Knox, November 17, 1775, in Force, *American Archives,* 4.3.1921. See also French, *First Year of the American Revolution,* 521–22.

35. Burbeck and Mason both declined the command of the regiment because of advanced age and recommended Knox, in Henry Burbeck's "Letter to Colonel Samuel Swett"; French, *First Year of the American Revolution,* 521. Washington's orders to Knox to go to Ticonderoga, November 16, 1775, in Force, *American Archives,* 4.3.1568. On qualifications for officers see John Adams to Henry Knox, November 11, 1775, expressing admiration for Knox and asking him to recommend candidates, Henry Knox Papers, 1719–1825, Massachusetts Historical Society Microfilm (1960), reel 1; Knox to Adams, August 21 and September 25, 1776, discussing general qualifications and specific individuals, reel 3, Knox Papers. See also Knox to Adams, May 13, 1776, reel 2, Knox Papers; Adams to Knox, August 25, 1776, reel 3, Knox Papers.

36. John Adams to James Warren, December 3, 1775, recommending Crafts and Trott, in *Warren-Adams Letters,* 1.186–87; Continental Congress accepted recommendations for Crafts and Trott on December 2, 1775, in Force, *American Archives,* 4.3.1939; Washington's remark on New England officers quoted in Brooks, "American Officer Development in the Massachusetts Campaign," 10; Washington to the president of Congress, December 14,

1775, on refusal of Crafts and Trott, in John C. Fitzpatrick, ed., *The Writings of George Washington,* 39 vols. (Washington, D.C., 1931–44), 4.160–62; Thomas Crafts Jr. to John Adams, December 16, 1775, in Robert J. Taylor, ed., *The Papers of John Adams* (Cambridge, Mass., 1979), 3.366–67; John Adams to Thomas Crafts Jr., February 18, 1776, in Smith, *Letters of Delegates to Continental Congress,* 3.273.

37. Samuel Adams to Joseph Palmer, April 2, 1776, on shortage of openings for New England men, in Smith, *Letters of Delegates to Continental Congress,* 3.473–74. John Adams's letter to Thomas Crafts Jr., February 18, 1776, mentioning Brewer, is incomplete, reading: "You know the State of Coll Brewer's Case—an experienced and a brave officer, removed from a Regiment and the General Officers thought" [rest of letter missing], in Smith, *Letters of Delegates to Continental Congress,* 3.272. For details on Brewer's court-martial on October 23, 1775, see Force, *American Archives,* 4.3.1155. See also James Warren to John Adams, December 11, 1775, on supporting "deserving" men like Thomas Crafts, William Burbeck, and Reverend Dr. Samuel Cooper, in *Warren-Adams Letters,* 1.194–95.

38. On the evacuation of Boston see Brooks, *Henry Knox,* 38–44 (Knox's phrase "a noble train of artillery" is from a letter to George Washington, December 17, 1775, quoted on 40); Parkman, *Army Engineers in New England,* 5–7; French, *The First Year of the American Revolution,* 654–71 (French, on pp. 656–57, including n. 19, claims that both Gridley and Knox laid out the works at Dorchester Heights); "A British Officer in Boston," pt. 2, *Atlantic Monthly,* 34 (May 1877): 553–54; *Boyle's Journal of Occurrences, New England Historical and Genealogical Register* 85 (January 1931): 119.

39. Henry Burbeck, "Extract of a Letter to Colonel Samuel Swett"; Heitman, *Historical Register,* 133; Parkman, *Army Engineers in New England,* 7. Washington expressed his disapproval of Burbeck's behavior in a letter to John Hancock, May 11, 1776, in Fitzpatrick, *Writings of Washington,* 5.34–35. On Revere's military appointments see *Massachusetts Soldiers and Sailors,* 13.121–22; Revere's military commissions in roll 1, Revere Papers. Several contemporary sources, including his obituary in the *Boston Intelligencer and Evening Gazette,* May 16, 1818, referred to him as Colonel Revere.

40. Revere to Lamb, April 5, 1777, Lamb Papers, quoted in Goss, *Life of Colonel Revere,* 1:280–81. On Lamb's military career, see Heitman, *Historical Register,* 338; *DAB,* 10.555–56.

8. No Laurels on His Brow

1. Paul to Rachel Revere, April 1775: "pray order him [Paul Jr.] . . . to keep at home" and "lett Isaac Clemens . . . take care of the shop," quoted in Forbes, *Paul Revere,* 272. On Isaac Clemens see Gregory Palmer, *Biographical Sketches of Loyalists of the American Revolution* (Westport, Conn., 1984), 160. On destruction during the siege of Boston see "Diary of Samuel Cooper, 1775–1776," *American Historical Review* 6 (January 1901): 338; "A Journal Kept During the Time Yt Boston Was Shut Up in 1775–1776 by Timothy Newell, Esq.," *MHS Collections,* 4th ser., 1 (1852): 269, 271; "Diary of Ezekiel Price, 1775–1776," *MHS Proceedings* 7 (November 1863): 215–16, 244–46; Horace E. Scudder, "Life in Boston in the Revolutionary Period," in *Memorial History of Boston,* ed. Winsor, 3.158; Forbes, *Paul Revere,* 294–96.

2. Stark, *Loyalists of Massachusetts,* 133–36 (list of Boston Tories who left Boston for

Halifax in March 1776); Foner, *Tom Paine and Revolutionary America*, chap. 4 ("Paine, the Philadelphia Radicals, and the Political Revolution of 1776").

3. On the Boston town meeting of March 29, 1776, see "Diary of Ezekiel Price," March 29, 1776, 247; *Boston Town Records*, 18.228.

4. Washington to the president of Congress, March 24 and April 4, 1776, in Fitzpatrick, *Writings of George Washington*, 4.424–26, 473. On British destruction at Castle Island and defensive preparations in Boston see also Washington to Governor Cooke of Rhode Island, March 27, 1776, in Force, *American Archives*, 4.4.522; orders for Colonel Whitney's regiment, April 23, 1776, in *Acts and Resolves of Massachusetts*, 19.340; "Diary of John Rowe," March 19, 20, 1776, 304–5; *Boyle's Journal of Occurrences*, March 19, 1776, *New England Historical and Genealogical Register* 85 (April 1931): 119.

5. *Boston Town Records*, 18.228, 233; "Records of the Boston Committee of Correspondence, Inspection, and Safety, May to November 1776," *New England Historical and Genealogical Register* 30 (July 1876): 381–82. Thomas Crafts, Edward Proctor, Captain John Pulling, and Thomas Hichborn of the North End Caucus were also chosen for the Committee of Correspondence.

6. John Revere was born on June 13 and died on June 27, 1776, in Nielsen, "The Revere Family," 301. On the Nantasket expedition see "Extract of a Letter from an Officer in the Colony Train at Nantasket under the Command of Colonel Crafts," in *Continental Journal and Weekly Advertiser*, June 20, 1776, *Dorr Collection*, 4.957; Frothingham, *History of the Siege of Boston*, 314–15.

7. On Paine see Foner, *Tom Paine and Revolutionary America*, chap. 1, 74–78; excerpts from *Common Sense* in Greene, *Colonies to Nation*, 270–83 (quoted material on 282, 272). See also Otis, "The Rights of the British Colonies Asserted and Proved," in Greene, *Colonies to Nation*, 28–33.

8. John to Abigail Adams, July 3, 1776, in Butterfield, *Adams Family Correspondence*, 2.29–31.

9. Text of the Declaration of Independence in Greene, *From Colonies to Nation*, 298–300; Abigail Adams to John Adams, July 21, 1776, in Butterfield, *Adams Family Correspondence*, 2.56.

10. Washington to the Massachusetts Legislature or Committee of Safety of the State, July 9, 1776, Fitzpatrick, *Writings of Washington*, 5.239. On the progress of the war see John Boyle's diary entries on August 11, 31, September 12, October 13, November 16, and December 12, 1776, and January 9 and February 27, 1777, in *Boyle's Journal of Occurrences*, *New England Historical and Genealogical Register* 85 (April 1931): 124–27; Alden, *The American Revolution*, 94–111.

11. On Knox see *DAB*, 10.476. Joseph Warren was born on April 30, 1777; Lucy was born on May 15, 1780, and died on July 9, 1780; and Harriet was born on July 20, 1782; in Nielsen, "The Revere Family," 301. On Revere's attendance at town meetings on March 10 and May 17, 1777, and his election as fire ward from 1777 to 1779 see *Boston Town Records*, 18.271, 281, and 26.4, 50. On his participation in Masonic festivals and his attendance at, and absence from, Grand Lodge meetings from December 1776 to December 1779, when he was on active military duty, see *Grand Lodge Proceedings*, 1733–92, 258–77. Masonic offices are listed in Steblecki, *Paul Revere and Freemasonry*, appendix 2, 103.

12. The House of Representatives met on September 6, 9, and 10, 1776, to arrange for Revere to recut the former colony plates and "to desire him to alter the word Colony, in the plate . . . and insert State in the room thereof," in *Journals of the House of Representatives of Massachusetts*, vol. 52, pt. 1 (Boston, 1985), 93, 95, 97. On Maresquelle's and Revere's work casting cannon for the Massachusetts Board of War see entries for December 11, 1776, January 11, February 28, March 15 and 20, 1777, *Board of War Minutes, 1776–77*, MAC 148.38, 106, 182, 207, 215; Revere's orders to Titicut (part of Bridgewater) from the War Office, February 28, 1777, in roll 1, Revere Family Papers, MHS; Forbes, *Paul Revere*, 308–9. On Louis de Maresquelle see Octavius J. Howe, "Massachusetts on the Seas in the War of the Revolution, 1775–1782," in Hart, *Commonwealth History of Massachusetts*, 3.40; *Massachusetts Soldiers and Sailors*, 10.227.

13. On news of events at Danbury, Connecticut, the Boston town meeting's actions regarding Tories, and the Test Act see John Boyle's diary entry, May 5, 1777, *Boyle's Journal of Occurrences, New England Historical and Genealogical Register* 85 (April 1931): 128; *Boston Town Records*, 18.280–82; Lawrence Shaw Mayo, "The Massachusetts Loyalists, 1775–1783," in Hart, *Commonwealth History*, 3.262–63.

14. Reverend John Eliot to Reverend Jeremy Belknap, May 20, 1777, Jeremy Belknap Papers, *MHS Collections*, 6th ser., 4 (1891): 113–16; entries for June 2 and 20, 1777, *Board of War Minutes, 1776–77*, MAC 148.342–43, 381; Forbes, *Paul Revere*, 311–17.

15. John Eliot to Jeremy Belknap, May 9, 1777, Jeremy Belknap Papers, *MHS Collections*, 6th ser., 4 (1891): 109.

16. Eliot to Belknap, May 9, 1777, Jeremy Belknap Papers, *MHS Collections*, 6th ser., 4 (1891): 111–12.

17. Deborah Revere's obituary in the *Boston Gazette*, May 26, 1777; Nielsen, "The Revere Family," 292–95, 298–301.

18. Henry Jackson to Henry Knox, July 29, 1776, Henry Knox Papers, 1719–1825, MHS Microfilm, reel 3; James Kimball, "Orderly Book of the Regiment of Artillery Raised for the Defence of Boston in 1776," *Historical Collections of the Essex Institute* 13 (January 1875), pt. 1. See orders of June 27, July 3, 9, and 13, 1777, on 119, 122, 125–26, 128–29.

19. Courts-martial of August 16 and 22, Crafts's comments on August 17, and his orders of August 24 are all in "Orderly Book of the Regiment of Artillery," *Historical Collections of the Essex Institute* 13 (July 1876): 239–44.

20. Samuel Adams to Paul Revere, July 28, 1777, in which Adams mentions receiving a letter from Revere on June 26 and one from Crafts, in Smith, *Letters of Delegates to Continental Congress*, 7.386–87.

21. Resolve Relating to Monopolizing and Giving Extravagant Prices for Provisions, January 30, 1777, and reference to committee appointed "to Consider the Whole Matter Respecting the Acts for preventing Monopoly and Oppression," June 27, 1777, in *Acts and Resolves of Massachusetts*, 19.789 and 20.49–50; Revere to Samuel Adams, August 24, 1777, quoted in Patterson, *Political Parties in Revolutionary Massachusetts*, 161; Adams to Samuel Phillips Savage, president of the Revolutionary Board of War in Massachusetts, July 3, 1778, S. P. Savage Papers, vol. 2, MHS. For background on legislation and wartime inflation see Patterson, *Political Parties in Revolutionary Massachusetts*, 160–61; Alden, *The American Revolution*, 214–16, 218–21.

22. Account of Ticonderoga and Stark's victory at Bennington in *Boyle's Journal of Occurrences,* July 17 and August 22, 1777, *New England Historical and Genealogical Register* 85 (April 1931): 129, 130; Revere's orders to march to Worcester to take charge of the prisoners, August 27 and September 2, 1777, in "Orderly Book of the State Artillery Regiment," *Historical Collections of the Essex Institute* 13 (July 1876): 245, 246. See also Alden, *The American Revolution,* 129–42.

23. On the Newport expedition see "Orderly Book of the State Artillery Regiment," September 21, 26, and November 3, 1777, *Historical Collections of the Essex Institute* 13 (July 1876): 248, 251; *Historical Collections* 14 (January 1877): 60; *Boyle's Journal of Occurrences,* November 1, 1777, *New England Historical and Genealogical Register* 85 (April 1931): 131. On Burgoyne's surrender and the "Continental Thanksgiving," see *Boyle's Journal of Occurrences,* October 22 and December 18, 1777, *New England Historical and Genealogical Register* 85 (April 1931): 131, 132. On details of two Battles of Freeman's Farm and events leading to Burgoyne's surrender at Saratoga see Alden, *The American Revolution,* 142–49; Greene, *Colonies to Nation,* 408–9.

24. Background and text of the French treaty in Greene, *Colonies to Nation,* 410–13; Alden, *The American Revolution,* 149, chap. 12 ("The Bourbons Enter the War").

25. Crafts's petition of September 1777, *Revolution: Petitions,* June 1777–February 26, 1778, MAC 183.120; petition of Revere and officers, complaining about clothing allowance, March 30, 1778, *Revolution: Resolves,* 1778, MAC 218.410; House authorization of the clothing allowance on April 30, 1778, *Journals of the House of Representatives of Massachusetts,* 1777–78, vol. 53, pt. 2 (Boston, 1988), 246; petition of Jonathan Edes, David Bradlee, William Todd, Benjamin White Jr., Josiah Audibert, Abel Moore, and Winthrop Gray requesting clothing allowance of April and September 1778 (petition undated but given a date of January 1, 1779, in the index), *Revolution: Petitions,* March 1778–February 11, 1779, MAC 184.297; Todd et al. to House, October 8, 1778, in *Journals of the Massachusetts House of Representatives,* vol. 53, pt. 2, p. 71; petition of Jonathan Edes and John Meinzies, dated September 9, 1778, and Daniel Ingersoll, September 11, 1778, *Revolution: Petitions,* MAC 184.210, 214, 218. Edes remained with the regiment until he resigned on February 26, 1779; Meinzies was granted a discharge on November 5, 1778; and Ingersoll was discharged on November 2, 1778, later serving as an officer of the Suffolk County militia at Fort Hill. See *Massachusetts Soldiers and Sailors,* 5.209–10; 10.609; 8.624.

26. General William Heath to Revere, March 1, 1778, roll 1, Revere Papers. On the continued disciplinary problems in the Massachusetts Artillery Regiment, the execution of Thomas Harrison, and Revere's orders to march to Providence see "Orderly Book of the State Artillery Regiment," in *Historical Collections of the Essex Institute* 14 (July 1877): 192, 193, 196–99, 201. William Norcutt was found guilty of neglect of duty on May 14, 1778, and sentenced to be whipped twenty stripes "with a burch Rod on his Naked Breech." Nicholas Brown was found guilty of "being Drunk on his post" on June 4, 1778, and sentenced to receive thirty-nine lashes with a cat-o'-nine-tails "on his Naked Back." On July 3, 1778, General Heath expressed his hope that the troops of the State Artillery Regiment had learned from the example of Harrison's execution to "avoid a Crime so Atrocious in its Nature and pernitious in its Consequences."

27. Sullivan's orders in "Orderly Book 1778," vol. 55, roll 15, Revere Papers. On partici-

pants in the second Newport expedition see Louis Hatch, "Massachusetts in the Continental Forces, 1776–1783," in Hart, *Commonwealth History of Massachusetts*, 3.122; references in "Diary of Ezekiel Price, 1777–1778" for August 1778, *New England Historical and Genealogical Register* 19 (October 1865): 334–35. The description of Lafayette is in a letter from Samuel Adams to Samuel Phillips Savage, September 14, 1778, S. P. Savage Papers, vol. 2, MHS.

28. Paul to Rachel Revere, August 1778, Revere Family Papers II, roll 4. Crafts had previously expressed his displeasure at serving under Crane in a letter to John Adams, December 16, 1775, in Taylor, *The Papers of John Adams*, 3.366–67.

29. "Orderly Book 1778," especially entries for August 13, 14, 15, 17, 18, 20, 24, 26, 28, roll 15, Revere Papers; "Diary of Ezekiel Price, 1777–1778," *New England Historical and Genealogical Register* 19 (October 1865): 334–37 (entries for July 25–September 15, 1778); *Boston Gazette*, August 17, 24, and especially 31, 1778. See also Alden, *The American Revolution*, 207; Hatch, "Massachusetts in the Continental Forces," 122–24. On pp. 123–24, Hatch mentions that the performance of Lovell's Brigade at Newport "won for General Lovell the Greek gift of the command of the army in the Penobscot expedition of the following year."

30. Copy of return to General Gates, January 31, 1779, roll 1, Revere Papers; William Dunlop to General Gates, February 9, 1779, asking to meet Gates to "learn the nature of my Offense," *Miscellaneous Bound Manuscripts*, MHS; details of case and ruling in *Revolution: Council Papers*, 2d ser., 1778–79, MAC 175.214, 215–17a; ruling of the Superior Court, Concord, April 1779, and other details of case in several documents dated February 26, April 6, 21, May 27, and June 8, 1779, in roll 1, Revere Papers. For background on privateering and "libelling," the process of laying claim to a ship or goods by drawing up the grounds for seizure in a document called a libel, see J. Franklin Jameson, *Privateering and Piracy in the Colonial Period* (1923; reprint, New York, 1970), xii; Gardner Weld Allen, *Massachusetts Privateers of the Revolution*, MHS *Collections* 77 (Boston, 1927): 14–60.

31. References to reports of House committees on June 10, 17, September 17, 21, October 10, 16, 1778, January 16 and 18, 1779, in *Journals of the Massachusetts House of Representatives*, 1778–79, vol. 54 (Boston, 1989), 22, 30, 42, 49, 75, 82, 101, 103. The petition of Crafts, Revere, and Todd is in *Revolution: Petitions*, MAC 184.416–18.

32. E.g., the council granted a petition of discharge for Increase Newhall, adjutant in the regiment, "as he now has an Opportunity and Inclination to serve his Country on the Sea service," October 23, 1778, and for Revere's cousin Captain Phillip Marett, who asked to be discharged to "serve his country in a more advantageous manner" on January 29, 1779, and on the following day was commissioned commander of a privateer. On Newhall see *Revolution: Council Papers*, 2d ser., December 1777–December 1778, MAC 174.480. On Marett see *Massachusetts Soldiers and Sailors*, 10.227. See also Hatch, "Massachusetts in the Continental Forces," 121; Forbes, *Paul Revere*, 331–33.

33. Resolve of February 25, resignations of February 26, and resolve of March 1, 1779, in *Journals of the Massachusetts House of Representatives*, vol. 54, pp. 157, 159, 162; petition of resignation, containing the notation that Revere was in Newbury, *Revolution: Resolves*, 1779, MAC 221.293–94a. Although Crafts resigned on February 26, he petitioned the council on March 30 asking for a settlement of his and his staff's pay and rations, to which

the council responded that they would not "pass upon the Rolls" until Crafts produced "a Certification that he has settled his account with the Board of War." His petition is in *Revolution: Council Papers*, 2d ser., 1778–79, MAC 175.213.

34. Revere's deposition to the "Honorable Committee to Investigate the Causes of the Failure of the Expedition to Penobscot, etc.," *Revolution: Penobscot Expedition*, MAC 145.335. Todd and Gray were two of the regiment's officers who petitioned the council on March 24, 1779, requesting a "speedy, just, and Honorable accounting . . . Wishing each of us to go to our different occupations," *Revolution: Council Papers*, 2d ser., 1778–79, MAC 175.201–201A.

35. On Revere's solution to the problem of desertion see Revere to council, March 27, 1779; council to Revere, March 29, 1779; Revere to council and council's response, April 9, 1779; all in *Revolution: Council Papers*, 2d ser., 1778–79, MAC 175.211, 210, 242, 243–243a. See also Forbes, *Paul Revere*, 331–33. Captain Hacker was commander of the sloop *Providence*, which participated in the Penobscot expedition. In a war council held on August 7, 1779, Hacker voted to continue the siege, while Revere voted against it. On Hacker's command during Penobscot see Gardner Weld Allen, *A Naval History of the American Revolution* (1913, 1940; reprint, New York, 1962), 2.420. On the war council of August 7 see *Revolution: Penobscot Expedition*, MAC 145.77–79.

36. Petition of Francis Gray to the House of Representatives, April 20, 1779, *Journal of the House of Representatives*, vol. 54 (Boston, 1989), 186; House committee appointed "to repair to Castle Island," June 25, 1779, *Journal of the House of Representatives*, vol. 55 (Boston, 1990), 67.

37. Revere's orders to prepare for the Penobscot expedition, June 26, 1779, roll 1, Revere Papers; Revere's description of the expedition in a letter to General William Heath, October 24, 1779, Heath Papers, *MHS Collections*, 7th ser., 4 (1904): 318–26 (quoted material on 324 and 318, respectively). See also Orderly Book (containing orders of General Solomon Lovell, correspondence between Lovell and the Massachusetts Council, and Council of War Minutes), Solomon Lovell's Letterbook, July 7–12, 1779, and "State of facts respecting the Penobscot Expedition" by William Todd, in Solomon Lovell Papers, MHS. For secondary sources see Allen, *Naval History of the American Revolution*, vol. 2, chap. 12 (The Board of War's order to Commodore Saltonstall on July 13 to "preserve the greatest harmony with the Commander of the Land Forces" is on 422); Goss, *Life of Colonel Revere*, vol. 2, chaps. 10 ("Penobscot Expedition"), 11 ("Revere's Diary of the Penobscot Expedition"), 12 ("Investigation, Testimony, and Vindication"); Octavius T. Howe, "Massachusetts on the Seas in the War of the Revolution," in Hart, *Commonwealth History*, 3.36–38; Russell Bourne, "The Penobscot Fiasco," *American Heritage* 25 (October 1974): 28–33, 100–101; William M. Fowler Jr., "Disaster in Penobscot Bay," *Harvard Magazine* 81 (July–August 1979): 26–31; Frederic Grant Jr., "The Court-Martial of Paul Revere," *Boston Bar Journal* 21 (April 1977): 5–13.

38. Allen, *Naval History of the Revolution*, 2.423–27 (Lovell's account of the "smart conflict" is on 426); Bourne, "The Penobscot Fiasco," 29–33; Fowler, "Disaster on Penobscot Bay," 28; Revere to William Heath, October 24, 1779, Heath Papers, *MHS Collections*, 321.

39. The other officer Todd accused of "Backwardness" was Colonel Mitchell, who

"complained heavily of disorders." See "State of facts respecting the Penobscot Expedition" by William Todd, Solomon Lovell Papers, MHS. See also Major William Todd's deposition to the committee investigating Penobscot, September 28, 1779, *Revolution: Penobscot Expedition*, MAC 145.230–37.

40. Comments of General Lovell and Revere in council of war, August 7, 1779 MAC 145.123, 124; see also councils of war, July 27, August 7 and 13, 1779, *Revolution: Penobscot Expedition*, MAC 145.77–79 (August 7), 108 (August 13), 119 (July 27), 123–25 (August 7), 129 (August 13); Revere's explanation for the failure of the expedition in deposition to the Penobscot committee, *Revolution: Penobscot Expedition*, MAC 145.339. See also Allen, *Naval History of the Revolution*, 2.427–31; Fowler, "Disaster in Penobscot Bay," 29–30.

41. Depositions of Peleg Wadsworth and Revere, *Revolution: Penobscot Expedition*, MAC 145.275–82, 335–40 (quoted material on 278 and 335). See also Allen, *Naval History of the Revolution*, 2.431–38; Bourne, "Penobscot Fiasco," 100–101; Fowler, "Disaster in Penobscot Bay," 30–31; Grant, "The Court-Martial of Paul Revere," 7–8; Joseph Williamson, "The Conduct of Paul Revere in the Penobscot Expedition," *Collections and Proceedings of the Maine Historical Society*, 2d ser., 3 (1892): 379–92.

42. Council to Revere, September 6, 1779, *Revolution: Council Papers*, 2d ser., 1778–79, MAC 175.545; depositions of Thomas Jenners Carnes and William Todd, *Revolution: Penobscot Expedition*, MAC 145.274–274a, 230–37 (quoted material on 237). When Todd referred to Revere's inattendance at the "General's Marque," I think he meant "marquee," i.e., "a large field tent" or "any large tent or temporary structure for a special gathering (councils of war, etc.)," definition in *Webster's New Universal Unabridged Dictionary*, 2d ed. See also Grant, "Court-Martial of Paul Revere," 8; Goss, *Life of Colonel Revere*, 2.335–59.

43. Revere's deposition, Revere's questioning of General Lovell, Wadsworth's denial that he or General Lovell made the statement about Revere, and supporting depositions by Marett, Brown, and Nichols appear in *Revolution: Penobscot Expedition*, MAC 145.337, 320–21, 282, 250, 271–73, 303.

44. Gilbert Speakman's deposition, General Lovell's response to questioning by Revere that the only time Revere disobeyed an order was "the day after we retreated," and Revere's defense appear in *Revolution: Penobscot Expedition*, MAC 145.322–25, 320–21, 340. See also Lovell's letter to the council, dated August 29, 1779: "I should likewise beg if you would give Lieutenant-Colonel Revere a very severe reprimand for his unsoldierlike behavior in returning home without orders," Orderly Book, Solomon Lovell Papers, MHS.

45. Revere's deposition, *Revolution: Penobscot Expedition*, MAC 145.337–38.

46. Committee report of October 7, 1779, Revere's petition of October 8, 1779, and committee report of November 16, 1779, *Revolution: Penobscot Expedition*, MAC 145.350–51, 346–47, 375–76. See also "Proceedings of the General Assembly and Council of Massachusetts Relating to the Penobscot Expedition (1780)," Evans, *Early American Imprints*, no. 16847, 27–29; *Boston Gazette*, December 27, 1779.

47. Revere to William Heath, October 24, 1779, Heath Papers, *MHS Collections*, 324–26. Revere repeated his accusation of Todd's malice toward him because Revere accepted command of the state artillery regiment in his deposition to the committee investigating Penobscot, in *Revolution: Penobscot Expedition*, MAC 145.335–37. On Lieutenant John Marston see *Massachusetts Soldiers and Sailors*, 10.269–70.

48. Revere to council, September 9, 1779, requesting a court-martial, *Revolution: Letters,* 1779, MAC 201.281; Israel Keith to William Heath, September 26, 1779, Heath Papers, *MHS Collections,* 317–18; Revere's petition to the council for a court-martial, January 17, 1780, *Revolution: Council Papers,* 2d ser., 1779–80, MAC 176.109–11 (quoted material). See also petition of March 9, 1780, *Revolution: Resolves,* 1780, MAC 226.254–55; petition of January 22, 1781, *Revolution: Petitions,* 1781–82, MAC 187.20. In a letter to the *Boston Gazette,* March 25, 1782, Revere cited petitions of December 1779 and August 1780 in addition to the ones cited above. On Revere's entitlement, as a militia officer, to a court-martial under Continental regulations, see Grant, "The Court-Martial of Paul Revere," 8–9.

49. Proceedings of the General Court-Martial of Lieutenant-Colonel Paul Revere, February 19, 1782, *Revolution: Council Papers,* 1781–83, MAC 172.105–12. On Revere's "newspaper war" with Todd and Carnes see *Boston Gazette,* March 18, 1782 (Todd writing as Veritas), March 25 and April 1 (Revere's response, revealing Todd's identity on March 25), April 8 (Todd and Carnes), and April 15 (Revere).

9. Paul Revere, Esq.

1. Robert Pope's order, February 6, 1779, Epes Sargent's order, August 15, Dr. Phillip Godfrid Kast's order, August 29, and Stephen Metcalf's order, August 31, 1780, in Waste Book and Memoranda, vol. 1, roll 5, Revere Family Papers, MHS; Paul Revere to Mathias Rivoire, October 6, 1781 (date penciled in on manuscript), roll 1, Revere Papers.

2. Receipt signed by Phillip Marett, August 27, 1780, vol. 41, receipt book, Boston, 1780–1805, roll 12, Revere Papers; Epes Sargent's payment in goods, October 2, 1780, and Captain Mungo Mackay's payment on June 14, 1781, in Waste Book and Memoranda, vol. 1, roll 5, Revere Papers.

3. John Rivoire to Paul Revere, January 28, 1781, September 9, October 15, 1782, March 4, 1783; Mathias Rivoire to Paul Revere, April 8, 1781, and March 1782 (date penciled in on manuscript); Paul Revere to Mathias Rivoire, October 6, 1781 (date penciled in on manuscript); all in roll 1, Revere Papers.

4. Paul Revere to John Rivoire, July 1, 1782, roll 1, Revere Papers (letter addressed to "Dear Cousin," and the recipient is not identified, but in the letter Revere refers to John Rivoire's letter of January 28, 1781, in the Revere Papers, roll 1).

5. Revere to John Rivoire, July 1, 1782, roll 1, Revere Papers. The text of the Declaration of Independence is in Greene, *Colonies to Nation,* 298–300.

6. Revere to John Rivoire, July 1, 1782, roll 1, Revere Papers. For a comparison of Revere's pre- and post-Revolutionary shop see Federhen, "From Artisan to Entrepreneur," 75–89. Federhen notes the number of entries for cash taken out of the shop between 1783 and 1789 to fund Revere's other business ventures on p. 84, which may be seen in Revere's Waste Book and Memoranda, vol. 2 (1783–97), roll 5, Revere Papers. On Revere's resumption of the goldsmith's trade in 1781 see orders from pre-Revolutionary customers Stephen Bruce on January 10 and November 29, William Breck in April (no day), and Isaiah Thomas on May 10, in Waste Book and Memoranda, vol. 1, roll 5, Revere Papers.

7. On neoclassicism see E. P. Richardson, *Painting in America, 1502 to Present* (New York, 1965), 85–87, 93; Russel Blaine Nye, *The Cultural Life of the New Nation, 1776–1830*

(New York, 1960), 3–6, 268–92; Fales, *Early American Silver*, 28–31. Avery, *Early American Silver*, 84–88, terms Revere's silver "of varying quality." Both Skerry, "The Revolutionary Revere," 51–58, and Federhen, "From Artisan to Entrepreneur," 75–89, consider Revere to be a talented craftsman but an even better technological innovator and entrepreneur. Fairbanks et al., *Paul Revere's Boston*, 197–200, give Revere more credit for his artistic ability. On neoclassicism in Federal Boston and Revere's mastery of the style see Fairbanks et al., *Paul Revere's Boston*, 143–200.

8. Nathaniel Tracy ordered six silver goblets on April 15, 1782; Moses Michael Hayes (Revere lists the order under "M. M. Hayes"), who served with Revere in the Massachusetts Grand Lodge, ordered one of Revere's earliest neoclassical teapots on February 5, 1783, and placed several more orders, including one for silver goblets on March 12, 1792, in the 1780s and 1790s; Elias Hasket Derby, a Salem merchant, was another repeat customer in the 1780s and 1790s, ordering butter boats, canns, bowls, and a silver waiter; Perez Morton, who was also a member of St. Andrew's Lodge, placed several orders for a variety of spoons, sugar tongs, cream pots and "silver muggs" in the 1780s and 1790s; all in Waste Book and Memoranda, vol. 1 (1761–83) and vol. 2 (1783–97), roll 5, Revere Papers. On the type of objects Revere made for the mercantile and political elite see Federhen, "From Artisan to Entrepreneur," 75–76. On the display of luxury to assert status and convey gentility in a mobile society see Cary Carson, "The Consumer Revolution in Colonial British America: Why Demand?" in *Of Consuming Interest: The Style of Life in the Eighteenth Century*, ed. Cary Carson, Ronald Hoffman, and Peter J. Albert (Charlottesville, Va., 1994), 483–697, especially 523, 619–94. Nathaniel Tracy, a Revere customer, is an example of how fortunes could change in post-Revolutionary America. A member of a prominent pre-Revolutionary mercantile family in Newburyport, Massachusetts, Tracy lost nearly all his wealth in 1786 and had to sell most of his assets. See Labaree, *Patriots and Partisans: The Merchants of Newburyport, 1764–1815*, 11, 218–19.

9. On Revere's adoption of changes in techniques and changes in type of items he produced see Skerry, "The Revolutionary Revere," 53–54; Federhen, "From Artisan to Entrepreneur," 75–79. Solomon Munro (or "Munroe") charged Revere eight shillings "To one day work at putting up a plating mill," November 17, 1785, roll 1, Revere Papers.

10. Paul Revere Sr. noted his work in the margin of his ledgers with slanting, diagonal hatch marks or the notation "Revere, Senior." Paul Jr.'s work is noted with horizontal hatch marks or a cross. A circle and check mark also appear in the ledgers, possibly marks used by apprentices or journeymen in Revere's shop. There is not a mark in the ledger for every order, especially for large orders that involved the labor of several individuals. See Waste Book and Memoranda, vol. 1 and vol. 2, roll 5, Revere Papers. On Revere's ledgers and use of marks see Kathryn C. Buhler, "The Ledgers of Paul Revere," *Bulletin of the Museum of Fine Arts* 34 (June 1936): 38–45; Federhen, "From Artisan to Entrepreneur," 86–87.

11. On Revere's work for Stephen Emmery see entries for April 23, 1785, January 30 and August 4, 1787, September 5 and October 17, 1788, in Waste Book and Memoranda, vol. 2, roll 5, Revere Papers. Emmery is identified as a silversmith in the Thwing Index, MHS. On Simon and Aaron Willard see Waste Book and Memoranda, vol. 1, roll 5, Revere Papers; Fairbanks et al., *Paul Revere's Boston*, 182–83. Orders for Deacon Boardman and Son appear between 1783 and 1797, most steadily between 1788 and 1797. The hatter Wil-

liam Williams became a customer on April 16, 1792, and remained a regular customer until 1797. Revere also made hat bills for Charles Smith on November 15 and December 8, 1792, and January 24, 1795; in Waste Book and Memoranda, vol. 1 (for Deacon Boardman's orders in 1773 and 1774) and vol. 2 (all other orders), roll 5, Revere Papers. Federhen, "From Artisen to Entrepreneur," 81, credits Revere with an astounding total of over 17,000 hat bills between 1783 and 1797. John Dyer was a customer between 1786 and 1790, Zachariah Hicks between 1786 and 1792, John Winnick between 1788 and 1793, and Edward Cole between 1790 and 1793. They were Revere's biggest customers among saddlers and harness makers, but he made items for others, including Andrew Stimpson (several orders in 1792) and John Swift (July 18, 1789). See Waste Book and Memoranda, vol. 2, roll 5, Revere Papers; Federhen, "From Artisan to Entrepreneur," 79–81. Dyer, Hicks, and Winnick are all listed as saddlers in the 1789 *Boston Directory*, Evans, *Early American Imprints*, no. 22033, 16, 24, 44.

12. Federhen, "From Artisan to Entrepreneur," 84, cites a 1782 letter from Willard to Revere about their partnership. There are several letters from Willard to Revere in 1784 and especially in 1785, including the one cited above [February 1785], in roll 1, Revere Papers. Willard advertised that Samuel King and "Colonel Paul Revere, Boston" were selling his clock jacks in the *Independent Chronicle*, February 3, 1785. See also "Act Granting Simon Willard the Exclusive Privilege of Making and Vending Clock Jacks for Five Years," July 2, 1784, *Acts and Resolves of Massachusetts, 1784–1785* (Boston, 1890), 45; Revere to Captain Oaks, December 21, 1784 (Revere is sending "two of Willards' patent Jacks which be kinde enough to sell for me . . ."), Letterbook, 1783–1800, vol. 53, roll 14, Revere Papers; John Blagge to Paul Revere, April 26, 1787, roll 1, Revere Papers.

13. Receipt from Gideon Snow to Paul Revere for "part of Freight of goods in the *Rosamond,*" January 3, 1783, roll 1, Revere Papers; Revere to Geyer, June 30, September 5, November 3, 1783, Letterbook, 1783–1800, vol. 53, roll 14, Revere Papers. On contents of Revere's hardware shop see Account Book, 1783–88, vol. 9, roll 6, Revere Papers; Cash Books, Inventory, 1785, vol. 32, roll 11, Revere Papers; various receipts for merchandise in Book of Invoices, 1783–91, vol. 37, roll 11, Revere Papers; Revere's advertisements in the *American Herald*, May 23, and 30, 1785, and in the *Massachusetts Centinel*, December 10, 14, 17, 1785. On Frederick William Geyer, a Boston Tory merchant who was banished in 1778 but allowed to return to the United States in 1789, see Stark, *Loyalists of Massachusetts*, 350–51.

14. Revere's hardware customers are in Account Book, 1783–88, vol. 9, roll 6, and Boston Ledger, 1761–88, roll 7, Revere Papers. Perez Morton placed several silver orders, including an order for a cream pot and spoons on May 10, 1784, silver clasps on January 13, 1785, silver mugs on June 4, 1788, and a slop bowl on April 8, 1796; all in Waste Book and Memoranda, vol. 2, roll 5, Revere Papers. On Perez Morton, who became a member of St. Andrew's Lodge in 1776, see Palmer, *Centennial Memorial*, 234; Goss, *Life of Colonel Revere*, vol. 2, appendix C, 635 (North End Caucus members). Amos Lincoln married Deborah Revere on January 14, 1781. She died on January 8, 1797, and on May 24, 1797, Lincoln married her younger sister, Elizabeth. See Nielsen, "The Revere Family," 298, 300.

15. Revere's Masonic offices are listed in Steblecki, *Paul Revere and Freemasonry*, appendix 2, 103–4. The Massachusetts Grand Lodge originally issued a summons for a meeting

on March 7, 1777, but adjourned to the following night when only nine members responded to their call. Paul Revere was chosen Junior Grand Warden the same night that the Grand Lodge chose Joseph Webb as Grand Master. See *Grand Lodge Proceedings, 1733–92,* 259–60; Taylor, *Historical Sketch of the Grand Lodge of Massachusetts,* 6–7; Steblecki, *Paul Revere and Freemasonry,* 32–33.

16. *Grand Lodge Proceedings, 1733–92,* 284, 288–89; Bullock, *Revolutionary Brotherhood,* 114–17.

17. *Grand Lodge Proceedings, 1733–92,* 301–4.

18. The letter of the committee of five to Massachusetts Grand Lodge, February 25, 1783, is in a report by Charles W. Moore on the early history of St. Andrew's Lodge, in Palmer, *Centennial Memorial,* 39. The Massachusetts Grand Lodge appointed a committee to confer with St. Andrew's Lodge on December 24, 1782. The members included Perez Morton and James Avery, who had served with Revere on the committee that approved the independence of the Massachusetts Grand Lodge, in *Grand Lodge Proceedings, 1733–92,* 305. See also Steblecki, *Paul Revere and Freemasonry,* 36–38; Taylor, *Historical Sketch of the Grand Lodge of Massachusetts,* 8.

19. The vote of St. Andrew's Lodge is listed in Palmer, *Centennial Memorial,* 244. On the breakup of St. Andrew's Lodge, the formation of Rising States Lodge, and Revere's offices in Rising States Lodge see Steblecki, *Paul Revere and Freemasonry,* 38–43, appendix 2, 103. Revere was chosen president of the Masonic convention on March 10, 1785. The convention met at Free Masons Hall in Charlestown on May 26. On the continued refusal of St. Andrew's Lodge to join the Massachusetts Grand Lodge see James Carter, Master of St. Andrew's Lodge, and Elisha Sigourney, Senior Warden, to the Massachusetts Grand Lodge, May 23, 1785; all in *Grand Lodge Proceedings, 1733–92,* 460–61.

20. There remain different interpretations of the legitimacy of the actions of the Massachusetts Grand Lodge. Taylor, in *Historical Sketch of the Grand Lodge of Massachusetts,* 7–8, believes the action of the Massachusetts Grand Lodge in appointing Joseph Webb Grand Master in 1777 was "a mere assumption for practical ends and might well have been intended for a temporary expedient until such time as the military and Masonic atmosphere had cleared." Their act of assumption was "not new in the history of Masonry," and the Grand Lodge claimed "exclusive jurisdiction only over *Ancient* Masons." Henry Wilson Coil, in *Coil's Masonic Encyclopedia* (New York, 1961), 35–38, claims that the "American Doctrine" or doctrine of "Territorial Exclusiveness," i.e., the belief that "there can be but one recognized Grand Lodge in a state and that it must have exclusive jurisdiction therein" was "contrary to such precedents as existed" and was not "generally recognized in America until after the Revolution." Coil terms the actions of the Massachusetts Grand Lodge in electing Webb a "masonically questionable act" and "an act of sovereignty," since the death of the provincial Grand Master vacated the office until the Grand Master in Britain could appoint a successor.

21. For identifications of friends, neighbors, customers, and political associates who opposed Revere's vote to sever ties between St. Andrew's Lodge and the Grand Lodge of Scotland see Goss, *Life of Colonel Revere,* vol. 2, appendix C, 635–36 (North End Caucus); Waste Book and Memoranda, vol. 1, roll 5, Revere Papers (on Barrett and Graham);

Forbes, *Paul Revere,* 55, 163 (on Marston). Of the twenty-three members who voted for the Massachusetts Grand Lodge, fourteen had joined St. Andrew's Lodge within five years of casting their vote on January 22, 1784. Only Revere (1760), Robert Hichborn (1764), and Nathaniel Fellows (1768) had been members for more than fifteen years. Dates of Masonic membership may be found in either Palmer, *Centennial Memorial,* 231–36, or under member's names in "Parker Index." Rent receipts for Joseph Dunkerly ("Dunkerley"), July 19 and October 19, 1784, and January 19, 1785, in Waste Book and Memoranda, vol. 1, roll 5, Revere Papers. Revere paid Captain Nathaniel Fellows £20 in July 1783 for a variety of goods, including padlocks, warming pans, flat seam needles, plated spurs, and women's scissors, in Book of Invoices, 1783–91, vol. 37, roll 11, Revere Papers.

22. On the celebration of the peace treaty see the *Boston Gazette,* March 1, 1784. Merrill Jensen, *The New Nation: A History of the United States during the Confederation, 1781–1789* (1950; reprint, Boston, 1981), offers a strong rebuttal to the "Critical Period" thesis of the 1780s proposed in John Fiske's *The Critical Period of American History* (1888) and repeated by twentieth-century historians. Yet, in newspapers and letters, Americans expressed concern about the rise of luxury, self-interest, and factionalism in their midst and argued about the appropriate forms of national and state governments to foster prosperity and revive virtue. For an overview of American fears about the future of republicanism see Wood, *Creation of the American Republic,* 393–425.

23. See Revere and Samuel Adams's comments on greed and vice in chapter 8. On the economic and social dislocations created by the Revolution and John Adams's revival of the commonwealth ideal in the Massachusetts constitution see Oscar Handlin and Mary Flug Handlin, *Commonwealth: A Study of the Role of Government in the American Economy, Massachusetts, 1774–1861,* rev. ed. (Cambridge, Mass., 1969), 10–12, 28–31. On the moral dimension of republicanism see Wood, *Creation of the American Republic,* chap. 3 ("Moral Reformation").

24. On the Massachusetts constitution see Greene, *Colonies to Nation,* 345–57; Patterson, *Political Parties in Revolutionary Massachusetts,* chaps. 6–7. For greater detail on the creation of state governments and constitutions see Alan Nevins, *The American States During and After the Revolution, 1775–1789* (New York, 1924). On the necessity of constitutional conventions see Wood, *Creation of the American Republic,* 328–43 ("A Power Superior to the Ordinary Legislature"). Notice of defeat of the first constitution is in the *Boston Gazette,* October 12, 1778.

25. Handlin and Handlin, *Commonwealth,* 28–31; Patterson, *Political Parties in Revolutionary Massachusetts,* 218–26; Wood, *Creation of the American Republic,* 567–80.

26. Patterson, *Political Parties in Revolutionary Massachusetts,* 226–47; Nevins, *The American States During and After the Revolution,* 179–82; Handlin and Handlin, *Commonwealth,* 25–31; "An Address of the Convention . . . to their Constituents (1780)," attempting to "sell" the constitution to the people, in Greene, *Colonies to Nation,* 352–57; support for John Hancock's election in the *Boston Gazette,* October 23, 1780.

27. On Adams see his "Thoughts on Government (1776)" in Greene, *Colonies to Nation,* 306–11; discussion of his views as embodied in the Massachusetts constitution in Patterson, *Political Parties in Revolutionary Massachusetts,* 219–26. On Parsons see Patterson, *Political*

Parties in Revolutionary Massachusetts, 191–92 (quoted material from *Memoir of Theophilus Parsons* and the "Essex Result"); excerpts from "Essex Result" in Greene, *Colonies to Nation,* 352.

28. For a description of the master-apprentice relationship in theory and practice see Lemay and Zall, *Benjamin Franklin's Autobiography,* 10–17; Bridenbaugh, *Colonial Craftsman,* 130–34. On the importance of hierarchy and deference in Freemasonry see Bullock, "Ancient and Honorable Society," 54–59; Charter of St. Andrew's Lodge in Palmer, *Centennial Memorial,* 5–6. Revere began to assume leadership positions in church and political affairs in the late 1780s, when he was no longer just a goldsmith but an entrepreneur managing a goldsmith business, hardware shop, and foundry.

29. Charleston, South Carolina; New Haven, Connecticut; and several towns in New Jersey and Virginia were incorporated after the war. Opposition to incorporation was strong in both Philadelphia and Boston. For an overview of the subject see Jensen, *The New Nation,* 118–22. On incorporation in Boston see "An American," *Massachusetts Centinel,* June 16, 1784; *Massachusetts Centinel,* June 19, 1784 (Barrel's views expressed in town meeting of June 17, 1784); *Independent Chronicle,* June 17, 1784.

30. *Independent Chronicle,* June 24, 1784; *Massachusetts Centinel,* June 19, 1784; Adams's speech in *Massachusetts Centinel,* May 12, 15, 1784 (issues missing), quoted in Jensen, *The New Nation,* 119; Jeremy Belknap to Ebenezer Hazard, June 19, 1784, Jeremy Belknap Papers, *MHS Collections,* 5th ser., 2 (1877): 358–61. On failure of incorporation in the fall of 1785 and articles pro and con see *Massachusetts Centinel,* October 26, 29, November 2, 5, 9, 23, 26, 30, December 3, 1785; *American Herald,* October 31, November 7, 28, December 12, 1785.

31. Revere to Geyer, September 5, November 3, and December 25, 1783, April 15, August 5, December 5, 1784, April 15, 1786, complaining about the scarcity of money created by his own lack of cash and the absence of a bank in Boston; Revere to Cruger, Lediard, Mullette, August 21, 1784, expressing surprise "that the Bill on Blanchard and Lois is noted for non Acceptance, I cannot account how it could happen, as the drawer, Mr. Swan [James Swan, merchant], is of undoubted credit"; Revere to John Sampson, December 9, 1784; Revere to Captain Peter Cunningham, December 25, 1783, asking him to sell 5,000 flat-seam needles purchased in London; all in Letterbook, 1783–1800, vol. 53, roll 14, Revere Papers.

32. *Massachusetts Centinel,* March 12, 26, April 9, 13, 16, 1785.

33. *Massachusetts Centinel,* April 20, 1785.

34. *Massachusetts Centinel,* April 23, 27, 1785. On the response to British trade policies in 1785 and especially the development of a "mechanics' interest" see Gary J. Kornblith, "From Artisans to Businessmen: Master Mechanics in New England, 1789–1850" (Ph.D. diss. Princeton University, 1983), 54–71. On terminology, throughout the eighteenth century the terms "mechanic," "artisan," "craftsman," and "tradesman" were used interchangeably, sometimes to define a kind of work and sometimes to refer to social class. The term "mechanic" seems most often to be used when artisans organized for political purposes. They stressed their worth to the community by reminding their fellow citizens that theirs was a "life defined by productive labor" that contributed to the well-being of the commu-

nity. See Olton, *Artisans for Independence*, 7; Nash, "Artisans and Politics in Eighteenth-Century Philadelphia," 62–68.

35. Gibbens Sharp was a member of the North End Caucus and a Revere customer. He and Sarson Belcher, a member of the Committee of Correspondence, Inspection, and Safety, also dined with Revere at Liberty Tree in August 1769. For names of Committee of Tradesmen and Manufacturers who drew up resolutions on April 25, 1785, and members of Association of Tradesmen and Manufacturers, along with identifications, see *Massachusetts Centinel*, April 27 and May 25, 1785; Kornblith, "From Artisans to Businessmen," 62–63. "A Friend to Commerce," in the *Independent Chronicle*, August 12, 1784, called for "the necessity of promoting our own *manufacturers*" and an end to "our large importation of *gewgaws, ballooneries . . .* trifles." On the connection between luxury and the loss of virtue see Drew McCoy, *The Elusive Republic: Political Economy in Jeffersonian America* (1980; reprint, New York, 1982), 21–24, 94–95.

36. For several examples of Hancock's success at currying popular favor, especially in his attempt to become governor in 1780, see Patterson, *Political Parties in Revolutionary Massachusetts*, 186–87, 197–200, 214–17. On the election of 1785 and development of political factions between 1780 and 1785 see Nevins, *The American States During and After the Revolution*, 210–16; Anson Ely Morse, *The Federalist Party in Massachusetts to the Year 1800* (Princeton, N.J., 1909), 14–23, 26–32. "Philo-Civis" attacked the "vacillating" Hancock and lauded Bowdoin in the *Massachusetts Centinel*, May 25, 1785.

37. On Revere's personal reasons for disliking Hancock see his letter to William Heath, October 24, 1779, *MHS Collections*, 7th ser., 4 (1904): 318–26, discussed in chapter 8. See address to Governor Bowdoin by the Committee of Merchants and Traders, June 4, 1785, and by the Committee of Tradesmen and Manufacturers, June 7, 1785, in Bowdoin-Temple Papers, *MHS Collections*, 7th ser., 6 (1907): 50, 52–53; Thomas Wadsworth to Paul Revere, July 3, 1785, roll 1, Revere Papers.

38. Bowdoin's address to House and Senate, June 3, 1785, in *Massachusetts Centinel*, June 4, 1785; resolve recommending a convention to revise the Articles of Confederation, July 1, 1785, *Acts and Resolves of Massachusetts, 1784–1785*, 666. On Bowdoin's support for Revere see "An Act Giving to Paul Revere and John Noyes, The Exclusive Privilege of Erecting a Steam Engine, For Manufacturing Iron," March 14, 1786, *Acts and Resolves of Massachusetts, 1784–1785*, 557–58; "Message from Governor Bowdoin to Senate and House," February 8, 1786, recommending that Revere and Noyes be granted the privilege, *Acts and Resolves, 1784–1785*, 828–29. According to Bowdoin's message, Noyes "had gained a thorough knowledge" of "the new invented steam engine" and "several branches of manufacture in iron." Revere and Noyes were granted an exclusive fifteen-year privilege of manufacturing iron by steam engine provided that they established the manufactory in Massachusetts "within eighteen months." On Bowdoin's support for government involvement in manufacturing and internal improvements see Shipton, *Sibley's Harvard Graduates*, 11.542–43; Kornblith, "From Artisans to Businessmen," 65–67; Morse, *The Federalist Party in Massachusetts*, 31–32. For an overview of the role of Massachusetts state government in the economy see Handlin and Handlin, *Commonwealth*, chap. 3 ("To Encourage Industry and Economy").

39. The "Honestus" series appeared in the *Independent Chronicle* between March and June 1786 and was answered by several writers in the *Massachusetts Centinel*, e.g., "Anti-Honestus," as late as September 23. 1786. For an analysis of the brief life of the Association of Tradesmen and Manufacturers and the possible role of the "Honestus" controversy in its dissolution see Kornblith, "From Artisans to Businessmen," 62–71. See also Helen R. Pinkney, *Christopher Gore: Federalist of Massachusetts, 1758–1827* (Portland, Maine, 1969), 18–19. On Benjamin Austin Jr. see *DAB*, 1.431–32.

40. The most complete analysis of Shays's Rebellion is in David P. Szatmary, *Shays' Rebellion: The Making of an Agrarian Insurrection* (Amherst, Mass., 1980). For a brief analysis of grievances, excerpts from the Hampshire County Convention, chronology, and reaction to events in Boston see Greene, *Colonies to Nation*, 505–7; Handlin and Handlin, *Commonwealth*, 34–46; Myron F. Wehtje, "Boston's Response to Disorder in the Commonwealth, 1783–1787," *Historical Journal of Massachusetts* 12 (January 1984): 19–27.

41. See "Real Grievances," news of the Hampshire Convention, and report of the Boston town meeting's disapproval of western actions and "readiness to assist government, in every measure taken for the preservation of the constitutional rights of the people" in *Massachusetts Centinel*, September 9, 1786. See also *Massachusetts Centinel*, September 13 ("Address of Inhabitants of Boston to Friends and Fellow Citizens"), September 16 ("Address to Governor from the Inhabitants of Boston"), September 20 ("Miscellany from the *Essex Journal*"), and September 27 ("Anti-Honestus"). Revere's name was not listed in the Account of subscriptions for procuring supplies for the militia engaged in suppressing Shays's Rebellion, 1787, in Edward Payne Papers, MHS. On Revere's bowl for General Shepard see Forbes, *Paul Revere*, 365–66.

42. Henry Knox to George Washington, December 21, 1786; Knox to Stephen Higginson, January 28, 1787; several other letters to and from Knox concerning Shays's Rebellion; all in Henry Knox Papers, 1719–1825, Massachusetts Historical Society Microfilm, reel 19. George Washington shared Knox's concerns about "the disorders, which have arisen in these States" and wrote that "Vigilance in watching and vigor in acting is become in my opinion indispensably necessary. . . . I think with you, that the spring will unfold important and distressing scenes, unless much wisdom and good management is displayed in the interim." See Washington to Knox, December 26, 1786, in Greene, *Colonies to Nation*, 507–8. On economic reasons for strengthening the national government see Jensen, *The New Nation*, chaps. 14–17; E. James Ferguson, "The Nationalists of 1781–1783 and the Economic Interpretation of the Constitution," in *The Confederation and the Constitution: The Critical Issues*, ed. Gordon S. Wood (Lanham, Md., 1979), 1–14. On support for strengthening the Articles of Confederation in Boston see Myron F. Wehtje, "Boston and the Calling of the Federal Convention of 1787," *Historical Journal of Massachusetts* 15 (June 1987): 99–105.

43. On the Annapolis Convention, James Madison's outline of the defects of the confederation ("Vices of the Political System of the United States," April 1787), and "Debates in the Federal Convention in Philadelphia," see Greene, *Colonies to Nation*, 509–47. See also Madison, *Federalist Number Ten*, *The Federalist Papers*, New American Library ed. (New York, 1961), 84; Anti-Federalist arguments in Greene, *Colonies to Nation*, 558–68 (James Winthrop, "Agrippa" Letter 4, December 3, 1787, on 560–61).

44. Writer in the *Connecticut Courant*, commenting on Shays's Rebellion and the danger

of "men of sense and property" being replaced by "blustering, ignorant men," quoted in the *Massachusetts Centinel,* December 2, 1786; quote on "parasites and sycophants" from Hamilton, *Federalist Number Seventy-One,* 432. On Federalist concerns with restoring the proper men to leadership and Anti-Federalist obsessions with aristocracy see Gordon S. Wood, "The Worthy against the Licentious," in *The Confederation and the Constitution,* ed. Wood, 86–112. On the origin and definitions of "Federalist" and "Anti-Federalist" see Jackson Turner Main, *The Antifederalists: Critics of the Constitution* (1961; reprint, New York, 1974), viii–xii.

45. Madison, *Federalist Number Sixty-Three,* 389–90; Madison, *Federalist Number Forty-Eight,* 309; see also Madison, *Federalist Number Fifty-One,* 320–55. On the importance of popular sovereignty, representation, and separation of powers in the federal republic see Wood, *Creation of the American Republic,* 547–53, 596–615.

46. On the impact of Shays's Rebellion on the gubernatorial election of 1787 and ratification in Massachusetts see Richard D. Brown, "Shays's Rebellion and the Ratification of the Federal Constitution in Massachusetts," in *Beyond Confederation: Origins of the Constitution and American National Identity,* ed. Richard Beeman, Stephen Botein, and Edward C. Carter II (Chapel Hill, N.C., 1987), 113–27; Main, *The Antifederalists,* 200–209; Nevins, *The American States During and After the Revolution,* 219–20, 234–36; Morse, *The Federalist Party in Massachusetts,* 54–57. On the support of "Tradesmen and Mechanicks" for the Constitution see Kornblith, "From Artisans to Businessmen," 72–74. See also *Massachusetts Centinel,* March 31, 1787 ("Essex" writing in support of Hancock for governor), and January 9, 1788 ("Proceedings of TRADESMEN and MECHANICKS OF BOSTON").

47. Resolutions of "Tradesmen and Mechanicks of Boston" adopted January 7, 1788, quoted in *Massachusetts Centinel,* January 9, 1788. As a tradesman, mechanic, manufacturer, and holder of Continental securities (amount unknown), Revere had good reason to support a strong central government that would encourage trade, manufacturing, and sound economic practices. See Revere to James Young, March 14, 1786, and Revere to Mr. Bangs, October 15, 1788, referring to purchase of Continental certificates, Letterbook, 1783–1800, vol. 53, roll 14, Revere Papers.

48. *Massachusetts Centinel,* January 9, 1788. Kornblith, "From Artisans to Businessmen," 75–76, stresses the centrality of economic over ideological motives for Boston mechanics. I believe that for Revere, and perhaps for other mechanics, ideological and psychological reasons were equally, if not more, important.

49. Whether Bussey won the retailer's license over Revere's friend is unknown, since the existing records relating to the case contain only a petition from the Dedham Selectmen to the General Sessions of the Peace in Suffolk County, June 30, 1783, recommending that Bussey get the license. I suspect that he did win, and the license helped Bussey become successful. At his death in 1842 Bussey left a sizable estate, including "Woodland Hills," which he left to Harvard University. It became the Bussey Institution (now the Arnold Arboretum in Jamaica Plain, Massachusetts), dedicated to "instruction in practical agriculture, in useful and ornamental gardening, in botany, and in such other branches of natural science, as may tend to promote a knowledge of practical agriculture." Political differences may also have been a factor in Revere's dislike of Bussey, since Revere was a Federalist and Bussey was a Democratic-Republican, one of the original subscribers to the

State National Bank, founded by Democratic-Republicans and chartered in 1811. See Paul Revere to Stephen Metcalf, July 30, 1783, Bostonian Society Library, asking Metcalf to attend the court session. Revere wrote: "I should not be so pressing, or any way attempt to biass your Judgment, where you have a right to sit as Judge, did I not know how much you dispise Scoundrels." See also Dedham Selectmen to the Suffolk County General Sessions of the Peace, case no. 94468, reel 292, Suffolk County Supreme Judicial Court Files, Judicial Archives, Massachusetts Archives; "Will of Benjamin Bussey" and Thomas Gray, D.D., "A Tribute to the Memory of Benjamin Bussey, Esq. Who Died at Roxbury, January 13, 1842," in *Biographical Pamphlet Series,* vol. 10, nos. 16–17, Massachusetts State Library; "Sketches of Distinguished Merchants," art. 10, no. 4, Benjamin Bussey, of Roxbury, Massachusetts (1842), Harvard University Archives, HUG 1249; article on Bussey ("Harvard's Benefactor") in the *Boston Globe,* February 18, 1901; information on Bussey's involvement with the State National Bank in *Professional and Industrial History of Suffolk County* (Boston, 1894), 2.236–37.

50. John Rivoire to Paul Revere, March 9, 1786, and Paul Revere to John Rivoire, May 19, 1786, over claims to the estate of Paul Rivoire, "a Frenchman who lived near Philadelphia," in roll 1, Revere Papers.

51. *Debates, Resolutions, and other Proceedings of the Convention of the Commonwealth of Massachusetts . . . for the Purpose of Assenting to and Ratifying the Constitution Recommended by the Grand Federal Convention* (1788), Evans, *Early American Imprints,* no. 21242; news of ratification in *Massachusetts Centinel,* February 9, 1788.

52. Several contemporaries seemed to think that the mechanics' resolutions were a turning point in convincing Adams and Hancock, e.g., Christopher Gore to Rufus King, January 6, 1788: ". . . a meeting [of the tradesmen] to be held tomorrow night . . . this may possibly have effect on Mr. A. if not—it will effect his E[xcellency] who wavers" and Henry Jackson to Henry Knox, January 1788: "Mr. S. Adams has not yet come out, if he is against it I believe he will say but little, as the meeting of the mechanicks of this Town and their proceedings must and will have an influence over him," quoted in Morse, *Federalist Party in Massachusetts,* 51. In a speech at Pittsburgh on July 8, 1833, Daniel Webster attributed a rather grandiose speech to Paul Revere as he handed the mechanics' resolutions to Samuel Adams. When Adams asked how many mechanics were at the Green Dragon, Revere allegedly replied: "More, Sir, than the Green Dragon could hold." Adams: "And where were the rest, Mr. Revere?" Revere: "In the streets, Sir." Adams: "And how many were in the streets?" Revere: "More, Sir, than there are stars in the sky"; quoted in Goss *Life of Colonel Revere,* 2.452–54. For other explanations of why Adams and Hancock changed their minds see Jeremy Belknap to Ebenezer Hazard, February 3, 1788, Belknap Papers, *MHS Collections,* 5th ser., 3 (1877): 15; Morse, *Federalist Party in Massachusetts,* appendix E, 212–14; Kornblith, "From Artisans to Businessmen," 76–77.

53. Alfred F. Young claims that although artisans in several states participated in and helped plan parades celebrating ratification, along with other members of the community, only in Boston was the parade sponsored by a committee of tradesmen. See Young, "Plebeian Culture and Eighteenth-Century American Radicalism," in *Origins of Anglo-American Radicalism,* ed. Margaret Jacob and James Jacob (London, 1984), 185–212, espe-

cially 200–204. On descriptions of the parade see *Massachusetts Centinel*, February 9 and 13, 1788; Kornblith, "From Artisans to Businessmen," 77–78.

54. Revere to Messrs. Brown and Benson of Providence, Rhode Island, November 3, 1788, on opening of the foundry, in Letterbook, 1783–1800, vol. 53, roll 14, Revere Papers. Revere seems to have abandoned his retail trade in imported items by 1788, according to his Account Book, 1783–88, vol. 9, roll 6. The other members of the town meeting committee chosen on October 10, 1789, included John Lucas and Benjamin Russell, Revere's coleaders in drafting the mechanics' resolutions in favor of the Constitution; the Honorable Stephen Higginson, Esq.; the Honorable Caleb Davis, Esq.; and Joseph Barrell, the merchant who led the unsuccessful fight for incorporation in 1785. See *The New Brick Committee Book, 1761–1800*, Boston Public Library, Rare Books, Ms Bos. Z16 (2), by courtesy of the Trustees of the Boston Public Library; *Boston Town Records* (1784–96), 31.210 (appointment to committee on October 10, 1789), 272–73, 275. Ambivalence about luxury—whether it destroyed virtue or elevated society—is discussed in McCoy, *The Elusive Republic*, especially 21–32, 90–104. Revere's dual identities as a producer of both luxury items and utilitarian objects may have allowed him to reconcile the conflicting views of luxury.

10. A True Republican

1. On April 22, 1789, a meeting of tradesmen and manufacturers assembled at the Green Dragon Tavern and appointed Paul Revere to a committee of correspondence to revive the Association of Tradesmen and Manufacturers. By the time their petition for tariff relief reached the House of Representatives on June 5, the House had already passed tariff legislation. Gary Kornblith offers two reasons for Revere's failure to sign the petition: either a "falling out with the other Association organizers" or his wish "to keep a low profile while his bid for a federal appointment was pending." I would not completely discount his desire for federal appointment as a reason, but given that he and Benjamin Austin Jr. would find themselves on opposite sides of political issues throughout the 1790s and early 1800s, I suspect that political differences were the reason for Revere's withdrawal from the Association of Tradesmen and Manufacturers. See Kornblith, "From Artisans to Businessmen," 78–82 (quoted material on 81).

2. On artisans' collective identity and divergent interests see Nash, "Artisans and Politics in Eighteenth-Century Philadelphia," 62–88; Olton, *Artisans for Independence*, especially 7–18, 33–47. On the failure of artisan unity in the face of partisan differences see Kornblith, "From Artisans to Businessmen," 78–82 and chap. 3 ("Mechanic Ideology, 1789–1820"). Revere and Austin, an Anti-Federalist turned Democratic-Republican in the 1790s, were on opposite sides of several issues, which will be discussed later.

3. On Hamilton's program see John C. Miller, *The Federalist Era, 1789–1801* (New York, 1963), 39–69. In several letters in the 1780s, Revere complained about his shortage of money, difficulty in obtaining payment from customers, difficulties with Continental securities, and plans for his foundry. See Revere to Frederick William Geyer, November 3, 1783, April 15, 1784, April 15, 1786 (on scarcity of money); Revere to Laban Bates, January 12, 1789 (Bates owed Revere money, which he promised to pay in pork, butter, or pigs; Revere

replied: "That story has been told too often, if [you] mean to pay me, why have you not sent those articles to market and after they were sold pay me"); Revere to James Young, March 14, 1786, and to Mr. Bangs, October 15, 1788 (on buying Continental securities); all in Letterbook, 1783–1800, vol. 53, roll 14, Revere Family Papers, MHS.

4. On deference see J. G. A. Pocock, "The Classical Theory of Deference," *American Historical Review* 81 (June 1976): 516–23; Bushman, *King and People*, 55–63; Wood, *Radicalism of the American Revolution*, 57–77; Lisa B. Lubow, "Artisans in Transition: Early Capitalist Development and the Carpenters of Boston, 1787–1837" (Ph.D. diss., University of California, Los Angeles, 1987), 312–20; definitions of "deference" as "a courteous regard or respect" and "emulation" as the "desire or ambition to equal or surpass," in *Webster's New Universal Unabridged Dictionary*, 2d ed. In Revere's case, emulation was probably more a desire to be considered an equal of Washington, Adams, and others in terms of his credentials as a patriot and republican. Given his respect for deference and hierarchy, I do not think it likely that he entertained the notion of surpassing such men.

5. Fisher Ames to Paul Revere, April 26, 1789; Samuel A. Otis to Revere, May 7, 1789; Ames to Revere, January 24, 1791; all in roll 1, Revere Papers. Revere to President George Washington, February 5, 1791, Applications for Appointment to Federal Posts during the Washington Administration, United States Miscellany, 1789–1824, Manuscript Division, Library of Congress. Revere's admission that he had no "personal acquaintance" with Washington also refutes two myths: that Revere made false teeth for Washington and that Washington personally asked Revere to repair the cannon at Castle Island before the Continental Army left Boston in 1776. Ames and Otis referred Revere to the Revenue or Excise Department (Treasury) because it was the largest department in the federal government and offered the best chance for federal appointment. On the Treasury Department see White, *The Federalists: A Study in Administrative History*, 116–23.

6. Harrison Gray Otis to Revere, April 16, 1798, roll 1, Revere Papers.

7. On qualifications for federal office see Gaillard Hunt, "Office-Seeking during Washington's Administration," *American Historical Review* 1 (October 1895): 270–83; Hunt, "Office-Seeking during the Administration of John Adams," *American Historical Review* 2 (January 1897): 241–61; Sidney Aronson, *Status and Kinship in the Higher Civil Service: Standards of Selection in the Administrations of John Adams, Thomas Jefferson, and Andrew Jackson* (Cambridge, Mass., 1964), especially 3–6, chaps. 2, 4–6; White, *The Federalists*, 106–7, 259–90, 470–78. Secretary of the Treasury Alexander Hamilton, Secretary of War Henry Knox, Benjamin Lincoln, collector of the Port of Boston, and John Lamb, collector of customs of the Port of New York, had all been Continental Army officers. Knox and Lincoln had both served as secretary of war in the Confederation government, and Lincoln was also lieutenant governor of Massachusetts. In 1784 Lamb was appointed collector of customs by the New York State Legislature, of which he was a member, and retained the position in the Washington administration. See White, *The Federalists*, 125–27, 139–43, 152–53, 261, 304–5.

8. Washington made it clear that he alone was responsible for nominating candidates, but he would consult Congress on the worthiness of his choices. Adams had less control over his appointments and congressional influence. See White, *The Federalists*, 82–87. On Knox's influence see William Rickard to Knox, January 20, 1790, Henry Knox Papers, 1719–

1825, MHS Microfilm, reel 25; Benjamin Lincoln to Knox, July 18, 1789, reel 24; Benjamin Hichborn to Knox, July 28, 1789, reel 24; John Langdon to Knox, March 25, 1790, asking Knox to write to General Lincoln to get him a post in the Customs Department, "knowing the Intimacy and Friendship that subsists between you," reel 26; all in Knox Papers. John Lowell did receive a federal judgeship, and Hichborn's nephew Nathaniel Fosdick probably also received an appointment because he had risen to collector of customs in Portland by 1804. On Lowell see David Hackett Fischer, *The Revolution of American Conservatism: The Federalist Party in the Era of Jeffersonian Democracy* (New York, 1969), 251. On Nathaniel Fosdick see Revere to Thomas Ramsden, August 4, 1804, complaining about Fosdick's removal from office "because he was not a Democrat," roll 2, Revere Papers.

9. Knox's friend and fellow Continental Army officer Henry Jackson lobbied Knox shamelessly for appointments to several offices, e.g., Jackson to Knox, August 23, 1789, seeking a position in the Revenue Department, reel 24; Jackson to Knox, April 20, 24, 1791, on appointment as United States marshall, reel 28; Knox to Jefferson, on John Coffin Jones, December 10, 1788, reel 23; all in Knox Papers. There is no evidence in the Knox, Lincoln, Revere, or Washington Papers that Knox discussed Revere's suitability for a federal appointment.

10. Ames to Revere, January 24, 1791, roll 1, Revere Papers. Several letters attest to Lincoln's support in the highest Federalist ranks, e.g., Benjamin Lincoln to George Washington, February 20, 1789, seeking Federal appointment because of a series of financial losses; Theodore Sedgwick to Lincoln, August 1 and 3, 1789 ("I am the more pleased that the event was one ardently wished by all good men"); Henry Knox to Lincoln, August 4, 1789 ("Although I do not conceive the office . . . adequate to the merits of my friend . . . I sincerely congratulate you on the appointment"); John Spooner to Lincoln, September 9, 1791 (Lincoln's appointment as collector "is flattering to you evincing the Friendship of that illustrious man [Washington], who made the Appointment"). On Lincoln's influence over appointments see Lincoln to Washington, August 16, 1789, and Tobias Lear to Lincoln, April 8, 1791, on Lincoln's role in obtaining a post for Jonathan Jackson as inspector of the revenue for the survey of Massachusetts; all in Lincoln Papers, MHS. See also David Mattern, *Benjamin Lincoln and the American Revolution* (Columbia, S.C., 1995), 186–89.

11. Lincoln ordered spoons and sugar tongs on February 3, 1785, in Waste Book and Memoranda, vol. 2, roll 5, Revere Papers. He also placed three hardware orders on January 26, February 10, and April 28, 1785, for a Willard clock jack, brushes, warming pan, candlesticks, house bell, kettles, flat irons, and various kitchen items, in Account Book, 1783–88, vol. 9, roll 6, Revere Papers. Lincoln's next order was for a bell on September 1, 1803, in Boston Ledger, 1799–1804, vol. 14, roll 7, Revere Papers. On gubernatorial election and Revere's presumed support for Bowdoin see chapter 9. There is unfortunately no existing correspondence between Revere and Lincoln in either the Revere or Lincoln Papers at MHS to conclusively prove or disprove the theory that there may have been a connection between Revere's lack of support for Lincoln in the election of 1785 and his failure to obtain an appointment under Lincoln. Revere's listing of Lincoln as a reference in his letter of application to Washington suggests that he thought he could rely on Lincoln's support, but as in his quest for a Continental commission, he seems to have discovered the limits of "friendship."

12. On Revere's older children and their spouses see Nielsen, "The Revere Family," 298–300; "Parker Index," 200–201 (on Amos Lincoln); Federhen, "From Artisan to Entrepreneur," 87–88 (on Thomas Stevens Eayres).

13. Maria Revere was born on July 14, 1785, and John Revere was born on March 27, 1787. On enrollment of Revere's sons at Boston Latin see Jenks, *Catalogue of the Boston Public Latin School,* 373. On the education of Revere's younger daughters see chapter 1. For further information on the children of Revere's second marriage see Nielsen, "The Revere Family," 301–2; Grundy and Triber, "Paul Revere's Children."

14. Federhen, "From Artisan to Entrepreneur," 85–86; Fairbanks, *Paul Revere's Boston,* 166 (text accompanying illustration 245 on Chinese porcelain), 190–94 (including text on Derby's silver cups and Captain Bradford's urn), 200–201 (Hartt tea set), 207 (text on inspiration for Revere's silver pitcher). On Revere's adaptation of the Chinese porcelain bowl see Forbes, *Paul Revere,* 364–65. The inventory of Revere's estate lists three silver pitchers, a teapot, sugar pot, cream pot, porringer, two salts, a ladle, twelve tablespoons, twenty-two teaspoons, a sugar tong, and a cup. His waste books include an entry on December 29, 1786, for four silver teaspoons; a large order on May 30, 1789, for a coffeepot, teapot, cream pots, salt and pepper caster, punch strainer, teaspoons, tea tongs, silver canns, and gold earring tops; and orders for spoons in July and December 1793. See Suffolk Probate Court Record Books, case no. 25527, vol. 116, p. 315, microfilm reel 49, Judicial Archives, Massachusetts Archives; Waste Book and Memoranda, vol. 2, roll 5, Revere Papers.

15. Renee L. Ernay has carefully scrutinized Revere's business correspondence and records in an excellent analysis of the operation of Revere's foundry. She notes the financial assistance of Benjamin Hichborn, who provided Revere with £59.2.0 in eight installments between April and December 1787, and Samuel Hichborn, who paid for raw materials and carting of materials. Benjamin Hichborn sold the land on which the foundry was built to Revere on June 28, 1792. Revere also tried to interest Messrs. Brown and Benson, owners of the Hope Furnace in Providence, Rhode Island, in partial ownership of his foundry in exchange for a "constant and regular supply of Piggs from your furnace." Brown and Benson did not take Revere up on his offer, but they were one of his suppliers of pig iron. See Ernay, "The Revere Furnace, 1787–1800" (M.A. thesis, University of Delaware, 1989), 1, 5–8, on establishment of foundry with assistance of his cousins and list of products (quote on products from trade card of Revere and Son); deed from Benjamin Hichborn to Paul Revere for sale of land on Lynn Street, June 28, 1792, roll 1, Revere Papers; Revere to Messrs. Brown and Benson, November 3, 1788, announcing opening of foundry and offering a partnership. Letterbook, 1783–1800, vol. 53, roll 14; Revere Papers; Brown and Benson to Revere, April 11, 1788, and Revere to Brown and Benson, September 3, 1789, on supplying pig iron, roll 1, Revere Papers.

16. On "mechanic ideology" from 1789 to 1820 and its connection to republicanism see Kornblith, "From Artisans to Businessmen," chap. 3, especially 132–37. On the changes in American society brought about by the "celebration of commerce" see Wood, *Radicalism of the American Revolution,* chaps. 17 ("A World within Themselves") and 18 ("The Celebration of Commerce"). Renee Ernay divides Revere's foundry operation into two periods: 1787–93 (construction of the foundry and the production of cast iron goods) and 1794–1800

(Revere as a "defense contractor" supplying ordnance and ship fittings). See Ernay, "The Revere Furnace," 9–13, 20–51.

17. Jeremy Belknap to Ebenezer Hazard, March 23, 1793, Belknap Papers, *MHS Collections,* 5th ser., 3 (1877): 326. On the effects of the democratic revolution see Wood, *Radicalism of the American Revolution,* 230–43. On the importance of the intellectual skills that distinguished the mechanic from the common laborer see Kornblith, "From Artisans to Businessmen," 132–37.

18. For an enlightening discussion on how politics affected scientific inquiry in this period see Linda K. Kerber, *Federalists in Dissent: Imagery and Ideology in Jeffersonian America,* 2d ed. (Ithaca, N.Y., 1980), chap. 3 ("The Objects of Scientific Inquiry"); Daniel J. Boorstin, *The Lost World of Thomas Jefferson* (1948; reprint, with new preface, Chicago, 1981), 8–26, 213–25. Kerber cites contemporary opinion that the American Academy of Arts and Sciences was associated with Federalists and the American Philosophical Society with Jeffersonian Republicans or Democrats, as their Federalist opponents preferred to call them, and that the American Academy stressed mathematical and astronomical studies while the Philosophical Society concentrated on natural history. The Federalists also ridiculed Jefferson and other Democratic scientists as impractical visionaries, but as Boorstin reminds us, the Jeffersonians would have been equally vehement in their claims that the only reason for scientific inquiry was "the quest for useful knowledge." Revere's scientific pursuits, involving the natural history fields of chemistry and geology, mathematics, and the practical application of scientific principles, seems to draw on both Federalist and Democratic scientific traditions. As for Benjamin Lincoln, although his essays may have been read by educated gentlemen, he had only a common-school education and was a self-educated "man of intellect and science." On Revere's interest in science see Revere's Journal and Commonplace Book, 1777–1801, vol. 51, no. 1; Revere to Messrs. Brown and Benson, November 7, 1788, asking "Mr. N. Brown if he would send the Volume of Watsons Chimistry by the first opportunity," Letterbook, 1783–1800, vol. 53; Revere to Dr. Letsome, December 3, 1791, Letterbook, 1783–1800, vol. 53; all in roll 14, Revere Papers. On Richard Watson, bishop of Llandaff and author of the *Chemical Essays,* see Charles Coulston Gillispie, ed., *Dictionary of Scientific Biography* (New York, 1980), 13.191–92. On Lincoln see "Notices on the Life of Major General Benjamin Lincoln," *MHS Collections,* 2d ser., 3 (1815): 233–55.

19. On Revere's growing reputation as a metallurgist and expert in casting ordnance see Stephen Rochefontaine to Revere, June 22, 1795, roll 1, Revere Papers; Ernay, "The Revere Furnace," 22–51. On Rochefontaine see Parkman, *Army Engineers in New England,* 7–9.

20. References to Revere's work on the U.S.S. *Constitution* are scattered among his papers, e.g., bill for $3,820.33, dated October 28, 1797, and other entries in Cash and Memoranda, 1791–1801, vol. 9, roll 6; copper nails, bolts, and spikes, June 27, 1799, Waste Book and Memoranda, vol. 3 (1799–1804), roll 5; bill for copper bolts, spikes, nails, etc. supplied in 1802, Boston Ledger, 1799–1804, vol. 14, roll 7. On the launch of the *Constitution* see *Columbian Centinel,* October 25, 1797. Information on Revere's foundry customers may be found in various ledgers and journals in vols. 9–11, roll 6, and vols. 14–15, roll 7, Revere Papers; letters in roll 1, Revere Papers; Letterbook, 1783–1800, vol. 53, roll 14, Revere Papers. See also Revere to Benjamin Stoddard, December 31, 1798, Letterbook, 1783–1800, vol. 53, roll 14, Revere Papers.

21. Revere to Watson, February 21, 1790; Revere to Sheafe, October 28, 1795; Revere to an unidentified recipient (apparently a government official), February 7, 1796; Revere to Sheafe, January 7, 1799. Revere also informed John Brown of Providence on April 24, 1797, "that after considerable labour and expense," he had developed a sound method of making copper malleable and offered to supply copper bolts for a ship that Brown was building; all in Letterbook, 1783–1800, vol. 53, roll 14, Revere Papers. See also Ernay, "The Revere Furnace," 40–41.

22. A list of Revere bells cast between 1793 and 1801 is in Cash and Memoranda, vol. 9, roll 6, and another list of bells is in Stock Book, 1793–1828, vol. 40, roll 11, Revere Papers. See also Arthur H. Nichols, *The Bells of Paul and Joseph W. Revere* (Salem, Mass., 1911), 10–30; Edward Stickney and Evelyn Stickney, *The Bells of Paul Revere, His Sons and Grandsons* (Bedford, Mass., 1976). Both Paul Revere Jr. and Joseph Warren Revere made bells with their father, and after 1801 Paul Jr. cast bells on his own. The Revere Copper Company, under the direction of Joseph Warren Revere, ceased the production of bells in 1828. On the art and science of bell casting and how Revere learned his trade see Nichols, *The Bells of Paul Revere*, 1–6; Forbes, *Paul Revere*, 370–76. On Revere's first bell see entries for May 21 and October 8, 1792, in *The New Brick Committee Book,* Boston Public Library, Rare Books, by courtesy of the Trustees of the Boston Public Library; *The Diary of William Bentley* (1905–7; reprint, Gloucester, Mass., 1962), 1.387, 395 (entries for August 17 and September 19, 1792).

23. Revere to Heywood, Flag, and Stowell, July 5 and August 30, 1802, Letterbook, 1801–6, vol. 53, roll 14, Revere Papers; Heywood, Flagg, and Stowell to Revere, August 25, 1802, and Heywood and Flagg to Revere, December 21, 1802, roll 2, Revere Papers.

24. Silvester Gardiner to Revere, February 14, 1785, roll 1, Revere Papers; Thomas Wadsworth to Revere, May 27, July 3 and 23, 1785, roll 1, Revere Papers; Wadsworth's will, September 14, 1799, Thomas Wadsworth Papers, South Caroliniana Library, University of South Carolina; Susanna Cox to Revere, June 16, 1798, roll 1, Revere Papers. On Silvester Gardiner see Stark, *Loyalists of Massachusetts*, 313–15.

25. Thomas Shreve to Revere, September 3, 1789 (asking Revere to "collect every circumstance of this poor unfortunate woman's conduct"); Shreve to Revere, January 8, 1790, with note added May 26, 1790 (mentioning his wife's complaint "that she had been used very ill by Colonel Revere"). See also Shreve to Revere, June 25 and November 5, 1788, April 27, 1789; all in roll 1, Revere Papers.

26. Thomas Ramsden to Revere, December 30, 1796, Revere Family Papers II, roll 4, Revere Papers.

27. Most of Revere's letters are to Mrs. Ramsden, who was living in England. Captain Ramsden's whereabouts were often unknown, and Mrs. Ramsden complained to Revere about her long separation from her husband. Details of the case and Revere's actions on behalf of the Ramsdens are outlined in Revere to Thomas Ramsden, November 9, 1797; Revere to Ann Ramsden, March 21, May 14, June 20, September 23, November 17, 1798, April 1, 1799, October 11, 1800; Revere to Thomas Ramsden, September 3, 1801; Revere to Ann Ramsden, April 14 and May 27, 1802; Revere to Thomas Ramsden, November 15, 1802; several letters from Revere to Edward Edwards of Philadelphia between 1798 and 1800; all in Letterbook, 1783–1800, and Letterbook, 1801–6, vol. 53, roll 14, Revere Papers.

See also the inventory of Ramsden's items left in care of Thomas Woodhead, September 1797; Ann Ramsden to Paul Revere, December 31, 1797, enclosing another inventory in hope that Revere will be able "to secure this *small* part of our property"; Thomas Ramsden's grant of power of attorney to Edward Edwards of Philadelphia, January 22, 1798, and Edwards's substitution of power of attorney to Paul Revere, April 17, 1798; Ann Ramsden to Revere, July 26, 1798, February 20, 1799, February 6, 1801; all in roll 1, Revere Papers. Ann Ramsden to Revere, February 20, 1802, roll 2, Revere Papers.

28. Ann Ramsden to Revere, June 18, August 7, 1798; Thomas Ramsden to Revere, April 13, 1801; roll 1, Revere Papers.

29. For Revere's appointments to town meeting committees see *Boston Town Records* (1784–96), 31.210, 272–73, 275, 314; and (1796–1813), 35.2, 24, 34, 78. On Revere's service as coroner see his appointment, May 11, 1795 (signed by Governor Samuel Adams), roll 1, Revere Papers; Revere's accounts of cases as coroner, 1796–1801, Journal and Commonplace Book, 1777–1801, vol. 51, no. 1, roll 14, Revere Papers; Revere's letter of resignation as coroner to Governor Caleb Strong, January 28, 1801 ("I must either neglect my own, or, the publicks business, as I must be, a large proportion of my time, out of Town"), Boston Public Library, Rare Books, Ch.F.6.4; and thanks to Revere for his service, April 3, 1801, *Boston Board of Health Records, 1799–1816*, 3 vols., 1 (1799–1806), 176, Boston Public Library, Rare Books, Ms1328, both by courtesy of the Trustees of the Boston Public Library. His subscription to the Humane Society, December 1795, membership in Charitable Fire Society, June 30, 1796, subscription to the *Federal Orrery,* January–July 1795, subscription to *Massachusetts Magazine,* October 1, 1795, and dues for the Boston Library Society, December 9, 1797, are all in roll 1, Revere Papers. On the Boston Library Society see Caleb H. Snow, *A History of Boston the Metropolis of Massachusetts From Its Origins to the Present Period: with Some Account of the Environs* (Boston, 1828), 355.

30. On the importance of virtue, benevolence, and education in republican society see Wood, *Creation of the American Republic,* especially 53–70, 118–24, 426–27, 567–71; Wood, *Radicalism of the American Revolution,* 213–25.

31. On John Lamb see Countryman, *A People in Revolution,* 274–79; *DAB,* 10.555–56. On the development of political parties see Joseph Charles, *The Origins of the American Party System* (New York, 1961); William Nisbet Chambers, *Political Parties in a New Nation: The American Experience, 1776–1789* (1963; reprint, New York, 1969), chaps. 2–4; Richard Hofstadter, *The Idea of a Party System: The Rise of Legitimate Opposition in the United States, 1780–1840* (Berkeley, Calif., 1969), chap. 3; John R. Howe Jr., "Republican Thought and the Political Violence of the 1790s," *American Quarterly* 19 (Summer 1967): 147–65. Benjamin Hichborn's shifting political principles and colorful personality are discussed in Shipton, *Sibley's Harvard Graduates,* 17.36–44.

32. On town meetings of December 30, 1791, and January 26, 1792, see *Boston Town Records,* 31.272–73, 275. For articles against the reform of town government, some probably written by Benjamin Austin Jr., see *Independent Chronicle,* January 12, February 2, 1792, and *Boston Gazette,* January 16, 1792 (especially "A Northend Blacksmith" to his "Fellow Townsmen—particularly Brothers Mechanicks"), and January 23, 1792 ("A Mechanick and Friend to the Principles of '75"). On support for reform see *Columbian Centinel,* January 14, 18, 21, 1792. In his diary on February 2, 1792, Reverend William Bentley referred to Ben-

jamin Austin's speeches in "Edes' wretched Monday Gazette" and articles in the *Independent Chronicle,* where "the threats are noticed, and the alarming consequences intimated," *Diary of William Bentley,* 1.345.

33. Revere's speech is in roll 1, Revere Papers. On the vote of January 26, 1792, see *Boston Town Records,* 31.275. For a discussion of how the vote on town reform split Boston's artisan leaders see Kornblith, "From Artisans to Entrepreneurs," 104–7. For an analysis of why New England artisans were loyal to Federalism, "artisan Federalism" as a "distinctive brand of Federalism," and differences between "artisan Federalism" and "artisan Republicanism" see Kornblith, "Artisan Federalism: New England Mechanics and the Political Economy of the 1790s," in *Launching the "Extended Republic": The Federalist Era,* ed. Ronald Hoffman and Peter J. Albert (Charlottesville, Va., 1996), 249–72.

34. *Diary of William Bentley,* 1.3, 13. On Austin's support for the French Revolution see Kornblith, "From Artisans to Entrepreneurs," 107. On reaction to the French Revolution in Massachusetts see Charles Warren, *Jacobin and Junto; or, Early American Politics as Viewed in the Diary of Dr. Nathaniel Ames, 1758–1822* (Cambridge, Mass., 1931), 45–58 (quote on necessity of "Democratic Societies" from declaration sent out by the Massachusetts Constitutional Society on 53); James M. Banner Jr., *To the Hartford Convention: The Federalists and the Origins of Party Politics in Massachusetts, 1789–1815* (New York, 1970), 17–19. On the impact of the French Revolution on American politics see Miller, *The Federalist Era,* chap. 8.

35. On Madison's commercial legislation see Miller, *The Federalist Era,* 142–51; Stanley Elkins and Eric McKitrick, *The Age of Federalism: The Early American Republic, 1788–1800* (New York, 1993), 375–88. For a discussion of the alternative socioeconomic visions of Madison and Hamilton (Madison's "political economy of Anglophobia" versus Hamilton's admiration for the "mercantile utopia" of Great Britain) see Elkins and McKitrick, *The Age of Federalism,* 79–114. For a "republican" interpretation of Jeffersonian political economy see McCoy, *The Elusive Republic,* 166–78, 236–48; Lance Banning, *The Jeffersonian Persuasion: Evolution of a Party Ideology* (Ithaca, N.Y., 1980), 218–27, chap. 10. For a "liberal" interpretation of Jeffersonian political economy see Joyce Appleby, *Capitalism and a New Social Order: The Republican Vision of the 1790s* (New York, 1984). On support for Madison's proposals in the Boston town meeting see Kornblith, "From Artisans to Entrepreneurs," 107–8; Kornblith, "Artisan Federalism," 263–64.

36. *Boston Town Records,* 31.347–48; *Columbian Centinel,* February 12, 1794 ("A Merchant"), February 26, 1794 ("A Citizen" listed those in favor and those against Madison's resolutions). Massachusetts Congressman David Cobb and William Eustis, a member of the town meeting committee that debated Madison's resolutions, both of whom opposed the resolutions, discussed the issue in a series of letters in the David Cobb Papers, MHS: Cobb to Eustis, February 22, 1794; Eustis to Cobb, February 26, 1794; Cobb to Eustis, February 26 and March 1, 1794; Eustis to Cobb, March 2, 1794. See also Kornblith, "From Artisans to Entrepreneurs," 107–8; Kornblith, "Artisan Federalism," 263–64.

37. The personal and political antipathy between Benjamin Austin Jr. and Benjamin Russell, which degenerated into a spitting incident and lawsuit resulting from the meeting to reform town government in 1792 and their partisan use of the press, is discussed in Kornblith, "From Artisans to Entrepreneurs," 104–7; Kornblith, "Artisan Federalism."

J. S. J. Gardiner, assistant rector of Boston's Trinity Church, caricatured Austin and Crafts in his *Remarks on the Jacobiniad* in 1795. Austin and Jarvis were both libeled in "The Lyars— a Political Eclogue," published in the *Federal Orrery,* September 10, 1795. For a colorful discussion of the harsh political rhetoric over reaction to the French Revolution, constitutional societies, and Jay's treaty, see Warren, *Jacobin and Junto,* 45–70 (quotes from Gardiner's satire and "The Lyars" on 54–55).

38. The constitution refers to the Associated Mechanics and Manufacturers of the Commonwealth of Massachusetts, but in early records and correspondence the organization was usually called the Boston Mechanic Association. In 1806 the organization was incorporated under the name of the Massachusetts Charitable Mechanic Association. Revere was unanimously elected president on April 16, 1795, after Edward Tuckerman declined the office. Revere was reelected annually until he declined another term in 1798. See Joseph T. Buckingham, *Annals of the Massachusetts Charitable Mechanic Association* (Boston, 1853), 3–6, 11; Jerome Carter Hosmer, *The Beginnings of the Massachusetts Charitable Mechanic Association, 1795–1808* (Boston, 1906), 3–5.

39. Revere's cashbooks are filled with Moseley's debts, and eventually Revere was appointed guardian of his estate. In 1808 Revere asked to be relieved of his guardianship of Moseley, "a Person Wasting his Estate by Excessive drinking." For an overview of Revere's difficulties with Moseley (sometimes spelled "Mosely") see Nielsen, "The Revere Family," 295–96; Federhen, "From Artisan to Entrepreneur," 87; Forbes, *Paul Revere,* 381. See also Revere's Cash and Memoranda Book, 1791–1801 (for the period 1796–98), and records for the Moseley estate, 1791–98, both in vol. 9, roll 6, Revere Papers. Revere and Moseley were also involved in a legal case in 1784, in which Revere successfully sued to recover real estate. See *Revere vs. Hill and Cunningham,* April 3, 1784, Suffolk County Court of Common Pleas Record Book, October 1783–April 1784, 171, Judicial Archives, Massachusetts Archives.

40. Of the original eighty-three members who signed the constitution of the Associated Mechanics and Manufacturers of the Commonwealth of Massachusetts, eleven were housewrights, constituting the largest occupational group. The other occupations were blacksmiths, coopers, and tailors (six each); bakers, hatters, and ropemakers (five each); bricklayers, cordwainers, and painters (three each); bookbinders, coppersmiths, hairdressers, printers, saddlers, and goldsmiths (two each; the goldsmiths were Paul Revere and Paul Revere Jr.); and bookseller, cabinetmaker, carpenter, cotton and woolen cardmaker, currier, engine builder, farrier, furrier, mason, pump and block maker, rigger, sailmaker, shipwright, silk dyer, turner, watchmaker, whitesmith, and Windsor chairmaker and paint seller (one each). Membership requirements, list of original members, officers, occupations, and brief biographies of members are in Buckingham, *Annals of the Massachusetts Charitable Mechanic Association,* 6, 10–11, 25 (Edmund Hartt), 37–39 (Zachariah Hicks), 40–41 (Thomas Stoddard Boardman and William Williams), 47–48 (John Bray), 48–49 (David Cobb). The most complete analysis of the establishment and early years of the Massachusetts Charitable Mechanic Association, particularly the economic status and political affiliation of its members, is in Kornblith, "From Artisans to Businessmen," 85–104, 108–9.

41. On May 5, 1795, Russell, Revere, and Tuckerman sent the constitution of the Me-

chanic Association with a request for support to twenty merchants. Stephen Higginson, John Codman, Daniel Sargent, William Little, and Joseph Blake were Revere's customers, and Nathaniel Fellows was a business associate and member of the Rising States Lodge. Customers' names may be found in the various waste books and ledgers in Revere's business papers, MHS. On Nathaniel Fellows see "Parker Index," 112–13. As Gary Kornblith points out, the lack of roll-call votes in the House journals for 1795–96 and the lack of knowledge about the politics of the committee that advised against incorporation of the Associated Mechanics and Manufacturers in February 1796 makes it difficult to determine conclusively whether Federalists or Democrats led the opposition. He believes, however, citing support from Benjamin Russell and Joseph Buckingham, that Federalists were behind the opposition. The petition of January 15, 1799, also suggests that Federalist leaders could have mistakenly feared the association was another of the "self-created societies" that Washington condemned. On incorporation of the Associated Mechanics and Manufacturers see Buckingham, *Annals of the Massachusetts Charitable Mechanic Association*, 12–13, 57; Kornblith, "From Artisans to Businessmen," 88–89, 109–12 (quoting Russell's address to the Massachusetts Charitable Mechanic Association, December 21, 1809).

42. Of the eighty-three original members, thirty-nine either voluntarily withdrew or forfeited their membership by violating the constitution of the association. Among those who withdrew were Paul Revere Jr. and Amos and Jedediah Lincoln. Of the eleven original housewrights in the association, nine withdrew. In 1804 Boston's master housewrights, who had played a major role in the Associated Mechanics and Manufacturers of Massachusetts, formed their own organization, the Associated Housewrights Society of the Town of Boston. On the decline of the association, including list of original members who withdrew, see Buckingham, *Annals of the Massachusetts Charitable Mechanic Association*, 10, 54; "From Artisans to Businessmen," 112–13. On the Associated Housewrights Society of the Town of Boston see Lubow, "Artisans in Transition" 450–67. On the Quasi-War, American defense preparations, and Revere's increase in business see Miller, *The Federalist Era*, 212–18; Ernay, "The Revere Furnace," 35–51 (see fig. 3 on ordnance production by year on p. 36).

43. Revere did not sign the January 15, 1799, petition for incorporation, and his name almost disappeared from the association's records after 1799. Membership of the association increased to 275 in 1800 (after the artisans' procession in Washington's memory), including a number of housewrights and carpenters and at least one prominent Jeffersonian, Bela Clap. The association finally got its charter on March 8, 1806, helped by the efforts of four of its members in the General Court and the Federalist leadership in the House and Senate. What needs much further investigation is a political analysis of the membership of these mechanics' associations. Did members withdraw from the Associated Mechanics and Manufacturers because its Federalist leanings no longer represented their interests? Were more Democrats joining the Associated Mechanics and Manufacturers in the late 1790s and early 1800s, and is that why Revere declined a leadership role? Were there political differences between members of the Associated Mechanics and the Associated Housewrights? See Buckingham, *Annals of the Massachusetts Charitable Mechanic Association*, 65–67, 94–97; Kornblith, "From Artisans to Businessmen," 112–18; Lubow, "Artisans in Transition," 375–492.

44. On the appeal of Freemasonry as a means of providing cultural stability and strengthening republicanism see Steven C. Bullock, "A Pure and Sublime System: The Appeal of Post-Revolutionary Freemasonry," *Journal of the Early Republic* 9 (Fall 1989): 359–73; Bullock, *Revolutionary Brotherhood*, 138–58; John L. Brooke, "Ancient Lodges and Self-Created Societies: Voluntary Association and the Public Sphere in the Early Republic," in *Launching the "Extended Republic*," ed. Hoffman and Albert, 273–377. Revere was appointed to a committee to "obtain a Union among Masons, respecting the choice of a Grand Master" on March 2, 1787; appointed to another committee to confer with the officers of St. John's Grand Lodge on the subject of "a Compleat Masonic Union" on December 5, 1791; and appointed one of seven electors to choose a Grand Master of the new Grand Lodge on March 5, 1792. On Revere's committee appointments, establishment of new Grand Lodge, and election as Grand Master see *Grand Lodge Proceedings, 1733–92*, 340, 380–81; *Grand Lodge Proceedings, 1792–1815* (Cambridge, Mass., 1905), 10–14, 61. Revere's speech at the laying of the cornerstone of the State House may be found in *Grand Lodge Proceedings, 1792–1815*, 74–76; Goss, *Life of Colonel Revere*, 2.483–84. On his term as Grand Master see Steblecki, *Paul Revere and Freemasonry*, chap. 9; Steblecki, "Fraternity, Philanthropy, and Revolution," 132–34.

45. On Revere's concerns over subordination of the lodges and the virtue of candidates and his final speech as Grand Master on December 11, 1797, see Steblecki, *Paul Revere and Freemasonry*, 53–59. Bentley discussed various Masonic disputes and alluded to disharmony within the lodges on March 5 and 20, 1793, and November 14, 1795, in *Diary of William Bentley*, 2.6–8, 11–12, 166.

46. John Brooke argues that by 1798 Republicans had infiltrated Freemasonry and could thus claim "the ceremonial center of the Moderate Enlightenment." Morse's attack against the Illuminati was then "a calculated attack upon the institutional base of the political opposition." On the Bavarian Illuminati controversy and its political background see Brooke, "Ancient Lodges and Self-Created Societies," 322–54 (quoted material on 326, 353); Banner, *To the Hartford Convention*, 155–56; Bentley's diary entries for August 14, 21, September 8, December 8, 1798, February 4, August 10, September 3, 1799, *Diary of William Bentley*, 2.278, 281–82, 291, 296, 315–16. On the Masonic procession in honor of Washington see *Diary of William Bentley*, 2.329–30; Brooke, "Ancient Lodges and Self-Created Societies," 355–56.

47. Revere to Otis, March 11, 1800, roll 1, Revere Papers; Revere to Otis, January 17, 1801, Letterbook, 1783–1800 (also contains letters from 1801), vol. 53, roll 14, Revere Papers. See also Revere to Navy Secretary Benjamin Stoddard, February 26, 1800, on plans to build a copper mill, Letterbook, 1783–1800, vol. 53, roll 14, Revere Papers.

11. "In My Last State, How Blest Am I, to Find Content and Plenty By"

1. Belknap originally told Revere that his letter would only be deposited in the Historical Society's library, but after reading it, he decided to publish the letter in the society's *Collections*. Revere's letter to Belknap, dated January 1, 1798, by Belknap, appeared in *MHS Collections*, 1st ser., 5 (1798): 106–12. The second version of the letter, with the complete

text, appeared in *MHS Proceedings* 16 (November 1878): 371–76. For a facsimile reproduction of Revere's letter to Jeremy Belknap and analysis by Edmund Morgan see *Three Accounts*. On Belknap's solicitation of Revere as acknowledgment that Revere's recollections were as significant as those of the Adamses or Hancock see Louis Leonard Tucker, *Clio's Consort: Jeremy Belknap and the Founding of the Massachusetts Historical Society* (Boston, 1990), 106.

2. Based on Governor Increase Sumner's recommendation in his speech on June 7, 1798, the Massachusetts General Court voted to cede the fortifications at Castle Island, once commanded by Paul Revere, to the United States government on June 25, 1797; Petition of Massachusetts General Court to President John Adams, June 7, 1798, in Adams Papers, reel 389, MHS. On the cession of Castle Island see *Massachusetts Mercury*, June 18, 1798; *Acts and Resolves of Massachusetts, 1798–1799* (Boston, 1897), 16; Triber, "Massachusetts and the Federal Garrison at Fort Independence," 46–55. The Massachusetts Grand Lodge's letter to President Adams, June 11, 1798, is in *Grand Lodge Proceedings, 1792–1815*, 130. See also Miller, *The Federalist Era*, 205–17.

3. On the increase in Revere's foundry business see Ernay, "The Revere Furnace," 35–40. Edgard Moreno cites the enormous capital investment required for a copper mill and the potential profitability. On the development of the American copper industry and an analysis of Revere's copper mill see Moreno, "Patriotism and Profit: The Copper Mills at Canton," in *Paul Revere—Artisan, Businessman, and Patriot*, 95–115 (especially 99–101).

4. There is some discrepancy over when Revere bought the Canton property. Moreno says that Revere bought the land in January 1800. Forbes cites a letter of late December 1800 in which Revere contracted for materials to build the mill, writing: "I have engaged to build me a Mill for Rolling Copper into sheets which for me is a great undertaking, and will require every farthing which I can rake or scrape." A lawsuit that Revere filed against Jonathan Leonard over water rights on his property in 1804 states that Leonard conveyed the land to Revere on January 23, 1801. Goss says that Revere bought the property on March 14, 1801. It seems unlikely that Revere would have purchased the property before January 1801, when he had successfully produced sheet copper, although he expressed his interest in erecting a copper mill in letters to government officials in early 1800. See Moreno, "Patriotism and Profit," 100–103; Forbes, *Paul Revere*, 407–10; Ephraim Williams, Esq., *Reports of Cases Argued and Determined in the Supreme Judicial Court of the State of Massachusetts from September 1804 to June 1805* (Northampton, Mass., 1805), 1.91–94; Goss, *Life of Colonel Revere*, 2.56; Revere to Benjamin Stoddard, February 26, 1800, on desire for government assistance to erect copper mill; Revere to Eben Lee, January 13, 1801; Revere to Stoddard, January 17, 1801, mentioning visit to Philadelphia the previous May and naval agent Stephen Higginson's promise of government assistance for the mill; all in Letterbook, 1783–1800 (also contains letters from 1801), vol. 53, roll 14, Revere Family Papers, MHS. See also Harrison Gray Otis to Revere, December 31, 1800 (Otis apologized for not having time to examine Revere's copper spikes and bolts but offered his services to "an ingenious and industrious fellow citizen and artisan"); Joshua Humphreys to Revere, February 26, 1801 ("happy to find you have succeeded in Smithing the Copper"), roll 1, Revere Papers.

5. On the Saint-Memin portrait see Revere to Edward Edwards of Philadelphia, Janu-

ary 20, 1800 (telling Edwards he paid "Mr. Memin" five dollars for the frame and glass for his portrait), and August 25, 1800 (asking Edwards to "call on the Frenchman, about my picture, he promised it in two or three months I paid him for the frame"), Letterbook, 1783–1800, vol. 53, roll 14, Revere Papers. The Copley and Saint-Memin portraits of Revere, with explanatory text, may be compared in Fairbanks et al., *Paul Revere's Boston,* 18–19, 196. The Reveres apparently rented out their North Square home much of the time after the Revolution while they lived in rented houses. Receipts for rent on North Square house from George DeFrance on May 27, 1780, and Joseph Dunkerly ("Dunkerley"), July 19, October 19, 1784, and January 19, 1785, in Waste Book and Memoranda, vols. 1 and 2, roll 5, Revere Papers; Revere's assessment in the United States Direct Tax of 1798, including his house and foundry on Lynn Street, valued at $750, in *Boston Town Records,* 22.4, 201; description of Charter Street house in Forbes, *Paul Revere,* 400–401. The value of Revere's property on Clark's Court put him on a par with his artisan cousins Samuel and Thomas Hichborn. In contrast, cousin Benjamin Hichborn, an attorney, was the owner and occupier of a brick dwelling measuring 2,404 square feet on Marlboro Street, situated on 5,612 square feet of land with thirty windows, valued at $7,500. See United States Direct Tax of 1798 in *Boston Town Records,* 22.217, 218, 336. For furnishings in Revere's Charter Street home see the inventory of his estate, Suffolk Probate Court Record Books, case no. 25527, vol. 116, p. 315, microfilm reel 49, Judicial Archives, Massachusetts Archives.

6. Miller, *The Federalist Era,* 228–77; Warren, *Jacobin and Junto,* 153; Stephen G. Kurtz, *The Presidency of John Adams: The Collapse of Federalism, 1795–1800* (Philadelphia, 1957), 374–408.

7. On Ames's disapproval of the Federalists and joy at the prospect of Jefferson's administration see Warren, *Jacobin and Junto,* 97–126, 146–59 (quoted material on 158).

8. Fisher Ames to Theodore Dwight, April 16, 1802, quoted in Warren, *Jacobin and Junto,* 160. On Federalist fears of anarchy and disorder under Jeffersonian democracy see Kerber, *Federalists in Dissent,* chap. 6 ("Images of the Social Order").

9. Revere's difficulty in obtaining the government loan was complicated by Jefferson's difficulty in finding a secretary of the navy. See Revere to Benjamin Stoddard, April 3, 1801; Revere to Levi Lincoln, April 21, 1801; Revere to Samuel Smith, April 21 and May 11, 1801; Revere to Robert Smith, May 24, 1802; all in Letterbook, 1801–6, vol. 53, roll 14, Revere Papers. Benjamin Stoddard to Revere, March 10, 1801, roll 1, Revere Papers; naval agent at Boston to Revere, June 7, 1802, confirming that Revere's copper to the amount of $10,000 advanced by the government will be accepted, and Revere's agreement with the Navy Department, June 29, 1801, roll 2, Revere Papers. See also Moreno, "Patriotism and Profit," 102. On Jefferson's difficulty in finding a navy secretary see Leonard D. White, *The Jeffersonians: A Study in Administrative History, 1801–1829* (New York, 1956), 270–71.

10. Joseph Warren Revere was seventeen years younger than Paul Revere Jr., but he had the close personal and business relationship with his father that Paul Jr. might have expected as the firstborn son. Paul Revere Jr. also did not have his younger brother's economic success. In 1783 and 1784 Paul Revere Sr. paid for his oldest son's rent and wood, and on September 11, 1811, Paul Jr.'s tax bill in the amount of $5.10 was added to his father's bill. See Revere's receipts for payment of Paul Jr.'s rent and wood in Waste Book and Memoranda, vol. 2, roll 5, and Receipt Book, Boston, 1780–1805, vol. 41, roll 12, Revere

Papers; tax bill in roll 2, Revere Papers. For biographical details on Paul Revere Jr. see Nielsen, "The Revere Family," 304–5; U.S. Direct Tax of 1798, *Boston Town Records*, 22.176; "Parker Index," 266; Federhen, "From Artisan to Entrepreneur," 69, 86–87; Forbes, *Paul Revere*, 168–69, 225, 272, 310, 357–58, 382, 385.

11. Joshua Revere's obituary in the *Columbian Centinel*, August 15, 1801, stated that he was "connected in business" with his father. See also Nielsen, "The Revere Family," 301.

12. In 1811 Revere turned over his business to Joseph Warren Revere, who presided over the business until his death in 1868. Joseph Warren and Joshua Revere were both "made" Masons in Massachusetts Lodge on February 10, 1800. On March 1, 1800, Joseph Warren Revere joined St. John's Lodge. He served in the Massachusetts Legislature in 1816, 1817, 1819, and 1840, where he was a member of committees on the establishment of Maine as a separate state, the incorporation of manufacturing firms, and the improvement of state prisons. As a member of the Boston Board of Aldermen in 1833, he served on a committee on prison expansion and improvement. Joseph Warren Revere married Mary Robbins on April 16, 1821, and family letters describe their fashionable life in genteel society. See articles of agreement between Paul Revere and Joseph Warren Revere, June 7, 1804 (for partnership to last for three years), and June 7, 1807 (renewing partnership until March 10, 1810); indenture dissolving partnership, March 1, 1811; all in roll 2, Revere Papers. Revere's will, November 15, 1816 ("And as I have at great pains and Expense with the assistance of my said Son Joseph Warren brought the Copper business to the state in which it now is," Revere offered his son the chance to buy the mill), Suffolk Probate Court Record Books, case no. 25527, vol. 116, p. 246, microfilm reel 49, Judicial Archives, Massachusetts Archives, and roll 3, Revere Papers. On Joseph Warren Revere's trip to England and the Continent to study copper works, 1804–5, see Revere's letter of introduction for his son, October 20, 1804, roll 2, Revere Papers; Paul Revere to Joseph Warren Revere in Gothenburg, Sweden, November 4, 1804 (regarding copper prices, Revere wrote: "As you will be nearer the spot than I shall, you can best tell wether the price will answer"), Letterbook, 1801–6, vol. 53, roll 14, Revere Papers. See also R. H. Williamson, "Paul Revere and the First United States Mint," *The Numismatist* 63 (December 1950): 792; Forbes, *Paul Revere*, 411; "Parker Index," 266–67 (on Masonic history); Nielsen, "The Revere Family," 309–10; Grundy and Triber, "Paul Revere's Children." On Mary Robbins Revere's kinship with Thomas Hutchinson see "Memoir of Governor Hutchinson," *New England Historical and Genealogical Register* 1 (October 1847): 300–302.

13. In addition to his Edinburgh thesis on mental illness, John Revere's other published works include "Account of the Yellow Fever in Baltimore in 1819, with Remarks on Treatment and Origin (1820)," "Case of Sudden Death in the Ninth Month of Pregnancy (1820)," "On Dyspepsia (1820)," "An Inquiry into the Origins and Effects of Sulphurous Fumigation in the Cure of Rheumatism, Gout, Diseases of the Skin, Palsy, etc. (1822)," and several lectures on the theory and practice of medicine and the state of medical education in the United States as compared with Europe. His published works are listed in the *National Union Catalog*. John Revere's bill for the Independent School in Lexington, May 7, 1801, is in roll 1, Revere Papers. On John Revere's career see sources cited above in chapter 1, n. 26.

14. Revere to Thomas Ramsden, August 4, 1804, roll 2, Revere Papers. *Boston Directories* in 1806–7 list the bell foundry on 13 Lynn Street; the *Directory* in 1809 lists the foundry on Charter Street, and by 1813 Revere and Son is listed on 10 Kilby Street. See *Boston Directories*, 1789–1821, Boston Public Library, microfilm roll 1. See also Forbes, *Paul Revere*, 411–12.

15. The agents for building the State House paid Revere and Son a total of $4,232, beginning with the first payment of $2,000 on October 14, 1802, in Waste Book and Memoranda, vol. 3 (1799–1804), roll 5, and Boston Ledger, 1799–1804, vol. 14, roll 7, Revere Papers. Several orders for the *Constitution* may be found in Waste Book and Memoranda, vol. 3, roll 5, and Boston Ledger, vol. 14, roll 7. During this period, Revere and Son also produced copper spikes and bolts for the United States Navy's gunboats on April 8, 1805, sheet copper for the North Church on September 19, 1806, and a variety of ship fittings for James and Thomas Handasyd Perkins between 1804 and 1811, in Boston Waste Book, 1804–11, vol. 4, roll 5; six brass cannon for Amasa Davis, quartermaster general for Massachusetts, December 13, 1806, Boston Ledger, 1804–11, vol. 15, roll 7; a bell for the town of Barnstable, October 9, 1806, Boston Journal, 1804–11, vol. 11, roll 6; various copper spikes, bolts, and sheet copper to customers in New York, Baltimore, and Philadelphia, in Boston Waste Book, 1804–11, vol. 4, roll 5, and correspondence in Letterbooks, roll 14. Records for the Canton copper mill are scattered among various waste books, ledgers, and journals in the Revere Papers. See Boston Waste Book, 1804–11, vol. 4, roll 5; Boston Journal, 1804–11, vol. 11, roll 6; Boston Ledger, 1804–11, vol. 15, roll 7; Canton Ledger, 1802–6, vol. 29, roll 10; Canton Ledger, 1805–14, vol. 30, roll 10. On sales of sheet copper and profitability of the Canton mill see Moreno, "Patriotism and Profit," 108–12 (including table 2, "Sales of Sheet Copper"); Forbes, *Paul Revere*, 409–10.

16. Revere to Navy Secretary Smith, June 10 and July 1, 1803; Revere to Francis Coffin, August 15, 1803, shipping a cargo of "Yellow bales Nankins," the proceeds to buy copper in Leghorn; Revere to Beck and Harvey of Philadelphia, August 25, 1803; Revere to John Amory, August 29, 1803, re buying copper in Leghorn; Revere to Brown and Ives, Providence, September 12, 1803, re supplying copper; Revere to Harmon Hendricks of New York, September 15, 1803: "We will take all the 24 and 25 oz. Copper you have"; all in Letterbook, 1801–6, vol. 53, roll 14, Revere Papers. On Revere and Son's relationship with Harmon Hendricks see Mark Bortman, "Paul Revere and Son and Their Jewish Correspondents," *Publication of the American Jewish Historical Society* 43 (1953–54): 199–229; Maxwell Whiteman, *Copper for America: The Hendricks Family and a National Industry, 1755–1939* (New Brunswick, N.J., 1971), 55–56, 62–65, 100. Payment in old copper is noted in Revere's journals and ledgers.

17. In a draft petition to Congress in 1807, Revere denied seeking monopolistic privileges, claiming he sought only "a reasonable protecting duty" and protection from competition "with the long established and wealthy manufacturing establishments of England." If Revere and Son's petition was granted, it would encourage other copper manufacturers "under the confident expectation that the protection of government will be extended to them as well as to other manufacturers"; roll 2, Revere Papers. See also Revere to Albert Gallatin, April 3, 1806, roll 2, Revere Papers; and Revere and Son to Committee on

Commerce and Manufacturing, February 10, 1808, Letterbook, 1805–10, vol. 53, roll 14, Revere Papers. There are also several other letters and petitions from Revere and Son requesting tariff legislation in roll 2. On Report of the Committee of Commerce and Manufacturing, January 21, 1808, considering the petitions of Revere and Son and the coppersmiths and braziers of Philadelphia and New York, see Bortman, "Paul Revere and Son and Their Jewish Correspondents," 223–28. See also Whiteman, *Copper for America*, 75–79, on role of Harmon Hendricks in preventing Revere's petition for tariff relief from being granted by expressing doubt about Revere and Son's ability to supply the domestic market for copper.

18. Leonard and Kinsley successfully sued Revere for raising his dam, and Revere countersued but lost his case. Depositions of Revere and Abner Crane, who surveyed the land sold by Leonard and Kinsley, and receipt from Silas Kinsley, January 1, 1805, for payment from Revere "to satisfy two executions in favour of Jonathan Leonard and Adam Kinsley," roll 2, Revere Papers; "Cash paid on account of our Law Suit with L and K ($59.25)," October 4, 1806, Boston Journal, 1804–11, vol. 11, roll 6, Revere Papers; "Paid Execution Leonard and Kinsley ($81.25)," February 4, 1807, Canton Waste Book, 1805–12, vol. 20, roll 8, Revere Papers; Williams, *Reports of Cases Argued and Determined in the Supreme Judicial Court of the State of Massachusetts*, 1.94–95 (Norfolk County, Dedham, October term 1804, *Paul Revere vs. Jonathan Leonard and another*).

19. Petition from Revere and Son to Canton selectmen, February 20, 1808 (addressed from Boston), roll 2, Revere Papers. The dispute between Revere and Leonard and Kinsley took a new direction on April 20, 1808, when Leonard and Kinsley threatened to bring a lawsuit against Revere because he was "keeping your triphammer dam considerable higher," which "does us much damage by causing the back water to flow against our forge, grindstone and gristmill wheels"; roll 2, Revere Papers.

20. Paul Revere to Thomas Ramsden, August 4, 1804, roll 2, Revere Papers. On Federalist condemnation of the French Revolution and criticism of Republican naïveté see Kerber, *Federalists in Dissent*, 115–26 (including quotes from John Adams and Fisher Ames), 192–93, 199–212. In a Fourth of July speech in 1800 Benjamin Lincoln struck at what he considered the Republicans' misguided attempt to link the American and French Revolution. From "a residence amongst us," the French had gained only a superficial understanding of "the principles and effects of a free constitution." What they overlooked, in Lincoln's assessment, was "the very sinews of the system—*the diffusion of knowledge and the morals of the people. . . . Vanity* and *Ambition* led them astray"; in Lincoln Papers, MHS.

21. Thomas Ramsden to Paul Revere, May 30, 1804, and Revere to Ramsden, August 4, 1804, roll 2, Revere Papers. On terminology, the Federalist Paul Revere used the pejorative term "Democrats" instead of "Republicans," thereby blaming the Republicans for the introduction of partisanship and social anarchy in American society and depriving them of their contention that they were the true heirs of the republican revolution. For a broader discussion of the use of political terminology in this period see Kerber, *Federalists in Dissent*, 194–99. Revere's implicit criticism that the Democrats were appointing incompetent men to office was more explicitly stated by the southern Federalist John Rutledge Jr., who wrote to Harrison Gray Otis, "I feel for the honor of my country. The unjust displacement of able virtuous men, many of them eminent in the revolution, is a scandalous abuse

of power. . . . The appointment of unfit characters in other cases is degrading." See Rutledge to Otis, September 15, 1801, Otis Papers, MHS.

22. Details of Jefferson's first administration may be found in Marshall Smelser, *The Democratic Republic, 1801–1815* (New York, 1968), 53–57, 83–103 (on the Louisiana Purchase). Drew McCoy, in *The Elusive Republic*, discusses the Republican Party's rhetoric and actions to ensure "a truly republican political economy." See especially 121–32, 152–61, 185–208. Elkins and McKitrick, in *The Age of Federalism*, describe Hamilton's policies as "the political economy of Anglophilia" on p. 123. The phrase "a wise and frugal government" is from Jefferson's First Inaugural Address. Jefferson's description of "cultivators of the earth" as "the most valuable citizens" is from a letter to John Jay, August 23, 1785. In his "Notes on the State of Virginia," Jefferson also said: "Those who labour in the earth are the chosen people of God . . . whose breasts he had made his peculiar deposit for substantial and genuine virtue." Jefferson quotations are in Merrill D. Peterson, ed., *The Portable Thomas Jefferson* (1975; reprint, New York, 1977), 293, 384, 217.

23. On Republican electoral victories see Smelser, *The Democratic Republic*, 51, 81; Paul Goodman, *The Democratic-Republicans of Massachusetts: Politics in a Young Republic* (Cambridge, Mass., 1964), 128–53; Banner, *To the Hartford Convention*, 362 (appendix 2, table 5, "Representation in the Massachusetts House, 1800–1815"). On Federalist reaction to the Jeffersonian era see Kerber, *Federalists in Dissent;* Fischer, *The Revolution of American Conservatism;* Banner, *To the Hartford Convention*, 72–83 and chap. 6 ("The Genesis of Party Organization"). On the need for Federalists to respond through their party and the press see John Rutledge Jr. to Harrison Gray Otis, September 15, 1801; Theodore Sedgwick to Otis, May 14, 1802; Rutledge to Otis, April 3, 1803; all in Harrison Gray Otis Papers, MHS. Christopher Gore to Rufus King, December 28, 1807, quoted in Pinkney, *Christopher Gore*, 99.

24. On August 23, 1785, Jefferson, in a letter to John Jay, had called artificers "the panders of vice and the instruments by which the liberties of a country are generally overturned"; in Peterson, *The Portable Thomas Jefferson*, 384. The description of mechanics and other productive classes ("farmers, merchants . . . and common laboring men") as having a "common interest" against "the great landholders and monied men" is from "Scrutator," *New York Journal*, April 19, 1797, quoted in Alfred Young, "The Mechanics and the Jeffersonians: New York, 1789–1801," *Labor History* 5 (Fall 1964): 271. On Republican criticism of Federalist political economy and their creation of a republican political economy see McCoy, *The Elusive Republic*, especially 14–47, 157–78, 236–48; Banning, *The Jeffersonian Persuasion*, 127–60, 220–30. For arguments that the Republicans created an economy of "liberal capitalism" beginning in the 1790s see Appleby, *Capitalism and the New Social Order;* Steven Watts, *The Republic Reborn: War and the Making of Liberal America, 1790–1820* (Baltimore, 1987), especially 6–16, 65–70, 224–39.

25. On New York Republican mechanics see Young, "The Mechanics and the Jeffersonians," 247–76; Young, *The Democrat-Republicans of New York: The Origins, 1763–1797* (Chapel Hill, N.C., 1967), 398–412, 405–7, 566–82.

26. Biographical information on Dearborn in *DAB*, 3.174–76. The hostile relationship between Dearborn and Massachusetts Federalists, who dubbed Dearborn the "God of War," is discussed in Triber, "Massachusetts and the Federal Garrison at Fort Indepen-

dence," 63–67, 70–78, 90–111. On the contrast between Federalist and Republican regions and on Maine as a Republican stronghold see Banner, *To the Hartford Convention*, 168–215; Goodman, *Democratic-Republicans of Massachusetts*, 97–127.

27. Both Paul and Joseph Warren Revere had to deal with employees who came late and left early, were frequently absent from work, were tardy in arriving and returning from transporting goods to and from Boston, quit after short periods, or were discharged for drunkenness or "making disturbance." Records of employee salaries and work habits are in Canton Waste Book, 1805–12, vol. 20, and Canton Waste Book, 1812–14, vol. 21, roll 8, Revere Papers; Canton Waste Book, 1814–18, vol. 22, roll 9, Revere Papers; Canton Ledger, 1805–14, vol. 30, roll 10, Revere Papers. See also Revere to Joshua Humphreys, December 19, 1803, in Letterbook, 1801–6, vol. 53, roll 14, Revere Papers. On the operation of the Canton mill, including analysis of Revere's labor force, see Moreno, "Patriotism and Profit," 105–8 (including table 1, "Employment Records, 1802–1810").

28. For more on the Federalist condemnation of Republicans for corrupting American society see Kerber, *Federalists in Dissent*, chap. 6 ("Images of the Social Order"). Republicans, too, feared that their approval of equality and individual ambition could lead to self-interest and a love of luxury that would destroy American society. Republican solutions included Benjamin Rush's educational ideas to instill self-control in republican citizens (*Thoughts on Education*, 1786), an emphasis on the practice of benevolence through associations, and, on an individual basis, the spread of evangelical Christianity (perhaps an unintended solution for Jefferson and other Republican Deists), and even what Steven Watts has termed the "social regeneration" of the War of 1812. See Watts, *The Republic Reborn*, especially 93–100, 110–60, 218–24, 275–321.

29. On the importance of benevolence in Freemasonry see Bullock, "The Ancient and Honorable Society," especially Masonic addresses on 50–51; Bullock, "A Pure and Sublime System," 359–73; Bullock, "The Revolutionary Transformation of American Freemasonry, 1752–1792," *William and Mary Quarterly*, 3d ser., 47 (July 1990): 347–69; Bullock, *Revolutionary Brotherhood*, 3–5, 57–58. On the importance of benevolence as a republican ideal see Wood, *Radicalism of the American Revolution*, 213–25.

30. Forbes writes that Eayres's mental condition exhibited itself in a mania for flute playing and a phobia toward dirt. Eayres's father, Joseph Eayres, was a Son of Liberty, Tea Party participant, and member of the Massachusetts Artillery Train with Revere. On Eayres see Forbes, *Paul Revere*, 121, 190, 385–87; Nielsen, "The Revere Family," 299. See Revere to Eayres's family (addressed to "My friends"), June 9, 1799, informing them of his daughter's death and of their duty to take care of Eayres, in Letterbook, 1783–1800, vol. 53, roll 14; Revere to Dr. Willard, June 6, 1801, on complaints about expense of Eayres's medical care; Revere to Willard, November 16, 1801, approving of his medical treatment; Revere to Willard, April 4, 1802, instructing Willard to put Eayres on the stage to New York ("when he gits with his Brothers and Sisters they must take care of him"); another letter to the Eayres family on caring for their relative, September 26, 1802; all in Letterbook, 1801–6, vol. 53, roll 14, Revere Papers. See also Dr. Willard to Revere, June 2 and 15, 1801, roll 1, Revere Papers.

31. The court declared Eayres *non compos mentis* on October 25, 1802, and appointed Jedediah Lincoln guardian on November 8, 1802, with Paul Revere and Paul Revere Jr.

bound for "the faithful performance of his trust." In his letter to Davis on April 5, 1803, Revere referred to Davis's refusal to answer his letters of January 24 and March 8 because they were "too severe." When Aaron Burr became Jefferson's vice president, he strenuously campaigned for a political appointment for Davis, but knowledge of Burr's political machinations during the Republican electoral victories in New York in 1800 made Jefferson reluctant to grant Burr's request. The issue of the Davis appointment created one of the Jefferson administration's most distasteful patronage episodes and contributed to the rupture between Jefferson and Burr. On Revere's care of Eayres see Matthew Davis to Revere, June 28, 1799, roll 4, Revere Papers; Revere to Mrs. Nancy Collings (Eayres's sister), January 2, 1802, and Revere to Matthew Davis, April 5, 1803, Letterbook, 1801–6, vol. 53, roll 14, Revere Papers; Nielsen, "The Revere Family," 299. On Matthew Livingston Davis see *DAB*, 3.138–39; Young, "The Mechanics and the Jeffersonians," 270; notice of his marriage in Boston to Sarah Eayres of Boston, *The Weekly Museum* (New York), April 23, 1796, and William Kelby (1841–98), "Notes on Trinity Church Yard Families," genealogical information on Matthew Davis, New York Historical Society; Noble E. Cunningham Jr., *The Jeffersonian Republicans in Power: Party Operations, 1801–1809* (Chapel Hill, N.C., 1963), 38–43 (on patronage dispute involving Davis, Burr, and Jefferson).

32. Revere to Secretary of War Eustis, February 20, 1804, *Miscellaneous Bound Manuscripts*, MHS; Deborah (Sampson) Gannett to Paul Revere, February 22, 1806, roll 2, Revere Papers. See also Forbes, *Paul Revere*, 415–17.

33. I am hesitant to push the political overtones of Revere's letter too far, because his language is familiar in Masonic discourse, as can be seen by perusing the *Grand Lodge Proceedings*, but it takes on added significance in this time period. In his letter of praise to Reverend George Richards, Revere added in parentheses that he had made a bell for the Universal Church in Portsmouth for which he had not yet been paid. He asked Richards, "Will you not enquire into the matter and write us." See Revere to Richards, May 20, 1806, Letterbook, 1805–10, vol. 53, roll 14, Revere Papers.

34. Details of the case appear in *Trail of Thomas O. Selfridge ... For Killing Charles Austin* (shorthand report of the trail, 1807), Evans, *Early American Imprints*, no. 13740; Thomas O. Selfridge, *A Correct Statement of the Whole Preliminary Controversy Between Thomas O. Selfridge and Benjamin Austin, also a Brief Account of the Catastrophe in State Street . . .* (January 7, 1807), Evans, *Early American Imprints*, no. 13566. The best account of the political background and aftermath of the Selfridge case is in Warren, *Jacobin and Junto*, chap. 7 ("A Political Murder"). See also Samuel Eliot Morison, *Harrison Gray Otis, 1765–1848: The Urbane Federalist* (Boston, 1969), 277–79; Carl Seaburg and Stanley Paterson, *Merchant Prince of Boston: Colonel T. H. Perkins, 1764–1854* (Cambridge, Mass., 1971), 172–76; Pinkney, *Christopher Gore*, 96–98; entry on Benjamin Austin Jr., in *DAB*, 1.431–32.

35. *Trial of Thomas O. Selfridge*, especially 14, 28–37, 54; Selfridge, *Correct Statement*, especially 13–26, 39; Warren, *Jacobin and Junto*, 183–90; Morison, *Harrison Gray Otis*, 277–78; Seaburg, *Merchant Prince of Boston*, 172–73; Pinkney, *Christopher Gore*, 96–97.

36. *Trial of Thomas O. Selfridge*, especially Gore's defense and Dexter's stunning closing argument; Selfridge, *Correct Statement*, especially his arguments on the absolute necessity of defending his honor and the honor of the court and jurors, 33, 42 to the end. On the trial and the political aftermath see Warren, *Jacobin and Junto*, 196–214; Morison. *Harrison*

Gray Otis, 278–79; Seaburg and Paterson, *Merchant Prince of Boston*, 173–76; Pinkney, *Christopher Gore*, 97–98. Additional information on Theophilus Parsons, Samuel Dexter, and Thomas Handasyd Perkins in Fischer, *The Revolution of American Conservatism*, 254, 259, 271. On Dexter's wavering political views and dramatic summation in the Selfridge case see William T. Davis, "History of the Bench and Bar," in *Professional and Industrial History of Suffolk County Massachusetts*, 1.591–93.

37. *Independent Chronicle*, March 16, 26, 1807; *Columbian Centinel*, March 28, 1807. Revere's payment for "outstanding Debts Collected by our attorney Thomas Selfridge," February 26, 1806, is in Boston Waste Book, 1804–11, vol. 5, roll 5, Revere Papers. Revere and Son also paid Selfridge on October 7, 1814, in Cash Book, 1811–18, vol. 33, roll 11, Revere Papers.

38. In the *Independent Chronicle* of March 30, 1807 ("Truth vs. The Centinel"), Dow challenged Revere to deny his assertions "with his signature" and promised to give an affidavit in the presence of Revere or "any person he may authorize to act for him." See also *Independent Chronicle*, April 2, 1807.

39. *Independent Chronicle*, May 18, 1807; Thomas O. Selfridge to Paul Revere, May 12, 1807, roll 2, Revere Papers. See also "Extract of a letter from the country, to a friend in Boston" and "Extract of a Letter from a Gentleman in the Country to his Friend in Boston," repeating Dow's allegations and pressing Revere for a further explanation of his conduct in the Selfridge case, in the *Independent Chronicle*, April 23, June 23, 1807. Coverage of the Burr conspiracy and *Chesapeake-Leopard* incident superseded reaction to the Selfridge case in both the *Independent Chronicle* and *Columbian Centinel* beginning in May 1807. On the Burr conspiracy see Smelser, *The Democratic Republic*, 111–23. On the *Chesapeake-Leopard* incident and Federalist reaction see Smelser, *The Democratic Republic*, 157–59; Pinkney, *Christopher Gore*, 103–4; Seaburg and Paterson, *Merchant Prince of Boston*, 184–86.

40. The *Independent Chronicle* of July 2, 1807, referred to the "British Barbarity" and "British Outrage" in the *Chesapeake* affair. The other "Vice-Presidents" at the Federalist Fourth of July dinner were Josiah Quincy, "Hon. Messrs. Mason and Otis," Colonel Welles, Colonel Bradford, S[tephen] Codman, Esq., and Major Russell. At the July 10 meeting of Republicans and moderate Federalists, the Republican Elbridge Gerry was chosen moderator and the Republican Perez Morton, secretary. In contrast, at the July 16 town meeting, John Coffin Jones, a Federalist merchant, was chosen moderator, and Federalists Christopher Gore, Harrison Gray Otis, and Thomas Handasyd Perkins were appointed to the resolutions committee. See *Columbian Centinel*, July 8, 11, 18, 1807; *Independent Chronicle*, July 13, 20, 1807; Pinkney, *Christopher Gore*, 103–5; Seaburg and Paterson, *Merchant Prince of Boston*, 184–87.

41. Revere to Carson, July 20, 1807, March 1808, March 6, 1809, Letterbook, 1805–10, vol. 53, roll 14, Revere Papers. Revere was paid $1,361.55 for four brass cannon for a United States revenue cutter on November 18, 1808, in Boston Journal, 1804–11, vol. 11, roll 6, Revere Papers. On the embargo and Federalist reaction see Smelser, *The Democratic Republic*, 151–99; McCoy, *The Elusive Republic*, 209–33; Banner, *To the Hartford Convention*, 294–306; Pinkney, *Christopher Gore*, 104–20.

42. John R. Livingston sent Revere an order for copper to be forwarded to Fulton and

Robert R. Livingston on November 25, 1808, in roll 2, Revere Papers. Fulton and Livingston's order of March 31, 1809, and other orders are in Boston Waste Book, 1804–11, vol. 5, and Boston Waste Book, 1811–18, vol. 6, roll 5, Revere Papers. Revere and Son's relationship with Robert Fulton lasted until 1814, despite Fulton's complaints about the quality of the copper. The correspondence is in roll 2 (loose mss. 1802–13); roll 3 (1814–1964); Letterbook, 1805–10, Letterbook, 1809–10, Letterbook, 1810–11, Letterbook, December 1810–January 1812, Letterbook, 1811–14, all in vol. 53, roll 14; Letterbook and Journal, 1811–14, vol. 54, roll 15. Revere's correspondence with Joseph Carson reveals that the loss of English copper created a new market for Revere's copper among coppersmiths and braziers in Boston and Philadelphia. See Revere to Carson, March 6, 1809, Letterbook, 1805–10, vol. 53, roll 14; Carson to Revere, June 6, 1809, roll 2. Revere's assets on March 1, 1811, when he dissolved his partnership with his son, are in roll 2, Revere Papers. On sales revenue, profitability, and work force of Revere and Son see Moreno, "Patriotism and Profits," 105–12 (especially tables 1 and 2).

43. Minutes of meetings on April 18, 1808 (regulations on conveyance of wastewater), July 18 and 25 ("Committee on Colonel Revere's premises requests more time"), 1808, August 1, 1808; all in *Boston Board of Health Records*, 2 (1806–10), Boston Public Library, Rare Books, by courtesy of the Trustees of the Boston Public Library. Undated letter from Paul Revere and Son to president and members of the Board of Health, found after letter dated June 2, 1809, Letterbook, 1805–10, vol. 53, roll 14, Revere Papers. Binney owned eighty-two shares in the State National Bank, chartered by the Massachusetts General Court on June 27, 1811, in *Professional and Industrial History of Suffolk County*, 2.236–37.

44. Paul Revere to Joseph Warren Revere, July 20, 1810, roll 4, Revere Family Papers II, 1775–1964.

45. Revere's poem, 1811, is in roll 2, Revere Papers. Compare it with John Rutledge's letter to Harrison Gray Otis on October 22, 1811: ". . . at the Palace repeatedly, but . . . did not talk politics with the King [Madison]. He and Mr. Monroe had lately been at Monticello to take counsel of Mr. Jefferson who unfortunately still directs the affairs of the nation"; in Harrison Gray Otis Papers, MHS.

46. Revere's attendance at the Grand Lodge declined dramatically after 1800. He attended meetings or the installation of officers on December 8, 1800, December 27, 1802, June 11 and September 10, 1804, and December 27, 1808, his last appearance until he appeared before the Grand Lodge committee investigating Rising States Lodge on June 8, 1812. Possibly his absence was because of increasing business demands in Boston and Canton, but it may also have been related to personal and/or political disputes within Masonic circles. Revere disappeared from the *Grand Lodge Proceedings* after June 8, 1812, and he apparently did not have a Masonic funeral. See *Grand Lodge Proceedings, 1792–1815*, 174, 207, 239, 243, 397 (Revere's attendance at Grand Lodge, 1800–1808), 414–15, 417 (on admission of St. Andrew's Lodge to the Massachusetts Grand Lodge), 450–51, 492–99, 533–35, 541–42, 552–55 (dissolution of Rising States Lodge); *Grand Lodge Proceedings, 1815–25* (Boston, 1928), where Revere is not even listed in the index. See also Steblecki, *Paul Revere and Freemasonry*, 66–69; Steblecki, "Fraternity, Philanthropy, and Revolution," 137–38; Thomas Sherrard Roy, *Stalwart Builders: A History of the Grand Lodge of Masons in Massachusetts, 1733–1971* (Boston, 1971), 95–97.

47. "Cantondale," undated [c. 1810?], roll 2, Revere Papers.

48. Joseph Warren Revere paid Stuart $200 for the paintings on June 1, 1813, in Cash Books, 1811–18, vol. 33, roll 11, Revere Papers. Rachel Revere died of "bilious cholic" on June 26, 1813. The portraits, with explanatory text, are in Fairbanks et al., *Paul Revere's Boston,* 202–4. On the deaths of Rachel and Paul Revere Jr. see Nielsen, "The Revere Family," 296, 304. Revere's subscriptions to the *Centinel, Repertory, Gazette,* and *Palladium* and a bill for shoeing his horse in February 1815 are in Cash Books, 1811–18, vol. 33, roll 11, Revere Papers. Receipt for dues for the Boston Library, March 1817–March 1818, is in roll 3, Revere Papers. On petition signed by Revere and the North End mechanics see *MHS Proceedings* 58 (1880–81): 287–88; Goss, *Life of Colonel Revere,* 2.591–92.

49. Revere's obituary in the *Boston Intelligencer and Evening Gazette,* May 16, 1818.

50. Towns named after Revere are in Massachusetts, Pennsylvania, Minnesota, and Missouri. On Revere as a folk here see Triber, "The Midnight Ride of Paul Revere: From History to Folklore." See also William Tudor, *The Life of James Otis of Massachusetts* (1823; reprint, New York, 1970), 458. The phrase "posthumous panegyrick" is from Revere's obituary, in which the writer claimed that such a man as Colonel Revere "has undoubted title to posthumous panegyrick."

BIBLIOGRAPHY

Primary Sources/Manuscript Collections

Boston Public Library

Boston Board of Health Records, 1799–1816. 3 vols. Rare Books, Ms 1328.
The New Brick Committee Book, 1761–1800. Rare Books. Ms. Bos. Z16 (2).
Revere's letter of resignation as coroner to Governor Caleb Strong, January 28, 1801. Rare Books. Ch.F.6.4.

Bostonian Society Library

Paul Revere to Stephen Metcalf, July 30, 1783.

Grand Lodge of Massachusetts A.F. & A.M., Samuel Crocker Lawrence Library, Boston

Boston Tea Party File.
Membership File.
Parker, Henry J. "Index to Early Masons, 1733–1800" ("Parker Index"). Handwritten ledger compiled in 1886. Boston: Grand Lodge of Massachusetts A.F. & A.M.
Records of Tyrian Lodge File.
St. Andrew's File.

Houghton Library Harvard

"Petition to Selectmen of Boston, March 2, 1772." fMS Am1075.
"Petition to Selectmen of Boston, June 2, 1772." fMS Am1075.1.
Sparks Manuscripts X. New England Papers. Vol. 3.

Library of Congress

Revere to President George Washington, February 5, 1791. Applications for Appointment to Federal Posts during the Washington Administration. United States Miscellany, 1789–1824. Manuscript Division.

Massachusetts Archives

MASSACHUSETTS ARCHIVES COLLECTION (SCI, 45X)
Board of War Minutes, 1776–77. Vol. 148.
Revolution: Council Papers, 1781–83. Vol. 172.
Revolution: Council Papers, 2d ser., December 1777–December 1778. Vol. 174.
Revolution: Council Papers, 2d ser., 1778–79. Vol. 175.
Revolution: Council Papers, 2d ser., 1779–80. Vol. 176.
Revolution: Letters, 1779. Vol. 201.
Revolution: Miscellaneous, 1774–83. Vol. 138.
Revolution: Miscellaneous, 1775–88. Vol. 140.
Revolution: Penobscot Expedition, Vol. 145.
Revolution: Petitions, June 1777–February 26, 1778. Vol. 183.
Revolution: Petitions, March 1778–February 11, 1779. Vol. 184.
Revolution: Petitions, 1781–82. Vol. 187.
Revolution: Resolves, 1778. Vol. 218.
Revolution: Resolves, 1779. Vol. 221.
Revolution: Resolves, 1780. Vol. 226.

JUDICIAL ARCHIVES
Suffolk County Court of Common Pleas Record Book. October 1783–April 1784.
Suffolk County Supreme Judicial Court Files (microfilm).
Suffolk Probate Court Records Books (microfilm).

Massachusetts Historical Society (MHS)

David Cobb Papers.
Benjamin Lincoln Papers.
Solomon Lovell Papers.
Miscellaneous Bound Manuscripts.
Nonimportation agreement of July 31, 1769, Ms. L (cataloged under name of Harbottle Dorr).
Harrison Gray Otis Papers.
Edward Payne Papers.
Petition of Massachusetts General Court to President John Adams, June 7, 1798, in Adams Papers, reel 389.
Ezekiel Price Papers.
Revere Family Papers.
S. P. Savage Papers, S. P. Savage II Papers.

Thwing Index.
Washburn Autograph Collection.

New York Historical Society

Notice of marriage of Matthew Davis to Sarah Eayres. *The Weekly Museum* (New York), April 23, 1796.
William Kelby (1841–1898). "Notes on Trinity Church Yard Families," genealogical information on Matthew Davis.

New York Public Library

Boston Committee of Correspondence Records (Bancroft Collection). Manuscripts and Archives Division. Astor, Lenox and Tilden Foundations. Photostat at the MHS.

University of South Carolina

Thomas Wadsworth's will, September 14, 1799. Thomas Wadsworth Papers. South Caroliniana Library. University of South Carolina.

Published Primary Sources/Microfilm Collections

Acts and Resolves of Massachusetts, 1775–1800. Boston: Wright and Potter, 1890–1918.
"An Alphabetical List of the Sons of Liberty who dined at Liberty Tree, Dorchester, August 14, 1769." Written in the hand of William Palfrey. *MHS Proceedings* 11 (August 1869): 140–42
Babcock, Mary Kent (Davey). "Christ Church, Boston, Records." *New England Historical and Genealogical Register* 100 (January and April 1946): 24–33, 132–43.
Jeremy Belknap Papers. *MHS Collections,* 5th ser., 2 and 3 (1877) and 6th ser., 4 (1891).
Boston Directory. Boston: John Norman, 1789.
Boston Directory. Boston: Edward Cotton, 1806, 1807, 1809, 1813.
Boston Registry Department. *Report of the Record Commissioners: Boston Town Records.* 39 vols. Boston, 1876–1909.
Bowdoin-Temple Papers. *MHS Collections,* 7th ser., 6 (1907).
Boyle, John. *Boyle's Journal of Occurrences in Boston, 1759–1778. New England Historical and Genealogical Register* 84 (April, July, October 1930): 142–71, 248–72, 357–82; 85 (January and April 1931): 5–28, 118–33.
"A British Officer in Boston (Diary of Lieutenant John Barker)." *Atlantic Monthly* 34 (April and May 1877): 388–401, 544–54.
Butterfield, L. H., ed. *The Adams Family Correspondence.* Vols. 1 and 2. Cambridge: Belknap Press, 1963.
——. *Diary and Autobiography of John Adams, 1755–1770.* Vol. 1. Cambridge: Belknap Press, 1961.
Calcott's Candid Disquisition on the Principles and Practices of the Most Ancient and Honorable Society of Free and Accepted Masons. 1772. Evans, *Early American Imprints,* no. 12345.

"A Circumstantial Account of an Attack, that happened on the 19th of April, 1775, on His Majesty's Troops, by a Number of People of the Province of Massachusetts Bay" ("General Gage's Account"). April 29, 1775. Evans, *Early American Imprints,* no. 14192.

Cunningham, Anne Rowe, ed. *Letters and Diary of John Rowe, Boston Merchant.* 1903. Reprint, Ann Arbor, Mich.: University Microfilm, 1968.

Debates, Resolutions, and other Proceedings of the Convention of the Commonwealth of Massachusetts . . . for the Purpose of Assenting to and Ratifying the Constitution Recommended by the Grand Federal Convention. 1788. Evans, *Early American Imprints,* no. 21242.

The Diary of William Bentley, D.D. Pastor of the East Church, Salem, Massachusetts. 2 vols. 1904–7. Reprint, Gloucester, Mass.: Peter Smith, 1962.

"Diary of Samuel Cooper, 1775–1776." *American Historical Review* 6 (January 1901): 301–41.

"Diary of Mr. Thomas Newell of Boston, 1773–1774." *MHS Proceedings* 15 (October 1877): 335–63.

"Diary of Ezekiel Price, 1775–1776." *MHS Proceedings* 7 (November 1863): 185–262.

"Diary of Ezekiel Price, 1777–1778." *New England Historical and Genealogical Register* 19 (October 1865): 329–38.

Drake, Francis S. *Life and Correspondence of Henry Knox.* Boston: Samuel G. Drake, 1873.

——. *Tea Leaves: Being a Collection of Letters and Documents Relating to the Shipment of Tea to the American Colonies in the Year 1773, by the East India Company.* 1884. Reprint, Detroit: Singing Tree Press, 1970.

Elsey, George M., ed. "John Wilkes and William Palfrey." *Colonial Society of Massachusetts Publications* 34 (February 1941): 411–28.

"Extract of a Letter from General Henry Burbeck to Colonel Samuel Swett . . . March 18, 1848, on his father William Burbeck." *New England Historical and Genealogical Register* 12 (October 1858): 351–52.

A Fair Account of the Late Unhappy Disturbance at Boston in New England. London: B. White, 1770.

The Federalist Papers. New York: New American Library, 1961.

Fitzpatrick, John C., ed. *The Writings of George Washington.* 39 vols. Washington, D.C.: Government Printing Office, 1931–44.

Force, Peter, ed., *American Archives.* 4th ser., 6 vols., and 5th ser., 3 vols. Washington, D.C., 1837–53.

Ford, Worthington C., ed. *Copley-Pelham Letters. MHS Collections* 71 (1914).

——. *Journals of the Continental Congress.* 34 vols. Washington, D.C.: Government Printing Office, 1904–37.

Grand Lodge Proceedings, 1733–92. Boston: Grand Lodge of Massachusetts, 1895.

Grand Lodge Proceedings, 1792–1815. Cambridge: Caustic-Claflin, 1905.

Grand Lodge Proceedings, 1815–25. Boston: Caustic-Claflin, 1928.

Gray, Thomas, D.D. "A Tribute to the Memory of Benjamin Bussey, Esq., Who Died at Roxbury, January 13, 1842." Boston: I. R. Butts, 1842. In *Biographical Pamphlet Series,* vol. 10, no. 17. Boston: Massachusetts State Library.

Harbottle Dorr Collection of Annotated Massachusetts Newspapers, 1765–1776. MHS Microfilm (1966). 4 vols.

William Heath Papers. *MHS Collections*, 7th ser., 4 (1904).

Heitman, Francis B. *Historical Register of Officers of the Continental Army during the War of the Revolution, April 1775 to December 1783*. 1914. Reprint, Baltimore: Genealogical Publishing, 1967.

"A Journal Kept During the Time Yt Boston Was Shut Up in 1775–1776, by Timothy Newell, Esq." *MHS Collections*, 4th ser., 1 (1852): 260–76.

Journals of the House of Representatives of Massachusetts, 1776–79. Boston: MHS, 1984–90.

Kimball, James. "Orderly Book of the Regiment of Artillery Raised for the Defence of Boston in 1776." *Historical Collections of the Essex Institute* 13 (January 1875 and July 1876): 115–34, 237–52; 14 (January, April, July 1877): 60–76, 110–28, 188–211.

Henry Knox Papers, 1719–1825. MHS Microfilm (1960). 55 reels.

Lemay, J. A. L., and P. M. Zall, eds. *Benjamin Franklin's Autobiography*. New York: W. W. Norton, 1986.

"Letters of John Andrews." *MHS Proceedings* 8 (1864–65): 316–412.

Lincoln, William, ed. *Journals of the Provincial Congress of Massachusetts, 1774 and 1775*. Boston: Dutton and Wentworth, 1838.

"List of the Committee of 63 (including Paul Revere)." *MHS Proceedings* 12 (1898): 139–42.

Longfellow, Samuel, ed. *Life of Henry Wadsworth Longfellow, with Extracts from his Journals and Correspondence*. 3 vols. Boston: Houghton Mifflin, 1891.

McGlenen, Edward W., comp. *Boston Marriages from 1700 to 1809*. 1903. Reprint, Baltimore: Genealogical Publishing, 1977.

Massachusetts Soldiers and Sailors of the Revolutionary War. 17 vols. Boston: Wright and Potter, 1896–1908.

Mather, Samuel. *The Life of the Very Reverend and Learned Cotton Mather*. 1729. Evans, *Early American Imprints*, no. 3188.

Matthews, Albert, ed. "Letters of Dennys DeBerdt, 1757–1770." *Colonial Society of Massachusetts Publications* 13 (March 1911): 293–461.

Mayhew, Jonathan. *A Discourse Concerning Unlimited Submission and Non-Resistance to the Higher Powers: With Some Reflections on the Resistance Made to King Charles I and on the Anniversary of his Death, delivered January 30, 1749/1750, West Church Boston*. Evans, *Early American Imprints*, no. 6549.

"Memoir of Governor Hutchinson." *New England Historical and Genealogical Register* 1 (October 1847): 297–310.

Memorial Services of Commemoration Day, Held in Canton, May 30, 1877 under the Auspices of Revere Encampment, Post 94, GAR. Boston: William Bense, 1877.

"Minutes of the Tea Meetings, 1773." In handwriting identified as that of Town Clerk William Cooper. *MHS Proceedings* 20 (November 1882): 10–17.

A Narrative of the Excursion and Ravages of the King's Troops Under the Command of General Gage on the Nineteenth of April 1775, Together with the Depositions Taken by Congress To Support the Truth of It. May 22, 1775. Reprint, New York: Arno Press, 1968.

"Notices on the Life of Major General Benjamin Lincoln." *MHS Collections*, 2d ser., 3 (1815): 233–55.

Paul Revere's Three Accounts of His Famous Ride: A Massachusetts Historical Society Picture Book. Boston: MHS, 1976.

Peterson, Merrill D., ed. *The Portable Thomas Jefferson.* 1975. Reprint, New York: Penguin Books, 1977.

Petition signed by Paul Revere and North End mechanics volunteering to strengthen Boston's defenses during the War of 1812. September 8, 1814. *MHS Proceedings* 58 (1880–81): 287–88.

The Poetical Works of Longfellow. Cambridge ed. Boston: Houghton Mifflin, 1975.

Proceedings in Masonry: St. John's Grand Lodge, 1733–1792, and Massachusetts Grand Lodge, 1769–1792. See *Grand Lodge Proceedings, 1733–92.*

"Proceedings of the General Assembly and Council of Massachusetts Relating to the Penobscot Expedition." 1780. Evans, *Early American Imprints,* no. 16847.

"Record of the Boston Committee of Correspondence, Inspection, and Safety, May to November 1776." *New England Historical and Genealogical Register* 30 (July 1876): 380–89; 31 (January 1877 and July 1877): 31–33, 290–94; 33 (January 1879): 23–25; 34 (January, April, July 1880): 14–20, 167–70, 251–53.

Selfridge, Thomas O. *A Correct Statement of the Whole Preliminary Controversy Between Thomas O. Selfridge and Benjamin Austin, also a Brief Account of the Catastrophe in State Street. . . .* January 7, 1807. Evans, *Early American Imprints,* no. 13566.

Seybolt, Robert Francis. *The Town Officials of Colonial Boston, 1634–1775.* Cambridge: Harvard University Press, 1939.

A Short Narrative of the Horrid Massacre in Boston. Boston: Edes and Gill, 1770.

Shurtleff, Nathaniel B., comp. *Records of the Governor and Company of the Massachusetts Bay in New England.* Vol. 1. Boston: William White, 1853.

"Sketches of Distinguished Merchants." Art. 10, no. 4. Benjamin Bussey, of Roxbury, Massachusetts. 1842. Harvard University Archives, HUG 1249.

Smith, Paul H., ed. *Letters of Delegates to the Continental Congress.* 15 vols. Washington, D.C.: Library of Congress, 1976–88.

Taylor, Robert J., ed., *The Papers of John Adams.* Vol. 3. Cambridge: Harvard University Press, 1979.

Trial of Thomas O. Selfridge . . . For Killing Charles Austin. Shorthand report of the trial, 1807. Evans, *Early American Imprints,* no. 13740.

Tudor, William. *The Life of James Otis.* 1823. Reprint, New York: Da Capo Press, 1970.

Upton, L. F. S. "Proceedings of Ye Body Respecting the Tea." *William and Mary Quarterly,* 3rd ser., 22 (April 1965): 287–300.

Voye, Nancy S., ed. *Massachusetts Officers in the French and Indian Wars, 1748–1763.* Boston: Society of Colonial Wars in the Commonwealth of Massachusetts, Office of the Secretary of the Commonwealth of Massachusetts and the New England Historical and Genealogical Society, 1975.

Ware, Henry. *Two Discourses Containing the History of the Old North and New Brick Churches United as the Second Church in Boston.* Boston: James W. Burditt, 1821.

Warren-Adams Letters. Vol. 1: 1743–77; vol. 2: 1778–1814, appendix. *MHS Collections* 72–73 (1917–25).

Washburn, Emory. "Memoir and Orderly Book of Colonel William Henshaw." *MHS Proceedings* 15 (October 1876): 65–160.

"Will of Benjamin Bussey of Roxbury." Boston: J. H. Eastburn, 1859. In *Biographical Pamphlet Series*. Vol. 10, no. 16. Boston: Massachusetts State Library.

Williams, Ephraim, Esq., *Reports of Cases Argued and Determined in the Supreme Judicial Court of the State of Massachusetts from September 1804 to June 1805*. Vol. 1. Northampton, Mass.: S. and E. Butler, 1805.

Wyman, Thomas, Jr., comp. "Records of the New Brick Church." *New England Historical and Genealogical Register* 19 (July 1865): 230–35.

Newspapers

American Herald (Boston).
Boston Gazette.
Boston Globe.
Boston Intelligencer and Evening Gazette.
Boston Newsletter.
Columbian Centinel (Boston).
Independent Chronicle (Boston).
Massachusetts Centinel (Boston).
Massachusetts Mercury (Boston).
New York Gazette and Weekly Mercury (New York City).
Pennsylvania Chronicle (Philadelphia).

Secondary Sources

Adams, Randolph G. "New Light on the Boston Massacre." *American Antiquarian Society Proceedings* 47 (October 1937): 259–354.

Ahlstrom, Sydney E. *A Religious History of the American People*. Vol. 1. Garden City, N.Y.: Image Books, 1975.

Alden, John E. "John Mein: Scourge of Patriots." *Colonial Society of Massachusetts Publications* 34 (February 1941): 571–99.

Alden, John Richard. *The American Revolution, 1775–1783*. New York: Harper Torchbook, 1962.

Allen, Gardner Weld. *Massachusetts Privateers of the Revolution*. MHS Collections 77 (1927).

——. *A Naval History of the American Revolution*. Vol. 2. 1913, 1940. Reprint, New York: Russell and Russell, 1962.

Anderson, Fred. *A People's Army: Massachusetts Soldiers and Society in the Seven Years' War*. Chapel Hill: University of North Carolina Press, 1984.

Andrews, Charles M. "The Boston Merchants and the Non-Importation Movement." *Colonial Society of Massachusetts Publications* 19 (February 1917): 159–259.

Appleby, Joyce. *Capitalism and a New Social Order: The Republican Vision of the 1790s*. New York: New York University Press, 1984.

——. "Liberalism and the American Revolution." *New England Quarterly* 49 (March 1976): 3–26.

———. "The Social Origins of American Revolutionary Ideology." *Journal of American History* 64 (March 1978): 935–58.

Aronson, Sidney. *Status and Kinship in the Higher Civil Service: Standards of Selection in the Administrations of John Adams, Thomas Jefferson, and Andrew Jackson.* Cambridge: Harvard University Press, 1964.

Arvin, Newton. *Longfellow: His Life and Work.* Boston: Atlantic Monthly Press, 1962, 1963.

Avery, C. Louise. *Early American Silver.* New York: Century, 1930.

Bailyn, Bernard. *Education in the Forming of American Society: Needs and Opportunities for Study.* Chapel Hill: University of North Carolina Press, 1960.

———. *The Ideological Origins of the American Revolution.* Cambridge: Belknap Press, 1967.

———. *The Ordeal of Thomas Hutchinson.* Cambridge: Belknap Press, 1974.

Bancroft, George. *History of the United States.* Vol. 7. Boston: Little, Brown, 1858.

Banner, James M., Jr. *To the Hartford Convention: The Federalists and the Origins of Party Politics in Massachusetts, 1789–1815.* New York: Alfred A. Knopf, 1970.

Banning, Lance. *The Jeffersonian Persuasion: Evolution of a Party Ideology.* Ithaca, N.Y.: Cornell University Press, 1980.

Barrow, Thomas C. *Trade and Empire: The British Customs Service in Colonial America, 1660–1775.* Cambridge: Harvard University Press, 1967.

Barry, John Stetson. *History of Massachusetts.* 3 vols. Boston: Henry Barry, 1855–57.

Baxter, W. T. *The House of Hancock: Business in Boston, 1724–1775.* 1945. Reprint, New York: Russell and Russell, 1965.

Beeman, Richard, Stephen Botein, and Edward C. Carter, II, eds. *Beyond Confederation: Origins of the Constitution and American National Identity.* Chapel Hill: University of North Carolina Press, 1987.

Boorstin, Daniel J. *The Americans: The Colonial Experience.* New York: Vintage Books, 1958.

———. *The Lost World of Thomas Jefferson.* 1948. Reprint, with new preface, Chicago: University of Chicago Press, 1981.

Bortman, Mark. "Paul Revere and Son and Their Jewish Correspondents." *Publication of the American Jewish Historical Society* 43 (1953–54): 199–229.

Bourne, Russell. "The Penobscot Fiasco." *American Heritage* 25 (October 1974): 28–33, 100–101.

Bridenbaugh, Carl. *Cities in Revolt: Urban Life in America, 1743–1776.* 1955. Reprint, New York: Oxford University Press, 1971.

———. *Cities in the Wilderness: Urban Life in America, 1625–1742.* 3d ed. New York: Capricorn Books, 1964.

———. *The Colonial Craftsman.* New York: Oxford University Press, 1950.

Brigham, Clarence S. *Paul Revere's Engravings.* New York: Atheneum, 1969.

Brooke, John L. "Ancient Lodges and Self-Created Societies: Voluntary Association and the Public Sphere in the Early Republic." In *Launching the "Extended Republic": The Federalist Era,* ed. Ronald Hoffman and Peter J. Albert. Charlottesville: University Press of Virginia, 1996.

Brooks, Noah. *Henry Knox: A Soldier of the Revolution.* 1900. Reprint, New York: Da Capo Press, 1974.

Brooks, Victor Daniel. "American Officer Development in the Massachusetts Campaign, 1775–1776." *Historical Journal of Massachusetts* 12 (January 1984): 8–18.

Brown, Richard D. *Revolutionary Politics in Massachusetts: The Boston Committee of Correspondence and the Towns, 1772–1774.* Cambridge: Harvard University Press, 1970.

Buckingham, Joseph T. *Annals of the Massachusetts Charitable Mechanic Association.* Boston: Crocker and Brewster, 1853.

Buhler, Kathryn C. "The Ledgers of Paul Revere." *Bulletin of the Museum of Fine Arts* 34 (June 1936): 38–45.

——. *Paul Revere, Goldsmith.* Boston: Museum of Fine Arts, 1956.

Bullock, Steven C. "The Ancient and Honorable Society: Freemasonry in America, 1730–1860." Ph.D. diss., Brown University, 1986.

——. "A Pure and Sublime System: The Appeal of Post-Revolutionary Freemasonry." *Journal of the Early Republic* 9 (Fall 1989): 359–73.

——. *Revolutionary Brotherhood: Freemasonry and the Transformation of the American Social Order.* Chapel Hill: University of North Carolina Press, 1996.

——. "The Revolutionary Transformation of American Freemasonry, 1752–1792." *William and Mary Quarterly*, 3d ser., 47 (July 1990): 347–69.

Bushman, Richard L. *King and People in Provincial Massachusetts.* Chapel Hill: University of North Carolina Press, 1985.

Carson, Cary. "The Consumer Revolution in Colonial British America: Why Demand?" In *Of Consuming Interest: The Style of Life in the Eighteenth Century*, ed. Cary Carson, Ronald Hoffman, and Peter J. Albert. Charlottesville: University Press of Virginia, 1994.

Cary, John. *Joseph Warren: Physician, Politician, Patriot.* Urbana: University of Illinois Press, 1961.

Chambers, William Nisbet. *Political Parties in a New Nation: The American Experience, 1776–1789.* 1963. Reprint, New York: Oxford University Press, 1969.

Charles, Joseph. *The Origins of the American Party System.* New York: Harper Torchbook, 1961.

Christie, I. R. *Crisis of Empire: Great Britain and the American Colonies, 1754–1783.* New York: W. W. Norton, 1966.

Coil, Henry Wilson. *Coil's Masonic Encyclopedia.* New York: Macoy Publishing and Masonic Supply, 1961.

——. *A Comprehensive View of Freemasonry.* Richmond, Va.: Macoy Publishing and Masonic Supply, 1973.

Colbourn, Trevor, ed. *Fame and the Founding Fathers: Essays by Douglass Adair.* New York: W. W. Norton, 1974.

Cole, Robert Glenn. "The Lodge of Saint Andrew: Headquarters of the Revolution." In his *Masonic Gleanings: From American and Masonic History.* Chicago: Kable Printing, 1954, 1956.

Cordell, Eugene F. *Medical Annals of Maryland, 1799–1899.* Baltimore: Williams and Wilkins, 1903.

Countryman, Edward. *A People in Revolution: The American Revolution and Political Society in New York, 1760–1790.* New York: W. W. Norton, 1989.

Cress, Lawrence Delbert. *Citizens in Arms: The Army in American Society to the War of 1812.* Chapel Hill: University of North Carolina Press, 1982.

Cunningham, Noble E., Jr. *The Jeffersonian Republicans in Power: Party Operations, 1801–1809.* Chapel Hill: University of North Carolina Press, 1963.

Day, Alan, and Katherine Day. "Another Look at the Boston Caucus." *Journal of American Studies* 5 (April 1971): 19–42.

Dictionary of American Biography. Ed. Dumas Malone. New York: Charles Scribner's Sons, 1926–36.

Dictionary of Scientific Biography. Ed. Charles Coulston Gillispie. Vol. 13. New York: Charles Scribner's Sons, 1980.

Drake, Samuel Adams. *Old Landmarks and Historic Personages of Boston.* 1900. Reprint, Detroit: Singing Tree Press, 1970.

Egnal, Marc. *A Mighty Empire: The Origins of the American Revolution.* Ithaca, N.Y.: Cornell University Press, 1988.

Elkins, Stanley, and Eric McKitrick. *The Age of Federalism: The Early American Republic, 1788–1800.* New York: Oxford University Press, 1993.

Ernay, Renee L. "The Revere Furnace, 1787–1800." M.A. thesis, University of Delaware, 1989.

Fairbanks, Jonathan, et al. *Paul Revere's Boston, 1735–1818.* Boston: Museum of Fine Arts, 1975.

Fales, Martha Gandy. *Early American Silver.* New York: Funk and Wagnalls, 1970.

Fischer, David Hackett. *Paul Revere's Ride.* New York: Oxford University Press, 1994.

———. *The Revolution of American Conservatism: The Federalist Party in the Era of Jeffersonian Democracy.* New York: Harper Torchbook, 1969.

Foner, Eric. *Tom Paine and Revolutionary America.* New York: Oxford University Press, 1976.

Forbes, Esther. *Paul Revere and the World He Lived In.* Boston: Houghton Mifflin, 1942.

Fowler, William M., Jr. "Disaster in Penobscot Bay." *Harvard Magazine* 81 (July–August 1979): 26–31.

French, Allen. *The Day of Concord and Lexington.* Boston: Little, Brown, 1925.

———. *The First Year of the American Revolution.* 1934. Reprint, New York: Octagon Books, 1968.

———. *General Gage's Informers: New Material upon Lexington and Concord.* 1932. Reprint, New York: Greenwood Press, 1968.

Frothingham, Richard. *History of the Siege of Boston.* 6th ed., 1903. Reprint, New York: Da Capo Press, 1970.

Gipson, Lawrence Henry. *The Coming of the American Revolution, 1763–1775.* New York: Harper Torchbook, 1962.

Goodman, Paul. *The Democratic-Republicans of Massachusetts: Politics in a Young Republic.* Cambridge: Harvard University Press, 1964.

Goss, Elbridge Henry. *The Life of Colonel Paul Revere.* 2 vols. Boston: Joseph George Cupples, 1891.

Grant, Frederic, Jr. "The Court-Martial of Paul Revere." *Boston Bar Journal* 21 (April 1977): 5–13.

Greene, Jack P. *Pursuits of Happiness: The Social Development of Modern British Colonies and the Formation of American Culture.* Chapel Hill: University of North Carolina Press, 1988.

——, ed. *Colonies to Nation: A Documentary History of the American Revolution.* 1967. Reprint, New York: W. W. Norton, 1975.

Gross, Robert A. *The Minutemen and Their World.* New York: Hill and Wang, 1976.

Grundy, Elizabeth, and Jayne E. Triber. "Paul Revere's Children: Coming of Age in the New Nation." Unpublished manuscript at the Paul Revere Memorial Association, Boston. 1983.

Hall, David D. "The World of Print and Collective Mentality in Seventeenth-Century New England." In *Colonial America: Essays in Politics and Social Development,* ed. Stanley N. Katz and John M. Murrin. 3d ed. New York: Alfred A. Knopf, 1983.

Handlin, Oscar, and Mary Flug Handlin. *Commonwealth: A Study of the Role of Government in the American Economy, Massachusetts, 1774–1861.* Rev. ed. Cambridge: Belknap Press, 1969.

Hart, Albert Bushnell. *Commonwealth History of Massachusetts.* vols. 2–3. 1928–29. Reprint, New York: Russell and Russell, 1966.

Hoerder, Dirk. "Boston Leaders and Boston Crowds, 1765–1776." In *The American Revolution: Explorations in the History of American Radicalism,* ed. Alfred F. Young. DeKalb: Northern Illinois University Press, 1976.

Hofstadter, Richard. *America at 1750: A Social Portrait.* New York: Alfred A. Knopf, 1971.

——. *The Idea of a Party System: The Rise of Legitimate Opposition in the United States, 1780–1840.* Berkeley: University of California Press, 1969.

Holland, Henry Ware. *William Dawes and His Ride with Paul Revere.* Boston: J. Wilson and Son, 1878.

Hosmer, Jerome Carter. *The Beginnings of the Massachusetts Charitable Mechanic Association, 1795–1808.* Boston: Fort Hill Press, 1906.

Howe, John R., Jr. "Republican Thought and the Political Violence of the 1790s." *American Quarterly* 19 (Summer 1967): 147–65.

Hunt, Gaillard, "Office-Seeking during the Administration of John Adams." *American Historical Review* 2 (January 1897): 241–61.

——. "Office-Seeking during Washington's Administration." *American Historical Review* 1 (October 1895): 270–83.

Jameson, J. Franklin. *Privateering and Piracy in the Colonial Period.* 1923. Reprint, New York: Augustus M. Kelley, 1970.

Jenks, Henry F. *Catalogue of the Boston Public Latin School, with an Historical Sketch.* Boston: Boston Latin School Association, 1886.

Jensen, Merrill. *The New Nation: A History of the United States during the Confederation, 1781–1789.* 1950. Reprint, Boston: Northeastern University Press, 1981.

Jones, E. Alfred. *The Loyalists of Massachusetts: Their Memorials, Petitions, and Claims.* London: St. Catherine Press, 1930.

Kaplan, Sidney. "Rank and Status among Massachusetts Continental Officers." *American Historical Review* 56 (January 1951): 318–26.

Kelly, Howard A., and Walter L. Burrage. *Dictionary of American Medical Biography*. New York: D. Appleton, 1928.

Kerber, Linda K. *Federalists in Dissent: Imagery and Ideology in Jeffersonian America*. 2d ed. Ithaca, N.Y.: Cornell University Press, 1980.

Kloppenberg, James T. "Christianity, Republicanism, and Ethics in Early American Discourse." *Journal of American History* 74 (June 1987): 9–33.

Kohn, Richard. *Eagle and Sword: The Federalists and the Creation of the Military Establishment in America, 1783–1802*. New York: Macmillan, 1975.

Kornblith, Gary. "Artisan Federalism: New England Mechanics and the Political Economy of the Federalist Era." In *Launching the "Extended Republic": The Federalist Era*, ed. Ronald Hoffman and Peter J. Albert. Charlottesville: University Press of Virginia, 1996.

——. "From Artisans to Businessmen: Master Mechanics in New England, 1789–1850." Ph.D. diss., Princeton University Press, 1983.

Kramnick, Isaac. "Republican Revisionism Revisited: Liberal and Classical Ideas in the New American Republic." *American Historical Review* 87 (June 1982): 629–64.

Kurtz, Stephen G. *The Presidency of John Adams: The Collapse of Federalism, 1795–1800*. Philadelphia: University of Pennsylvania Press, 1957.

Labaree, Benjamin Woods. *The Boston Tea Party*. 2d ed. Boston: Northeastern University Press, 1979.

——. *Patriots and Partisans: The Merchants of Newburyport, 1764–1815*. New York: W. W. Norton, 1975.

Labatut, André J. "Some New Information about the Ancestry of Paul Revere." *New England Historical and Genealogical Register* 143 (July 1989): 235–39.

Labatut, André J., and Pamela Labatut. "Paul Revere's Paternal Ancestry: The Rivoires: A Hugenot Family of Some Account." *New England Historical and Genealogical Register* 150 (July 1996): 277–98.

Lambert, Frank. "Subscribing for Profits and Piety: The Friendship of Benjamin Franklin and George Whitefield." *William and Mary Quarterly*, 3d ser., 50 (July 1993): 529–48.

Leake, Isaac Q. *Memoir of the Life of General John Lamb*. Albany, N.Y.: Joel Munsell, 1850.

Leehey, Patrick, et al. *Paul Revere—Artisan, Businessman, and Patriot: The Man behind the Myth*. Boston: Paul Revere Memorial Association, 1988.

Lemon, James T. *The Best Poor Man's Country: A Geographical Study of Early Southeastern Pennsylvania*. New York: W. W. Norton, 1972.

Little, David B. *America's First Centennial Celebration*. Boston: Houghton Mifflin, 1974.

Lubow, Lisa B. "Artisans in Transition: Early Capitalist Development and the Carpenters of Boston, 1787–1837." Ph.D. diss., University of California, Los Angeles, 1987.

McCoy, Drew. *The Elusive Republic: Political Economy in Jeffersonian America*. 1980. Reprint, New York: W. W. Norton, 1982.

McKay, Derek, and H. M. Scott. *The Rise of the Great Powers, 1648–1715*. London: Longman, 1983.

Maier, Pauline. *From Resistance to Revolution: Colonial Radicals and the Development of American Opposition to Britain, 1765–1776*. New York: Vintage Books, 1974.

——. *The Old Revolutionaries: Political Lives in the Age of Samuel Adams.* New York: Vintage Books, 1982.

Main, Jackson Turner, *The Antifederalists: Critics of the Constitution, 1781–1788.* 1961. Reprint, New York: W. W. Norton, 1974.

——. *The Social Structure of Revolutionary America.* Princeton, N.J.: Princeton University Press, 1965.

Mattern, David B. *Benjamin Lincoln and the American Revolution.* Columbia: University of South Carolina Press, 1995.

Miller, John C. *The Federalist Era, 1789–1801.* New York: Harper Torchbook, 1963.

Morgan, Edmund S., and Helen M. Morgan. *The Stamp Act Crisis: Prologue to Revolution.* 2d ed. New York: Collier, 1963.

Morison, Samuel Eliot. *Harrison Gray Otis, 1765–1848: The Urbane Federalist.* Boston: Houghton Mifflin, 1969.

Morse, Anson Ely. *The Federalist Party in Massachusetts to the Year 1800.* Princeton, N.J.: Princeton University Library, 1909.

Murrin, John M. "The Legal Transformation: The Bench and Bar of Eighteenth-Century Massachusetts." In *Colonial America: Essays in Politics and Social Development,* ed. Stanley N. Katz and John M. Murrin. 3d ed. New York: Alfred A. Knopf, 1983.

Nash, Gary B. "Artisans and Politics in Eighteenth-Century Philadelphia." In *The Craftsman in Early America,* ed. Ian M. Quimby. New York: W. W. Norton, 1984.

——. *The Urban Crucible: Social Change, Political Consciousness, and the Origins of the American Revolution.* Cambridge: Harvard University Press, 1979.

Nevins, Alan. *The American States During and After the Revolution, 1775–1789.* New York: Macmillan, 1924.

Nichols, Arthur H. *The Bells of Paul and Joseph W. Revere.* Salem, Mass.: Essex Institute, 1911.

Nielsen, Donald M. "The Revere Family." *New England Historical and Genealogical Register* 145 (October 1991): 291–316.

Nye, Russel Blaine. *The Cultural Life of the New Nation, 1776–1830.* New York: Harper and Row, 1960.

Olton, Charles S. *Artisans for Independence: Philadelphia Mechanics and the American Revolution.* Syracuse, N.Y.: Syracuse University Press, 1975.

Palmer, Ezra, et al. *The Lodge of St. Andrew and the Massachusetts Grand Lodge Centennial Memorial (Centennial Memorial).* Boston: Grand Lodge of Massachusetts, 1870.

Palmer, Gregory. *Biographical Sketches of Loyalists of the American Revolution.* Rev. ed. of Sabine. Westport, Conn.: Mecklin Publishing, 1984.

Parkman, Aubrey. *Army Engineers in New England: The Military and Civil Work of the Corps of Engineers in New England, 1775–1975.* Waltham, Mass.: U.S. Army Corps of Engineers, 1978.

Patterson, Stephen E. *Political Parties in Revolutionary Massachusetts.* Madison: University of Wisconsin Press, 1973.

Phinney, Elias. *History of the Battle of Lexington on the Morning of the 19th of April 1775.* 1825. Reprint, Society for the Preservation of Colonial Culture, 1968.

Pinkney, Helen R. *Christopher Gore: Federalist of Massachusetts, 1758–1827.* Portland, Maine: Anthoensen Press, 1969.

Pocock, J. G. A. "The Classical Theory of Deference." *American Historical Review* 81 (June 1976): 516–23.

Porter, Roy. *English Society in the Eighteenth Century.* New York: Penguin Books, 1982.

A Pride of Quincys: A Massachusetts Historical Society Picture Book. Boston: MHS, 1969.

Pringle, James R. "Address on the History of Tyrian Lodge on the Occasion of Its 150th Anniversary." *Grand Lodge Proceedings,* 1920, pp. 27–37.

Professional and Industrial History of Suffolk County Massachusetts. Vols. 1 and 2. Boston: Boston History Company, 1894.

Richardson, E. P. *Painting in America, 1502 to the Present.* New York: Thomas Y. Crowell, 1965.

Ripley, Ezra. *History of the Fight at Concord on the 19th of April, 1775.* 1927. Reprint, Society for the Preservation of Colonial Culture, 1968.

Robbins, Chandler. *A History of the Second Church, or Old North in Boston, To Which Is Added a History of the New Brick Church.* Boston: John Wilson and Son, 1852.

Roberts, Oliver Ayer. *History of the Military Company of the Massachusetts Now Called the Ancient and Honorable Artillery Company of Massachusetts, 1637–1800.* Vol. 2 (1738–1821). Boston: Alfred Mudge and Son, 1897.

Rock, Howard B. *Artisans of the New Republic: The Tradesmen of New York City in the Age of Jefferson.* New York: New York University Press, 1979.

Rodgers, Daniel T. "Republicanism: The Career of a Concept." *Journal of American History* 79 (June 1992): 11–38.

Roy, Thomas Sherrard. *Stalwart Builders: A History of the Grand Lodge of Masons in Massachusetts, 1733–1971.* Boston: Grand Lodge of Massachusetts, 1971.

Schlesinger, Arthur M., Sr. "The Aristocracy in Colonial America." *MHS Proceedings* 74 (1942). Reprinted in *The Social Fabric: American Life from 1607 to the Civil War,* vol. 1, 2d ed., ed. John H. Cary and Julius Weinberg, 72–85. Boston: Little, Brown, 1978.

Seaburg, Carl, and Stanley Paterson. *Merchant Prince of Boston: Colonel T. H. Perkins, 1764–1854.* Cambridge: Harvard University Press, 1971.

Seybolt, Robert Francis. *The Public Schools of Colonial Boston, 1635–1775.* 1935. Reprint, New York: Arno Press, 1969.

Shalhope, Robert E. "Republicanism and Early American Historiography." *William and Mary Quarterly,* 3d ser., 39 (April 1982): 334–56.

———. "Toward a Republican Synthesis: The Emergence of an Understanding of Republicanism in Early American Historiography." *William and Mary Quarterly,* 3d ser., 29 (January 1972): 49–80.

Shaw, Peter. *American Patriots and the Rituals of Revolution.* Cambridge: Harvard University Press, 1981.

Shipton, Clifton K. *Sibley's Harvard Graduates.* 14 vols. Boston: MHS, 1993–75.

Smelser, Marshall. *The Democratic Republic, 1801–1815.* New York: Harper Torchbook, 1968.

Snow, Caleb H. *A History of Boston the Metropolis of Massachusetts From Its Origins to the Present Period: with some Account of the Environs.* Boston: Abel Bowen, 1828.

Stark, James H. *The Loyalists of Massachusetts and the Other Side of the American Revolution.* 1910. Reprint, Clifton, N.J.: Augustus M. Kelley, 1972.

Steblecki, Edith J. *Paul Revere and Freemasonry.* Boston: Paul Revere Memorial Association, 1985.

Stickney, Edward, and Evelyn Stickney. *The Bells of Paul Revere, His Sons and Grandsons.* Bedford, Mass., 1976.

Taylor, Earl W. *Historical Sketch of the Grand Lodge of Massachusetts.* Boston: Grand Lodge of Massachusetts, 1958.

Tourtellot, Arthur B. *Lexington and Concord: The Beginning of the War of the American Revolution.* New York: W. W. Norton, 1963.

The Transactions of the American Medical Association. Philadelphia: T. K. and P. G. Collins, 1850.

Triber, Jayne E. "Massachusetts and the Federal Garrison at Fort Independence, 1798–1815: The Propriety of a Standing Army in a Republic." M.A. thesis, University of Massachusetts, Boston, 1985.

——. "The Midnight Ride of Paul Revere: From History to Folklore." Boston: Paul Revere Memorial Association, 1981 (publication and unpublished manuscript with research notes in the library of the Paul Revere Memorial Association).

Tucker, Louis Leonard. *Clio's Consort: Jeremy Belknap and the Founding of the Massachusetts Historical Society.* Boston: Northeastern University Press, 1990.

Wagenknecht, Edward. *Henry Wadsworth Longfellow: Portrait of an American Humanist.* New York: Oxford University Press, 1966.

Warden, G. B. *Boston, 1689–1776.* Boston: Little, Brown, 1970.

——. "The Caucus and Democracy in Colonial Boston." *New England Quarterly* 43 (March 1970): 19–45.

Warren, Charles. *Jacobin and Junto; or, Early American Politics as Viewed in the Diary of Dr. Nathaniel Ames, 1758–1822.* Cambridge: Harvard University Press, 1931.

Watson, John Lee. "Paul Revere's Signal: The True Story of the Signal Lanterns in Christ Church, Boston." *Boston Daily Advertiser,* July 20, 1876. Reprinted in *MHS Proceedings* 15 (1876): 164–77.

Watts, Steven. *The Republic Reborn: War and the Making of Liberal America, 1790–1820.* Baltimore: Johns Hopkins University Press, 1987.

Weigley, Russell F. *History of the United States Army.* 2d ed. New York: Macmillan, 1980.

Wehtje, Myron F. "Boston and the Calling of the Federal Convention of 1787." *Historical Journal of Massachusetts* 15 (June 1987): 99–105.

——. "Boston's Response to Disorder in the Commonwealth, 1783–1787." *Historical Journal of Massachusetts* 12 (January 1984): 19–27.

White, Leonard D. *The Federalists: A Study in Administrative History.* New York: Macmillan, 1956.

——. *The Jeffersonians: A Study in Administrative History, 1801–1829.* New York: Macmillan, 1956.

Whitehill, Walter Muir. *A Topographical History of Boston.* 2d ed. Cambridge: Belknap Press, 1968.

Whiteman, Maxwell. *Copper for America: The Hendricks Family and a National Industry, 1755–1939.* New Brunswick, N.J.: Rutgers University Press, 1971.

Whittemore, Bradford Adams. *Memorials of the Massachusetts Society of the Cincinnati.* Boston: Society of the Cincinnati, 1964.

Wilentz, Sean. *Chants Democratic: New York City and the Rise of the Working Class, 1788–1850.* New York: Oxford University Press, 1984.

Williamson, Joseph. "The Conduct of Paul Revere in the Penobscot Expedition." *Collections and Proceedings of the Maine Historical Society,* 2d ser., 3 (1892): 379–92.

Williamson, R. H. "Paul Revere and the First United States Mint." *The Numismatist* 63 (December 1950): 789–801.

Wills, Garry. *Cincinnatus: George Washington and the Enlightenment.* Garden City, N.Y.: Doubleday, 1984.

Winsor, Justin, ed. *The Memorial History of Boston.* Vols. 2 and 3. Boston: James R. Osgood, 1881.

Wolkins, George G. "Daniel Malcolm and Writs of Assistance." *MHS Proceedings* 58 (October 1924): 5–84.

Wood, Gordon S. *The Creation of the American Republic, 1776–1787.* New York: W. W. Norton, 1969.

——. *The Radicalism of the American Revolution.* New York: Alfred A. Knopf, 1992.

——, ed. *The Confederation and the Constitution: The Critical Issues.* Lanham, Md.: University Press of America, 1979.

York, Neil L. "Freemasons and the American Revolution." *The Historian* 55 (Winter 1993): 315–30.

Young, Alfred F. *The Democratic-Republicans of New York: The Origins, 1763–1797.* Chapel Hill: University of North Carolina Press, 1967.

——. "George Robert Twelves Hewes (1742–1840): A Boston Shoemaker and the Memory of the American Revolution." *William and Mary Quarterly,* 3d ser., 38 (October 1981): 561–623.

——. "The Mechanics and the Jeffersonians: New York, 1789–1801." *Labor History* 5 (Fall 1964): 245–76.

——. "Plebeian Culture and Eighteenth-Century American Radicalism." In *Origins of Anglo-American Radicalism,* ed. Margaret Jacob and James Jacob. London: Allen and Unwin, 1984.

Zobel, Hiller B. *The Boston Massacre.* New York: W. W. Norton, 1970.

INDEX

Abercromby, Gen. James, 24
Acts of Trade, 33
Adams, Abigail, 26
Adams, John, 82, 86, 118, 151, 176, 185, 191; and
    Boston Massacre, 83; on common people,
    68; in Continental Congress, 110, 124; on
    the Declaration of Independence, 125; on
    education, 14, 68; and Massachusetts Con-
    stitution, 149–50; on Otis's argument
    against writs of assistance, 33; as patriot
    leader, 35, 62, 68, 88, 118; on political cau-
    cuses, 34; presidency of, 161, 177–78, 179; on
    qualifications for leadership, 13–14, 114,
    118–19, 120–21; in quiet years, 84; on re-
    publican spirit, 97; and Revere's failure to
    obtain a Continental commission, 114, 118–
    19, 120–21, 122; on Revere's value as cou-
    rier, 98; on Ebenezer Richardson, 74; role
    in choosing Continental Army officers,
    114, 118–19, 120–21, 122; and Stamp Act cri-
    sis, 43; on Dr. Warren's death, 117
Adams, Samuel, 13, 82, 86, 99, 108, 151, 177;
    and Boston Massacre, 78, 83; and Boston
    Tea Party, 94, 95; in Continental Congress,
    99, 110, 124; as governor, 159, 175; and
    Hutchinson letters, 91; on Lafayette, 132;
    and nonimportation, 59, 62, 73, 81; opposes
    incorporation of Boston, 151; as patriot
    leader, 19, 35, 49–50, 62, 64, 68, 87; in quiet
    years, 84–85; and Revere, 88, 98, 117–18,
    119, 122–23, 129–30; Revere's engraving of,
    96; and Revere's ride to Lexington, 102,
    103, 104; and Christopher Seider's funeral,
    75; and Stamp Act crisis, 43, 48; on stand-
    ing armies, 66; on Suffolk Resolves, 100;
    and U.S. Constitution, 157, 158, 256 n. 52
Administration of Government Act, 97. *See
    also* Coercive Acts
Alien and Sedition Acts, 179
Allen, Ethan, 120
American Academy of Arts and Sciences, 165
American Philosophical Society, 165
Ames, Fisher, 159, 185, 186; on Jefferson, 179–
    80; and Revere's failure to obtain a fed-
    eral appointment, 160–62; and trial of
    Thomas O. Selfridge, 190
Ames, Dr. Nathaniel, 179
Amory, Thomas, 84
Ancient and Honorable Artillery Company,
    9, 113
Andrew, John, 84
Andrews, John, 94, 97–98, 108
Andros, Sir Edmund, 23
Anne Street, 8

Anti-Federalists, 156–57, 170

Appleton, Nathaniel, 87

Argument, Shewing that a Standing Army Is Inconsistent with a Free Government (Trenchard and Moyle), 66

Arnold, Benedict, 131

Articles of Confederation, 155

Artisans: and American Revolution, 2, 35–36, 40–46, 47–48, 53, 59–64, 68–69, 81, 82, 95; appeal of Freemasonry to, 4, 29, 30–31; divisions among, in New Republic, 154–55, 159–60, 170–75, 186–87, 252 n. 34; oppose incorporation of Boston, 151–52; and republicanism, 2, 4, 31, 53, 157; and Republican Party, 186; social position and mobility of, 4, 9–11, 15–17, 35, 43, 45, 61–63, 87–88; support for U.S. Constitution, 156–58; urge protection for American manufactures, 152–54

Association of Tradesmen and Manufacturers, 153–55, 159

Austin, Benjamin, Jr.: as Anti-Federalist and Republican leader, 157, 170–72; and Association of Tradesmen and Manufacturers, 153, 159; as Honestus, 154–55; opposes incorporation of Boston, 170–71; supports French Revolution, 171, 172; supports Madison's trade resolutions, 172; and trial of Thomas O. Selfridge, 189–90

Austin, Charles, 189, 190

Austin, Jonathan T., 152, 153

Avery, James, 147

Avery, John, 26

Avery, John, Jr. (Loyal Nine), 43, 44, 45

Baker, John, 60

Balch, Nathaniel, 68, 91

Bank of the United States, 160, 170

Bant, William, 114

Barber, Nathaniel, 53, 57, 64, 65, 86, 87

Barker, Lt. John, 108–10, 121

Barnard, Joseph, 38

Barre, Col. Isaac, 47, 91

Barrell, Joseph, 151

Barrell, William, 94

Barrett, Col. James, 108–9

Barrett, Samuel, 29, 30, 37, 40, 148, 152

Bartlett, Josiah, 176

Bass, Henry: and Boston Massacre, 76, 78; and Boston Tea Party, 93; and Loyal Nine, 43, 45, 48; protests troops on Boston Common, 85–86

Baum, Lt. Col. Friedrich, 130

Bavarian Illuminati, 176

Beck and Harvey (Revere copper customers), 184

Belcher, Sarson, 153

Belknap, Jeremy, 128; on democracy, 151, 164–65; and Revere's ride to Lexington, 103, 115, 177

Beney, Thomas, 41

Benney, Capt. Barnabas, 26

Bennington, battle of, 130

Bentley, Rev. William, 167, 171, 175, 176

Bernard, Gov. Francis, 66, 69; arrival of, in Boston, 32; attacked by Dr. Warren in press, 55; on *Boston Gazette*, 48; departure of, from Boston, 68; on Stamp Act, 41, 44

Billings, William, 80

Bill of Rights, 171

Binney, Capt. Amos, 192

Bird, Asa, 191

Blagge, John, 145

Blake, Increase, 40

Boardman, Thomas, 173

Boardman, Deacon William, 96, 145

Boit, John, 60, 62, 148

Boston, 134

Boston (in colonial and Revolutionary periods): arrival of British troops in, 66; crowd action in, 18–19, 43–44, 56–57, 63–64, 69–71; establishes Committee of Correspondence, 87; impact of war and royal policies on, 17–18, 21–25, 27, 31–32, 37–39; and nonimportation, 47, 48–49, 58–61, 62–63, 69–71, 73–75, 81, 82, 83–84, 98, 99, 100; opposition to royal salaries in, 86–87; origins of political caucuses in, 61–62; Pope's Day celebrations in, 17, 47, 74; and resistance to Coercive Acts, 97–100; siege and evacuation of, 110, 121, 123–24; and the Stamp Act, 40–53; and the Townshend Acts, 58–

60, 62, 64–66, 69–71, 81. *See also* Boston
  Massacre; Boston Tea Party
Boston (in the New Republic): celebrates
  peace, 148; debate over incorporation, 151–
  52, 170–71; debate over Madison's trade
  resolutions, 171–72
Boston Board of Health, 169, 192
Boston Chronicle, 69
Boston Committee of Correspondence: and
  Boston Tea Party, 92–95; employs Revere
  as courier, 95, 98, 100, 101, 228 n. 18,
  229 n. 25; and North End Caucus, 87–88,
  92–95; origins and members, 87; proposes
  Solemn League and Covenant, 99; supports independent postal system, 97
Boston Gazette: on Boston Massacre, 75, 79,
  85; on Boston Tea Party and Revere's ride
  to New York, 90, 95, 96; on colonial support for Boston, 98; on customs commissioners, 60; as forum of colonial resistance,
  48, 52; on *Liberty* riots, 63; on Newport
  expedition, 132; on James Otis's brawl in
  Royal Coffee House, 69; on post-war
  depression, 38; on Stamp Act, 44, 47, 48;
  supports John Hancock for governor, 150;
  supports independent postal system, 97;
  supports nonimportation, 73; supports
  refusal to rescind circular letter, 64; on trial
  of Thomas O. Selfridge, 190
Boston Grenadier Corps, 118
Boston Independent Company, 132
Boston Latin School, 13, 15, 181, 182
Boston Library Society, 15, 169, 194
Boston Massacre: background, 75–76; commemorations of, 85, 96; described, 76–77;
  patriot propaganda on, 77–80; Revere's
  diagram and engravings of, 78–80; trials, 83
Boston Mechanic Association, 173–75,
  265 n. 38. *See also* Massachusetts Charitable
  Mechanic Association
Boston Neck, 103, 111
Boston Port Act, 97–99. *See also* Coercive
  Acts
Boston Tea Party: background, 91–94;
  destruction of tea, 94–95; of March 1774,
  96; Revere spreads news of, 95. *See also*

Boston Committee of Correspondence;
  North End Caucus; St. Andrew's Lodge
Bouve, Gibbons, 84, 148
Bowdoin, James, 13, 153–54, 155, 156–57
Boyle, John: on Boston Massacre, 78; on
  Boston Port Act, 97; on fall of Quebec, 32;
  on *Liberty* riots, 63; on Newport expedi-
  tion, 130–31; on post-war depression, 38;
  on Revere carrying news of Boston Tea
  Party, 95; on Revolutionary War, 126; on
  Stamp Act protest, 43; on Townshend
  Acts, 58, 60
Brackett, Joshua, 16, 26, 36, 38, 68, 69
Braddock, Gen. Edward, 23–24
Bradford, Capt. Gamaliel, 163
Bradstreet, Gov. Simon, 9
Brattle, Thomas, 55
Brattle Square Church, 76
Brattle Street, 9, 76
Bray, George, 30
Bray, John, 173
Breck, Samuel, 152
Breed's Hill, 117
Brewer, Col. David, 121
Bridgewater, Mass., and cannon casting in
  Revolutionary War, 127
Broaders, Benjamin, 78
Brown, James, 137
Brown, Capt. (John), 101–2
Brown, Nicholas, 243 n. 26
Brown, Solomon, 103
Bruce, Stephen, 69, 93, 95
Buckingham, Joseph T., 174
Buckman's Tavern, 104
Bulfinch, Charles, 175
Bunker Hill, battle of, 116–17, 119
Burbeck, Henry, 113, 236 n. 16
Burbeck, John, 236 n. 16
Burbeck, Joseph, 236 n. 16
Burbeck, Thomas, 236 n. 16
Burbeck, William: charter member of St.
  Andrew's Lodge, 30; and criticism of
  Revere's command at Castle Island, 178;
  and dispute over St. Andrew's charter, 89–
  90; and establishment of Continental
  artillery regiment, 112, 113, 114, 120, 121,

Burbeck, William (*cont.*)
236 n. 16; opposes independence of Massa-
chusetts Grand Lodge, 147; prepares fire-
works to celebrate Stamp Act's repeal, 50;
and Revere's failure to obtain a Conti-
nental commission, 114
Burgoyne, Gen. John, 116, 130, 131
Burr, Aaron, 179, 188, 191
Bussey, Benjamin, 157–58, 255 n. 49
Butcher's Hall, 80
Bute, Lord (John Stuart), 43, 48, 50
Buttrick, Maj. John, 109
Butts, Samuel (Revere's apprentice), 205 n. 19
Byles, Rev. Dr. Mather, 128

Caldwell, James, 77
Cambridge, Mass.: Committe of Safety
meets in, 107; fieldpieces seized in, 99;
mandamus councillors resign in, 99
Canton, Mass., and Revere's copper mill, 178,
180, 184–85
"Cantondale" (Revere's poem), 193–94
Captain Cook's Voyage, and Revere's engrav-
ings for, 96
Carnes, Capt. Thomas Jenners, 136–38
Carr, Patrick, 77, 78, 79
Carson, Joseph, 192
Carter, James, 148
Castine, Maine, 135
Castle Island, 101, 112, 124, 126, 131, 132, 133,
136, 138
Castle William, 90, 94
Cato (servant and Boston Massacre witness), 78
Cato's Letters (Trenchard and Gordon), 66
Censor, The, 84
Chamberlain, Mellen, 78
Champney, Caleb, 62–63
Chardon, Peter, 86
Charles I, 17, 20, 23, 48
Charles II, 23
Charles River Bridge, 183
Charlestown, Mass.: and battle of Bunker
Hill, 116–17; gunpowder seized in, 99;
retreat of British troops to, 110; and
Revere's ride to Lexington, 102, 103
Charter Street, 179, 183

Chase, Thomas, 43, 45, 69, 93, 95
Chauncy, Dr. Charles, 100
Cheetham, James, 186
Cheever, Ezekiel, 93
Chesapeake-Leopard incident, 191
Christ Church, 11, 29, 103. *See also* Old North
Church
Church, Dr. Benjamin, 87, 89, 92; as traitor,
84, 115, 177; writes text for Revere's political
cartoon, 65
Clark, Dr. John, 7, 21
Clark, Rev. Jonas, 103
Clark, William, 10
Clarke, Richard, 92, 93
Clark-Frankland house, 10
Clark's Court, 179
Clark Street, 7
Clark's Wharf, 7, 9, 10, 11, 16, 26, 27, 68, 71
Clemens, Isasc, 123
Clermont, 192
Cleverly, Stephen, 43
Clinton, Gen. Henry, 116, 117, 133
Cobb, David, 173, 264 n. 36
Coburn, John, 26–27, 96
Cochran, Capt. Samuel, 26
Coercive Acts, 97, 100. *See also* Boston Port
Act; Quartering Act
Coffin, Capt., 55
Cole, Edward, 145
Collier, Sir George, 136
Collings, Capt. John, 16, 26
Collins, Ezra, 29, 60, 91
Colombier, Denis, 163
Colonies: attitude toward standing armies in,
23–25; education and social mobility in, 13–
15; impact of war and royal policies on, 17–
25, 27, 31–34, 37–39; interpretation of rights
and obligations of, 18–20, 23–25, 33–34;
social structure and mobility in, 9–15. *See
also* Revolution, American
Colson, Adam, 55, 63, 68, 69, 93, 95
Columbian Centinel (Boston): on death of
Joshua Revere, 181; defends Revere's honor
in trial of Thomas O. Selfridge, 190; as
Federalist newspaper, 172; on Republican
inroads into Freemasonry, 176

Commerce in post-war United States: artisans urge protection for American manufactures, 153; effect of British trade policies on, 149, 152–53; impact of currency shortage on, 152; merchants urge protection for import trade, 152–53; support for tighter congressional control over, 152–53, 154. *See also* Constitution (U.S.)

Committee of Correspondence (Massachusetts House of Representatives), 91

Committee of Correspondence, Safety, and Inspection, and Revere's role on, 124, 127–28

Committee of Inspection (1768–70), and nonimportation, 73

Committee of Merchants (1768–70), and nonimportation, 59

Committee of Merchants and Traders (1785), 152–54

Committee of Safety, 110, 115; established by Massachusetts Provincial Congress, 101; makes defense preparations, 102; orders fortifications at Bunker Hill, 116; and Revere's role as courier, 107, 110–11, 115; role of, in raising army and choosing officers, 111–13, 118

Committee of 63, and Revere's service on, 100, 101

Committee on Ways and Means, 99

Common Sense (Paine), 123–25

Conant, Col. (William), and arrangement of lantern signals for Revere's ride to Lexington, 102, 103

Concord, battle of: background, 107–8; British search for munitions, 108–9; confrontation at North Bridge, 109; retreat, 109. *See also* Lexington, battle of

Condy, James Foster, 93

Coney, John, 7, 8

Confederation period: commercial problems during, 148–49, 152–53, 154, concern over declining virtue and disorder in, 149, 155–56; defects of national government in, 155–56; impact of Shays's Rebellion in, 155–57. *See also* Constitution (U.S.)

Congress, U.S., and tariff legislation, 184

Connecticut, and support for Boston's resistance to Port Act, 98

Connecticut Courant, 156

Connor, Charles, 77

Constitution (U.S.): artisan support for, 156–58, 159; and bicameralism, 156; and democracy, 156; ratification in Massachusetts, 156–58; and republicanism, 156–57; as response to commercial problems, 156, 157; as response to Shays's Rebellion, 155–56; as response to state politics, 156; and Revere's support for, 157–58; and separation of powers, 156

Constitution, U.S.S., and Revere, 166, 183

Constitutional Society, 171

Continental Army: establishment of and choosing officers in, 111–14, 116, 118–22, 239 n. 33; and progress of Revolutionary War, 126, 130–31, 132–33, 134–36; republicanism and choice of officers in, 112; and Revere's failure to obtain a commission in, 112–15, 118–22, 235 n. 13

Continental Association, 100

Continental Congress, 110, 111, 117; adopts Continental Association, 100; approves Declaration and Resolves, 100; approves Declaration of Independence, 125; approves Suffolk Resolves, 100; and attitude toward militia, 129; chooses officers for Continental Army, 112, 116, 118–22; chooses George Washington commander of Continental Army, 116; directs Massachusetts to organize new government, 116; establishment of, 99; Revere's role as courier to, 98, 100

Cook, John, 115

Cooke, Elisha, Jr., 34

Cooper, Dr. Samuel, 61, 123

Cooper, William, and "Journal of Transactions in Boston," 66

Copley, John Singleton, 37, 38, 53–54, 93, 179

Cornhill, 76, 77

Cox, Susanna, 168

Cox (Edward) and Berry (John), merchants, 66–67

Crafts, Thomas, Jr.: and command of Massachusetts Artillery Regiment, 122, 128–33; on Committee of Correspondence, Safety, and Inspection, 127–28; and failure to obtain a Continental commission, 120–21; as Freemason, 29, 44, 67–68; political split with Revere after the Revolution, 172; reads Declaration of Independence in Boston, 126; as Son of Liberty, 43, 60, 99, 124

Crane, John, 113, 120, 132

Cromwell, Oliver, 23

Cromwell Head Tavern, 16

Crown Point, 22, 25

Cunningham, Capt. Peter, 152

Currency Act, 39

Cushing, Thomas, 49–50, 59, 91, 154

Customhouse, and Boston Massacre, 76, 77

Dalrymple, Lt. Col. William, 76

Dalton, Tristram, 61

Dana, Judge Richard, 36

Danbury, Conn., British burning of, 127, 128

Danforth, Dr. Samuel, 30, 84, 89, 96, 128, 188

Danforth, Judge Samuel, 99

Dartmouth, earl of (William Legge), 102

Dartmouth (tea ship), 93, 94

Dashwood, Capt. Samuel, 70

Davies, Sgt. Maj. William, 76

Davis, Amasa, 271 n. 15

Davis, Deacon Caleb, 127, 152

Davis, Edward, 70

Davis, Frederick William, 182

Davis, Capt. Isaac, 109

Davis, Matthew Livingston, 186, 188, 275 n. 31

Dawes, Thomas, 34

Dawes, William: ride to Lexington, 103, 104, 108, 232 n. 44; supports nonimportation, 59

Dearborn, Henry, 187

DeBerdt, Dennys, 59, 64

De Berniere, Ensign (Henry), 101–2

Debt, funding and assumption of state, 160, 170

Declaration and Resolves, 100

Declaration of Independence, 125–26, 142

Declaratory Act, 50, 51

DeFoe, Daniel, 11

DeFrance, George, 30

De Grey, William, 57

de Maresquelle, Louis, 127

Democracy, 128, 149–50, 151, 155–58, 164–65, 170–72, 185–87

Democratic-Republican Party. *See* Republican Party

Dennie, William, 87

Derby, Elias Hasket, 163

D'Estaing, Admiral Count, 132

Devens, Richard: on committee to gather depositions on battle of Lexington and Concord, 111; and Revere's ride to Lexington, 103

Dexter, Samuel, 190

Dexter, Thomas (Revere's great-great-grandfather), 9

Dickinson, John: "Letters from a Farmer in Pennsylvania," 63, 71; support for Boston's resistance to Coercive Acts, 98

Discourse Concerning Unlimited Submisson and Non-Resistance to the Higher Powers . . . (Mayhew), 20

Dock Square, 8, 76

Dorchester Heights, 111, 116, 121

Dorr, Harbottle, 41, 42, 59, 85, 100, 128; criticizes government, 83; documents "cruel treatment of the colonies," 71; encourages Stamp Act resistance, 41, 48; opposes royal salaries, 86; praises James Otis, 62; supports nonimportation, 83; on Tea Party of March 1774, 96

Dow, Levi, 190–91

Drowne, Deacon Shem, 8

Dulany, Daniel, 41–42

Dumaresq, Philip, 83, 84, 123

Dunkerly, Joseph, 30, 148

Dunlop, William, 133

Dyer, John (saddler), 145

Dyer, John (waxworks), 11

Eager (tavern keeper in Thomas O. Selfridge case), 189

East India Company, 90, 92, 93, 97

Eayres, Joseph, 274 n. 30

Eayres, Thomas Stevens (Revere's apprentice and son-in-law), 163, 188

Eayres, Thomas Stevens (grandson), 181

Edes, Benjamin, 45, 86, 115; and meeting to oppose royal salaries, 88; opposes Stamp Act, 43, 45, 48; opposes Tea Act, 93. *See also Boston Gazette;* Edes and Gill

Edes, Capt. Jonathan, 131

Edes (Benjamin) and Gill (John), publishers of *Boston Gazette:* and Boston Massacre, 78, 79, 80; and business relationship with Revere, 75, 79, 80, 81, 84, 222 n. 18. *See also Boston Gazette*

Edinburgh, University of, 15, 182

Eliot, Ephraim, 65

Eliot, Rev. John, and criticism of Paul Revere, 127–28

Embargo, and impact on Revere's business, 191–92

Emmons, Thomas, 84

Endecott, John, 9

Enlightenment, 29, 31, 82, 118

Erving, Capt. John, 71

Erving, John, Jr., 59

Essex Gazette, 94

Essex Street, 43

Eustis, William, 189, 264 n. 36

Eve, Oswell, 119

Fair Account of the Late Unhappy Disturbance at Boston (Tory version of Boston Massacre), 78, 220 n. 7

Faneuil, Andrew, 8

Faneuil, Peter, 8

Faneuil Hall, 8, 73, 93, 151, 153

Federalist Party: financial program of, 170, 172; and French Revolution, 170, 171, 172; as opposition party, 179–80, 185–87, 191, 192–193; policies and principles of, 156–58, 160, 170–72, 187

Federal Orrery, 169

Fellows, Capt. Nathaniel, 148

Field, Joseph, 43

First Lodge, 81

Flagg, Josiah, 29, 40

Flagg, Samuel, 167

Fleeming, John, 70

Fleet Street, 10, 181

Fletcher, Thomas, 41

Flucker, Thomas, 83

Forbes, Esther, 3, 53

Fort Carillon. *See* Fort Ticonderoga

Fort George, 135

Fort Oswego, 25

Fort Stanwix, 130

Fort Strong, 194

Fort Ticonderoga, 25, 120, 121, 130

Fort Washington, 126

Fort William and Mary, 101

Fort William Henry, 22, 113

Fosdick, Maj. Nathaniel, 162, 185

Fosdick, Nathaniel, 36, 76, 77, 78

Fosdick, Thomas, 36

Foster, John, 10

Fowles, Gunner Nathaniel, 129

Franco-American alliance, 131

Frankland, Sir Charles Henry, 10

Franklin, Benjamin: education and social mobility of, 12–13, 14, 82; on French and Indian War, 23–24; and Hutchinson letters, 91; and reorganization of Continental Army, 119

Franklin, Josiah, 12–13

Freeman's Farm, battle of, 131

Freemasonry: and American Revolution, 4, 31, 44–45, 46, 67–68, 93, 94, 95, 208 n. 33; and artisans, 29, 31; and deference, 4, 46, 53, 95, 114–15, 150–51; and Enlightenment, 29, 31; in the New Republic, 146–48, 175–76, 189, 193; origins and ideals, 4, 28–29, 31, 67–68; and republicanism, 4, 31, 175–76; schism between Ancient and Modern Masons, 29–30, 81–82, 113–14, 147, 175, 207 n. 26; and social mobility, 27–29, 30–31, 61, 67–68. *See also* Massachusetts Grand Lodge; Revere, Paul: Masonic Career; St. Andrew's Lodge

French, Jeremiah, 67

French and Indian War, and impact on colonies, 22–25, 113. *See also* Seven Years' War.

French Revolution: and impact on political parties, 170, 171, 172; Revere on, 185

Friendship Lodge, 30
Fulton, Robert, 192

Gage, Gen. Thomas, 83, 100; arrival of, in
    Boston, 97; and battles of Lexington and
    Concord, 108, 110, 111; orders Capt. Brown
    and Ensign De Berniere on scouting mis-
    sion, 101–2; plan to fortify Dorchester
    Heights and Bunker Hill, 116; receives
    orders for expedition to Lexington and
    Concord, 102; seizes gunpowder and field-
    pieces in Charlestown and Cambridge, 99
Gallatin, Albert, 184
Gardiner, J. S. J., 172
Gardiner, Dr. Silvester, 168
Garrick, Edward, 76
Gates, Gen. Horatio, 131
Genet, Edmund, 171
George III, 32, 50–51
Gerry, Elbridge: on Thomas Jefferson, 3; and
    Revere's failure to obtain federal appoint-
    ment, 161; Revere's ridicule of, 193; on
    Revere's role in designing gunpowder mill,
    119; urges Washington's appointment as
    commander of Continental Army, 116
Geyer, Frederick William, 152
Gill, John, 48, 86, 88. See also Boston Gazette;
    Edes and Gill
"Glorious Ninety-Two, The," 64–65
Glorious Revolution, 19
Glover, Brig. Gen. John, 132
Goddard, William, 97
Godfrey, Thomas, 14
Goldfinch, Capt. Lt., and Boston Massacre,
    76
Goldthwait, Ezekiel, 84
Goodwin, Capt. Joseph, 39, 55, 57
Gordon, Rev. William, 44, 107
Gore, Christopher, 186, 190, 191
Graham, James, 30, 148
Grand Lodge of England, 29–30, 67
Grand Lodge of Scotland, 29–30, 67, 82, 89,
    90, 147–48
Grand Turk, 163
Grant, Moses, 93
Graves, Admiral (Samuel), 111, 117

Gray, Francis, 134
Gray, John, and Gray's Ropewalks, 75–76,
    77
Gray, Samuel, 77
Gray, Thomas, 49–50
Gray, Capt. Winthrop, 133, 134
Green, Thomas, 38
Green, William, 75, 76
Green Dragon Tavern, 34, 90, 95, 101, 153, 157,
    173
Greene, Benjamin, 16, 26, 73
Greene, Gen. Nathaniel, 115, 132
Greene, Ned, 138
Greenleaf, Joseph, 87, 96
Greenleaf, Sheriff Stephen, 56, 93
Greenleaf, Thomas, 96
Greenough, Newman, 179
Greenwood, Isaac, 26, 78, 96
Gregory, John, 129
Grenville, George, 39, 47, 49, 50, 51
Gridley, Jeremiah, 29, 30, 112, 206 n. 23
Gridley, John, 69
Gridley, Richard, 22, 29, 206 n. 23; and battle
    of Bunker Hill, 117; and establishment of
    Continental artillery regiment, 112–14,
    119–20, 121, 236 n. 16; and Revere's failure
    to obtain a Continental commission, 113–
    14; skill as engineer, 112, 118, 121
Gridley, Samuel, 113, 119, 236 n. 16
Gridley, Scarborough, 113, 119, 236 n. 16
Griffin's Wharf, 94, 95
Griffith, Sgt. John, 129

Hacker's Island, 137
Hallowell, Benjamin, Jr.: as Freemason, 31;
    and Liberty riots, 63; and Daniel Malcolm,
    56, 57; Revere's confrontation with, 81
Hallowell, Robert, 31
Hamilton, Alexander, 161, 171, 186; financial
    program of, 160; and support for U.S.
    Constitution, 156
Hancock, John, 42, 108, 118, 132, 177; accused
    of violating nonimportation, 69; at Conti-
    nental Congress, 100; as governor, 150, 152,
    153–54; inherits uncle's fortune, 12; member
    of Committee of Merchants and Traders,

152; as patriot leader, 49–50, 68, 92, 96; in quiet years, 84; and Revere, 138, 154; Revere's engraving of, 96; and Revere's ride to Lexington, 102, 103, 104; seizure of sloop *Liberty*, 63; and St. Andrew's Lodge, 29; and U.S. Constitution, 157, 158

Hancock, Lydia (Henchman), 12

Hancock, Thomas, 11–12, 18

Hanover Street, 10, 179

Harrison, Joseph, 64

Harrison, Thomas, 132

Hartt, Edmund, 163, 166, 167, 173

Harvard College, 15, 182

Hayes, Moses Michael, 143

Hazard, Ebenezer, 164

Heath, William, 110, 131, 138

Heininburge, Countess of, 11

Henchman, Daniel, 12

Henry, Patrick, 41

Heywood, Benjamin, 167

Hichborn, Benjamin (cousin): comparison with Revere, 9, 114, 119; and Newport expedition, 132; as Republican, 185; and Shays's Rebellion, 155; solicits federal appointment for nephew, 162, 185; supports Revere's business, 146, 163

Hichborn, Frances (cousin), 36

Hichborn, Nathaniel (cousin), 26, 29, 71

Hichborn, Robert (cousin), 26, 93, 148

Hichborn, Samuel (cousin), and Revere's foundry, 163

Hichborn, Thomas (grandfather), 9

Hichborn, Thomas, Sr. (uncle), 16, 26, 69

Hichborn, Thomas, Jr. (cousin), 26, 38, 69

Hichborn, William (cousin), 26, 38

Hichborn Family, 9

Hichborn Wharf, 9

Hicks, Zachariah, 145, 173

Higginson, Stephen, 155, 180

Hill, Deacon Thomas, 37, 38, 40

Hiller's (Mrs.), waxworks, 11

Hillsborough, Lord (Wills Hill), 80

Hillsborough paint, 74

Hinckley, Capt. John, 141

Hobart, Aaron, 167

Honestus (Benjamin Austin Jr.), 154

Hooper, Robert "King," 61, 66–67

Hopkins, Capt. Caleb, 30, 37, 38, 42, 57, 67

Hosmer, Pvt. Abner, 109

Howard, Robert, 10, 71

Howe, Admiral Lord Richard, 133

Howe, Gen. William, 116, 117, 121, 123

Hubbart, Tuthill, 78

Hudson, Capt. Joseph, 84

Hughes, Hugh, 82, 87, 170

Huguenots, in Boston, 7–8

Hulton, Henry: allege criticism of James Otis, 69; Revere's confrontation with, 81

Humphreys, Joshua, 178, 179

Hunting, John, 179

Hurd, Nathaniel, 21, 26

Huske, John, 47, 48

Hutchinson, Elisha, 73, 91

Hutchinson, Foster, 56, 123

Hutchinson, Col. Thomas, 13

Hutchinson, Gov. Thomas, 10, 13, 66, 71, 159, 182; appointed governor, 83; and Boston Massacre, 77, 83; and Boston Tea Party, 93, 94; as enemy of the people, 19–20, 32–34; leaves Boston, 98; letters to Thomas Whately, 91; on *Liberty* riots, 63–64; and nonimportation, 73; in quiet years, 84; and Stamp Act, 42–44; supports royal salaries, 87; upholds writs of assistance, 32–34

Hutchinson, Thomas, Jr., 73, 91

Hutchinson house, 10

Independent Cadets, 9

Independent Chronicle (Boston), as Republican newspaper, 171, 172, 189, 190–91

Independent School (Lexington, Mass.), and John Revere, 182

Industry, 163

Ingersoll, Lt. Daniel, 131

Ingram, Capt. 70

Intolerable Acts. *See* Coercive Acts

Irvin, Capt., 115

Jackson, Henry, 128–29, 132, 162

Jackson, Dr. James, 182

Jackson, James, 30, 147

Jackson, Richard, 42
Jackson, William, 74
Jacobin Club, 171
James II, 23
Jarvis, Dr. Charles, 172
Jay's Treaty, 172
Jefferson, Thomas, 3, 142, 161, 162, 165; and
creation of Republican Party, 170, 171; and
Declaration of Independence, 125–26; and
election of 1800, 179; and embargo, 183;
presidency of, 185–86, 191–92; Revere's dis-
like of, 176, 185–88, 193
Jefferson Medical College (Philadelphia),
and Dr. John Revere, 182
Johonnot, Peter, 84, 123
Johonnot, Zacariah, 37, 40, 55, 84
Jones, John Coffin, 152, 162
"Journal of Transactions in Boston"
(Cooper), 66
Joy, John, 75, 84, 96
"Joyce, Jr.," 152
Juteau, John, 147

Kast, Dr. Philip Godfrid, 39, 40, 84, 89, 128,
141
Keith, Col. Israel, 138
Kilroy, Pvt. Matthew, 77, 83
King George's War, 17–18, 21
King's Chapel, 9
King Street, 69, 70, 76, 77, 78, 126
Kinsley, Adam, 178, 184–85
Knowles, Commo. Charles, 18–19
Knox, Henry, 14, 96, 115, 128; and Boston
Massacre, 77, 78; military career of, 118, 121,
126; organization of Continental artillery
regiment, 114, 118, 119–21; and Revere's
failure to obtain a Continental commis-
sion, 120; and Revere's failure to obtain a
federal appointment, 161–62; on Shays's
Rebellion, 155–56
Knox, Thomas, 74

Lamb, John: as Anti-Federalist, 170; as federal officeholder, 161; military career of, 115,
122, 204 n. 12; as Son of Liberty, 96, 97, 99,
100, 101

Larkin, Deacon (John), and Revere's ride to
Lexington, 103
Larrey, Baron Dominique Jean, and Dr. John
Revere's translation of his surgical essays,
182
Laurie, Capt. (Walter), 109
Lee, Maj. Gen. Charles, 118
Lee, Eben, 178
Lee, Joseph, 99
Leonard, Jonathan, 178, 184–85
Leslie, Col. (Alexander), 101
Letsome, Dr., 166
"Letters from a Farmer in Pennsylvania"
(Dickinson), 63
Lexington, battle of: confrontations at Lex-
ington green, 104–5, 107–8; retreat to
Boston, 110; and Revere's ride, 102, 103,
104. See also Concord, battle of
Liberty (sloop), riots, 63–64
Liberty Bowl, 64–65
"Liberty Song, The," 63, 68
Liberty Tree, 43, 48, 50, 70, 75, 83, 123, 212 n. 17
Liberty Tree dinner, 68–69
Life of the Very Reverend and Learned Cotton
Mather, The (Mather), 8
Lillie, Theophilus, 73, 74
Lincoln, Amos (son-in-law), 146, 148, 162–
63, 173, 175, 181, 249 n. 14
Lincoln, Benjamin, 165, 185; as gubernatorial
candidate, 154, 159; role in Revere's failure
to obtain a federal appointment, 161–62,
259 n. 11; and Shays's Rebellion, 155
Lincoln, Jedediah (son-in-law), 173, 181, 188
Lincoln, Levi, 180, 185
Livingston, Robert R., 192
Locke, John, 82
Longfellow, Henry Wadsworth, 1, 4–5, 102–
3, 195
Long Island, battle of, 126
Loudoun, John Campbell, fourth earl of, 24–
25
Louis XVI, 171
Louisburg, 12, 17, 18, 112
Love Lane, 7
Lovell, Gen. Solomon, 132, 135–38
Lowell, John, 92, 147

Loyal Nine: expands into Sons of Liberty, 47; Revere's connections to, 44–45; and Stamp Act protests, 43, 45, 47–48

Lucas, John, 157, 170

Lynn Street, 163, 183

McAlpine, William, 123

McIntosh, Ebenezer, 43–44, 45, 47, 48, 53, 59

Mackay, Capt. Mungo, 141

Mackay, Capt. William, 56, 64

McLean, Brig. Gen. Francis, 135

McNeil, Capt., 77

MacNeil's Ropewalks, 75

Madison, James: and creation of Republican Party, 170, 171–72; Revere's dislike of, 191–93; and U.S. Constitution, 156

Magabagaduce (Bagaduce) Peninsula, 135

Magna Charta, 49

Malcolm, Capt. Daniel, 56–57, 64, 74

Manufactures, Hamilton's Report on, 160

Marett, Phillip (cousin), 131, 137, 141, 244 n. 32

Marshall, Lt. Col. Thomas, 70, 76, 78, 124

Marston, Lt. John, 133, 138

Marston, Manasseh, 148

Maryland Institute, and Dr. John Revere, 182

Maryland Medical Recorder, and Dr. John Revere, 182

Mason, David, 113, 114, 120

Mason, George, 69

Mason, Jonathan, 70, 78

Masonry. *See* Freemasonry

Massachusetts: and nonimportation, 58–61, 81, 82, 83–84; opposition to Thomas Hutchinson in, 19–20, 32–34, 91; opposition to royal salaries in, 86–87; opposition to Tea Act in, 92–95; opposition to Townshend Acts in, 58–62, 64–66; in quiet years, 83, 84–88; ratification of U.S. Constitution and Revere's role in, 156–58; resistance to Coercive Acts, 97–102; and Seven Years' War, 22–25, 27, 31, 32, 37–39. *See also* Massachusetts Board of War; Massachusetts council; Massachusetts General Court

Massachusetts Artillery Regiment, 121–22; duties at Castle Island, 126, 128–30; escorts

prisoners captured at Bennington, 130; Newport expeditions, 130–31, 132–33; Penobscot expedition, 134–39; problems of, 129–34; seizure of *Minerva*, 133. *See also* Massachusetts council; Massachusetts General Court

Massachusetts Board of War: asks Revere to cast cannon, 127; confines Tory Dr. Mather Byles to home, 128; and state artillery regiment, 131

Massachusetts Centinel (Boston): on effects of post-war British trade policies, 152; support for incorporation of Boston, 151

Massachusetts Charitable Fire Society, 169

Massachusetts Charitable Mechanic Association, 173–75, 181, 265 n. 38. *See also* Boston Mechanic Association

Massachusetts Constitution: and John Adams, 149–50; aristocracy in, 150; and balanced government, 149–50; bicameralism in, 149; bill of rights in, 150; democracy in, 149–50; divisions over, 149–50; and representation, 149–50; and republicanism, 149–50

Massachusetts council: and Massachusetts Artillery Regiment, 131, 133–35; and Penobscot expedition, 136–39

Massachusetts General Court: controversy over convening outside Boston, 84; forms Committee of Correspondence, 91; impeaches Chief Justice Peter Oliver, 99; issues circular letter opposing Townshend Acts, 58–59, 64–65; and Massachusetts Artillery Regiment, 131, 133–35; passes price-fixing act during Revolutionary War, 130; passes resolution approving Continental Congress, 99; publishes Hutchinson letters, 91; supports President Adams's defense measures, 178

Massachusetts Government Act, 97. *See also* Coercive Acts

Massachusetts Grand Lodge: and dispute over St. Andrew's charter, 89–90; establishment of, 67; and independence from Grand Lodge of Scotland, 146–48, 250 n. 20; and investigation of Rising

Massachusetts Grand Lodge (*cont.*)
States Lodge, 193; Revere's offices in, 67, 86, 126–27, 146–48, 175; Revere's role in uniting Masons in new Grand Lodge, 175; as source of Revere's business, 30; supports President Adams's defense measures, 178. *See also* Freemasonry; Revere, Paul: Masonic Career; St. Andrew's Lodge

Massachusetts Historical Society, 177

Massachusetts House of Representatives. *See* Massachusetts General Court

Massachusetts Humane Society, 169

Massachusetts Magazine, 169

Massachusetts Mutual Fire Insurance Company, 169

Massachusetts Provincial Congress: creation of, 100; establishes Committee of Safety, 101; organizes government and defense, 101, 102; publicizes patriot version of battles of Lexington and Concord, 111; raises army and chooses officers, 111–13; Revere's work designing gunpowder mill for, 119; Revere's work engraving currency for, 115–16

Massachusetts Spy, 84, 96

Massachusetts Supreme Judicial Court, 184

Master's Lodge, 112

Matchett, John, 74

Mather, Cotton, 8, 12

Mather, Samuel, *Life of the Very Reverend and Learned Cotton Mather*, 8

Maverick, Samuel, 76, 77

May, Mehitable, 59

Mayhew, Dr. Jonathan, 20, 56, 123

Mechanics. *See* Artisans

Medical Society of Maryland, and Dr. John Revere, 182

Mein, John, 63, 69–71, 76, 78

Meinzies, Capt. Lt. John, 131

Meridian Lodge, 176

Metcalf, Matthew (Revere's apprentice), 205 n. 19

Metcalf, Stephen, 141, 255 n. 49

Minerva, 133

Minott, Samuel, 26

Mitchell, Major (Edward), 104

Modern Lodge, 81

Molesworth, Ponsonby, 67

Molineux, William, 81, 87; and attack on John Mein, 70; confrontation with customs commissioners, 91; on *Liberty* riots, 64; supports nonimportation, 73

Montcalm, Marquis de (Louis Joseph), 32, 112

Montesquieu, 82

Montgomery, Pvt. Hugh, 83

Montreal, surrender of, 32

Morgan, Daniel, 131

Morris, Robert, and letter of introduction for Revere, 119

Morristown, N.J., Washington's winter headquarters, 126

Morse, Rev. Jedediah, 176

Morton, Eleazer, 191

Morton, Perez, 143, 146, 147, 170, 172, 181

Moseley, David (apprentice and brother-in-law), 173

Munroe, Sgt. William, and Revere's ride to Lexington, 103

Murray's Barracks, 76

Narrative of the Excursion and Ravages of the King's Troops . . . , 111

National Mint, 161

Nautilus Island, 135

Neoclassical style, and Revere's mastery of, 143

New Brick Church, 7, 8, 9, 27, 68, 71, 158

Newburyport, Mass., and support for nonimportation, 98

Newell, Thomas, 99

Newell, Timothy, 123

New England Psalm-Singer (Billings and Revere), 80

Newhall, Increase, 244 n. 32

Newman, Robert, 103, 232 n. 40

New North Church, 8, 127

Newport (R.I.) expeditions, 130–31, 132–33

New York: Assembly's defiance of Quartering Act, 58; British capture of, 126; opposition to Tea Act and support for Boston Tea Party, 91–92, 95, 98

New York University, and Dr. John Revere, 182

Nichols, Peleg, 137

Noddle's Island, 194

Nonimportation: of 1765–66, 47, 48–49; of 1768–70, 58–61, 62–63, 69–71, 81, 82, 83–84; of 1774–75, 98, 99, 100

Norcutt, William, 243 n. 26

North, Lord (Frederick), 97

North Bridge (Concord, Mass.), 107, 109

North End, 7–8, 9–11, 179

North End Caucus, 71, 74, 76, 77, 78, 148, 151; and Boston Committee of Correspondence, 87–88, 92–95; and Boston Massacre commemorations, 85–86; and Boston Tea Party, 92–95; and Committee of Correspondence, Safety, and Inspection, 124, 241 n. 5; and nonimportation, 59–60, 62; origins and members, 34–35, 42, 61–63, 87; and Revere, 34–35, 92–95; as source of Revere's customers, 57, 84, 146; and St. Andrew's Lodge, 31

North Square, 71, 73–74, 121, 123, 179

North Street, 7

North Writing School, 7, 13, 14, 15

Old Brick Church, 76

Old Brick Meetinghouse, 124

Old Granary Burying Ground, 75, 78, 91

Old North Church, 102. See also Christ Church

Old North Meeting House, 71, 123

Old South Meeting House, 93, 96, 123, 148

Old West Church, 20, 123

Oliver, Andrew, 42–43, 47–48, 83

Oliver, Peter, 99

Oliver, Thomas, 99

Orange Street, 43

Oriskany, battle of, 130

Orr, Col. Hugh, 127

Otis, Harrison Gray, 169, 176, 186; and Revere's failure to obtain a federal appointment, 161; and trial of Thomas O. Selfridge, 190

Otis, James, Sr., 32

Otis, James, Jr., 61, 82–83, 118, 125, 151; and brawl at Royal Coffee House, 69; as patriot leader, 35, 48, 49–50, 62, 68, 87–88; in quiet years, 84; and Revere, 29, 88;

Rights of the British Colonies Asserted and Proved, 39–40; and Stamp Act crisis, 43; and writs of assistance, 33–34, 64–65

Otis, Samuel Allyne, 152, 160–61

Paddock, Adino, and Paddock's Company, 113, 132

Page, John, 169

Paine, Robert Treat, 191

Paine, Thomas, author of Common Sense and framer of Pennsylvania government, 123–24, 125

Paine, Dr. William, 89

Palfrey, William, 57, 65, 74, 83, 94, 147

Palmer, Joseph Pierce, 96

Palmes, Richard, 77, 78

Parker, Judge Isaac, 190

Parker, Capt. John, 104, 108

Parsons, Capt. (Lawrence), 109

Parsons, Theophilus, 149–50, 190

Parsons, William, 14

Parties, political, development of, 170–72. See also Federalist Party; Republican Party

Patronage, in Washington administration, 161–62, 258 n. 7, 258 n. 8

Patterson, Robert, 77, 78

Paul Revere and Son, 181, 183, 184, 192

Paxton, Charles, 66

Payne, Edward, 44, 59, 78, 152

Peck, Samuel, 93

Pelham, Henry, 80, 222 n. 17

Penobscot expedition, 134–39, 158, 195

Percy, Hugh, Earl, 109–10

Perkins, James, 271 n. 15

Perkins, Thomas Handasyd, 190, 271 n. 15

Perkins, William, 113

Philadelphia, opposition to Tea Act and support for Boston Tea Party, 91–92, 95, 98

Phillips, Nathan, 94

Phillips, Capt. Turner, 131

Phillips, William, 86

Piemont, John, 76

Pitcairn, Maj. John, 108–10

Pitt, William (Lord Chatham): on colonial resistance, 58; denies Parliament's right to tax colonies, 50, 51; and Seven Years' War, 31

Plains of Abraham, 32, 111

Plymouth (Mass.) Committee of Correspondence, and opposition to royal salaries, 87

Point Shirley Works, Winthrop, Mass. (Revere Copper), 182

Pond, Eliphalet, 89

Pope, Robert, 141

Pope's Day, 17, 47, 74

Prescott, Dr. Samuel, and ride to Concord, 103, 104, 108

Prescott, Col. William, 116, 117

Preston, Capt. Thomas, 77, 80, 83

Price, Ezekiel, 124

Princeton, battle of, 126

Proctor, Edward: as Revere's Masonic brother and customer, 40, 67, 84, 94, 147; as Son of Liberty, 53, 69, 74, 84, 93, 95

Providence (Continental frigate), 134

Providence (sloop), 134

Pulling, John, 103, 232 n. 40

Pulling, Richard, 30

Putnam, Col. Israel, 114, 117

Putnam, Lt. Col. Rufus, 118, 121

Pym, John, 48

Quarry-Hill (Charlestown), 99

Quartering Act: of 1765, 58; of 1774, 97

Quasi-War, 174, 177–78

Quebec, fall of, 31–32

Quebec Act, 97

Quiet Years, 83, 84–88

Quincy, Edmund, Sr. (IV), 29, 60–61, 206 n. 23

Quincy, Edmund, Jr., 29, 206 n. 23

Quincy, Josiah, 60, 73, 83, 84, 87, 99

Quincy, Rev. Samuel, 29, 206 n. 23

"Rallying Song of the Tea Party at the Green Dragon," 36, 95

Ramsden, Ann, 168–69

Ramsden, Capt. Thomas, 3, 168–69, 182, 185

Ramsden, Thomas (nephew of Capt. Thomas Ramsden), 168–69

Remick, Christian, 80

Republicanism, 1–4, 81, 82, 97, 112, 129–30, 149, 161, 168–76; artisans and, 2, 4, 31, 53, 57;

Freemasonry and, 4, 31, 175–76; and Massachusetts Constitution, 149–50; opposing interpretations of, 3, 149–50, 151–52, 156–58, 170–76, 179–80, 185–88; and U.S. Constitution, 156–57. *See also* Artisans; Federalist Party; Republican Party; Revere, Paul: Beliefs and Personality

Republican Party: artisan support for, 186; and election of 1800, 179–80; and French Revolution, 170, 171; and Jefferson administration, 185–86, 191–92; in New York, 186; and opposition to Hamilton's financial program, 171–72; policies and principles of, 170–72, 185–87. *See also* Jefferson, Thomas

Revere, Deborah Hichborn (mother), 7, 9, 21, 91, 128

Revere, Deborah (daughter), 25, 91, 128, 162–63, 249 n. 14

Revere, Elizabeth (sister), 173

Revere, Elizabeth (daughter), 83, 223 n. 26, 249 n. 14

Revere, Frances (daughter), 55, 163, 188, 214 n. 1

Revere, Harriet, 15, 126, 163, 241 n. 11

Revere, Isanna (daughter), 89, 91

Revere, John (son), 124, 241 n. 6

Revere, John (son): birth of, 260 n. 13; education of, 15, 163; medical career of, 163, 182, 270 n. 13

Revere, Joseph Warren (son), 128, 192; birth of, 117, 241 n. 11; career of, 181–82, 183, 270 n. 12; education of, 15, 163; named in memory of Dr. Joseph Warren, 117

Revere, Joshua (son), 128; birth of, 101, 231 n. 34; death of, 181; education and accomplishments, 15, 163, 181

Revere, Lucy (daughter), 126, 241 n. 11

Revere, Maria (daughter), birth of, 260 n. 13; education of, 15, 163

Revere, Mary (daughter), 214 n. 1

Revere, Mary (daughter), 223 n. 26

Revere, Paul, Sr. *See* Apollos Rivoire

Revere, Paul

    BELIEFS AND PERSONALITY: ambition, 2–3, 4–5, 15, 30–31, 42, 61, 67–68, 80, 114–16, 122, 128, 129, 133–39, 145, 160–61,

164–67, 186–87, 196–97; artisanal culture, 2, 4, 5, 35–36, 42, 45, 62–63, 159–
60, 170–75; benevolence, 3, 4, 28, 31,
35, 61, 68, 80, 168–69, 174–75, 187–89,
194–95; boldness and ingenuity, 36, 54,
104, 114, 161, 195; deference and hierarchy, 4, 32, 46, 53, 62, 95, 114–15, 118,
122, 150–51, 153, 160, 173–74, 187; democracy, 3, 157–58, 170–72, 185–88, 189; education, 13–15, 32, 53, 82–83, 150–51, 160,
163, 165–66, 169, 174–75, 181, 182, 193–
94; Enlightenment ideals, 28–29, 31, 53,
82, 174–75; equality, 2, 3, 4, 5, 61, 164–
66, 185–87; Federalist Party, 3, 156–58,
160, 170–74, 187, 191–93; Freemasonry,
4, 27–29, 30–31, 35–36, 46, 53, 61, 80, 95,
117–18, 122, 150–51, 175–76, 189; gentility, 15, 29, 30–31, 46, 61, 68, 139, 145,
163, 181–82; honor, 2–3, 31, 35–36, 46,
61, 68, 80, 112, 115–16, 118, 129–30, 134–
39, 157–58, 167–69, 175, 190–91; liberty,
2, 3–4, 5, 42, 62–63, 64–65, 85, 99–100,
185; philosophy of life, 193–94; republicanism, 1–5, 31, 53, 115–16, 122, 127–28,
129–30, 138–39, 149, 150–51, 157–58, 160,
164, 168–76, 185–89, 192–93, 194–96;
virtue, 2–3, 28–29, 31, 35, 36, 46, 59, 60,
61, 80, 115–16, 118, 129–30, 138, 149, 153,
160, 164, 173–74, 189, 195, 196
EARLY LIFE: apprenticeship, 15–16; attendance at Dr. Mayhew's sermon, 20;
birth, 7; education, 13–15; English
ancestry, 9; Huguenot ancestry, 3–4, 7–
9; impact of father's death, 21; impact
of political events, 17–22; residence in
North End, 7–11; service in French and
Indian War, 22–25; social class and
mobility, 9–15
MARRIAGE AND HOME: marriage to and
death of Sara Orne Revere, 25, 90–91;
marriage to and death of Rachel
Walker Revere, 92, 194; residences during marriage, 25, 71, 179, 269 n. 5. See
also entries for Revere's children
MASONIC CAREER: appeal of Freemasonry,
4, 27–29, 30–31; benefits to business, 30,

39, 40, 57, 146; Freemasonry and Revo-
lutionary activity, 4, 31, 36, 44–45, 46,
53, 59–60, 67–68, 89–90, 93, 94, 95;
Freemasonry and social mobility, 27–
29, 30–31, 37, 61, 67–68, 86, 126–27; in
Massachusetts Grand Lodge, 67, 86,
126–27, 146–48, 175; participation in
Masonic disputes, 89–90, 146–48; in
Rising States Lodge, 148, 193; as a
Royal Arch Mason, 67; in St. Andrew's
Lodge, 27, 37, 46, 67, 83, 86, 89–90, 114,
126, 146–48; strengthens ties to artisans,
28, 29; term as Grand Master, 175; and
Tyrian Lodge, 86; withdraws from
Freemasonry, 193, 277 n. 46. See also
Freemasonry; Massachusetts Grand
Lodge; St. Andrew's Lodge
MASTER ARTISAN: business with fellow
silversmiths, 26–27; connection between business and politics, 57, 63, 66–
67, 83–84, 89, 96; customers and range
of work, 16–17, 26–27, 37, 38–39, 40–41,
60–61, 81, 83–84, 95–96; dentistry, 16,
60, 61, 75, 80–81, 83, 96; description of
goldsmith's trade, 15–17; economic fluctuations of business, 16, 35, 37, 40–41,
55, 57, 60–61, 66–67, 75, 83–84, 89,
209 n. 44, 220 n. 6, 225 n. 1; engraving,
16, 30, 37, 40–41, 63, 75, 80, 83–84, 96;
establishes silver shop, 25–27; Masonic
customers, 30, 40; mastery of rococo
style, 16, 27; social class and mobility
of, 2, 9–11, 15–17, 35–36, 45–46. See
also Revolutionary Activity: political
cartoons
MERCHANT: conflict with republican
principles, 153, 164, 257 n. 54; connection
between silver and hardware customers,
146; customers and products, 146; dual
identity as artisan/merchant, 141, 143,
145–46, 151–53, 257 n. 54; opens hardware store, 146; problems affecting
business, 145, 152; social status as, 151–53;
transition to manufacturer, 158, 257 n. 54
POST-REVOLUTIONARY SILVER SHOP:
artistic achievements of, 143, 158, 163;

commemorative commissions, 163, 164; engraving, 145; market innovations, 143–45; mastery of neoclassical style, 143; and new elite market, 143–44; and pre-Revolutionary customers, 141, 143, 145; producing saddle parts and harness fittings, 145; resumes business, 141, 143; role of Paul Revere Jr. in, 145; silver for personal use, 163; technological improvements, 143, 145; and upward mobility, 141, 143–45, 163, 179

REVERE'S BELL AND CANNON FOUNDRY: appeal of Hamilton's financial program for, 160; begins foundry operation, 158, 163–64, 257 n. 54, 260 n. 16; bells, 163, 164, 165, 167–68, 183; cast iron goods, 163, 164, 183; exclusive privilege to manufacture iron, 154; ordnance and ship fittings, 163, 164, 166–67, 178, 183; Quasi-War, and impact on business, 178; and republicanism, 158, 164, 173–75, 257 n. 54; reputation as metallurgist, 163–68; and upward mobility, 164–66; work on U.S.S. *Constitution*, 166

REVERE'S COPPER MILL: combines copper and foundry operations in Canton, 183; customers and products, 182–83, 192, 271 n. 15; employees at, 187; establishment of, 176, 178, 180–81; and Fulton's steamboats, 192; impact of embargo policies on, 183, 191–92; and legal disputes, 184–85, 272 n. 18, 272 n. 19; profitability of, 182–83, 191–92; retirement from, 182, 192, 193–94; role of Joseph Warren Revere in, 181–82, 183; sheathing for dome of State House, 183; shortage of raw copper for, 183–84; and United States government, 176, 178, 180–81, 183, 192; work on U.S.S. *Constitution*, 183

REVOLUTIONARY ACTIVITY: appeal of Revolutionary ideology, 2, 42, 61–63; assets as artisan leader, 16, 35–36, 53–54, 61–62; Boston Massacre commemoration, diagram, and engravings, 78–80, 85, 225 n. 17; economic condition as motive for, 38–39, 40–41, 42; emergence during Stamp Act crisis, 40–50, 53–54; and Freemasonry, 31, 36, 45, 46, 53, 67–68, 93, 94, 95; impact of Seven Years' War on, 25, 31–34, 37–39; Liberty Tree dinner, 68–69; makes Liberty Bowl, 64–65; in North End Caucus, 34, 92–95; participation in crowd action, 56–57, 81, 91; petitions, 85–86, 99; political cartoons and tableaux, 48, 49, 50, 65, 80, 85, 96; refusal to serve as grand juror, 99; role in Boston Tea Party, 92–95, 96, 228 n. 18; and social mobility, 61–62, 67–68, 81–83, 87, 88, 92–95, 98, 100, 101; supports independent postal system, 97; supports nonimportation, 59–60, 100; writings on American Revolution, 96–97, 99–100, 102–5, 107, 111, 115, 142–43

RIDES FOR BOSTON COMMITTEE OF CORRESPONDENCE: carries news of the Boston Tea Party to New York, 95, 228 n. 18; carries proposal for nonimportation and copy of Boston Port Act south to Philadelphia, 98, 229 n. 25; carries Suffolk Resolves to Congress, 100; reputation as express rider, 101; rides to New York and Philadelphia (September 30, 1774) with news of patriotic spirit in Boston, 100; rides express to Portsmouth, N.H., 101; rides express to Exeter, N.H., 101

RIDE TO LEXINGTON: accounts of, by Revere, 102–5, 107, 111, 177, 231 n. 36, 233 n. 1, 267 n. 1; arranges lantern signals, 102; earlier ride to Lexington, 102; immortalized by Henry Wadsworth Longfellow, 1, 102–3, 195–96, 278 n. 50; intelligence gathering by Revere, 101–2; lands in Charlestown and borrows horse, 103; reaches Lexington, 103; rides toward Concord, 103; role of William Dawes, 103–4; role of Dr. Samuel Prescott, 103–4; seized by British and released in Lexington, 104; witness to opening shots at Lexington, 104–5, 107

SERVICE IN THE REVOLUTIONARY WAR: appointed militia officer, 121–22; casts cannon, 127; courier for Committee of Safety, 107, 110–11, 115; designs gunpowder mill, 119, 238 n. 32; engraves currency, 115–16, 127, 237 n. 23; escorts prisoners captured at Bennington, 130; failure to obtain Continental commission, 112–15, 118–22, 235 n. 13; impact of Dr. Warren's death, 117–18; monitors Tory activity on Committee of Correspondence, Safety, and Inspection, 124, 127–28; Nantasket expedition, 125; Newport expeditions, 130–31, 132–33; Penobscot expedition, court-martial, and vindication, 134–39; problems in state artillery regiment, 128–34; promoted to commander of regiment, 133–34; repairs cannon at Castle Island, 124; seizure of *Minerva*, 133; social mobility, limits of, 112–14, 119–21, 127–28, 129–30; town offices, 124, 126

"USEFUL CITIZEN" OF THE NEW REPUBLIC: artisan leader, 157–58, 170–71, 173–75; Association of Tradesmen and Manufacturers, 159; benefactor and friend, 168–69, 188–89, 194–95; business and the public good, 158, 164, 178; concern over Jeffersonian democracy and future of republicanism, 149, 157–58, 170–74, 176, 184–89, 192–93; contemporary views of Revere, 168–69, 190, 194–95, 196; death of, 194; failure to obtain federal patronage appointment, 160–62; Massachusetts Charitable Fire Society, 169; Massachusetts Charitable Mechanic Association, 173–75, 265 n. 38; Massachusetts Humane Society, 169; Massachusetts Mutual Fire Insurance Company, 169; New Brick Church, 158, 167; president, Boston Board of Health, 169; Selfridge trial, 189–91, 276 n. 37; social status and mobility, 160–63, 179, 181–83; Suffolk County coroner, 169; supports incorporation of Boston, 170–71; supports U.S. Constitution and Federalists, 150–51, 157–58, 160, 170–74, 187, 191; town committees, 158, 169, 170–71, 263 n. 29; view on slavery, 168; volunteers to build fort during War of 1812, 194

Revere, Paul, Jr.: birth of, 210 n. 1; death of, 194; life and career of, 181; remained in Boston during siege, 115, 123; role in father's business, 145, 163

Revere, Paul, III (grandson), 181

Revere, Rachel Walker (wife), 92, 101, 115, 126, 128, 132, 181, 194

Revere, Sarah (daughter), 128, 210 n. 1

Revere, Sara Orne (wife), 25, 90–91

Revere, Thomas (apprentice and brother), 21, 25

Revere (Mass., Minn., Mo., and Pa.), 278 n. 50

Revolution, American: artisans and, 2, 35–36, 40–46, 47–48, 53, 59–64, 68–69, 81, 82, 87–88, 95; economic conditions leading to, 37–39, 40–41, 42, 45–46, 57; Parliamentary sovereignty, 33, 39–40, 46–47, 51, 100; representation and taxation, 39–40, 41–43, 46–47, 50–51, 58, 66; republicanism, 2, 4, 31, 82, 96–97, 112, 115–16, 129–30; rights and liberties, 42, 47, 58, 66, 86–87, 90, 92, 126; Seven Years' War and, 37–39. *See also* Parliament acts and events of period

Rhode Island, and support for Boston's resistance to Port Act, 98

Richardson, Ebenezer, 74–75, 77

Rickard, William, 161–62

Rights of the British Colonies Asserted and Proved (Otis), 39–40

Riocaud, France, 7

Riordan, Capt. John, 84, 94, 96

Rising States Lodge: creation of, 148; dissolution of, 193

Rittenhouse, David, 14, 161

Rivington, James, 96

Rivoire, Apollos (father), 7–9, 15, 20, 21, 26

Rivoire, John (cousin): exchanges political views on Revolution with Revere, 15, 141, 142, 143; questions Revere's honor, 158; on Revere's reputation as express rider, 101

Rivoire, Mathias (cousin), 141

Rivoire, Simon (great-uncle), 7

Robbins, Edward Hutchinson, 182

Robbins, Mary (Mrs. Joseph Warren Revere), 182

Robinson, John, 66, 69, 78

Rochefontaine, Lt. Col. Stephen, 166

Rockingham, Marquis of, 51

Rococo style, and Revere's mastery of, 16, 27

Romans, Capt. Bernard, 96

Rosamond, 146

Rotch, Francis, 93, 94

Rousseau, Jean Jacques, 83

Rowe, John: defeated for Massachusetts General Court, 49–50; disapproval of radicalism of patriot cause, 81–82; disapproval of Revere, 81–82, 91; as Freemason, 29, 31; as moderate patriot, 59, 64, 99

Roxbury, fortifications at, 118

Royal American Magazine, 87, 96

Royal Coffee House, 69

Royal Exchange Lane, 76

Royal Exchange Tavern, 47

Ruddock, Abiel, 60, 92

Ruddock, John, 49–50

Ruggles, Timothy, 65

Russell, Benjamin, 157, 172, 174

Russell, Ezekiel, 84

Russell, Thomas, 152

St. Andrew's Lodge: and Boston Tea Party, 93, 94, 95, 228 n. 17; dispute over charter, and Revere's role in, 89–90, 114; dissolution of, and Revere's role in, 146–48; and Massachusetts Grand Lodge, 67, 81–82; origins and members, 27–31; Revere's offices in, 37, 46, 67, 83, 86, 126, 146–47; and Revolutionary activity, 31, 36, 44–45, 59–60, 93, 94, 95; as source of Revere's customers, 30, 39, 40, 57, 146. *See also* Freemasonry; Massachusetts Grand Lodge; Revere, Paul: Masonic Career

St. George's Field Massacre, 75

St. John's Grand Lodge, 29–30, 67, 175

St. Leger, Lt. Col. Barry, 130

Saint-Memin, Charles Balthazar Julien Fevret de, 179

Salem (Mass.) Committee of Correspondence, and support for nonimportation, 98

Saltonstall, Commo. Dudley, 135–36

Salutation Tavern, 34, 68

Sampson, Deborah (Gannett), 188–89

Sampson, John, 152

Sanderson, Elijah, 111, 235 n. 11

Saratoga, battle of, 131

Sargent, Epes, 40, 66, 141

Sargent, Epes, Jr., 89

Sargent, Capt. Winthrop, 55

Savage, Arthur, Jr., 40

Savage, Samuel Phillips, 40, 48, 130

Scollay, John, 38

Scott, Joseph, 38

Sears, Col. Isaac, 127

Seider, Christopher, 74–75, 85

Selfridge, Thomas O., manslaughter trial of, 189–91; Revere's role in, 190–91, 276 n. 37. *See also* Austin, Benjamin, Jr.

Seven Years' War, 31–32, 37–39. *See also* French and Indian War

Sewall, Chief Justice Stephen, 32

Sharp, Gibbens, 42, 53, 57, 62, 153

Shattuck, Job, 155

Shays, Daniel, 155

Shays's Rebellion, 155–57

Sheafe, Jacob, 166–67

Sheafe, William, 56

Shepard, Gen. William, 155

Shirley, Gov. William, 12, 18; and French and Indian War, 22, 24; and impressment riots, 19; on "mobbish spirit" in town meeting, 33

Short Narrative of the Horrid Massacre in Boston (patriot version), 78, 220 n. 7

Shreve, Rev. Thomas, 168

Shurtleff, Robert. *See* Sampson, Deborah (Gannett)

Sigourney, Elisha, 148

Smith, Lt. Col. Francis, 108–10

Smith, John, 43

Smith, Robert, 181, 183

Smith, Samuel, 181

Social status and mobility: and American Revolution, 4, 43–46, 47–48, 61–63, 81, 87–88, 112, 120–21; of artisans, 4, 9–11, 15–17,

35, 43, 45, 61–63, 81, 157; in colonial society, 9–15; education and, 13–15; in the New Republic, 151, 153, 157, 160–63, 248 n. 8
Solemn League and Covenant, 99. *See also* Nonimportation
Sons of Liberty: and Boston mobs, 64; commission Liberty Bowl, 64; Freemasonry and, 67; at Liberty Tree dinner, 68–69; and Daniel Malcolm incident, 57; and nonimportation, 47, 48–49, 59–60, 69–71, 76, 81, 82; origins and members, 42, 47–50, 61–62; and propaganda for Boston Massacre, 77–80; and resistance to Tea Act, 91–95, 96–97; and Christopher Seider's funeral, 74–75; and Stamp Act, 47–50, 83. *See also* Loyal Nine
Speakman, Gilbert, 137
Stacy, George, 30
Stamp Act, 40–41; colonial opposition to, 41–42, 48; and Thomas Hutchinson, 42–45; and nonimportation, 47; opposition in Boston, 42–46, 47–53; repeal of, 50–51; and Stamp Act Congress, 46–47
Stark, Gen. John, 136
State House (Bulfinch or New), 175, 183
State House (Old), 126, 148
State National Bank, 192
Stoddard, Asa, 42, 84, 148
Stoddard, Benjamin, 166, 178, 179, 180
Story, William, 43
Stoughton, Mass., site of Revolutionary gunpowder mill, 119
Stowell, Abel, 167
Strong, Gov. Caleb, 194
Stuart, Gilbert, 194
Suffolk County, Revere as coroner of, 169
Suffolk Resolves, 100
Sugar Act, 39, 40
Sullivan, James, 190
Sullivan, Maj. Gen. John, 132–33
Summary of Physiology (Magendie), translation by Dr. John Revere, 182
Sutherland, Lt. William, 108
Swift, John, 193
Swift (leader of North End mob), 47
Symmes, John, 57, 60, 148

Tea Act, 90, 91–94. *See also* Boston Tea Party
Test Act, 127
Thacher, Oxenbridge, 33
Thacher, Rev. Peter, 8
Thomas, Isaiah, 84, 94, 96
Tileston, Thomas, 93
Todd, William: and problems in Massachusetts Artillery Regiment, 131, 133, 134; role in Penobscot expedition and Revere's court-martial, 135–39
Tory, Capt. William, 26
Townshend, Charles, 58
Townshend Acts: and colonial opposition to, 58–59, 63; and Massachusetts circular letter (1768), 58, 64–65; opposition to, in Boston, 58–62, 64–66, 69–71; partial repeal of, 81. *See also* Nonimportation
Tracy, Nathaniel, 143
Transactions of the American Medical Association, on Dr. John Revere, 182
Tree, Capt. Francis, 94
Trenchard (John) and Gordon (William), *Cato's Letters*, 66
Trenchard (John) and Moyle (Walter), *Argument, Shewing that a Standing Army Is Inconsistent with a Free Government*, 66
Trenton, battle of, 126
Trott, George, 43, 120–22
Tuckerman, Edward, 174
Tudor, William, 98, 114; on Revere, 196
Turner, William, 15
Tyler, Royall, 61, 68
Tyrian Lodge, 86, 89

Urann, Thomas, 67, 93, 95, 148
U.S. Navy, and Paul Revere and Son, 178, 181, 183

Vassall, John, 118
Voltaire, 15, 82

Wadsworth, Peleg, 132, 135–39, 195
Wadsworth, Thomas, 168
Ward, Gen. Artemas, 118
Warner, George, 186

War of 1812, 194

Warren, James, 117, 119, 121

Warren, John, 147

Warren, Dr. Joseph, 82, 86, 99, 123, 151, 159, 160; and Boston Tea Party, 92–93, 95; death of, 117–18; impact of death on Massachusetts Grand Lodge, 146–48; as patriot leader, 19, 35, 55, 62, 64, 68, 85, 87; organizes army and government in Massachusetts, 110–11, 116; relationship with Revere, 29, 36, 53, 67, 88, 91–92, 114–15, 117–18; and Revere's ride to Lexington, 102, 103; and Revere's role as courier for the Committee of Safety, 107, 110–11; and Suffolk Resolves, 100

Washington, George, 158, 171, 174, 176; and criteria for federal officeholders, 161–62; Revere's admiration for, 158; and Revere's failure to obtain a federal appointment, 161; and Revolutionary War, 124, 126; and role in choosing Continental Army officers, 114, 116, 118–21; on Shays's Rebellion, 254n. 42

Watertown, Mass., headquarters for Massachusetts Provincial Congress, 111, 115

Watson, Rev. Richard, 15, 166

Webb, Joseph, 40, 146–47

Welles, Henry, 43, 45

Welsteed, Rev. William, 8

Wemms, Pvt. William, 77

Wethersfield, Conn., letter on Revere's alleged death after ride, 107

Whately, Thomas, 41, 91

Wheelwright, Nathaniel, 38

White, Pvt. Hugh, 76, 77

White, Isaac, 86

White Plains, battle of, 126

Whitney, Col. Josiah, 124

Wilkes, John, 64–65, 68

Willard, Aaron, 145

Willard, Dr. Samuel, 188

Willard, Simon, 145, 146

Williams, John, 64

Williams, William, 145, 173

Winnick, John, 145

Winslow, Gen. John, 24

Winthrop, James, 156

Winthrop, John, 93

Winthrop, John, Jr., 127

Wolfe, Gen. James, 31–32, 112

Woodhead, Thomas, 169

Writs of assistance, 32–34; and John Adams, 33; and Thomas Hutchinson, 32–34; and Capt. Daniel Malcolm, 56–57; and James Otis, 33–34

XYZ Papers, 177

Young, Dr. Thomas: opposes royal salaries, 86–87; as patriot leader, 73, 85, 87, 92; on republican spirit, 81, 82, 86–87; and Revere, 81, 82–83, 88, 117–18; role in framing Pennsylvania government, 123–24; on value of artisans to American Revolution, 81, 82

Young Ladies' Academy of Woburn, and Maria Revere, 15